I0885475

Transformations in Twentieth Century Korea

This edited collection traces the social, economic, political, and cultural dimensions of Korea's dramatic transformation since the late nineteenth century. Taking an interdisciplinary approach, the chapters examine the internal and external forces which facilitated the transition towards industrial capitalism in Korea, the consequences and impact of social change, and the ways in which Korean tradition continues to inform and influence contemporary South Korean society.

Transformations in Twentieth Century Korea employs a thematic structure to discuss the interrelated elements of Korea's modernization within agriculture, business and the economy, the state, ideology and culture, and gender and the family. Unlike other literature in the field which focuses on a particular era of Korea's twentieth century history, the essays in this volume encompass the Chosŏn dynasty, the colonial period, and postcolonial Korea. Collectively, they provide us with an original and innovative approach to the study of modern Korea, and show how knowledge of the country's past is critical to understanding contemporary Korean society.

With contributions from a number of prominent international scholars working in the disciplines of sociology, economics, history, and political science, *Transformations in Twentieth Century Korea* incorporates a global framework of historical narrative, ideology and culture, and statistical and economic analysis to further our understanding of Korea's evolution towards modernity.

Steven Hugh Lee is Associate Professor in the Department of History at the University of British Columbia. His previous publications include *Outposts of Empire: Korea, Vietnam and the Origins of the Cold War, 1949–1954* (1995), and *The Korean War* (2001). **Chang Yun-Shik** is Professor Emeritus in the Department of Sociology at the University of British Columbia. He was director of the Centre for Korean Research at UBC from 1994 to 2001, and has authored several edited books and numerous articles, including "Mutual Help and Democracy in Korea" in Daniel Bell and Ham Chaibong, eds, *Confucianism for the Modern World* (2003).

Routledge advances in Korean studies

1 **The Politics of Economic Reform in South Korea**
A fragile miracle
Tat Yan Kong

2 **Market and Society in Korea**
Interest, institution and the textile industry
Dennis McNamara

3 **Social and Economic Policies in Korea**
Ideas, networks and linkages
Dong-Myeon Shin

4 **North Korea in the World Economy**
Edited by E. Kwan Choi, Yesook Merrill and E. Han Kim

5 **Legal Reform in Korea**
Edited by Tom Ginsburg

6 **Women, Television and Everyday Life**
Journeys of hope
Youna Kim

7 **Transformations in Twentieth Century Korea**
Edited by Chang Yun-Shik and Steven Hugh Lee

Transformations in Twentieth Century Korea

Edited by Chang Yun-Shik and
Steven Hugh Lee

Routledge
Taylor & Francis Group
LONDON AND NEW YORK

First published 2006
by Routledge
2 Park Square, Milton Park, Abingdon, Oxon, OX14 4RN

Simultaneously published in the USA and Canada
by Routledge
270 Madison Ave, New York NY 10016

Routledge is an imprint of the Taylor & Francis Group, an informa business

Transferred to Digital Printing 2009

Typeset in Baskerville by Wearset Ltd, Boldon, Tyne and Wear

British Library Cataloguing in Publication Data
A catalogue record for this book is available from the British Library

Library of Congress Cataloging in Publication Data
A catalog record for this book has been requested

ISBN10: 0-415-38065-0 (hbk)
ISBN10: 0-415-54695-8 (pbk)

ISBN13: 978-0-415-38065-2 (hbk)
ISBN13: 978-0-415-54695-9 (pbk)

Contents

Illustrations

Figures

Tables

Contributors

Mary C. Brinton is Reischauer Institute Professor of Sociology at Harvard University. She is the author of *Women and the Economic Miracle: Gender and Work in Postwar Japan* (1994), and editor of *Women's Working Lives in East Asia* (2001). Currently, she is researching the effects of Japanese employment restructuring on young people's work lives.

Larry L. Burmeister is Associate Professor of Sociology at the University of Kentucky, where he teaches courses on international development, the sociology of agriculture, and East Asian political economy. He is the author of *Research, Realpolitik, and Development in Korea: The State and the Green Revolution* (1998).

Chang Yun-Shik is Professor Emeritus in the Department of Sociology at the University of British Columbia. He was Director of the Center for Korean Research at UBC from 1994 to 2001, and has authored several edited books and numerous articles, including "Mutual Help and Democracy in Korea" in Daniel Bell and Ham Chaibong, eds, *Confucianism for the Modern World* (2003).

Daniel Chirot is Professor of International Studies and Sociology at the University of Washington. His published work has examined ethnic violence, migration, and modern tyrannies. He has been the recipient of grants from the Mellon Foundation, the Guggenheim Foundation, and the Woodrow Wilson Center.

Minja Kim Choe is Senior Fellow at the East-West Center, the University of Hawaii. Her research interests include marriage and motherhood, fertility and reproductive health, and the health behavior of adolescents.

Moonkyung Choi is full-time Lecturer in the Department of Sociology at Kukmin University, Korea. Her current research interest is the sociology of information and technology.

Sheila Miyoshi Jager is Luce Assistant Professor of East Asian Studies at Oberlin College. In 2003, she published *Narratives of Nation-building in*

Korea: A Genealogy of Patriotism, and she is currently co-editing *Ruptured Histories: War, Memory and the Post-Cold War in Asia* with Rana Mitter.

David Kang is Associate Professor in the Government Department at Dartmouth College. His first book, *Crony Capitalism: Corruption and Development in South Korea and the Philippines*, was published in 2002. He is also co-author, with Victor Cha, of *Nuclear North Korea: A Debate on Engagement Strategies* (2003).

Uchang Kim is Professor of English at Korea University. He has written many books on Korean literature and culture. Translations of his works have appeared in French, English, Japanese, and German.

Seung-Ho Kwon is a Senior Research Fellow in the School of International Business at the University of New South Wales, Australia. He has published on Korean labor and business issues, and co-authored, with Michael O'Donnell, *The Chaebŏl and Labour in Korea* (2004).

Paul W. Kuznets is Professor Emeritus of Economics at the College of Arts and Sciences, Indiana University, Bloomington. He is an expert on the Korean economy and has written several books, including *Korean Economic Development: an Interpretive Model* (1994).

Steven Hugh Lee is Associate Professor of History at the University of British Columbia. His published work includes *Outposts of Empire* (1995) and *The Korean War* (2001). His current project is a book on twentieth century global history.

John Lie is Dean of International and Area Studies and Class of 1959 Professor at the University of California, Berkeley. His publications include *Multiethnic Japan* (2001) and *Han Unbound: The Political Economy of South Korea* (1998). His most recent book is *Modern Peoplehood* (2004).

Gi-Wook Shin is Associate Professor of Sociology, Director of Korean Studies, and Director of the Shorenstein Asia-Pacific Research Center, all at Stanford University. He is the author or (co)-editor of six books, including *Peasant Protest and Social Change in Colonial Korea* (1996). He is currently writing a book on mass media and US–ROK relations.

Chung-sok Suh is Associate Professor in the School of Organization and Management at the University of New South Wales, Australia. His work focuses on multinational companies, Korean businesses, and management in Asia. He has published articles on East Asian capitalism, globalization, and foreign direct investment.

Acknowledgments

This book is the product of a series of interdisciplinary and international conferences organized through the Center for Korean Research at the University of British Columbia. The conferences commemorated the fiftieth anniversary of the founding of the *Kyŏnghyang Sinmun*, a newspaper well known for its opposition to authoritarian regimes. It is fitting, therefore, that our discussions were organized around the theme of Korea's twentieth century transformations. We are pleased to express our appreciation to the *Kyŏnghyang Sinmun*, which generously funded the conferences and reported the proceedings to their readership. The newspaper's support has established a benchmark precedent for the promotion of Korean studies overseas. We would like to acknowledge and thank Ahn Sin-bae, President of the newspaper, Kim Hak-su, Director of the Planning Office, reporter Ju Jae-pak, and especially Kim Yoo-kyong, Director of the Cultural Bureau. Director Kim played an instrumental role in initiating the process which brought the newspaper and the university together. Additional funding was provided by the UBC Center for Korean Research, and we thank the Director, Don Baker, for his help and encouragement. At Routledge, our thanks go to Stephanie Rogers and Helen Baker for their dedicated work. Ann King, our copy-editor, did a fine and meticulous job, for which we are very appreciative. We would also like to thank Georgina Boyle, our production editor, for her valuable editorial contributions to the volume.

Note on romanization

We have used the McCune-Reischauer system of romanizing Korean. We deviated from this rule in cases where individuals or institutions have themselves preferred a different romanization of their names.

Introduction

Korea's twentieth century transformation

Steven Hugh Lee

The dramatic and defiant declaration "You can cut off my head, but never my hair" was a popular slogan of the *Ulmi* Righteous Army Movement and part of the organized resistance against King Kojong's 30 December 1895 haircutting edict that required Korean males to cut off their topnots or braids and to wear their hair Western-style. The antagonism generated by the King's order reflected the depth of influence of classical learning and culture in the late Chosŏn dynasty: his decree violated the custom of showing respect to the body inherited from one's parents, and undermined the integrity of *Chungwha*, the notion that China was the cultural center of the universe. Protests against the edict, mainly involving scholars and peasants, were widespread and sometimes violent. They forced the kingdom to issue a defensive statement in January 1896 saying that haircutting was not compulsory for the general population.[1]

The haircutting decree was part of a broader series of modernizing bills and edicts known as *Kabo* reforms which were introduced by the Yi dynasty in the mid-1890s, in response to the revolutionary challenges posed by the anti-dynastic Tonghak rebellion and Japanese and Western forms of modernity and power. This example of Korea's early experience with reform is a microcosm of many aspects of Koreans' engagement with socio-economic change in the twentieth century. Resistance and protest often accompanied efforts associated with the modernization of society, and efforts to alter existing social conditions were frequently initiated by the government in conjunction with a small number of the political elite. The role played by the state in setting the tone for societal change was thus not unique to either colonial or post-colonial Korea, though the ability of post-1910 Korean governments to mobilize the population for their modernizing projects quickly overtook the very limited reformist capacity of the late Chosŏn dynasty. Our example also underlines the point that the state's attempt to alter social norms has had successes, at least on its own terms. The kingdom's troops had defeated the *Ulmi* Righteous Armies by the fall of 1897, and within a decade more people came to associate the cutting of hair not with the breakdown of a moral order, but with the defense of the dynasty against growing Japanese influence in

Korea. By the late 1930s, Korean historian Mun Il-p'yŏng could write: "From today's perspective, the fact that people risked their lives to resist the Haircutting Decree is something we can laugh away" (Jang 1998: 26).

Although the resistance to the haircutting edict may be interpreted as a movement countering Western embodiments of modernity, it foreshadowed trends in Korea's twentieth century experience in which moral issues motivated the population to join popular movements opposing governmental policy. Indeed, for most of the century, the Korean state in its numerous forms – dynastic, colonial, occupational, and military – was itself a contradiction, both espousing social and economic change, yet also refusing to reform itself, and acting in an authoritarian fashion. In a number of instances, mass movements from below contained powerful progressive elements which succeeded in transforming repressive situations into ones which facilitated political and social reform. The 1919 March First Movement protesting colonial rule, the 1946 peasant uprisings, the 1960 student and urban unrest which toppled the Syngman Rhee government, and the popular call for democracy in the 1980s were only the most prominent examples of this dimension of Koreans' efforts to improve their socio-economic and political conditions in the twentieth century. Contemporary South Korean society is thus also a product of mass movements from below which have resisted rigid or undemocratic political regimes and their alliances with conservative elites.

The changing responses in Korea to Western hairstyles were only a minute part of the fundamental transformations that Koreans experienced in so many aspects of their daily lives since the late nineteenth century. Chosŏn Korea's ruling ideology, culture, and foreign relations were intimately linked to Chinese classical learning and the Qing dynasty's tributary system. After the 1870s a number of external and internal forces dismantled the Chosŏn kingdom's *yangban*–peasant social structure and agricultural economy and replaced them – at least in the area that became South Korea – with an industrial society and class structure associated with capitalist forms of labor and enterprise.

Indeed, the emergence of an industrial society over the course of the twentieth century was a defining feature of Korea's transformation, and the source of much conflict, for the imposition of a system of mass forms of production and the new consumer culture which this fostered resulted in the radical restructuring of people's lives and their relationships with one another. Some commentators have argued that the global spread of Western capitalism and culture resulted in a "Westernization" of the globe and the loss of traditional values and world views (see von Laue 1989). Although the chapters in this volume would support this contention to some degree, they also point to the unique aspects of Korea's transformation, and the ways in which local culture intermixed with globalizing trends associated with capitalism, nationalism, colonialism, and democracy to produce a society that does not conform to conventional ideas about Westernization. Collectively, the chapters show that Korea's modern condition is the culmination of a process born of significant social conflict, and that the Korean contribution to capitalist modernity has been original on its own terms. The volume thus underlines a non-Eurocentric methodology which emphasizes the interaction and interplay between Western and non-Western worlds, while also recognizing important similarities in capitalist structures between the two.

The chapters are concerned with tracing aspects of the genealogy of the dramatic and frequently traumatic process of change that Koreans have experienced since the late nineteenth century. They examine "agents" of Korea's twentieth century transformation, internal and external forces which facilitated the transition towards industrial capitalism, the consequences and impact of social change, and ways in which Korean "tradition" continues to inform and influence South Korean society. The volume looks at societal change thematically, highlighting five interconnected elements of Korea's transformation over the course of the twentieth century: agriculture, business and the economy, the state, ideology and culture, and gender and the family. In examining these dimensions of the modernization process, the book brings a multi-disciplinary perspective to Korea's socio-economic, political, and cultural transformation. It also adopts a novel approach to Korean development, as many works in the field focus either on the pre- or post-1945 eras. Although the bulk of the analysis focuses on South Korea since 1945, the chapters bridge the Chosŏn, colonial, and post-colonial periods. By taking this perspective the volume complements the extant literature on the evolution of Korean capitalism and modernity, and contributes to our understanding of the complexities that have underpinned that process (see e.g. Chung 2002: 18–59; Jang 1998, 2001; Jung 2000; Kim 1999, 2001; Shin and Robinson 1999; Yoo 2001).[2]

As Daniel Chirot points out in Chapter 10 of this volume, there is nothing inevitable about the modernization process itself, and radically different trajectories were possible. In this sense, the *Ŭlmi* righteous fighters should be viewed as expressing a form of anti-capitalist modernity within a Korean context. It is not my goal to treat Korea's contemporary modern world as a value in itself. To invoke a gender-based metaphor, if we denude the modernizing emperor of his clothes, we witness a plurality of directions in which Koreans from the late nineteenth century onwards defined their collective futures. North and South Korea today represent two of the many possible trajectories of Korean history. In other words, the history of conflict and negotiation has to be taken into account in any assessment of the evolution of Korea's transformation, as power relations are central to its processes, origins, and history.

The conventional linear chronology of (South) Korean history – late Chosŏn dynasty, colonial period, division and war, military rule, and democratization – serves as a helpful guide for reciting the narrative of modern Korea, yet it does not provide an analytical framework for understanding societal change as a process, and is inadequate in explaining or evaluating the fundamental reconfiguration of social relations that has occurred since the promulgation of the *Kabo* reforms in the mid-1890s. This chapter suggests that Korea's transformation may be divided into three interrelated periods of history. These are closely linked to the histories of the hegemonic powers which influenced Korean development over the last 100 years or so, but they take into account indigenous responses to the challenges and opportunities offered by the imperial powers which dominated Korea. The early phase, which I call an era of "nascent capitalism," lasted from the "opening" of Korea in the late nineteenth century to World War I. This period established the social, cultural, and economic groundwork for the emergence of capitalism on the peninsula. It witnessed the decline of the Chosŏn dynasty, the rise and consolidation of Japanese hegemony in Korea, the development of Korean nationalist thought, and the early beginnings of a Korean bourgeois entrepreneurial class. Chosŏn's ties to the East Asian trading network expanded in this period, partly as a result of the Qing dynasty's efforts to check its decline and partly to promote intra-Asian trade. In the 1890s a growing number of Chinese merchants in Korean ports competed with Japanese traders for local markets, but by the early 1900s the Japanese had asserted greater control over the peninsula and weakened their competition (Hamashita 2001; Kimura 2001). An elite group of Koreans also absorbed aspects of "Western" thinking during this era. New ideas included a faith in the power to improve society, social Darwinism, notions about "backward" and "advanced" civilizations, and a belief in hierarchies of peoples according to the linked categories of "race" and "nation" (Allen 2001; Huh 2001; Kim 2001). The carriers to Korea of these "modern" notions, for example, Japanese officials or Christian missionaries, embodied the social Darwinism and other irrational aspects of their own societies and cultures. We should be careful, therefore, not to equate the idea of the modern solely with enlightenment thinking based on "rationality." Korea's modernization process was bound up in the emergence of new forms of inequality.

The second era of Korea's transformation lasted from the early colonial period through to the 1970s. In this age of "foundational capitalism," Koreans, Japanese, and Americans established the bases for the emergence of a mature industrial capitalism in (South) Korea. These were years of extreme difficulties associated with the harsh experiences of colonial mobilization, the division of the peninsula in 1945, the Korean War, and a second epoch of compressed industrial revolution, especially in the 1960s and 1970s. Two interrelated and coterminous developments occurred in these decades: the expansion of industrial capitalism, and the transformation of the Korean countryside. In the north, Koreans redirected the social and industrial changes associated with the colonial era into a "revolutionary socialist modernity," a project which subordinated the region's colonial heavy industrial base to a postwar communist command economy.

In the Republic of Korea, the processes underpinning the country's foundational capitalism had reached a turning point by the 1980s, when a period of "pluralist capitalism" began to emerge. This era was characterized by industry moving into "higher technology" products, the deepening of the country's multilateral economic linkages with the rest of the capitalist world, democratization, and the export of "Korean" capital, production, and management strategies elsewhere on the globe.

The era of nascent capitalism, 1876–1914

Korea's societal transfiguration has been the product of a constant interplay of historical forces, often in competition with each other, which have been internally and externally driven and generated. While this is true of most countries, it is important to examine in each case the unique character, development, and relationship between these internal and external influences. We will begin by outlining several important aspects of socioeconomic change during Korea's era of nascent capitalism. These are shifts in ideology and thought which accompanied the end of the traditional tributary relationship with China and Japan's seizure of power on the peninsula, Korean modernization efforts, and the significance of agrarian social relations for understanding the social roots of industrial capitalism in Korea. Efforts to alter cultural practice and belief systems thus accompanied the gradual economic transformation of society.

Until the late nineteenth century, the Kingdom of Chosŏn had looked to Ming or Qing civilization as a point of reference for its culture, knowledge, and learning. In the aftermath of the *Kangwha* Treaty of 1876, and especially after the Sino–Japanese War of 1894–1895, when Korea formally entered the world of sovereign states, elite Koreans began to reconceptualize their cultural and diplomatic relationship with the country they began to conceive of as "China." The political and ritual linkages which had underpinned the two polities for centuries started to come under sustained criticism, and sharp contrasts began to be drawn between "old" classical learning, or *kuhak,* and "new," Western-based knowledge, referred to as *sinhak.*[3] This was a conflicted process, especially in the last decade of dynastic rule, when Japanese incursions into Korea complicated the perceived relationship between the new conceptual categories of "traditional" and "modern." Competing groups such as the Confucian Righteous Army Fighters, over 17,000 of whom died by 1910 battling the Japanese stationed on the peninsula, or those who supported Korean "self-strengthening" (*chagang*), vied either to retain or to eliminate elements of classical learning. As Andre Schmid has pointed out, the classical past was not rejected *in toto*; rather, selective elements of the kingdom's classical and ancient learning were held up as examples of things society should seek to recover (2002: 80–86). What was different was the means through which Koreans embarked on a new project of "enlightenment" (*kaewha*) and progress.

Urban reformers, intellectuals, and journalists led the effort to revolutionize the population's world view. One of the most prominent figures shaping the ideological trajectory of modern Korea was Sin Ch'ae-ho. In Chapter 9 of this volume Sheila Jager points out that for Sin, "the idea of a return to a time before the nation's corruption by Confucianism . . . constituted the basis for the nation's modern salvation." Sin's critique of classical learning was influenced by the direct challenges of Japanese modernity, but also by Qing reformers such as Liang Qichao who had spent time in Japan. Liang wanted the Qing dynasty to modernize, and he criticized corruption in the bureaucracy and foreign imperialism. The nationalism and sense of identity Sin C'hae-ho articulated were thus part of a wider discussion about "the modern" across Western and East Asian cultures in the period. Sin wanted to revitalize a "Korean civilization" which had been misled and corrupted partly by the classical Chinese past, but also by the conservative and formal ways in which Koreans had approached "Confucianism." Although he believed indigenous cultural practices had to be reformed, others, for example, Yi Kwang-su, argued that dynastic adherence to classical ritual had to be purged from society as it had been a major cause of dynastic decline. As more Koreans came to accept the view of "Chinese" civilization as decrepit, conservative, and ready to collapse, they expressed concern that instability in the middle kingdom could lead to social disruption and chaos on the peninsula. In this context, Western-based technology and learning was viewed increasingly as the new model to emulate. The Korean reform project to replace Confucian ritual with Western notions of progress and technology overlapped with the emergence of colonial rule on the peninsula.

As Kim Uchang elaborates in his chapter on Confucianism in twentieth century Korea (Chapter 8), even as the external context for Korea's political, economic, and cultural development changed radically, residues of the Chosŏn dynasty's classical heritage remained as a kind of inert force in society, available as a resource to serve the modernization projects of reform-minded conservatives and the authoritarian state. In this way, Koreans such as Sin modified the existing internal–external dynamic of "traditional" Chosŏn and produced new concepts of Korean society within a substantially altered internal–external nexus of power.

The ideological and cultural changes in Koreans' world views were accompanied by very gradual shifts in the economy and social sphere which laid the groundwork for the emergence of capitalist modes of production. The era from 1876 to 1914 was characterized by several key economic developments in the evolution of Korea's nascent capitalism. These included the accelerated commercialization of agriculture, a dramatic increase in trade with Japan in agricultural products, the creation of a national communications and transportation system, the establishment of a modern financial and monetary system, the emergence of Japanese businessmen as the dominant capitalists in Korean economic life, and the development of a native bourgeoisie out of a group referred to as *kaekchu*, wholesale merchants and entrepreneurs who initially played critical "middlemen" roles between foreign traders – especially Chinese and Japanese – and Korean producers. By the early twentieth century some of these merchants were involved in more complex economic transactions involving partnerships with Japanese businessmen or other *kaekchu*.[4] As Carter Eckert has pointed out, during this period, "Korea's economic position as a Japanese granary and export market for manufactured goods provided the basis for the accumulation of capital by a significant number of enterprising Koreans, who gradually became the core of a native bourgeoisie" (Eckert 1991: 11).

A number of developments which accompanied the era of nascent Korean capitalism began prior to the onset of formal colonial rule, and especially in the decade or so after the *Kabo* reforms. One Korean entrepreneur involved in modernization efforts in this era was Pak Ki-jong, a *kaekchu* from Pusan who supported a number of railway-building programs in the late 1890s. His sons went to Japan to learn about modern technologies in mining and railways. Other Korean entrepreneurs set up banking, trading, shipping, and textile enterprises, often with Japanese partners. Another prominent figure of the period was Yi Yong-ik, a mining entrepreneur from North Hamgyŏng province who held a number of significant economic and business ministerial portfolios in the Korean court after 1897. In the late 1890s and early 1900s Yi involved the Chosŏn dynasty in efforts to establish a Korean central bank, to construct railway lines from Seoul to Ŭiju and Seoul to Wŏnsan, and to modernize Korea's military. The dynasty also developed plans to standardize the monetary system, to adopt a gold standard, to produce convertible bills, and to allow Japanese currency to circulate (Duus 1995: ch. 4).

These efforts were significantly hampered by the inadequacies of the existing tax system, the regressive social structure, factionalism at court, and the unavailability of domestic capital to meet the needs of reform projects. External forces, including imperialist rivalries, Korean competition from Japanese merchants, a Japanese sense of superiority over "backward" Koreans, and Japanese government efforts to promote its strategic and economic interests in the Chosŏn kingdom also exacerbated factional rivalries in the dynasty and significantly weakened the ability of Koreans to pursue consistent strategies for modernizing society.

Although Japanese merchants, businessmen, and government officials dismissed Korean modernization efforts, writing them off as emanating from a corrupt and inefficient state, it is significant that Japanese officials accelerated their imperial hold on Korea precisely in this era of reform. The establishment of the protectorate in 1905 and colony in 1910 were critically linked to Japanese governmental efforts to strengthen the role of Japanese merchants and businessmen on the peninsula, and to weaken potential competition from Korean sources. Komura Jutaro, Japanese Foreign Minister from 1901 to 1906, stated in the early 1900s that, "even though it amounts to only ¥8 million, the Korean trade differs from the China trade or trade with America in that the export and shipping of goods is handled entirely by the Japanese" (Duus 1995: 249–250). This statement may not have been entirely accurate as there was a dramatic growth in the number of Chinese merchants in Korean ports in the period – their numbers went from about 160 in the early 1880s to almost 12,000 at the onset of colonial rule. This trend itself was an indication of the vigorous inter-Asian trade which was developing at the time, but Japanese diplomats viewed the presence of Chinese merchants as a threat to their commercial interests in Asia (Hamashita 2003: 40). Japan's goal was to eliminate, absorb, or make into junior partners its competitors so that its merchants and traders would benefit most from the commercialization of the peninsula. As we have seen, some Koreans did align themselves with Japanese businessmen, and Komura's statement was an indication prior to the signing of the protectorate treaty that leading figures in the Japanese state were intent on protecting the Korean market as much as possible for Japanese economic interests.

Japanese capitalists, though often reluctant or concerned about investing in Korea, especially prior to 1920, did have privileged industries on the peninsula. The Dai-Iichi bank and the Mitsubishi Shipping Company were two such enterprises (Duus 1995: 250–253). Japanese textile companies, especially ones from Osaka, were also prominent in Korean trade. They faced stiff competition in the early twentieth century, not so much from Korean manufacturers as from British empire-based ones. As late as 1910, for example, high-quality British textiles took up 37 percent of the Korean cotton textile import market. Japanese capitalists and government officials viewed strategic and economic threats as interlinked challenges to their interests: political control, security, and economic development went together. The logic which led Japanese statesmen to annex Korea succeeded in achieving its aims. By 1914, Japanese cotton textile exports to Korea made up 97 percent of Korea's imported cottons. The onset of colonial rule significantly weakened foreign competitors, and in this context allowed Japanese capitalists, together with a small Korean collaborating elite, to develop their economic interests in Korea, and later, Manchuria, relatively free from indigenous Korean and other Great Power competition (Duus 1995: 287; Eckert 1991; Haggard *et al.* 1997: 871).

Foundational capitalism: the era of Japanese hegemony

The long period of "foundational capitalism" evolved in two interrelated yet distinct phases. The first ended and the second began in 1945, the year the Korean peninsula experienced a sudden and dramatic change in the hegemons that dominated it. Taken together, the two phases established a mature form of industrial capitalism based on the consolidation of private property ownership, the destruction of the aristocracy, the transformation of urban and rural family life, the emergence of wage labor and a working class, and the establishment and growth of Korean conglomerates. Foundational capitalism was the product of two hegemonic powers' influence on the peninsula.

In the following discussion of the first phase of foundational capitalism I use the term "hegemony" as it pertains to Japan's power relationship with "Korea", and the dominance of Japanese state structures and private capital within the colony. The term is not used to suggest that Japan was globally hegemonic, but that it emerged as a regional hegemon in Northeast Asia in the early twentieth century. In many ways, Japan itself had a subordinate role within a broader capitalist global economy dominated by American, British, and European money and technology (see Arrighi *et al.* 2003; Cumings 2002). Until the 1930s, Japanese businessmen often worked closely with European and American multinational corporate executives in developing and gaining financial backing for their enterprises in Northeast Asia. The thrust of the Japanese empire, however, particularly following the early 1930s, was designed to break out of Anglo-American global economic hegemony.

Prior to 1920, Korea had served primarily as a market for Japanese manufactured goods. World War I significantly altered Japan's economic position in the world and its relationship with colonial Chōsen. During the conflict, Japanese production, trade, and shipping increased tremendously. Japan's GNP went up by 40 percent. Over the next decade, the country went from having a largely agricultural and small industry-based economy to one dominated by heavy industry and urban-based factory production. Most of the population still lived in rural areas – people living in cities accounted for 50 percent of the total population in 1950 – but by the late 1920s, for the first time, the value of manufacturing in Japan's GDP was higher than the value of agricultural goods (McClain 2002: 359–360).

During the war, inflation in Japan increased more than wages, culminating in major rice riots in 1917. That year was also a turning point for strikes as the numbers of disputes almost quadrupled over the previous year. Those involved in protests went from about 8,400 workers in 1916 to 66,500 in 1918 (McClain 2002: 372, table 11.7).[5] With growing pressure from domestic labor for higher wages, Japanese capitalists began to locate companies in Chōsen. The result was the abolition in 1920 of the Company Law, which restricted all investment in Chōsen to those companies that received a license from the Government General. This decision made possible limited Korean participation in the industrialization of the colony and empire (see Eckert 1991; McNamara 1990). Despite

Japanese discrimination, some Koreans formed their own companies and worked as subordinate partners with Japanese capital. In 1911 there were 152 companies registered in Korea and by 1940 there were 5,413. Five percent of the larger of these businesses, numbering about 2,000, were owned by Koreans, while just under 30 percent were jointly owned by Koreans and Japanese (McNamara 1990: 53). In 1937 there were approximately 2,300 Korean-operated enterprises, about 7 percent of which had more than fifty employees (Eckert 1991: 55).

As a result of Japan's economic transformation during the war and the empire's accelerated industrialization following the seizure of Manchuria in 1931, there was an intensification in the regional economic integration of Korea into a Japan-dominated Northeast Asia. Japanese businessmen and officials oriented Korean industrialization towards accelerating Japan's economic development within an expansive, and, especially following the onset of the Sino–Japanese War in 1937, increasingly autarchic and militaristic empire. Large numbers of Koreans, amounting to 10 percent of the entire Korean population by 1940, migrated out of the colony in search of work. Many went to Japan, especially Osaka, where in 1940, the 215,000 Koreans living there made up the third largest urban concentration of Koreans anywhere in the world (Taeuber and Barclay 1950: 287). Korea's regional integration in this era, however, was mostly tied to Japanese policies in Manchuria. Economic linkages between Manchuria and Chōsen had grown in the aftermath of the Russo–Japanese conflict when rice shipped from Inchŏn into Dairen and other Manchurian ports began to supplant supplies previously arriving from Shanghai (Duus 1995: 271). Financially, the most important banking institution promoting Japanese imperial expansion in Manchuria was the Bank of Chōsen. Significant amounts of Japanese industrial capital also moved into northern Korea after the mid-1920s: steel, petrochemical, fertilizer, gunpowder, and hydroelectric companies were among the larger corporations established by Japanese industrialists such as Noguchi Jun, co-founder and executive director of Nitchitsu, the main builder of hydroelectric and chemical plants in the colony. Compared with Japan, Korea had lower costs of electricty, labor, and taxes (Molony 1990: 158–166).

Korean businessmen welcomed the acquisition of Manchukuo, and Japanese officials encouraged an accelerated Korean migration to the region. In the early 1930s, Manchukuo agreed to accept an annual intake of 10,000 Korean families. By 1940 there were about 1.4 million Koreans living there (Eckert 1991: 167–181; Jones 1949; McNamara 1990: 43; Taeuber and Barclay 1950: 286). Koreans also invested in Manchuria, and it was the location of some large Korean businesses by the end of the war. Entrepreneur Min Kyu-sik, for example, put up 46 percent of the capital needed to establish the Tōhō development company, which purchased and developed land in northern Korea and Manchuria for Japanese, Korean, or Manchurian farmers. Kim Yŏn-su operated the large

Kyŏngbang textile company in Mukden which employed 3,000 workers by the end of the war, but he also invested in numerous Manchurian businesses, including the Mukden Bank of Commerce, the Manchurian Real Estate and Development Company, the Manchurian Paper Company, the Manchurian-Mongolian Woolen Company, and the Dairen Machine Works (Eckert 1991: 179–181; McNamara 1990: 71). Between 1933 and 1939 Korea's external trade with areas outside Japan grew tremendously, and most of it occurred as a result of increased commerce with Manchuria. As Carter Eckert pointed out, "with the establishment of Manchukuo, Korean exports enjoyed a boom that eventually allowed Korea to move from an almost total trade dependency on Japan to a more diverse trade structure" (Eckert 1991: 171). This late colonial era of regional economic integration thus marked a brief moment when Korean capitalists gained experience with pluralist trade linkages under Japanese hegemony.

Korean industrialization produced a small working class in this era. Over the course of the 1930s Koreans engaged in factory work doubled. By 1940 there were almost 703,000 workers in the colony, and the number reached 1.32 million by 1943 (Eckert *et al.* 1990: 311). This did not include the substantial numbers of Koreans slaving away in Manchuria or Japan. Most Koreans were forced to work as unskilled laborers, and were paid less than Japanese doing the same job. Korean women were generally exploited the harshest, as their salaries were often half of those given to Korean men. Up to 20 percent of women working in factories were under the age of sixteen, and for those working in textiles the figure was 10 percent higher. Women aged under sixteen earned even less – often about one-seventh of adult males (Chŏng 1988: 49–101). In Noguchi Jun's Chōsen Chisso chemical plant, for example, in 1945 male Japanese workers earned 7.33 yen per day while Korean men and women earned 3.58 and 1.46 yen respectively (Molony 1990: 165).

A small white-collar group of workers also emerged in the 1930s and 1940s. The outbreak of the Sino–Japanese War in 1937 led to labor shortages in the colony and to larger numbers of Koreans occupying managerial and engineering jobs. Some women obtained white-collar work: the number of female nurses in 1943 was just over 2,000, while over 2,000 women were employed as teachers in 1938 (Eckert 1996). Although relatively small in number, the middle and working classes of employees reflected the changing social composition of the colony.

In the face of colonial industrialization and tensions in the countryside, Korean peasants left their villages to seek work in cities or other parts of Korea (especially the north), Japan, or Manchuria. In the process, Korea's rural and urban worlds were recast. Urbanization accelerated following the onset of the second Sino–Japanese War, but even in the first half of the 1930s, industrial development combined with economic hardship in the countryside to produce an out-migration of about 350,000 men from villages. In the following decade, as many as 2.2 million men left villages in search of work. Hundreds of thousands of women also left villages, many for factory work in textile mills. The southern Korean cities of Seoul (Kyŏngsŏng), Inchŏn, and Pusan were also popular destinations for rural migrants in the 1930s and 1940s. Although not all Koreans who left the countryside went to live in cities, the urban composition of the country accelerated, approximately doubling between 1920 and 1935 to 7 percent of the population at the end of the period, and almost doubling again by the end of World War II. By 1940, Seoul had 1.1 million people, its population having increased by about 800,000 people in fifteen years. Kyŏngsŏng became a "fascinating example of a growing modern urban space ... with an infrastructure of a budding urban population, popular culture, and the penetration of modern technology and values through modern education" (Park 1999: 17). There were significant limitations to Korea's urban modernity in the colonial era. Relatively few people lived in cities and Kyŏngsŏng experienced a compressed form of colonial development unequaled in any other city in the colony. As Yoo Sun-young (2001: 426) argues,

> although rapid urbanization occurred during the colonial period, the gaps and lags between Kyongsong and other regions in terms of economic, social and cultural modernization were so great that Kyongsong was the only city in the process of modernization in Korea. The collective desire for modern things and images therefore, took its shape mostly in the streets of Kyongsong.

Improvements in health standards and life expectancy during the colonial period could also be taken as indicators of the new foundations of capitalist growth in Korea, though research done on these topics suggests that the introduction of modern health programs, not improvements in the standard of living, were primarily responsible for lowered mortality rates. As Haggard and colleagues have pointed out, "real average farm income changed little during 1915–37, real wages for agricultural labor declined, and consumption of major staple foods and caloric intake from them fell" (Haggard *et al.* 1997: 870; see also Kwon 1977, ch. III). Furthermore, the wartime suffering, the uprooting of the population, mass mobilization of society, and social conflict in the countryside are critical to understanding the broader psychological and social contexts in which foundational capitalism appeared in colonial Korea. To ignore the tremendous psychological stresses and social dislocations of the modernization process in this era would be to distort both its impact and the political conditions in which it evolved. Moreover, the social upheavals of the postwar era meant that capitalism on the Korean peninsula continued to evolve under conditions of profound social and psychological pain.

Korea's agricultural transformation: the agrarian roots of foundational capitalist modernity

Gi-Wook Shin's contribution to this volume (Chapter 1) provides us with a rich perspective on the broader societal changes that occurred in early twentieth century Korea. He demonstrates that the changing power relationships between peasants and landlords were a critical element of the history and evolution of Korean capitalism. The commercialization of agriculture that resulted from significantly increased exports to Japan after 1876 did not alter late dynastic Korea's social structure or the relationship between lord and peasant. Indeed, in the first couple of decades of the twentieth century, the fundamental power relations in the countryside became more favorable to the *yangban* elite. Important changes in socio-economic ties between landlord and peasant occurred only after the 1920s and they accelerated in the 1930s and 1940s.

Shin also shows that the colonial state and private capital were only partly responsible for the transformations besetting Korea. In the 1920s, the emergence of peasant protest provided an important impetus for the transition towards capitalism. The peasant union movement of this era challenged landlord authority by demanding changes in the terms of agricultural contracts, land tenure, and rents. In the 1930s, Japanese officials abandoned some of their previous support for Korean *yangban*, and peasants used newly enacted colonial legislation designed to mediate social conflict in the countryside successfully to dispute traditional spheres of landlord power. This weakening of the influence of the landowning class in rural areas provided incentives for them to invest in non-agricultural pursuits and to establish modern *nongjang* farms, thus accelerating the country's evolution towards a modern capitalistic social structure. The social and economic changes that resulted from the peasant–landlord power struggle therefore reflected the needs and responses of social classes under pressure, as well as the dialectics of power in colonial Korea.

In highlighting the role of non-state factors which shaped Korea's transformation and arguing that agrarian conflict was critical in laying the foundations for major societal change in twentieth century Korea, Shin contributes to our understanding of the significance of arguments put forth by Carter Eckert, Dennis McNamara, and others. By providing a nuanced framework for interpreting the "colonial origins" debate for the development of Korean capitalism, Shin reminds us not to exaggerate Chōsen's early twentieth century industrial accomplishment or the role of the colonial state as a factor in the country's longer term transfiguration. A fuller picture of capitalist development in twentieth century Korea requires us to take into account the interrelationship between socio-economic changes in agriculture and manufacturing.

Rival modernities: North and South Korea

The Soviet and American occupations facilitated the creation of two rival Korean states by the end of 1948, but the two Koreas were not simply Westernized or communized along pre-existing models. The northern system, even more than the southern, inherited an industrial base. What emerged was a command-style economy blended with colonial industry. According to Charles Armstrong, the northern economy, "like many other aspects of revolutionary transformation at the time, combined Japanese colonial legacies and Soviet models and influence to create a new, distinctively Korea communist system with great strengths as well as glaring weaknesses" (Armstrong 2003: 136). As part of an effort at self-legitimization, and to gain more autonomy within the communist world, the North Korean state projected itself as a revolutionary society *par excellence.* Especially from the mid-1950s onwards, northern writers and propagandists depicted Kim Il Sung as an heroic and legendary communist-nationalist, offering him to the world as a model for the future of all human revolution. Northern themes of revolutionary socialist modernity thus contrasted sharply with those articulated in the southern part of the peninsula.

In both North and South Korea, the colonial era fundamentally shaped the outlook of politicians; it informed their rhetoric, and the way they acted and reacted to domestic and international events. Like Kim Il Sung, Syngman Rhee articulated an anti-Japanese and anti-colonial meta-narrative, but Rhee's vision for Korea was a conservative, Christian, and capitalist country working closely with the West, and with the USA in particular. His goal was not only forcefully to rejoin the north and south, but, more generally, to eliminate the threat of secular, international communism. This counter-revolutionary project, which congealed in the wake of the Korean conflict, dovetailed with anti-communist aspects of colonial rule and the cold war to create a line of ideological continuity with the colonial era which did not exist in the north.

Foundational capitalism: the era of American hegemony, 1945–1970s

Korea's social and economic transformation was far from complete in 1945. As late as 1940, less than 6 percent of Korean laborers worked in manufacturing enterprises. Furthermore, employment and real wages in this sector declined over the next five years. Agricultural production still dominated the economy, and about three-quarters of the population lived in rural areas.[6] Exports increased dramatically in the decade of the 1930s – from 266.5 million yen in 1930 (approximately 133 million dollars) to over 1 billion yen (approximately 250 million dollars) in 1939 – but their value dropped for the remainder of the war, in part due to declines in agricultural productivity. By 1945, agricultural output in Korea had reverted back to 1933 levels.[7]

The partition of the country in 1945 and the repatriation of some 435,000 Japanese from southern Korea left the new American mandate with a hollowed industrial structure and created serious economic difficulties, particularly in the areas of power and resources.[8] Shortages of coal, electricity, fertilizer, chemicals, and paper significantly limited industrial production after the war (General Headquarters Supreme Commander for the Allied Powers 1983a). These problems were further exacerbated by the lack of skilled personnel and labor.

Indeed, the rapid dismantling of the colonial system and the division of the peninsula left Korea's political and economic future uncertain. During the colonial era the Japanese had limited Koreans' ability to accumulate capital, and to operate and manage industrial enterprises. Now the division of the peninsula at the 38th parallel created more barriers to Korean modernization. In short, the longer term viability of capitalism on the peninsula could not be assured in 1945. The end of the colonial era bequeathed to southern Korea a largely agrarian economy which had been cut off from its external markets, which faced shortages of indigenous technical expertise, and which had seriously inadequate resources and industrial chemicals. In March 1946, for example, American authorities had to import liquid chlorine and aluminum ammonium sulphate from Japan to purify southern Korea's drinking-water (General Headquarters Supreme Commander for the Allied Powers 1983b). Shortages resulted in declines in industrial productivity. In 1946, half of the factories in the American zone that had been in operation in 1944 were no longer functioning, and those that were were producing at only about 20 percent of their earlier rate. The numbers of Koreans employed in manufacturing industries south of the 38th parallel dropped from 300,520 in June 1945 to 122,159 in December 1949. In mid-1949 unemployment was about 900,000 in a population of just over twenty million (Haggard *et al.* 1997: 872; Kuznets 1977).

Despite the negative economic impact of partition, the processes of social and economic change involved in developing (South) Korea's industrial economy continued after 1945.[9] The period from the 1920s through to the 1970s as a whole was characterized by the decline of regressive landlord–peasant hierarchies, the elimination of landlords as a political and economic force in society, the emergence of an urban-based society, and the building up of a domestic consumer goods manufacturing capacity based on machine production and industrial processes. Korea ceased to be a predominantly agrarian society only in the mid-1970s, and only in the early 1970s did its secondary and manufacturing industries account for a higher percentage of the country's GNP than did agriculture. In these ways, Korea's societal transformation reached a turning point in the 1970s.

The hegemonic transitions which occurred in 1945 – the global, between the United States and Britain, and the regional, in Northeast Asia between the United States and Japan – did not alter the basic characteristics of Korea's social revolution which originated in the late Chosŏn dynasty. The transition from Japanese to American overlordship in post-World War II South Korea, however, did alter the political relationship between the new client state and the hegemon. This is significant, since after 1945 capitalism in South Korea evolved under a more loose form of hegemony-empire. In contrast to Japanese colonial rule, American hegemony was global in scope, and American power, more nuanced and diffused throughout the globe, exercised indirect as well as direct influence over South Korea through pressures on a nominally independent government. This political relationship encouraged Korean participation in the processes of capital accumulation and development much more than did the regional autarchy of the Japanese empire. The structural limits to this postwar framework of Korean development largely related to the US goal after 1946 to "link up"[10] Korea's economy with Japan. The reverse course in Japan in 1948 and the rebuilding of the Japanese economy in the 1950s had tremendous long-term implications for South Korean economic development, since once Japan resumed its position as the outstanding Asian capitalist power, the United States tied Korea more actively into its former colonial master's economic nexus (see Chapter 6, this volume). This occurred in part because of the attractiveness of its postwar economic success and because of the economic and strategic imperatives of the United States' cold war policy. Japan's growing economic prominence from the mid-1950s informed official American thinking about Korea.

For most of the postwar era, Korean governance was authoritarian in character. American policy-makers, moreover, accepted the repressive bent of these regimes, providing them with substantial economic and political support. As I argue in Chapter 6, US officials were more supportive of the Park Chung Hee junta than they were of the Second Republic, precisely because Park's economic objectives seemed to coincide more closely with their own. By embracing the new military government, American officials self-consciously cultivated a greater role for Japan in Korea's external system. After 1965, the year of the normalization treaty, Japan once again played an important role in Korea, but this was a Japan subordinate to American hegemony and firmly within a new "defensive perimeter" security framework for Asia. The result was increased Japanese influence on the military government, and on the evolution of Korean capitalism. The normalization of relations foreshadowed the pluralist capitalism that was increasingly to characterize Korean economic growth and the country's linkages with the advanced and developing economies of the world system. The grooming of Japan as a partner in America's informal empire on the peninsula diluted American hegemony in Northeast Asia, but these consequences were understood and welcome to American policy-makers. Authoritarian rule and domestic capital accumulation were thus two interrelated strains of South Korea's foundational capitalist modernity during the period of American hegemony.

Bureaucratic authoritarianism and foundational capitalism

For about a decade after 1945, American and South Korean economic objectives were designed to achieve pre-war production levels. Neither American nor Western planners, however, initially envisaged South Korea with an advanced industrial economy. South Koreans themselves often pushed for this strategy, not infrequently against the skepticism of officials in the various American aid agencies. In the 1950s, the Rhee government's industrialization program hoped to establish in South Korea defining elements of the northern economy: heavy industry and plant machinery which could produce hydroelectricity, fertilizer, and even steel. The Park regime then implemented and accelerated a number of the modernization programs that had been conceived in the late 1950s. A major factor underpinning South Korea's postwar economic development was the role of the state, and several chapters in this book contribute to our understanding of the dynamics and significance of what social scientists have labeled Korea's "strong" or "developmental" state.[11]

In his discussion of the major factors which have promoted South Korean growth, Paul Kuznets argues that the developmental state's most important contribution to economic growth was the succession of five-year plans which were produced by military governments from 1963 onwards. These plans targeted particular industries, while the Korean bureaucracy, including the economic planning board, the finance ministry, and the ministry of commerce and trade, oversaw their implementation and execution. These agencies and departments helped the large conglomerate *chaebŏl* to obtain technologies and access to domestic and international credit, and protected the domestic market from foreign competition.

David Kang (Chapter 7) and John Lie (Chapter 5) address questions related to who influenced the decisions of bureaucrats and what interests state employees sought to further or to protect. Far from being an autonomous, neutral agent, the Korean bureaucracy has been closely linked to state politics. As political scientist T.J. Pempel has noted, "developmental state theorists too often treat the national bureaucracy as totally depoliticized, socially disembodied, and in rational pursuit of a self-evident national interest – in short, the embodiment of Weber's 'idealized' bureaucracy" (Pempel 1999: 144). John Lie emphasizes the role of state patronage and the intricate social networks between *chaebŏl* owners and the bureaucracy as factors shaping the success of Korean business. Kang also explores the relationship between the state and large corporations in Korea, challenging some of the existing literature on the developmental state. He argues that there was more continuity in the Korean bureaucracy from the Rhee to the Park regimes than has been suggested, and that Park carefully monitored the bureaucracy to promote the goals and interests of the ruling junta. Although the state supported the growth of the *chaebŏl*, both parties became dependent on each other and in effect "mutual hostages" of each others' power and policies. In other words, Kang, complementing Shin's arguments in this volume, points to some of the limits of the power of the post-colonial developmental state. The state was not always able to achieve its goals, and the influence of big business *vis-à-vis* the state grew in the 1970s and 1980s (see also Haggard 1998: 85). As Kang shows, state efforts to "rationalize" the power and automobile industries in the 1970s and 1980s were failures largely because they were successfully resisted by those companies targeted for merger or elimination.

John Lie, David Kang, and Paul Kuznets agree that the postwar era produced more significant economic growth than did the colonial period, and that the 1970s was a critical decade for accelerating Korea's industrial development. For Lie, the importance of the postwar years is symbolized in the post-World War II history of Korea's *chaebŏl*, large corporations and powerful agents themselves in shaping Korea's twentieth century transformation. The *chaebŏl* had roots in the colonial period, but by the 1980s all but two of them had begun their corporate lives after 1945. According to Kuznets, the state prized the *chaebŏl* for their size and economies of scale. Suh Chung-sok and Kwon Seung-Ho provide us with a case study of the state–*chaebŏl* relationship in their chapter on the structural and managerial history of the Hyundai business enterprise (Chapter 4). These authors show a pattern of government support for Hyundai as a favored *chaebŏl*. Beginning in the 1950s, state contracts were an essential element of Hyundai's economic growth. The conglomerate's dependence on these sources of funding grew in the 1960s. The Korean government also supported the company when it faced periods of economic difficulty or crisis. For example, the fall-off in construction associated with the end of the Vietnam War was made up by a series of government contracts to the Hyundai Construction and Civil Engineering Company in the 1970s. Further, when the Hyundai car company was hit by a second oil crisis in the late 1970s, the military government of Chun Doo Hwan granted exclusive rights to Hyundai Motor Company and Hyundai Heavy Industries to build compact automobiles and certain large marine engines. The company's earnings at home contributed in the 1970s to its move into the Middle Eastern construction scene. In this way Hyundai facilitated the geographical and spatial movement of Korean capital in the 1970s, a process which reflected the nascent pluralist geometry of capitalism in Korea in the American era.

As many analysts of Korea's political economy have remarked, the Korean state's economic policy after the 1960s encouraged high indebtedness and overcapacity, structural problems which contributed to periodic economic crises, including the one in the late 1990s. Many people worked hard and for long hours, but structural problems in the *chaebŏl* extended to white-collar management, as John Lie shows (Chapter 5). *Chaebŏl* managers were not always effective in monitoring employees, and employees sometimes pretended to look busy in lieu of doing work. Lie's conclusions accord with those articulated by James Palais, who argues that factors other than "Confucianism" were primarily responsible for the hard work undertaken by white- and blue-collar workers in Korea (Palais 2002).

We therefore need to examine the relationship between the state's repressive policies towards labor and the growth of Korea's global trading networks. A major goal of the *Yusin* constitution of 1972 was to keep workers' demands within prescribed boundaries so as to make Korean *chaebŏl* and capitalism competitive not only on a local, but also on a worldwide scale. The military dimensions of Korea's post-World War II modernization program are discussed by John Lie who traces the strict discipline in the factory workplace to the militarization of the society in the Park Chung Hee era. Military rule tended to legitimize managerial authoritarianism, and military-style methods were employed to discipline blue-collar workers. Management carefully monitored industrial workers in order to maximize production and to meet the export-promotion goals of the state and *chaebŏl*. Military mobilization was thus a significant aspect of South Korea's economic growth, and men's experiences in the army were a harbinger of the work discipline put to use in the country's factories. In the second military era, the themes of competition and work were emphasized as part of a state discourse designed to mobilize workers for national greatness. Although *Yusin* was designed to meet economic needs, it also responded to external challenges posed by North Korea, *détente*, the Nixon doctrine, America's greater reliance on protectionism, and cutbacks in global US military spending. All these threatened to destabilize Korean society and economy. Park equated capitalist development with national strength, or to put it somewhat differently, national greatness.[12] His was not a critique of colonialism, but of societies that lacked the will and capacity to industrialize:

> So far, our export commodities have been made up largely of primary industrial goods, semi-finished products and light industrial items. From now on, we have to shift the pattern to increase drastically exports of finished products, heavy and chemical industrial items, and capital goods. At the same time, we have to broaden our export market to include all countries if possible, instead of relying lopsidedly on a few countries as we are doing now. We also have to make a major shift in our export endeavor to explore overseas markets for our capital and technology. Exports represent the index of national strength.
>
> (Park n.d.: 132)

Yusin thus provided a critical pivot and transitional phase for the movement towards pluralist capitalism for Korea. Moreover, it coincided with a turning point in America's postwar hegemony, the year 1971, when the

Bretton Woods system collapsed. Events going on in Korea were thus part of broader processes related to the changing character of international capitalism after 1945 and to changes in the global structure of power, but they were also influenced by the particular vision of President Park's military government.

The Park regime also facilitated the transformation of South Korean agriculture, as Larry Burmeister demonstrates (Chapter 2). His study of the National Agricultural Cooperative Federation (*nonghyeŏp*) draws parallels between the post-World War II agricultural cooperative's bureaucratic organization and its precursors' in the colonial period. The pre-war agencies included councils for rural revitalization, financial cooperatives, and mutual aid associations; they dealt with such things as financial problems associated with Korean agriculture and improving crop yields. They also provided technical training and social leadership in rural society (Shin and Han 1999). While the post-1961 system shared similarities with the work of the revitalization campaign of the 1930s, the level of state penetration in the countryside was greater. After the 1961 coup, the top-down relationship between the cooperative and various state departments such as the Ministry of Home Affairs or the Ministry of Agriculture and Fisheries reflected the authoritarian style of the military government, which utilized the agricultural cooperative to mobilize the rural population in support of the regime's rural development programs and industrialization efforts. In the 1970s, for example, the agricultural cooperative became a means to implement a government program designed to increase the country's food self-sufficiency. Under this scheme, foreign exchange otherwise spent on food imports would be redirected into investment in industry. The international context in which the cooperative operated was also different. In particular, the United States now provided some of the money and investment needed to launch the new government's development program for agriculture. Major funding for fertilizer plants came from the US government through aid, and later from private corporations such as Gulf Oil and Dow Chemical. In this way, American public aid facilitated the spread of US private capital investment on the peninsula.

Social change in the era of pluralist capitalism

Korea's pluralist capitalist era was characterized by continued reliance on the US–Japanese alliance; a shift towards more complex forms of industry, ones which required more intensive levels of technology and capital input; increased Korean capital investment around the world; growing multilateral trade linkages; and internal political reforms associated with the democracy movement. A number of factors in the 1960s and 1970s helped to lay the groundwork for these developments. They included the relative decline in America's global power, the re-emergence of Japan as a factor in Korean economic development, Korean participation in the Vietnam War, the success of the initial five-year plans, and the incorporation of Korea into the General Agreements on Tariffs and Trade (GATT), and later, the World Trade Organization. There are numerous books and articles on Korea's recent economic development and "globalization." The articles in this volume are largely interested in the ideological dimensions and social consequences of this era of capitalism on the peninsula, and we will begin with a discussion of the impact of industrialization and urbanization upon the modern family structure.

As we have seen, the colonial era was a pivotal period for Korea's transfiguration towards a modern and industrial society. However, viewed in the framework of Korea's twentieth century transformation as a whole, colonial industrialization had a limited impact upon the lives of most Koreans prior to 1945. The urbanization of the country greatly accelerated in the post-World War II era. Several million people migrated from northern to southern Korea after the division, and the Korean War uprooted millions more from villages, towns, and cities. It was the post-Korean war reconstruction and the military government's industrialization drive, however, that shifted the balance of the population away from the countryside. As Paul Kuznets points out in Chapter 3, the population living in urban areas rose from 25 percent in 1955 to 82 percent in 2003. The turning point came in the mid-1970s, when about 50 percent of the population lived in urban areas.[13]

Changes in the urban–rural composition of Korea that began to occur in the 1920s and 1930s were greatly accelerated in the decades of compressed industrialization following 1961. Between 1965 and 1985 about eleven million men and women left farming areas for work in cities. In 1960 Seoul had a population of 2.6 million. By 1970, its population was already over 5.5 million, and about 70 percent of the increase came from people moving from both rural and urban areas of the country. The number of workers in the manufacturing sector also increased dramatically, from just over 250,000 in 1960 to almost one million at the time of the 1972 *Yusin* constitution, and to 2.5 million in 1980. In 2003 there were about 4.2 million workers in manufacturing industries across the country.[14] Many of these industrial workers were women. In pre-1945 Korea, the peak percentage of women factory workers was reached in 1932 when they comprised 34 percent of the manufacturing workforce; in the postwar era, the proportion of female workers in the manufacturing sector rose to higher levels. Women were particularly recruited in the textile and electronics industries, and in the mid-1970s – at the height of their participation rate – they comprised a small majority of all production workers in the country (Koo 2002: 35–36; Park n.d.: 31).

Minja Kim Choe (Chapter 11, this volume) examines the impact these urban and industrial developments have had upon postwar Korean families and cultural belief systems. In particular, she tracks changing attitudes towards marriage, divorce, and gender roles. As Choe illustrates, the growing number of divorces in South Korea in recent years underlines a decline in "traditional" attitudes. In the era of pluralist capitalism, Koreans adopted cultural norms more akin to societies with similar industrial social structures. Other statistics, including the dramatic decrease in the birth rate, reinforce this observation. In the early 1970s, the population grew at more than 2 percent per annum. It was 0.6 percent in 2002, and some observers predict zero population growth early in the third decade of the twenty-first century. Although there have been shifts in direction in the number of births per thousand over the past three decades, the general tendency is towards declining rates. Some of the most dramatic social changes have occurred over the past thirty years, and have thus accompanied the deepening of Korea's industrial and technological revolution. The fertility rate was 4.5 in 1970; this dropped to 1.2 in 2003. In addition, the percentage of three or four generations of a family living in the same accommodation has dropped. In the early 1980s just over 15 percent of all Korean households contained three generations of families; in 2000 there were only 8 percent of such households. The number of single-person households moved in the opposite direction, from 8 percent in 1980 to almost 16 percent in 2000 (Korea National Statistical Office). These statistics underline the impact that industrialization and modernization have had on family life in South Korea. However, while Choe argues that Korean society is now more accepting of working women by and large, Koreans "hold quite traditional views on gender roles, and tend to endorse the traditional division of labor" with the man working and the wife taking care of the children (see Chapter 11). Thus although the status of women in Korean society has changed significantly since divorce was first introduced and legalized by the colonial regime in 1918, social attitudes still reflect a generally conservative belief system.

Choe's conclusions are consistent with those articulated by Mary Brinton and Moonkyung Choi (Chapter 12), whose work underlines the incomplete character of changes in Korea's gendered division of work since the 1960s. They examine the impact that industrialization has had on women's work patterns and underscore some of the unique characteristics and challenges facing contemporary Korean women. The authors note, for example, that in 2000 Korea had the fifth lowest female labor participation rate within the Organization for Economic Co-operation and Development. The gap in employment between men and women is particularly evident among the highly educated. Even within other countries in East Asia, Korea's gendered employment statistics are not encouraging. Comparing the Republic of Korea with Taiwan and Japan, Brinton and Choi find that female Korean wage earners have the highest gender gap in salaries and that they have the lowest workforce rate among women of child-bearing age in all three countries. Professional women are somewhat better off; these workers have a greater likelihood than other Korean women of remaining in their jobs and attaining wages approaching those earned by men. Korea is also unique in the degree of rigidity in its formal employment sector. Korean women with less education and with less well-educated husbands are also more likely to work than other women. Furthermore, barriers to women's careers in white-collar occupations stem from male discrimination and male attitudes which block the hiring or career progress of women. The authors argue that these indicators support marginalization theory's predictions about the incorporation of women into the workforce. In short, despite some areas of progress, many Korean women have continued to experience male patriarchal attitudes and discrimination.

Brinton and Choi do, however, find a mixed pattern of experiences, some of which are not predicted by sociological theory. They find that younger women with more education did enter the formal sector during the intensive period of mobilization and industrialization following 1961. In addition, the percentage of urban women working in the formal sector has not been a good indicator of how successfully the country has incorporated women into the workforce. There are, the authors point out, a number of similarities between women working in the informal and formal sectors, but unique to Korea are differences between married and unmarried women. Most importantly, married women in the informal sector earn higher wages on average than do those in the formal sector. In the future, women's entry into the formal sector will depend on changes in the hiring practices of managers and corporations, and on the perceived relative benefits of formal versus informal work.

The decline of the developmental authoritarian state

By the mid-1980s the contradictions of pursuing economic development within a repressive political system were straining the regime's capacity to govern. The democracy movement which emerged during that decade contested the military government's interpretation of Korea's past and future. A mass coalition of students, workers, and religious organizations demanded democratic and responsible government and successfully challenged the authoritarian regime, forcing it to move towards a more open political system. In this context we may view Sheila Jager's examination of the ideological and social meaning of the country's war memorial museum, conceived under the last military ruler of South Korea, Roh Tae Woo, as an effort by the state to appropriate Korea's military legacy in order to legitimize its own political agenda. The museum's halls are filled with epitaphs linking South Korea's military history to the successful unification of the peninsula. In this view, modernity can only be constructed out of a martial race of men dedicated to strengthening, in a social Darwinian sense, Korean independence and national power. Jager (Chapter 9) reminds us that competition between North and South Korea continued to shape Korean perceptions after the cold war ostensibly ended in the early 1990s. The museum is a good example of how a synthesis of the past and a projected future are meant to influence Korean ideas about the modern world.

Kim Uchang (Chapter 8) discusses the relationship between Confucianism and democracy in contemporary Korea, which is part of a recent resurgence of interest in Asian classical learning (see Bell and Hahm 2003; Duncan 2002a, 2002b; Elman *et al.* 2002). Kim explores the philosophical and social bases of democracy in the West and Korea in an effort to discover if Korea's classical tradition can contribute to a strengthening of its modern civil society. He is interested in the role of Confucianism in Korea's twentieth century transformation, the position of the individual in Western democracies, and the problems associated with exporting a purely Western model of democracy to non-Western countries. He suggests the possibility of a Cartesian–Confucian synthesis for strengthening Korean civil society. Kim's project itself is a modernist one, since he argues that the classical inheritance contains resources which may be recovered to suit the needs of the new democracy. The ideological inheritance includes the classical emphasis on ethical and moral principles, along with its sense of collective ethos.

At this point we should recall the criticisms of classical culture made by individuals and social groups within Korea in the late twentieth century, since in many cases the struggle for democracy was also perceived as a fight against the oppressive legacies of "Confucian" society (Duncan 2002a, 2002b). Kim is aware of the pitfalls of invoking the historical legacy of Confucianism to serve as a model for Korean society, and he points out that the Confucian tradition has often stood in opposition to the movement towards modern forms and institutions. His analysis of the classical themes of authenticity, *kyung*, or apprehensive awareness, and morality are reminiscent of themes which are compatible with important strains in Western philosophy, and existentialism in particular. It may be that modern-day Korea's search for freedom in a political and moral sense will be enhanced by a renewed effort to understand its classical inheritance.

Conclusion

This chapter has suggested a chronology and framework for understanding Korea's societal transformation. Many of the dates highlighted – 1876, 1894, 1914, 1945, and 1971 – represent turning points in Korean history, but they were also significant years in the evolution of the modern international system itself. Korea's economic development has been influenced by local and global socio-economic and political structures of power. Moreover, they emerged as a product of the competition as well as partnership of two hegemonic powers in particular: Japan and the United States. The period between the 1910s and the 1970s was a turbulent age when the bases for Korea's societal transformation were established. Linking the history of colonial and post-colonial Korea might be controversial, partly because of the odium associated with Japan's harsh and violent colonial project. Unlike the celebratory accounts of South Korea's economic growth, however, this framework does not take for granted the emergence of modern capitalistic structures in Korea. Indeed, until late in the foundational era, Koreans recognized many social and political possibilities for their country's future. The chronology thus expresses the contingent character of Korean economic development, while capturing the uncertainty and sense of urgency which underpinned Korean actions throughout the period. In so doing, it suggests a fresh way of conceptualizing and understanding Korea's twentieth century transformation.

The chapters in this volume attest to the significant struggles within Korea which accompanied efforts to industrialize and modernize society. Agrarian disputes, mobilization and uprooting of people, ideological battles, and state repression have been defining features of Korea's modern history. The social and economic dislocations associated with dynastic decline, occupation, war, and authoritarianism were central to the transformative processes affecting the peninsula, as it was in these contexts that Koreans articulated ideas about themselves and the directions in which they wanted to take society. Over the course of the past 100 years the material life and world views of Koreans have changed dramatically. A mass-production, high-technology, and consumer-based economy has replaced the Chosŏn dynasty's craft industry and farmers' market; capitalist class structures dominate a highly urbanized society; associational groups with global networks work to improve the country's environment and to advance democratic practices and social rights; and China has turned to South Korea as well as to other industrialized states for its own development. Contemporary problems associated with the distribution of wealth, unemployment, social conflict, and poverty are discussed and mediated in an increasingly complex and internationally oriented democratic polity. Studying Korea is important now as ever. The developing world has turned to the republic as a partial model for its own modernization projects; a greater appreciation in the West of the dynamics of Korean history and society will also enhance our comparative understanding of the challenges facing industrial societies around the globe.

Acknowledgments

I would like to thank Yun-Shik Chang, Gi-Wook Shin, William Wray, and Avram Agov for their insightful comments and suggestions on earlier versions of this chapter. My work on this volume also benefited from a grant from the Social Sciences and Humanities Research Council of Canada.

Notes

1 For an analysis of the haircutting decree and its impact see Jang (1998). A very good discussion on the use of the terms "Confucianism" and "Neo-Confucianism" may be found in Elman (2002).
2 My thanks go to Jinyoung Yu for research assistance in Korean language sources.
3 For an excellent discussion of the transition in thought between the late Chosŏn and early colonial eras, consult Schmid (2002). The reference here is taken from pp. 56–57.
4 For a discussion on the role of the *kaekchu* see Eckert (1991: ch. 1). For the distinction between *kaekchu* and *yŏgak*, consult Duus (1995: 273–276).
5 Over the 1918 to 1928 period the average number of people involved in strikes per year was about 51,000.
6 In the first two decades of Japanese rule, grains had, on average, comprised almost 70 percent of colonial Korea's exports. From 1930 to 1938, a period generally of high exports, grains remained the single most important commodity export, accounting for some 55 percent of the total goods sent out of the colony. See McNamara (1996: 35).
7 Colonial statistics are derived from the Government-General of Tyosen of Keizo (Seoul) (1938: ch. 3) and McNamara (1996: 48 fn 43). Over the course of the 1930s, the yen's value went down about 50 percent. In 1930 the yen was worth about 49 cents. By 1939 it was worth about 25 cents. The low point occurred in late 1932 when it reached about 20 cents. See also Suh (1978: chs 2 and 5). For the decline in agricultural productivity during the war see Haggard *et al.* (1997: 869).
8 There were about 225,000 Japanese north of the 38th parallel in mid-August 1945. See Cumings (1981: 479, fn 70). In September 1945 American military authorities estimated that there were 7.4 million Japanese in occupied territory overseas. The vast majority of these returned over the course of 1945 and 1946. See General Headquarters Supreme Commander for the Allied Powers (1983a).
9 Despite the economic difficulties which beset the early postwar South Korean economy, Korean entrepreneurs furthered their economic prospects. As early as the fall of 1945, American occupation authorities observed that there had been "great public clamor to dispose of Japanese ownership of properties in Korea." Although the regulations governing such transfers were complex and cumbersome, "many Koreans are anxious to buy such properties" (General Headquarters Supreme Commander for the Allied Powers, 1983a).
10 The phrase is George Marshall's (see Cumings 1984).
11 See e.g. Woo-Cumings (1999).
12 For a discussion of some of these issues, consult Woo (1991: ch. 5).
13 In 1975 48 percent of Korea's population lived in urban areas. See United Nations Development Program, Human Development Indicators for Korea at http://www.undp.org/hdr2003/indicator/cty_f_KOR.html.
14 For internal migration patterns in the 1960s in Korea see Yu (1980); Koo (2002: ch. 2); Korea National Statistical Office, Statistical Handbook of Korea (2002, http://www.nso.go.kr/eng/handbook/chapter2.shtml).

References

Allen, Michael. 2001. "Ambivalent Social Darwinism in Korea," *International Journal of Korean History* 2: 1–24.

Armstrong, Charles. 2003. *The North Korean Revolution 1945–1950*, Ithaca, NY: Cornell University Press.

Arrighi, Giovanni, Po-Keung Hui, and Ho-Fung Hung. 2003. "Historical Capitalism, East and West," in Giovanni Arrighi, Takeshi Hamashita and Mark Selden (eds), *The Resurgence of East Asia – 500, 150, 50 year Perspectives*, New York: Routledge.

Bell, Daniel A. and Hahm Chaibong (eds). 2003. *Confucianism for the Modern World*, Cambridge: Cambridge University Press.

Chŏng, Chinsong. 1988. "Singminji Chabonchu ŭi wa Kwachŏngesŏ Yŏsŏngnotongui Pyŏnmo," *Han'gŭk yŏsŏnghak* 4: 49–101.

Chung, Youn-tae. 2002. "Refracted Modernity and the Issue of Pro-Japanese Collaborators in Korea," *Korea Journal* 42: 18–59.

Cumings, Bruce. 1981. *The Origins of the Korean War: Liberation and the Emergence of Separate Regimes 1945–1947*, Princeton, NJ: Princeton University Press.

——. 1984. "The Origins and Development of the Northeast Asian Political Economy: Industrial Sectors, Product Cycles and Political Consequences," *International Organization* 38: 1–40.

——. 2002. "The Korea-Centric Japanese Imperium and The Transformation of the International System from the 1930s to the 1950s," Paper prepared for the XIII Congress of the International Economic History Association at http://www.eh.net/XIIICongress/cd/papers/8Cumings414.pdf.

Duncan, John. 2002. "Uses of Confucianism in Modern Korea," in Benjamin Elman, John Duncan, and Herman Ooms (eds), *Rethinking Confucianism: Past and Present in China, Japan, Korea, and Vietnam*, Los Angeles, CA: Asia Institute.

——. 2002. "The Genealogy of Confucian *Moralpolitik* and Its Implications for Modern Civil Society," in Charles Armstrong (ed.), *Korean Society: Civil Society, Democracy and the State*, London: Routledge.

Duus, Peter. 1995. *The Abacus and the Sword: The Japanese Penetration of Korea, 1895–1910*, Berkeley: University of California Press.

Eckert, Carter. 1991. *Offspring of Empire: The Koch'ang Kims and the Colonial Origins of Korean Capitalism 1876–1945*, Seattle: University of Washington Press.

——. 1996. "Total War, Industrialization, and Social Change in Late Colonial Korea," in Peter Duus, Ramon Myers, and Mark Peattie (eds), *The Japanese Wartime Empire, 1931–1945*, Princeton, NJ: Princeton University Press.

Eckert, Carter, Ki-baik Lee, Young Ick Lew, and Edward Wagner (eds). 1990. *Korea Old and New: A History*, Seoul: Ilchokak.

Elman, Benjamin A. 2002. "Rethinking 'Confucianism' and 'Neo-Confucianism' in Modern Chinese History," in Benjamin A. Elman, John B. Duncan, and Herman Ooms (eds), *Rethinking Confucianism: Past and Present in China, Japan, Korea, and Vietnam*, Los Angeles, CA: Asia Institute.

General Headquarters Supreme Commander for the Allied Powers. 1983a. *Summation of Non-military Activities in Japan and Korea*, No. 1, 1945, Wilmington: Scholarly Resources Microfilm.

——. 1983b. *Summation of Non-military Activities in Japan and Korea*, Nos. 1–7, 1945–6, Wilmington: Scholarly Resources Microfilm.

Government-General of Tyosen. 1938. *Annual Report on Administration of Tyosen, 1937–38*, Seoul: Keizo.

Haggard, Stephan. 1998. "Business, Politics and Policy in East and Southeast Asia," in Henry S. Rowen (ed.), *Behind East Asian Growth: The Political and Social Foundations of Prosperity*, New York: Routledge.

Haggard, Stephan, David Kang, and Chung-in Moon. 1997. "Japanese Colonialism and Korean Development: A Critique," *World Development* 25: 871.

Hamashita, Takeshi. 2001. "Overseas Chinese Financial Networks and Korea," in S. Sugiyama and Linda Grove (eds), *Commerical Networks in Modern Asia*, London: Curzon.

——. 2003. "Tribute and Treaties: Maritime Asia and Treaty Port Networks in the Era of Negotiation, 1800–1900," in Giovanni Arrighi, Takeshi Hamashita and Mark Selden (eds), *The Resurgence of East Asia – 500, 150, 50 year Perspectives*, New York: Routledge.

Huh, Dong-hyun. 2001. "Forms of Acceptance of Social Darwinism by the Korean Progressives of the 1880–1890s: On the Materials of Yu Giljun and Yun Ch'iho," *International Journal of Korean History* 2: 41–63.

Jang, Sukman. 1998. "The Politics of Haircutting in Korea: A Symbol of Modernity and the 'Righteous Army Movement' (1895–1896)," *Review of Korean Studies* 1: 26–52.

——. 2001. "The Formation of Antiritualism in Modern Korea: Modernity and Its Critique of Confucian Ritual," *Korea Journal* 41: 93–113.

Jones, Francis Clifford. 1949. *Manchuria since 1931*, London: Royal Institute of International Affairs.

Jung, Tae-hern. 2000. "Economic Features of Colonial Modernity in Modern Korea," *International Journal of Korean History* 1: 39–60.

Kim, Gi-seung. 2001. "Embracing and Overcoming of Social Darwinism by Confucian Intellectuals in the Early 20th Century Korea: The Cases of Park Eun-Sik (1859–1925)," *International Journal of Korean History* 2: 25–40.

Kim Jinsŏng. 1999. *Hyundaesŏng ŭi Hyŏngsŏng Sŏul e Ttansŭhŭlŭl Hŏhara*, Seoul: Hyŏnsil Munwha yŏn'gu.

Kim Keong-il. 2001. "Modernity and Tradition in Everyday Life of the 1950s," *Seoul Journal of Korean Studies* 14: 263–297.

Kim, Sunhyuk. 2002. "Civil Society and Democratization", in Charles Armstrong (ed.), *Korean Society: Civil Society, Democracy and the State*, London: Routledge.

Kimura, Kenji. 2001. "Japanese Business Networks in Prewar Korea: The Case of the Enterprises of Kameya Aisuke," in S. Sugiyama and Linda Grove (eds), *Commerical Networks in Modern Asia*, London: Curzon.

Koo, Hagen. 2002. *Korean Workers: The Culture and Politics of Class Formation*, Ithaca, NY: Cornell University Press.

Korea National Statistical Office, http://www.nso.go.kr/eng.

Kuznets, Paul. 1977. *Economic Growth and Structure in the Republic of Korea*, New Haven, CT: Yale University Press.

Kwon, Tai Hwan. 1977. *Demography of Korea: Population Change and Its Components 1925–66*, Seoul: Seoul National University Press.

McClain, James L. 2002. *Japan: A Modern History*, New York: Norton.

McNamara, Dennis L. 1990. *The Colonial Origins of Korean Enterprise 1910–1945*, Cambridge: Cambridge University Press.

——. 1996. *Trade and Transformation in Korea, 1876–1945*, Boulder, CO: Westview Press.

Molony, Barbara. 1990. *Technology and Investment: The Prewar Japanese Chemical Industry*, Cambridge, MA: Harvard Council on East Asian Studies.

Palais, James. 2002. "Confucianism and Economic Development in South Korea," in Benjamin A. Elman, John B. Duncan, and Herman Ooms (eds), *Rethinking Confucianism: Past and Present in China, Japan, Korea, and Vietnam*, Los Angeles: UCLA Asia Pacific Monograph Series, pp. 489–517.

Park Chung Hee. n.d. "October Revitalizing Reforms and Our Future Goals," in Republic of Korea, *Major Speeches by President Park Chung Hee*, Seoul: Samwha Publishing, n.d. (*c*.1974).

Park Soon-Won. 1999. *Colonial Industrialization and Labor in Korea: The Onoda Cement Factory*, Cambridge, MA: Harvard University Asia Center.

Pempel, T.J. 1999. "The Developmental Regime in a Changing World Economy," in Meredith Woo-Cumings, *The Developmental State*, Ithaca, NY: Cornell University Press.

Schmid, Andre. 2002. *Korea Between Empires, 1895–1919*, New York: Columbia University Press.

Schumpeter, E.B. (ed.). 1940. *The Industrialization of Japan and Manchukuo: Population, Raw Materials and Industry*, New York: Macmillan.

Shin Gi-Wook and Do-Hyun Han. 1999. "Colonial Corporatism: The Rural Revitalization Campaign, 1932–1940," in Gi-Wook Shin and Michael Robinson (eds), *Colonial Modernity in Korea*, Cambridge, MA: Harvard University Asia Center.

Shin Gi-Wook and Michael Robinson (eds). 1999. *Colonial Modernity in Korea*, Cambridge, MA: Harvard University Asia Center.

Suh, Sang-Chul. 1978. *Growth and Structural Changes in the Korean Economy, 1910–1940*. Cambridge, MA: Harvard University Press.

Taeuber, Irene B. and George W. Barclay. 1950. "Korea and the Koreans in the Northeast Asian Region," *Population Index* 4: 287.

United Nations Development Program. 2003. *Human Development Indicators for Korea* at http://www.undp.org/hdr2003/indicator/cty_f_KOR.html.

von Laue, Theodore. 1989. *The World Revolution of Westernization: The Twentieth Century in Global Perspective*, Oxford: Oxford University Press.

Woo, Jung-en. 1991. *Race to the Swift: State and Finance in Korean Industrialization*, New York: Columbia University Press.

Woo-Cumings, Meredith (ed.). 1999. *The Developmental State*, Ithaca, NY: Cornell University Press.

Yoo Sun-young. 2001. "Embodiment of American Modernity in Colonial Korea," *Inter-Asia Cultural Studies* 2: 423–441J.

Yu, Eui-Young. 1980. "Internal Migration and Development of Cities," in Chang Yunshik (ed.), *Korea: A Decade of Development*, Seoul: Population and Development Studies Center, Seoul University.

Part I

The agrarian transformation

1 Neither "sprouts" nor "offspring"

The agrarian roots of Korean capitalism[1]

Gi-Wook Shin

Recent works on colonial industrialization have renewed the debate over the relationship between colonialism and development in Korea (An *et al.* 1989; Eckert 1991; Hori 1995; McNamara 1990; Park 1999). Their research challenges Korean nationalist scholarship that has depicted Japanese colonial rule as either destroying the "sprouts" of what was supposedly an incipient Korean capitalism or distorting Korea's path to capitalist development. They argue instead that not only was there colonial industrialization, but also substantial participation in it by Korean landlords and capitalists. Their view, while commended by some as enhancing current understanding of colonial and postcolonial development in Korea (Kohli 1994), has also encountered fierce criticism, especially from Korean scholars who interpret it as regressing to the "colonialist view (*singminjuŭi sagwan*)" of Japanese rule in Korea (see Chŏng 1997; Haggard *et al.* 1997; Sin 1997).

This chapter attempts to contribute to the debate by re-examining the historical process of Korea's transition from an agrarian to industrial nation since the late nineteenth century. Its central argument is that both nationalist and "colonial origins" explanations are inadequate for understanding Korea's transformation from an agrarian economy during the late dynastic era to its initial industrialization during the Japanese colonial period, and South Korea's more advanced levels of postcolonial development. As an alternative, I offer an explanation based on a theory of agrarian conflict that posits agrarian class structure, relations, struggles, and conflict resolution as key to economic change. Such attention to agrarian variables affords a more comprehensive historical explanation of the origins and processes of Korean capitalism. I begin, however, with a discussion of the debate between advocates of "sprouts" (*maeng'a ron*) or incipient capitalism theory and those who emphasize the colonial origins of Korean capitalism.[2]

The Korean debate: "sprouts" or "offspring of Empire"?

The sprouts school, represented by Korean nationalist historians, argues that increased commercialization and development of wage labor relations indicate capitalism had already emerged in eighteenth-century Korea, long before the arrival of Japanese imperialism. According to Kim Yongsŏp's (1960, 1970) influential analyses of land and tax registers (*yangan*), commercial capitalism, led by "managerial farmers (*kyŏngyŏnghyŏng punong*)," comparable to British yeomen, appeared in eighteenth-century Korea as a result of internal urban market growth and such technological innovations as double-cropping and transplanting. Unlike "feudal landlords" who increased income through high rent and usury and yields by expanding holdings (cultivated by slaves and tenants), managerial farmers adopted improved techniques to increase productivity and profit. Imperialist incursion, however, later skewed such development, reducing Korea to a "semi-feudal, semi-colonial" country and preventing the sprouts of its native capitalism from becoming full-grown capitalism. North Korean historians, who in the 1960s debated the origins of Korean capitalism, also agreed that capitalism infiltrated agriculture in the nineteenth century (see Ch'oe 1981; Doe 1991).

More recently, a number of scholars, notably in the United States and Japan, trace Korean capitalist origins only as far back as the colonial period (An *et al.* 1989; Eckert 1991; Hori 1995; Kohli 1994; McNamara 1990). They argue that rather than trampling the sprouts of capitalism, colonialism fostered industrial development, to the extent that by 1945 Korea was "an integral part of an imperial economic nexus that stretched from Japan across Korea to the Asian continent" (Eckert 1991: 67). For both political and economic reasons, Japanese colonial rule not only promoted industrialization, but also permitted and even encouraged the rise of a Korean capitalist class that came to play a crucial role in postcolonial industrialization. In Eckert's (1991: 255) view,

> Colonialism bequeathed to the postwar period not only a social basis for future development but also an historically based model of successful capitalist growth . . . the pivotal economic function of the state, the concentration of private economic power in the hands of a small number of large business groups . . . the emphasis on exports, and the threat or actuality of war as a stimulus of economic growth.

In short, integral to Korean capitalist development is its colonial legacy, both material and human-cultural.

While both the sprouts and colonial origins views represent major historical approaches to Korean backwardness and development, their explanatory power is weakened by a number of serious flaws. First, the sprouts school exaggerates the capitalist development *potential* in the emergence of managerial farmers and wage laborers. Commercialization of agriculture does not suffice for capitalism: commercialization may be stimulated by motives other than capitalist ones and certain agrarian class structures may prevent managerial farmers from becoming agricultural capitalists. As shown below, many managerial farmers, drawn to attractive returns on land and usury, became landlords rather than agricultural capitalists. The sprouts school is blind to such internal barriers, blaming colonialism for almost every aspect of Korea's underdevelopment. Although colonialism may have indeed skewed Korea's economic trajectory, the precolonial failure to develop capitalism was largely due to a regressive agrarian class structure. The sprouts school also falters in explaining the survival, despite supposed colonial suppression, of the "national capital (*minjok chabon*)" that undergirded postwar capitalist success (Cho 1982).

In contrast, the colonial origins view elucidates how colonialism fostered a particular model of economic growth, featuring the interplay of the state, foreign capital and technology. Its focus on colonial state *industrial* policy and its interaction with *exogenous* factors captures well the overall process of colonial industrialization, but is limited when it comes to understanding *endogenous* forces of industrialization and Korean participation in it. Explaining such participation is important because 40 percent of all firms were Korean, and the Korean share of total capital formation under colonial rule was about 13 percent. When one includes firms owned jointly by Koreans and Japanese (about 30 percent of all companies), Korean participation in colonial industrialization was even more substantial. More importantly, after the Japanese left in 1945, these experienced Koreans played key roles in postcolonial industrialization. Although some Korean capitalists, as the colonial origins proponents have shown, were progressives eager to take advantage of state industrial incentives, it remains to be seen whether they were representative of the whole class of Korean landlord-turned-capitalists. As Haggard *et al.* (1997) point out, the argument may suffer from "selection bias," since it is based on a very few cases selected from among the most successful Korean capitalists.

This suspicion stems primarily from the fact that many Korean landlords, who constituted the rural elite, maintained a Confucian valuation of agriculture over commerce or industry, a cultural heritage that would discourage their participation in colonial industrialization. In addition, Korean agriculture prospered throughout much of the 1930s, producing a higher overall profit margin than non-agricultural investment. Although some sectors of the latter may have been more profitable, non-agricultural investment was still risky in the 1930s, since much of it was lost in firms that went bankrupt within a few years. In fact, the majority of landlord investments, as detailed below, were made in small Korean firms, especially those owned by family members, relatives, and friends, as a method of "portfolio diversification" rather than capitalist enterprise (see Chang 1989; Hŏ 1989). These factors suggest that state industrial policy or economic incentives did not completely dictate landlord capital conversion; other non-economic social factors were also at work.

Finally, the colonial origins argument says little about how the supposed bequeathing of the colonial legacy to postcolonial development actually occurred throughout the turbulent years of the decolonization process, marked by U.S. occupation, division of the nation, popular revolts and rebellions, and war. The issue of historical continuity is important, since a group of scholars have argued that the legacy of colonial industrialization was "erased by intervening historical events," and thus could not contribute much to subsequent industrialization (Haggard *et al.* 1997: 3). As Kohli admits, "demonstrating parallels between historical and contemporary situations ... is clearly not enough to sustain an argument for historical continuity" (1994: 1285). We need an explanation that better specifies concrete mechanisms of historical continuity and discontinuity in Korean development.

This chapter explains Korea's transformation from an agrarian to an industrial nation since the late nineteenth century, using an agrarian conflict theory I have elaborated elsewhere (see Shin 1998). The theory, based on Marxist scholarship on the origins of Western and Japanese capitalism by such writers as Barrington Moore, Jr., Robert Brenner, and E.H. Norman, focuses on agrarian class structure, relations, struggles, and conflict resolution as underlying both economic backwardness and development. Its central claim is that the breakdown of regressive agrarian class structure is pivotal to the rise of capitalist production relations, and that this is achieved through class struggles and consequent conflict resolution that weaken the power of the landed class. In particular, attention to these agrarian variables helps identify structural conditions for economic backwardness, the historical process by which previously regressive class structure and relations can become compatible with capitalist development, and how such change in agrarian class structure and relations can facilitate capitalist transformation. Accordingly, this chapter examines: (1) how agrarian class structure and relations in late nineteenth-century Korea hindered the rise of agricultural capitalism despite increased commercialization; (2) how colonial-era agrarian class struggles and consequent conflict resolution broke up this structure and its relations, facilitating capital movement from land to industry, key to colonial industrialization; and (3) how continued agrarian conflict bred postcolonial land reform that deposed the regressive landed class and further impelled the crucial conversion of capital to industry.

Agrarian structure and the limits of modernity in pre-colonial Korea

In pre-colonial Korea, an agrarian class structure characterized by a powerful landed aristocracy, weak peasantry, and limited royal power promoted regressive methods of surplus extraction, impeding the rise of capitalist production relations. Despite a centralized agrarian bureaucracy, the monarchy had neither the organizational capacity to penetrate society nor effective autonomy from the dominant class. This was because the sources of power, wealth, and prestige were not controlled exclusively by the Crown; they were also based on inheritance of status and landownership. The landed *yangban* aristocracy monopolized landholdings, and its close association with the central bureaucracy effectively checked the power of the throne. Checks and balances between the throne and the aristocracy bequeathed a long period of political stability to the Chosŏn dynasty (1392–1910), but prevented the government from making meaningful reforms in times of domestic crisis and foreign challenge. As Palais indicates, the "fusion of aristocratic status with private landownership ... was almost as resistant to the fiscal encroachments of the central government as a bona fide feudal nobility" (1975: 58).

A powerful landed aristocracy entailed high land concentration and rural inequality. Studies show that not uncommonly about 10 percent to 20 percent of landholders owned one-half to two-thirds of the registered land and 60 percent to 70 percent of the rural population rented all or part of their land from landlords (Kim 1960; Shin 1973). Rental rates were high (around 50 percent of harvested crops) and lease renewal was often at the mercy of landlords, who also indebted their poor tenants through usury. Further, the landed class preserved a regressive land tax structure through connections with the central bureaucracy and kept their lands off tax registers by bribing local officials, at the expense of both the central government and the peasantry. Such inequity and corruption in the levying and collection of taxes often provoked peasant rebellions, such as the 1862 and 1894 peasant uprisings, but these did not seriously alter the dominance of the landed aristocracy. As Palais points out, the *yangban* aristocracy per se was not targeted because peasants did not think of the agrarian class structure and relations as the cause of their poverty. They instead acted against "corrupt officials who practiced extortion and bribery and registered and graded land falsely and inaccurately" (1975: 66). Even late nineteenth-century state reform (e.g., that led by the Taewŏn'gun or the Kabo reforms of 1894–1896) was not able to diminish landlord power. In short, a regressive agrarian class structure along with limited state power blocked significant reform or economic change, including the rise of rural capitalist relations.

In late nineteenth-century Korea, as in early modern Europe, two major forces emerged that had the potential for challenging traditional agrarian social order; that is, population change and the spread of market relations. It is well known that demographic change can greatly influence the course of the economy (see Postan 1972). In nineteenth-century Korea, population growth caused a steady decline in the land/man ratio that strained the agrarian system. Although the exact figures for cultivated land and population during the Chosŏn dynasty are undetermined, the trend seems clear: one study estimates that the land/man ratio decreased gradually from 0.25 *kyŏl* (1 *kyŏl* = 5 acres) per capita in 1666 to 0.19 *kyŏl* in 1807 (Shin 1973), and another reports a more rapid decline from 0.11 *kyŏl* in 1592 to

0.05 *kyŏl* in the early nineteenth century (Pak 1987). The decline in per capita landholding, however, did not break up the existing class structure. On the contrary, it led to increased land concentration and inequality; one estimate shows that the land concentration gini coefficient grew from 0.36 in 1830 to 0.54 in 1898–1899 (Kim 1994: 302). Simply put, demographic change caused increased competition for land among peasants, further weakening their position vis-à-vis the landed class.

Moreover, the abundance of cheap labor dissuaded labor-saving capital investment by the landed class, a situation reinforced by the lack of any substantial development of non-agricultural sectors that could have provided new outlets for surplus labor. Cultivation was of a small amount of owned land, leased land, or both, and since most poor peasants could not meet subsistence needs, they often hired out their labor for supplemental income (Hŏ 1965; Kim 1992). Conversely, neither did wage labor alone suffice to support a family. A typical poor peasant in late nineteenth-century Korea owned little or no land, leased a small amount from others, and labored for wages. Many were compelled to hire out in crucial seasons, at the cost of inadequate or untimely work on their own small farms (Ch'oi 1985). Taking advantage of this labor surplus and their powerful position in society, Korean landlords further consolidated feudal class relations, burdening their tenants with high rent and rates of tenancy transfer.

Another powerful factor in late nineteenth-century Korea was the growth of market relations. While pre-modern Korea (prior to the *Kanghwa* Treaty of 1876) possessed a large number of markets, they were predominantly local: lack of a coherent currency system prevented market integration, and state policy forbade private foreign trade; but the *Kanghwa* Treaty shattered Korea's commercial isolation. Korea not only became a market for foreign manufactured goods, but also an exporter of crops – especially rice and beans – to Japan. Over the thirty years from 1881 to 1910 Korean exports increased fifteenfold and, as a result, prices rose dramatically; between 1901 and 1910 alone, the price of rice increased 79 percent and that of beans 64 percent. Whether interpreted as a free trade system based upon comparative advantage or a typical core–periphery system, the Korean economy was gradually integrating into the world (or, more specifically, Japanese) market.

Market expansion facilitated commercialization of Korean agriculture. Main subsistence crops such as rice and beans rapidly commercialized, joining older commercial crops such as cotton and tobacco. Not only landlords but also owner-cultivators and relatively well-to-do tenants and owner-tenants actively pursued commercial trade. A 1910 survey shows that landlords sold 71.9 percent of their crops and owner-tenants 42.4 percent. Rice commercialization was led by landlords, while the upper strata of owner-tenants and tenants led the development of trade in beans (Miyajima 1974). Those who resided near such port cities as Mokp'o and

Kunsan benefited especially from trade with Japan. For instance, the landlord Yun family in Haenam county of South Chŏlla province, geographically benefiting from proximity to Mokp'o, increased profits by exporting rice; as a result its land holdings almost doubled between 1895 and 1919. Kim's (1972) study of the landlord Kim family on Kanghwa island of Kyŏnggi province and Hong's (1986) case study of the landlord Yi family in Posŏng county of South Chŏlla show that expanding markets facilitated agricultural commercialization. They not only leased land to tenants but cultivated it themselves, hiring wage laborers.

For our purposes, however, the crucial issue is to what extent such signs of increased commercialization indicate that the capitalist mode of production emerged in the countryside. The sprouts school, as described above, argues that commercialization and the emergence of managerial farmers and wage laborers evince the rise of capitalism in nineteenth-century Korea. While this argument demonstrates that the Korean economy was not stagnant prior to imperialist intrusion and that emergent managerial farmers employed improved techniques using hired labor, it remains unclear whether this could have fostered a new *social class* of agricultural capitalists. In addition, the existence of wage labor does not, in itself, indicate the emergence of a capitalist mode of production. As Huang (1985) points out in the case of North China, the emergence of a wage labor force in an overpopulated, non-industrialized society such as Korea would not be sufficient to prove the existence of a qualitative change in mode of production, though it would seem to belie economic stagnation.

Further, agricultural commercialization does not necessarily augur a transition to capitalism. Moore (1966) makes it clear that the *form* of commercial agriculture was just as important as commercialization itself in the rise of Western capitalism. In parts of France, for instance, agricultural commercialization, instead of developing into agricultural capitalism, left peasant society largely intact, while in Eastern Germany Junkers reduced formerly free peasants to serfdom to grow and export grain. Huang (1985) concurs with Moore when he says agricultural commercialization can be stimulated by "subsistence pressures" (subsistence commercialization) or "external intrusion" (dependent commercialization) as much as by the sorts of entrepreneurial efforts (entrepreneurial commercialization) that led to Western capitalism. Although it is difficult to determine the relative importance of each form, it appears that motivations for commercialization were diverse in late nineteenth-century rural Korea: Miyajima's (1974) study of rice commercialization shows that tenants were forced to market rice to obtain subsistence cash, whereas landlords marketed it for profit.

Accordingly, the argument of sprouts theorists that axiomatically links agricultural commercialization to the rise of capitalist relations is problematic. Whether the former leads to the latter is *contingent* on existing class structure and relations. As in modern Eastern Europe, a powerful, regressive landlord class, most of whom relied heavily on high rent and usury for their income, impeded the development of capitalist production relations in nineteenth-century Korea, despite increased agricultural commercialization. High rental rates may have discouraged managerial efforts to develop new technology and improve productivity, and interest on loans in rural Korea ran so high as to be more profitable than income from land. As a result, even managerial farmers increased their fortunes not only by applying improved technology with hired labor, but perhaps preponderantly through usury and commerce (Hong 1981, 1985, 1986; Pak 1983). Taking advantage of attractive returns on land and usury, many, in fact, were becoming landlords rather than agricultural capitalists.[3] In short, Moore's observation about India, where "a class of parasite landlords [who] skimmed off, together with the money lenders, much of what the peasants did not eat themselves, greatly inhibited capital accumulation and industrial growth," appears to describe Korea as well (1966: 430). As late as the turn of the nineteenth century, the economic power of the Korean landed class was closely fused with political power, and their separation from each other, a prerequisite to the development of capitalism, had to wait another generation. Simply put, capitalism as a mode of production had not yet replaced the old social and economic order in pre-colonial Korea.

Colonialism, agrarian conflict, and industrialization

The central point of contention in the sprouts vs. colonial origins debate is the role of colonialism in Korean development. The former claims that colonial rule destroyed incipient forms of capitalism and promoted "colonial landlordism (*singmin chijuje*)." By contrast, the latter recognizes substantial colonial industrialization, especially after the 1930s, with active Korean participation. While I agree with the colonial origins view in this regard, its emphasis on the interplay of the colonial state and Japanese capital and technology ignores preceding historical changes in Korea that weakened barriers to capitalism – specifically, changes in agrarian class structure and relations conducive to colonial industrialization. This section examines how rural conflict and consequent colonial policy changes transformed agrarian class structure and relations in ways that facilitated capital conversion from land to non-agricultural sectors, enhancing colonial industrialization by Korean landlords and capitalists despite a Confucian cultural heritage that discouraged such involvement in mercantile matters.

When Japan annexed Korea in 1910, it did little to change the existing agrarian class structure. While Japanese colonizers reformed corrupt and inefficient taxation to increase their financial base and improve revenue collection, they largely retained the earlier characteristics of land tenure–private ownership, highly unequal land distribution, and extensive tenancy. Refuting earlier claims by nationalist scholars of radical change, recent studies show that the colonial government cadastral survey (1910–1918) served mainly to reaffirm the existing Korean agrarian class structure (Cho 1988; Gragert 1994; Pae 1988). The Japanese, as Cumings attests, found it to "their advantage to ally with the non-entrepreneurial landed class in Korea which resided in every village," whom they could "encourage . . . to govern the countryside for them" (1984: 492). As a concrete step to enlist Korean landlords as a social basis of colonial rule, the government established landlord associations and even promoted limited participation in local politics after 1920: of provincial council members elected in 1920, the overwhelming majority were large landlords (i.e., those who owned more than fifty chŏngbo [1 chŏngbo = 2.45 acres]) (see Chang 1989). Although the Korean landlord class ceased to be the state's competitor for power, its social and economic power vis-à-vis cultivators did not undergo any substantial decline in the early years of colonial rule.

In addition, land investment remained far more profitable than other investments. As late as 1929, return rates from paddy-field and dry field land investment amounted to 8.2 percent and 8.8 percent respectively, whereas the rate for corporate stocks was 7.1 percent (Chang 1980). Strong rice prices (especially prior to the late 1920s' depression) and high rental rates were the primary reasons for higher land profit. Landlords also continued to amass fortunes from poor peasants through usury (see Ch'oi 1985; Hong 1985, 1986; Kim 1972, 1978; Pak 1983). As a result, while many landless tenants and semi-tenants were impoverished, landlords, especially large landlords, prospered: a 1925 government survey of rural income showed that landlords with more than twenty chŏngbo of land (0.3 percent of the rural population) had an average *surplus* income of 5,582 wŏn, while average *total* income for the landless and semi-tenants was only 500 and 587 wŏn, respectively (Chōsen sōtokufu 1929: 35–38). As shown below, however, when conditions changed, it was these large landlords who came to actively participate in colonial industrialization.

Such landlord accumulation was greatly abetted by growing Japanese demand for Korean crops (particularly rice), which boosted prices, stimulated production and exports, facilitated market growth, and encouraged commercialization. Between 1910 and 1920, rice prices rose fourfold and rice production grew 43 percent; between 1912 and 1925 rice exports to Japan increased more than threefold (see Suh 1978). Yet, as discussed earlier, mere increases in output or commercialization do not necessarily presage agricultural capitalism. During the early colonial period, Korean agricultural production increased without a comparable increase in productivity; from 1920 to 1930 total output increased by 5 percent, but productivity decreased slightly by 1 percent (Ban 1979). That is, increases in labor input (8.1 percent from 1920 to 1930), crop area (9.2 percent from 1920 to 1930), double-cropped area (from 17 percent to 23.1 percent in paddy fields from 1915 to 1927), and crop diversification boosted output without improving productivity (see Shin (1996, ch. 3) for details). In addition, to survive, poor peasants were often forced to market their crops, a great portion of which went to Japan, constituting a phenomenon which Korean scholars term "famine export" (*kia such'ul*) (Cho 1979).

Thus in early colonial Korea, market expansion and increased commercialization did not *qualitatively* transform agriculture. Instead, as Brenner (1977) points out for early modern Poland, the growth of surplus extraction in response to the market, without transformation of the mode of production, only intensified use of – indeed "used up" – labor power. Landlord dominance and traditional class relations remained virtually intact; tenants still paid high rent "in kind" under insecure tenancy terms (mostly set in oral agreements). Despite the emergence of "enterprising landlords" interested in agricultural improvement and production, most landlords retained traditional methods of surplus extraction, employing "maximization of rents through pressure on tenants" (Eckert 1991, p. 22). Even colonial government campaigns to boost agricultural production, such as the Program to Increase Rice Production launched in 1920, largely worked through the existing class structure.

Agrarian class structure and relations, however, began to meet strong tenant challenge after the 1920s. Tenants no longer meekly accepted landlord domination and authority in rural villages; instead they protested collectively against their landlords to protect and promote such interests as reduced rent, more secure land tenure, and better contract terms. In particular, the "cultural policy" that Japanese pursued after 1920 facilitated organization and mobilization of tenants for collective action against their landlords. For instance, in 1924, 181 worker/peasant unions organized to press tenancy disputes; by 1926 in South Chŏlla province alone (the geographical center of 1920s disputes), eighty-three peasant unions with 11,938 members formed (Asada 1973: 182; Lee 1978: 24). Stressing that "tenants' welfare could not be improved by expecting benevolent action from landlords, but only through tenants' collective action" (quoted in Kim and Kim 1986: 69), these unions initiated collective disputes (see Shin 1996). These challenges mostly took collective non-violent forms such as threat of non-cultivation, refusal to harvest, and rent withholding, actions that mobilized village tenants for a month or two. However, at times tenant protests involved violence and police arrest, mobilized hundreds of tenants across several villages, and lasted for more than a year (see Shin 1996). Colonial government statistics show a total of 4,804 instances of tenant–landlord conflicts involving 74,581 tenants and landlords nationwide from 1920 to 1932, with over 90 percent occurring in six southern provinces (see Table 1.1). The colonial government, well aware of similar conflict in Japan, was greatly concerned about this growing unrest and cited it as a "constant phenomenon" of rural Korea (Chōsen sōtokufu 1929, 1934).[4]

To be sure, this assertiveness did not aim for a social revolution but

Table 1.1 Summary of tenancy disputes, 1920 to 1939

	1920–1932	*1933–1939*
1 *Disputes*	4,804	136,175
2 *Participants*	74,581	322,673
3 *Main issue*		
Tenancy rights or leased land	53%	81%
Rent-related	41%	17%
Other	6%	2%
4 *Outcome*		
Complete tenant victory	16%	58%
Partial tenant victory or compromise	41%	24%
Demand withdrawn	14%	12%
Unresolved or tenant defeat	29%	7%
5 *Disputes in six provinces*[a]	92%	75%

Sources: Chōsen sōtokufu (1929: 58–61; 1940a: 8–9, 21–24, 26–28, 36–39, 43–44).

Note

a Includes North and South Ch'ungch'ŏng, North and South Kyŏngsang, and North and South Chŏlla provinces.

rather for the procurement of better terms within existing relations. In addition, tenant challenge alone, despite some early success in lowering rental rates and obtaining better tenancy terms, did not break up the existing agrarian class structure. Nonetheless, the widespread eruption of tenancy disputes in the 1920s greatly concerned colonial policy-makers and exerted an unequivocal impact upon rural policy. In particular, Ugaki Kazushige, who became Governor-General in the summer of 1931 and who was quite worried about growing rural unrest, attempted to quell it through a social policy (*sahoe chŏngch'aek*) approach that encouraged state intervention (see Shin and Han (1999) for more details on Ugaki's social policy orientation in colonial Korea). Most significant in terms of agrarian class structure and relations was government abandonment of its earlier practice of support for landlordism and non-intervention in disputes, and the formulation of measures to appease rural discontent and reorganize rural society through more direct government involvement in local affairs. Fully cognizant of tenancy problems in Japan, Ugaki and other policy-makers feared socialist influence on disputes and therefore sought "thorough-going solutions for the tenancy problems" through "adequate laws and regulations" (Lee 1936: 178).

A major outcome of such colonial government effort to resolve rural conflict was the 1932 Tenant Arbitration Ordinance, patterned on the 1924 Japanese measure. It enabled either landlords or tenants to submit claims to non-binding arbitration by local representatives of county tenancy offices.[5] Although it did not seek to prevent disputes but to settle them, it was the first step towards appeasement of rural discontent and institutionalization of agrarian conflict at the expense of earlier landlord-based policy (Chŏng 1991; Pak Sŏp 1988). Two years later in 1934, the government further constrained landlord rights by passing the Agricultural Lands Ordinance, despite strong landlord resistance. It guaranteed contract lengths of at least three years (Article 7), allowed tenants to propose reduction or remission of rent upon crop failure (Article 16), made contracts renewable unless violated by tenants (Article 19), and forbade agreements in which the tenant waived certain rights (Article 6) (Cho 1979). It made county tenant councils created in 1933 under the Arbitration Ordinance permanent and empowered them directly, or by referral from appropriate courts, to hear and arbitrate disputes (Chōsen sōtokufu 1940a).

Such measures crucially altered agrarian class relations; they provided legal grounds for tenants' complaints and as a consequence constrained landlords' rights. William R. Langdon (1934), American consul in Seoul, in his report to the Secretary of State, described the Land Ordinance as "a good measure of protection to the tenant" and its "political significance ... [as] one of the first measures to set the interests of the mass of the Korean peoples above those [of Japanese and Korean landlords]." The report predicted "some important change in the social and economic structure of the country" and even that it would destroy "the ancient incubus of landlordism." Both ordinances markedly reoriented colonial policy. They resulted from Japan's recognition of a deteriorating rural situation and of the difficulty of "maintaining peace and order among the people unless effective measures to weaken and reduce landlordism were taken" (Langdon 1934).

These land laws further encouraged tenant activism, though within institutionalized frameworks. From 1933 to 1939, 136,175 disputes (an annual average of 19,454 disputes) occurred, a fiftyfold increase over the 1920 to 1932 period. The disputes during this seven-year period involved 322,673 tenants, landlords, and agents, and in most cases were initiated by the tenants (see Table 1.1). An American consulate report shows that over 96 percent of the 9,370 cases reported in 1936 were initiated by the tenants and cited as major reasons for the rapid increase in "both the effectiveness of the ordinances and the satisfaction of tenant farmers with the decisions rendered" (Marsh 1937). While dispute issues and geographical distribution changed little from the earlier period (98 percent of the disputes entailed tenancy rights or rent, and 75 percent occurred in the six southern commercialized areas), tenant activism was far more successful than before – in more than 80 percent of the disputes tenants obtained partial or complete victory. By contrast, only 10 percent of the disputes over leased land or tenancy rights, the major categories of disputation, were decided in favor of landlords, who were thereby empowered to retake land or change tenants (see Chōsen sōtokufu 1940a: 8–9, 28–29, 36–39).

Besides these land laws, the colonial government initiated a comprehensive rural revitalization campaign known as *nongch'on chinhŭng undong.* Launched in the fall of 1932, the campaign was aimed primarily at economic improvement in villages ravaged by agricultural depression through debt reduction and other relief programs. The campaign offered low interest rate loans through financial co-ops and provided selected households with detailed plans for economic rehabilitation. It also stressed complete utilization of available labor, crop diversification, and rational land management. Yet the program did not limit its scope to raising rural living standards; it also attempted to reorganize villages torn by class conflict through promoting "spiritual welfare" expressed in such community virtues as social harmony, mutual assistance, and self-sufficiency. To carry out the rural campaign, the colonial government created and mobilized a number of semi-official organizations such as councils for a revitalization campaign, financial co-ops (*kŭmyung chohap*), and mutual aid associations (*siksan'gye*). By 1940 more than two-thirds of all rural households were members of *kŭmyung chohap* and by 1943 83 percent were *siksan'gye* members, indicating the extent of rural reorganization and state penetration into rural society. The campaign also sought to create new village leadership (*chunggyŏn inmul*) that was expected to serve as a new social base for colonial rule in the countryside in place of landlords. According to official statistics, between 1936 and 1940 about 9,600 "mainstays" were trained at 148 long-term (one year) and short-term (one month) training sites. Candidates were "physically strong" and "ideologically healthy" educated youths (aged eighteen to twenty-five, with at least ordinary school education) largely from non-landlord classes (see Shin and Han (1999) for a detailed discussion of the rural revitalization campaign).[6]

The campaign touched almost every aspect of rural economic and social life, from food and debt problems to lifestyle and relations to the state, and involved extensive rural mobilization through official and semi-official organizations. Of particular importance in terms of rural class relations was a reorientation away from previous reliance on landlords as the main social base for colonial rule and a shift towards more direct mobilization of rural society with a new village leadership. Engaged in the Manchurian adventure launched in 1931 and preparing for another war, Japan undoubtedly adopted these social policy measures lest rural unrest impede labor and resource mobilization.

Tenant activism, new land laws, and the rural revitalization campaign all combined to undermine landlords' rights and position. Landlords now faced challenges not only from their tenants over economic issues but also from state-supported *chunggyŏn inmul* over village leadership. They could no longer displace tenants or increase rental rates at whim, and often, as discussed above, lost to tenants in legal disputes. Government statistics indicate a steady decline in rental rate beginning in the mid-1930s: between 1933 and 1938, the average rental rate dropped from

48.6 percent to 47.8 percent in paddy-fields and from 38.9 percent to 37.2 percent in dry fields. Furthermore, the extent of reduction seemed to reflect the degree of tenant activism: the four southern provinces, which had the most disputes during the 1920s and 1930s, showed the greatest rate reductions, from 48.7 percent to 47.2 percent in paddy-fields and 31.3 percent to 28.1 percent in dry fields during the same five-year period. By contrast, five northern provinces, with far fewer disputes, showed little change (see Chōsen sōtokufu 1940b). Although many landlords managed to keep their *economic* wealth, due to increased agricultural productivity, their *social* power as rural elites was clearly on the decline, making regressive ways of surplus extraction increasingly difficult to maintain. Intensifying tenant activism and land laws set clear limits on how far landlords could press tenants, and their traditional hegemony in village affairs was under fire as well.

In response, landlords adopted two measures that had implications for colonial industrialization: (1) establishment of a modern farm (*nongjang*) system, and (2) capital conversion from land to non-agricultural sectors. *Nongjang* farm systems, common among Japanese landlords, used both hired workers and tenants, but even when using tenant labor, tenant–landlord relations were strictly modeled on employee–employer ones based on written contracts to reduce sources of conflict. *Nongjang* had an organizational structure similar to a modern industrial company, with specialized bureaus in agricultural production, marketing, and finance, each of which further oversaw several departments. It also hired agricultural technicians to improve land productivity through the use of improved seeds and chemical fertilizers as well as rationalization of production processes (see Choi 1985; Hong 1986, 1992; Kim 1992; Pak 1983). In a study of the Kwan'guk *nongjang* of landlord Yi in South Chŏlla province, Kim attests: "Landlord Yi's farm no longer followed feudal practices of land management. On the surface the farm was similar to the old landlord system, but its content and practice showed a clear departure from the past. Landlord Yi was transforming himself into an agricultural capitalist" (1976: 59–60). Kim claims Yi's conversion from landlord to agricultural capitalist was a not uncommon response at the time to spreading tenancy disputes. Farm establishment was particularly popular among large landlords in southern provinces: for instance, the Koch'ang Kim family of North Chŏlla established nine *nongjang* between 1924 and 1938 (Kim 1978).

The emergence of *nongjang* influenced both colonial and postcolonial industrialization in several ways. First, farm management increased landlord income by raising agricultural productivity, which provided the material base for landlord participation in colonial industrialization, discussed below. Between 1935 and 1939, an agricultural output increase of 31 percent accompanied labor and land productivity growth of 22 percent and 29 percent.[7] A second consequence was significant consolidation of landholdings and reduced use of tenant labor. In turn, many former tenants moved to urban areas where, as in modern England, they provided the labor force crucial for industrialization. During the same five years, urban population increased by 91 percent, while tenant population declined, especially in southern provinces where *nongjang* were widespread (Chōsen sōtokufu 1940a: 139). Finally, the *nongjang* system provided an organizational model for later industrial corporations (see Eckert 1991), and experience in farm management became a valuable asset for postcolonial capitalist activity, as shown below.

In a second, more consequential response to tenant challenge and newly unfavorable colonial policy, many landlords moved their capital into non-agricultural sectors, especially commerce and industry. While their rights were substantially constrained, large landlords still enjoyed extensive economic resources (again, decline in rental rates did not necessarily reduce actual rental income, owing to increased agricultural productivity). However, realizing the limits on previous methods of wealth accumulation (e.g., exploiting tenants by raising rents or changing tenure), many responded to colonial promotion of industry, especially through conversion of land capital into commercial and industrial stocks. As English landlords took advantage of the international wool market, so Korean landlords exploited opportunities for industrial investment. As Hori points out, "[T]he upper class of the Korean landlords had a significantly close relationship with the commercial and industrial spheres of the society" (1994: 16).

Recent studies by Korean economic historians confirm landlord investment in non-agricultural sectors in 1930s Korea. Chang's (1989) examination of 880 large landlords in four provinces reveals that 37 percent made non-agricultural investments, averaging 2.8 instances of investment (see Table 1.2). Half of these investments were made in commerce or finance

Table 1.2 Investment in non-agricultural sectors by province

Province	*Total no. of landlords* (A)	*No. of landlords with non-agricultural investments* (B)	(B)/(A)	*No. of non-agricultural investments* (C)	(C)/(B)
Kyŏnggi	349	117	34%	330	2.8
S. Ch'ungch'ŏng	110	65	59	179	2.8
N. Chŏlla	162	51	31	133	2.6
S. Chŏlla	259	90	35	247	2.7
Total	880	323	37	889	2.8

Source: Chang (1989: 163).

Note

Numbers of landlords for Kyŏnggi and South Chŏlla provinces indicate those with over fifty chŏngbo and for South Ch'ungch'ŏng and North Chŏlla those with over 100 chŏngbo.

and more than a quarter in industry. Two-thirds of the investments were made in Korean companies and 17 percent of landlords with non-agricultural investments received more income from them than from rent, including Kim Sŏng-su and Yŏn-su of North Chŏlla and Pak Hŭngsik and Min Kyu-sik of South Ch'ungch'ŏng provinces, cases selected by Eckert (1991) and McNamara (1990) to demonstrate colonial origins of Korean capitalism. Similarly, Hŏ's (1989) study of 1,508 large landlords shows that 523, or about 35 percent, participated directly or indirectly in corporate management between 1926 and 1939. In contrast to England, where yeomen became the core agricultural capitalists and then industrial bourgeoisie, Korean capitalists were predominantly large landlords who accumulated wealth through landholdings. Even while making substantial non-agricultural investments, many retained their land, leading McNamara to conclude that "the interplay of agriculture and industrial investment . . . represents a curious blend of old and new in the process of socioeconomic development" (1990: 118).

However, one should not exaggerate the progressive nature of Korean landlords or their embrace of state incentives to invest in industry. Even in the 1930s many Korean landlords maintained a traditional Confucian respect for agriculture above commerce and industry, and therefore eschewed capital conversion on cultural grounds. A landlord in South Chŏlla remembers that his clan so strongly condemned his commercial involvement as a violation of Confucian ethics that despite economic success it took years for him to receive positive recognition from kin for his activities (Kim 1992). Another landlord in South Kyŏngsang province recalls with regret that he did not embrace industrial opportunities in the 1930s because of "Confucian teachings and his family's *yangban* tradition" (Pak Sŏktu 1988). He adds that he had such good tenant relations that he deemed capital movement unnecessary.[8] Even when Korean landlords invested in non-agricultural sectors, they did so mainly in firms owned by family members, relatives, friends, or other significant others (see Chang 1989) as a strategy of "diversifying their portfolio" (see Hŏ 1989).

In addition to cultural barriers to industrial investment, another deterring factor was that land still remained highly profitable. As Table 1.3 shows, productivity, profitability, and prices of land all increased constantly throughout the 1930s, and the pace of agricultural recovery from the depression was faster than that in industry, as indicated by prices of agricultural and industrial goods. Reflecting these facts, overall return on land exceeded that from stocks, a gap that widened over the years (for paddy-fields: 7.7 percent versus 6.9 percent in 1931, and 8.0 percent versus 6.5 percent in 1937),[9] although a few sectors of industry, such as textiles, may have produced higher margins of return. Chang's (1989) study also shows that two-thirds of landlord investment was made in Korean firms, which were far smaller in scale than Japanese ones. (While the number of Korean firms constituted about 40 percent of all firms,

Table 1.3 Indices of land and industry related items, 1930 to 1940

	1931	*1932*	*1933*	*1934*	*1935*	*1936*	*1937*	*1938*	*1939*	*1940*
Land productivity	100	103	105	108	117	121	117	118	122	111
Agricultural crop price	100	113	116	142	148	156	156	177	220	264
(Manufactured product price)	100	104	113	111	119	118	147	184	206	225
Land profitability[a]	100	122	128	140	182	214	224	242	269	337
Land prices[a]	100	104	111	130	159	196	215	230	267	344

Sources: Ban (1979: table k-1b); Chang (1989: 39); Suh (1978: 169).

Notes
a Paddy fields.
Profitability = rent income − (tax and public dues + management fee).

their share of total capital formation in colonial Korea was only about 13 percent (Hŏ 1989).) Moreover, 41 percent of landlords' non-agricultural investments were made in companies that went bankrupt within a few years (see Hong (1981, 1985) for detailed description of concrete cases). Such realities warn us against overstressing the progressive nature of capital movement and attractiveness of state incentives for commercial or industrial investment in the 1930s. The evidence supports claims of Korean landlord participation in colonial industrialization, but their capital movement to non-agricultural sectors involved more than economic considerations; social and political factors that were strong enough to override cultural obstacles equally or even more crucially shaped landlords' decisions to move capital into non-agricultural sectors. Recent studies of the colonial origins of Korean capitalism that emphasize the crucial role of colonial industrial policy in attracting Korean capital are based too heavily on a few highly successful capitalists such as Kim Yŏn-su and Pak Hŭngsik (e.g., Eckert 1991; McNamara 1990), and suffer from what Haggard *et al.* (1997) consider a "selection bias."

For many landlords smaller than Kim or Pak, growing rural unrest and consequent land policy colored their decisions. No comprehensive statistics detail how much capital transfer occurred for these reasons, but recent case studies show that their influence was not uncommon. For instance, landlord Kim on Kanghwa Island of Kyŏnggi province in 1928 sold all his land to found a linen and cotton shop (Kim 1972), and landlord Cho in Koksŏng county of South Chŏlla province sold part of his land to invest in a mining company in 1937 for the same reasons, that is, spreading tenant unrest and unfavorable policy measures (Hong 1985). Such circumstances similarly influenced another Kanghwa Island landlord, Hong, to sell his land to found the Choyang Spinning and Weaving Company in 1936, and landlord Mun in South Chŏlla province to establish two managed farms and invest in three companies during the 1930s (see Hong 1981; Pak 1983).

The colonial government report on current tenancy customs published in 1930 also recognized the "recent phenomenon" of the popularity among landlords of investment in finance, commerce, and industry, and related it to the rising number of disputes with tenants and consequent rural unrest (Chōsen sōtokufu 1930, vol. 1). William Langdon (1934), American consul in Seoul, agreed that "with the landlord's rights curbed and the tenant's rights extended [by the ordinances], no doubt land will lose some of its attractiveness as an investment, diverting capital and savings to manufacturing and other industrial lines." Consequently, the number of large landlords declined over the 1930s: between 1930 and 1942, the number of Korean landlords with over 100 chŏngbo decreased from 800 to 488, and those with between fifty and 100 chŏngbo from 1,438 to 1,351 (Chang 1989). Thus it is evident that agrarian conflict and its resolution through new land laws and the rural revitalization campaign facilitated the establishment of *nongjang* and/or capital movement from land to non-agricultural sectors, contributing to colonial industrialization.

Decolonization, revolt, war, and reform

Despite the significance of the immediate occupation and wartime periods (1945–1953), both the sprouts and colonial origins arguments leave it largely unexplored. They stress the contribution to postcolonial development of either "national capital" that somehow managed to survive colonial discrimination, or the "material" and "human-cultural" legacy of colonial industrialization. Neither view closely examines how national capital or the colonial legacy were transmitted to later industrialization. Simply asserting continuity or discontinuity is not enough; we need to explicate specific mechanisms that maintain or disrupt links between the colonial and post-1945 periods. The immediate postcolonial era, marked by decolonization, American occupation, peasant revolts, civil war, and land reform, should be considered integral to the historical process of Korea's industrial transformation.

The end of Japanese rule did not resolve the agrarian question. Rural Korea remained highly unequal in land ownership; as of late 1945, landlords who constituted about 3 percent of the rural population owned 63.4 percent of the land, while 49 percent of the rural population owned no land at all. Accordingly, most grass-roots organizations that appeared after 1945 sought to redress inequity and unfair practices in rural society. For instance, Chŏnnong, a major national peasant organization, urged that (1) "land be distributed to peasants," (2) "transfer of land ownership be prohibited," (3) "Japanese and national traitors' owned land be confiscated," and (4) "landlords' land exceeding five chŏngbo be confiscated and if they want to cultivate land themselves, the same amount of land as peasants be allowed to them" (*Chosŏn inminbo*, March 16, 1946). It also advised tenants to pay only 30 percent of the crop as rent (the 3/7 system) until land reform was instituted. As a result, even though prevailing rental rates dropped to one-third of the crop and tenants not uncommonly paid less, landlords were unable to oust tenants, especially in areas with a history of tenant protest (Chang 1985; Hong 1986; Pak Sŏktu 1988). Previously undermined by colonial-era regulations, the Korean landed class was hard-pressed to defend its traditional rural elite position. In Cumings' (1981) view, rural South Korea was on the verge of an "agrarian revolution" that would eliminate the landed class.

However, American occupation complicated the situation. The American military government suppressed popular organizations such as people's committees (*inmin wiwŏnhoe*) and peasant unions (*nongmin chohap*) as being communist and restored much of the Japanese colonial framework. Most of the Korean officials and policemen who had served in the colonial administration assumed key positions, and Japanese economic agencies and programs including rice collection were revived (see Cumings 1990).[10] While the military government restricted rental rates to one-third of the crop to pre-empt the Chŏnnong's 3/7 system, it had no administrative enforcement mechanism and thus the rent restriction was "widely violated," except in areas where tenants had some power and, in fact, had already been paying only about one-third of their crop (Gayn 1948; Mitchell 1951). Although Americans appeared to recognize the importance of land reform to contain communist influence in the countryside, they were "reluctant to participate in a reform that involved a substantial element of expropriation of private property.... There was no clear and consistent American position on Korean land reform" (Ban *et al.* 1980: 284–285). American reporter Mark Gayn even opined after his visit to Korea in the fall of 1946 that everyone in the U.S. military government, from military Governor-General Archer Lerch down to the "Korean interpreters," seemed "opposed to any land reform."

Among the peasants, American restoration of colonial systems and lack of any substantial reform bred despair, frustration, and anger. As one in Kangwŏn province declaimed, "Since we went through the terrible years under the Japs, we have been trying to be patient with the current situation.... But how long should we stand?" (*Hansŏng ilbo*, June 24, 1946). Lack of land reform similar to that promulgated in North Korea particularly exacerbated peasant frustration.[11] Peasants expressed their discontent by refusing to comply with government programs, carrying out raids on government agencies, and engaging in disputes with landlords: by September 1946, only 12.6 percent of the scheduled rice was collected, eighty-one police stations and twenty-three government agencies throughout the south were attacked, and in North Kyŏngsang province alone, 1,552 disputes erupted between tenants and landlords (Chŏng 1988; Hwang 1985). Peasant discontent and grievances escalated continuously, exploding into the major agrarian rebellions of twentieth-century Korea in the fall of 1946.

What began as an urban riot on October 1, 1946 in Taegu, a major south-central city, escalated into an agrarian rebellion that swept through the countryside in North Kyŏngsang, then South Kyŏngsang, South and North Ch'ungch'ŏng, Kyŏnggi, and South and North Chŏlla provinces over a three-month period. Mobilized through local peasant unions and people's committees, the peasants attacked big landlords, police stations, and local government offices. To cite just an example, in Yŏngch'ŏn county, near Taegu, an estimated 10,000 protesters attacked the county police station, killing the county executive and some twenty "reactionaries and landlords" (Cumings 1981: 358). By the end of 1946, a full 30 percent of the counties in the south – or about forty witnessed uprisings – involved an estimated 2.3 million participants (mostly peasants). The largest and most significant agrarian uprising since the 1894 Tonghak peasant wars, the 1946 rebellion clearly showed the urgent need for a new social and political course, especially land reform. Again, in the words of reporter Mark Gayn, the rebels "stumped the country, demanding ... land for the sharecroppers" (1948: 399).

What, then, was the outcome of the 1946 rebellion, especially in regard to agrarian structure and class relations? From one perspective it may be said that the rebellion met with prompt and severe opposition from the national police under the auspices of the American military government, failed to achieve any immediate, tangible outcomes, and was over by the end of 1946. The uprisings claimed about 1,000 protesters' lives, while another 30,000 were arrested, creating chilling memories of repression in the countryside. Nonetheless, the rebellion unmistakably influenced American military government policy, especially land policy (see Hwang 1985; Yi Kyŏngsuk 1987). On February 5, 1947, for the first time since the onset of American occupation, the military Governor made a "definite statement about the future of the 'enemy farm lands'" in a memorandum to the Secretary of the Interim Legislative Assembly, depicting land reform as "essential to the solution of the vital problem of Southern Korea" (cited in Cho 1964: 69). Americans could no longer overlook the urgency of land reform and began preparations for the distribution of formerly Japanese-owned lands or "vested lands" (*kwisok nongji*) that they controlled. This American plan was not satisfactory to Korean leaders both left and right, who argued that land reform should be the prerogative of the imminent Korean government (see Korea Institute of Rural Economy 1989: 320–323). Nonetheless, realizing the risk of further delays in land reform, the military government went ahead and distributed vested lands in the spring of 1948.

However, American distribution did not resolve the land question, which continued to be a crucial social and political issue for the Korean government established in the summer of the same year. Besides the fact that American distribution affected only 18.7 percent of the total land targeted, the land issue was closely tied to the interests of divergent social and political groups in the new regime. Although almost no group denied the necessity of land redistribution per se,[12] there existed a great deal of disagreement over such questions as *how* to distribute the land, and *whether* and *how* to compensate landlords for it. For instance, peasant organizations and progressive politicians argued for "free distribution with no compensation," as in North Korea, whereas the Korean Democratic Party, which represented landed interests, demanded high compensation to landlords who would lose their lands. Despite President Syngman Rhee's strong desire to pass a land reform bill,[13] such disagreements produced a series of heated debates that led to stalemate in the National Assembly (see chs 3–4 in Korea Institute of Rural Economy 1989).

Land reform finally did pass the National Assembly in June 1949. According to the law, each family would be allowed to own land up to three chŏngbo, and peasants would make a five-year payment to the government for the distributed land in the amount of 150 percent of the annual crops from the land. The government would compensate expropriated landlords with land bonds it hoped would be invested in industry. This plan would cover approximately 80 percent of landlord-held land that was not Japanese-owned. Yet continued stalemate in the process of legislating follow-up regulations necessary to execute the reform further delayed actual implementation until the spring of 1950. In the meantime, approximately half of landlord-held land was privately sold.[14]

There exists a controversy over *when* South Korean land reform was actually executed, especially as to whether it occurred before or after the Korean War. Bruce Cumings, for instance, asserts that "not a single acre had changed hands by June 25" (1990: 455), whereas most South Korean sources indicate that implementation of reform occurred before the war broke out (see Korea Institute of Rural Economy 1989; Pak 1996, vol. 2). Part of this disagreement stems from different understandings of what land distribution involved. Land reform required a series of stages to complete (distribution, compensation, and registration), and no doubt neither compensation nor registration (therefore, no legal transfer of land) occurred prior to the war. On the other hand, by the spring of 1950 the Korean government had prepared a detailed plan as to *which land was to be redistributed to whom*, and actually had both landlords and peasants review and confirm this document to remove potential sources of dispute following redistribution. It would have been only a matter of time to formally *legalize* new landownership, a process that was interrupted by the war. From this perspective it could be said that land reform was already underway, though one must acknowledge local variations (see chs 5–6 in Korea Institute of Rural Economy 1989 for the reform's concrete processes).[15]

With the outbreak of the war, many suppressed people's committees (PCs) revived and, under the auspices of the North Korean army, carried out "revolutionary" land reform. Largely following the North Korean model, it called for expropriation of landlord-held land without compensation. Local PCs functioned as the main organization executing actual land redistribution, although North Korean party cadres oversaw the whole process. It is claimed that by the end of August 1950 land reform was completed in the provinces of Kyŏnggi, North and South Ch'ungch'ŏng, North Chŏlla, and in most of South Chŏlla (Cumings 1990), and it was estimated that by the time the North Korean Army left, 573,000 chŏngbo, or 95 percent of the land to be redistributed according to the government land bill, had been redistributed (Yi Taegŭn 1987: 82). Whether or not land reform was underway before the war, there is little question that wartime events dealt a final blow to the old agrarian social order.[16]

As the North Korean Army retreated, the Rhee government wasted no time in finalizing the previously planned land reform. It not only had to appease peasant discontent but also requisition badly needed crops (paid to the government by the peasants for their redistributed land) to provide food for the military (see Yi Taegŭn 1987). Land reform proceeded as planned in the midst of war: by April 15, 1951, about 71.5 percent of the targeted land was redistributed to peasants. When Korea was decolonized in 1945, big landlords, 3 percent of the rural population, owned almost two-thirds of the land; a remaining 80 percent of the rural population were either landless tenants or semi-tenants with little land. However, by 1957, following the war and reform, 88 percent of the rural population were full owner-cultivators. The once-powerful landlord system had collapsed.

How, then, did agrarian conflict resolution through land reform affect subsequent industrialization? To answer this question requires understanding the nature of South Korean land reform. In contrast to their northern counterparts, South Korean landlords were compensated for lost interests with land bonds; that is, financial assets that could be invested elsewhere. Furthermore, despite a series of political debates and objections, the government encouraged use of land bonds for industrial capital formation, as illustrated by Article 10 of the reform bill which stated in part that "landlords who sell land according to this law will be given priority to participate in business that can contribute to national economic development" (see Korea Institute of Rural Economy 1989). In particular, the government encouraged using land bonds to purchase vested enterprises; unlike Taiwan, where most vested properties were nationalized, the Korean government made most available to the private sector. More than two-thirds of the vested enterprises were sold after 1950 (Kim Yunsu 1988), and it is estimated that 53.6 percent of land bonds were used to purchase vested enterprises, which played a key role in post-reform capital formation and industrialization (Korea Institute of Rural Economy 1989).[17]

This is not meant to suggest that most landlords successfully became industrial capitalists. On the contrary, many small and medium landlords had to sell their bonds, especially during the war, at a discount to brokers or others who went on to purchase vested properties. For some of them, land reform was a total loss. Even so, land bonds clearly constituted a crucial part of the "primitive capital formation needed for Korean industrialization,"[18] and many landlords, especially large ones, used land bonds profitably to fund the transition to their new role as capitalists. The agrarian contribution to industrialization is confirmed by a 1975 survey of 311 Korean "private entrepreneurs" by the Harvard-Korean Development Institute Project, which concluded that "the industrial elite was recruited from the pre-capitalist elite, landlords, rather than from society as a whole" (Jones and SaKong 1980: 228).

Yi's (1994) recent study substantiates the historical process of landlord capital conversion to industry in the post-reform period. He shows that of 418 landlords in the Chŏlla region with at least twenty chŏngbo of land subject to redistribution, forty-six (11 percent) came to own at least one enterprise in the 1950s (20 percent for those with over fifty chŏngbo) through purchase of vested or other enterprises with their bonds. Thirteen other former landlords established educational foundations with their bonds.[19] These foundations were closely tied to enterprises run by the landlords. Nine other landowners had already owned at least one enterprise at the time of reform through prior land sales. Together, these landlord-turned-capitalists comprised 14 percent of the landlords examined. However, this excludes absentee owners (such as the well-known Kim of Kyŏngbang – see Eckert 1991) and those who did not own enterprises but invested as shareholders. Including these investors, Yi estimates that about 30 percent of the former landlords in the Chŏlla region participated one way or another in 1950s industrialization.

Further, Yi shows that colonial experience in farm establishment and/or non-agricultural investment proved crucial to successful capital conversion to industry following land reform. For instance, 60 percent of the landlord-turned-capitalists had either established *nongjang*, or invested in commerce or industry during the colonial period. In addition, landlords involved in any form of commercial or industrial activities under colonial rule were more likely than those without such experience to emerge as capitalists in the postwar era, 25 percent versus 6 percent. More specifically, 43 percent of the landlords who owned at least one enterprise during the colonial period became capitalists in the postcolonial era. Yi's study demonstrates, in short, that those who had been large landlord capitalists during the colonial period were better positioned to emerge as post-reform industrial capitalists.[20]

Such findings challenge the prevailing emphasis within South Korean scholarship on the failure of landlords to become industrial capitalists (Kim 1990; Kong 1994; Korea Institute of Rural Economy 1989). There seems no question that most "pure" landlords (those who had no previous experience in non-agricultural investment) failed to convert into industrial capitalists. However, as discussed above, a substantial proportion of

Korean landlords, especially large ones, had already invested in non-agricultural sectors during the colonial period and many emerged as industrial capitalists after land reform. Accordingly, if we include the "part-landlord part-capitalist" in the category of landlords, we find that a much higher proportion of Korean landlords became industrial capitalists. In fact, Kim's study of "disposal of Japanese property," while siding with the conventional view, also acknowledges that "landlords with experience in commercial or financial investment during the colonial period more easily transformed into capitalists after 1945 than those landlords without such experience" (1990: 250; see also Kong 1994). All in all, it appears indisputable that colonial experience in non-agricultural investment significantly assisted the transformation of landlords into industrial capitalists in the post-reform era.

Conclusion: the agrarian roots of Korean capitalism and modernity

This chapter shows the central role of agrarian factors in hindering or promoting capitalist development. In pre-colonial Korea, regressive agrarian class structure and relations were responsible for economic backwardness. As a result, even increased agricultural commercialization and the rise of wage labor, contrary to the sprouts argument, did not foster agricultural capitalism. Strong landlordism favored exploiting high rent, usury, and abundant cheap labor over investment in new technology or land management. Without a fundamental change in class structure, capitalism held little allure for landlords. The sprouts school, while pointing out correctly that the Korean economy was not stagnant prior to colonialism, is inherently limited in appreciating such internal barriers to capitalist development in pre-colonial Korea.

This chapter also challenges the colonial origins argument for its exclusive focus on the colonial state's *industrial* policy and *exogenous* factors such as Japanese capital and technology, without considering their counterparts, *agrarian* and *endogenous* factors. While the argument shows correctly that both colonial industrialization and Korean participation were significant, it does not adequately address how Korean landlords overcame cultural barriers to embrace economic risk in joining colonial industrialization. Even in the 1930s, many Korean landlords held the Confucian valuation of agriculture above commerce or industry, land remained highly profitable, and investment in non-agricultural sectors was risky. In other words, state industrial policy or economic incentives did not dictate landlord participation in colonial industrialization; other non-economic social factors were crucial as well. In particular, this chapter reveals that agrarian activism and subsequent policy measures that constrained landlord rights were instrumental to such a historic shift in economic (investment) behavior. Put another way, growing rural unrest or social "pushing" factors were as crucial as state promotion of industry or economic "pulling" factors in Korean participation in colonial industrialization.

Further, both the sprouts and colonial origins views do not adequately explain how the colonial legacy was incorporated into postcolonial development throughout the turbulent years of decolonization, occupation, revolts, war, and reform. The former simply argues that national capital which survived harsh colonial suppression financed later industrial success, while the latter supposes that colonial industrialization offered a model for post-1960s capitalist development. Neither view adequately specifies concrete mechanisms of historical continuity/discontinuity in the process of Korean industrial transformation. One important mechanism was agrarian activism. Agrarian conflict was not only a key factor behind Korean landlord participation in colonial industrialization; it also paved the way for the postcolonial agrarian radicalism that necessitated the enactment of land reform. Such reform then facilitated landlords' capital conversion into commercial and industrial sectors, contributing to "primitive capital formation" crucial to subsequent industrialization. Colonial experience in non-agricultural investment also facilitated the transition for landlords of operating capitalistic forms of enterprise.

That Korean industrialization occurred under colonial rule should not suggest that Japan "modernized" Korea or that the Korean transformation is merely an "offspring of empire." The recent debate over whether or not Japanese modernized Korea (see An 1997; Cho 1997; Chŏng 1997; Sin 1997) focuses on what Japanese did (either exploited or modernized Korea) with the unfortunate, though unintended, consequence of overlooking Korean agency in the nation's transition to modernity. Although Japanese took a key part in colonial industrialization, they did not simply dictate the whole process; on the contrary, as shown above, Koreans (peasants, landlords, capitalists) played equally crucial roles. Denying their role would be to remove the Korean side of the story. Similarly, although Korean development was not entirely indigenous, it was not simply transplanted from outside either. Strictly speaking, excluding England, industrial development elsewhere (including Korea) has been more or less "transplanted" and thus not indigenous. Accordingly it would be fruitless to debate whether Japanese modernized or exploited Korea, or whether the Korean transformation was indigenous or transplanted. Instead, as Steven Lee suggests in the Introduction to this volume, attention should be paid to the complex processes in which both indigenous and foreign forces interacted to produce the particular path that Korea took in its transition to modernity.

Notes

1 This is a significantly modified version of an article that appeared as "Agrarian Conflict and the Origins of Korean Capitalism" in *American Journal of Sociology* 103.5 (March 1998). It has been revised extensively to address the Korean debate.
2 There also exists a group of scholars who criticize theories of colonial modernization (*singmingji kŭndaehwaron*), but they do not offer any alternative explanation of Korea's capitalist origins. See Chŏng (1997) and Sin (1997).
3 Note also that Confucian valuation of agriculture over commerce or industry must have facilitated this process of landlordization.
4 Colonial Korea witnessed other forms of peasant protest such as the red peasant union movement. However, these were not class conflicts between peasants and landlords but targeted local government officials over taxes and interference in village affairs and were concentrated in the northeast region. They were also short-lived. See Shin (1996) for details.
5 As a result, in 1933, 150 county tenant councils were established in Korea.
6 No comprehensive statistics profile the class background of these *chunggyŏn inmul* but one source indicates that among 979 trainess in three places, 32 percent came from the owner-cultivator, 44 percent from the semi-tenant, and 24 percent from the landless tenant class (see Shin and Han 1999).
7 Major factors in productivity gains were increased use of chemical fertilizers and new varieties of crops, more commonly by large farms than by small tenancies.
8 With land reform, however, he was "forced to become a capitalist ... not an easy thing to swallow" (see Pak 1988).
9 The figures for dry fields were 8.3 percent in 1931 and 8.5 percent in 1937. Rates of return on paddy- and dry-fields in Japan were 3.9 percent and 3.7 percent in 1931 and 4.9 percent and 5.5 percent in 1937, respectively, much lower than in Korea. See Suh (1978: 85).
10 For instance, about 85 percent of the notorious Korean policemen were retained, and the Oriental Development Company and Chosen Food Distributing Company re-emerged as the New Korea Company and Korean Commodity Company (U.S. Army [1948] 1988, vol. 3: 142–143).
11 North Korea carried out land reform in the spring of 1946 and stories of "joy and satisfaction of North Korean peasants with land reform" were reported in many newspapers in the south. See, for instance, *Haebang Ilbo* of March 12 and 19, and *Tongnip Sinbo* of August 6 and 7.
12 Article 86 of the Constitution specified that lands be distributed to peasants.
13 Rhee was highly supportive of land reform since it would not only remove a major source of social and political instability in Korea but also enhance autonomy of the central government from the old rural elite and its political organization, the Korean Democratic Party.
14 Anticipating land redistribution, landlords sold their land to their tenants and others, but the terms of their land sales were not necessarily better than what they would have received as compensation from the government after redistribution. Some term this pre-reform selling "indirect land distribution" in comparison to the "direct" one instituted by the government (see Korea Institute of Rural Economy 1989).
15 I thank Steve Lee and Young Ick Lew for urging me to look into this process more carefully.
16 Hong's (1992) study of a village in South Chŏlla province shows the process vividly. With the outbreak of war, a PC was restored in the village and redistributed landlord-held land to tenants without compensation, and seven or eight

"reactionary" landlords were killed. The war experience was so devastating that most village landlords left their homes, never to return.

17 Since vested enterprises were only part of Korean industrial facilities, including conversion of land bonds into non-vested enterprises would increase the figure for contribution of land bonds to Korean capital formation.

18 In addition, American aid provided capital for Korean industrialization. The relative contribution of domestic and foreign capital merits further research.

19 Land used for the establishment of educational foundations was compensated at a higer rate, sometimes as much as twice the compensation paid for other land.

20 Some of them may have learned valuable lessons from earlier failures in industrial investment.

References

An, Pyŏngjik, Yi Dae-kŭn, Nakamura Satoru, and Kajimura Hideki. 1989. *Kŭndae Chosŏn ŭi kyŏngje kujo* [The Economic Structure of Modern Korea]. Seoul: Pibong Press.

——. 1997. "Han'guk kŭn hyŏndaesa yŏn'gu ŭi saeroun p'aeradaim [New Paradigms in the Studies of Modern and Contemporary Korea]." *Ch'angjak kwa pip'yŏng* 25(4): 39–58.

Asada, Kyoji. 1973. *Nihon teikokushugika no minzoku kakumei undō* [National Revolutionary Movements under Japanese Imperialism]. Tokyo: Miraisha.

Ban, Sung Hwan. 1979. "Agricultural Growth in Korea, 1918–1971," in Y. Hayami *et al.* (eds). *Agricultural Growth in Japan, Taiwan, Korea, and the Philippines.* Honolulu: University Press of Hawaii, pp. 90–116.

——, Pal Yong Moon, and Dwight Perkins. 1980. *Rural Development.* Cambridge, MA: Harvard University Press.

Brenner, Robert. 1977. "The Origins of Capitalist Development: A Critique of Neo-Smithian Marxism." *New Left Review* 104: 25–91.

——. 1989. "Economic Backwardness in Eastern Europe in Light of Developments in the West," in Daniel Chirot (ed.). *The Origins of Backwardness in Eastern Europe.* Berkeley/Los Angeles: University of California Press, pp. 15–52.

Chang, Sanghwan. 1985. "Nongji kaehyŏk kwajŏng e taehan silchŭngjŏk yŏn'gu [An Empirical Study of Korean Land Reform]," in *Haebang chŏnhusa ŭi insik* [Perspectives on Korean History in the Pre- and Post-War Eras]. Seoul: Han'gilsa, pp. 292–358.

Chang, Siwŏn. 1980. "Singminjiha Chosŏn ŭi pan ponggŏnjŏk t'oji soyu e kwanhan yŏn'gu [A Study of Semi-feudal Land Ownership in Colonial Korea]." *Kyŏngje sahak* 4: 38–139.

——. 1989. "Ilcheha tae chiju ŭi chonjae hyŏngt'ae e kwanhan yŏn'gu [A Study of Large Landlords under Japanese Imperialism]." Ph.D. dissertation, Department of Economics, Seoul National University.

Cho, Jae Hong. 1964. "Post–1945 Land Reforms and Their Consequences in South Korea." Ph.D. dissertation, Department of Economics, Indiana University.

Cho, Kijun. 1982. *Han'guk chabonjuŭi sŏngnipsaron* [History of Formation of Korean Capitalism]. Seoul: Taewangsa.

Cho, Sŏggon. 1988. "Chosŏn t'oji chosa saŏp e issŏsŏ ŭi soyugwŏn kwajŏng e kwanhan han yŏn'gu [A Case Study of the Investigation Process of Land Ownership in the Cadastral Survey in Korea]," in Chang Siwŏn (ed.). *Han'guk kŭndae nongch'on sahoe wa nongmin undong* [Rural Society and Peasant Movements in Modern Korea]. Seoul: Yŏlŭmsa, pp. 9–55.

——. 1997. "Sut'allon kwa kŭndaehwaron ŭl nŏmŏsŏsŏ (Beyond the Theory of Exploitation and Theory of Modernization)." *Ch'angjak kwa pip'yŏng* 24(2): 355–370.

Cho, Tonggŏl. 1979. *Ilcheha han'guk nongmin undongsa* [A History of Peasant Movements under Japanese Colonialism]. Seoul: Han'gilsa.

Ch'oe, Youngho. 1981. "Reinterpreting Traditional History in North Korea." *Journal of Asian Studies* 40(3): 503–523.

Ch'oi, Wŏn'gyu. 1985. "Hanmal-Ilcheha ŭi nongŏp kyŏng'yŏng e kwanhan yŏn'gu – Haenam Yunssiga ŭi sarye [A Case Study of Farm Management in the Late Chosŏn and Early Colonial Korea – The Haenam Yun Family]." *Han'guksa yŏn'gu* 50/51: 275–318.

Chŏng, Haegu. 1988. *10wŏl inmin hangjaeng yŏn'gu* [A Study of the October People's Uprisings]. Seoul: Yŏlŭmsa.

Chŏng, T'aehŏn. 1991. "1930 nyŏndae singminji nongŏp chŏngch'aek ŭi sŏnggyŏk chŏnhwan e kwanhan yŏn'gu [A Study of Rural Policy Change in 1930s Korea]," in *Ilchemal Chosŏn sahoe wa minjok haebang undong* [Colonial Korea and National Liberation Movements during the Last Years of Japanese Rule]. Seoul: Ilsongjŏng, pp. 56–107.

——. 1997. "Sut'allon ŭi songnyuhwa soge sarajin singminji (Colony That Disappeared in the Midst of a Trivializing Theory of Exploitation)." *Ch'angjak kwa pip'yŏng* 24(3): 344–357.

Chōsen sōtokufu [Government-General of Korea]. 1929. *Chōsen no kosaku kanshū* [Tenancy Customs in Korea].

——. 1930. *Chōsen no kosaku kankō* [Tenancy Customs in Korea], 2 vols.

——. 1934. *Chōsen ni okeru kosaku ni kansuru sankō jikō tekiyō* [A Briefing on Tenancy-related Issues in Korea].

——. 1940a. *Chōsen nōchi nenpō* [Annual Report on Korean Agricultural Lands].

——. 1940b. *Nōka keizai gaikyō chōsa – kosaku nōka, 1933–1938* [Survey of the Peasant Economy – Tenant Households, 1933–1938]. Keijo.

Cumings, Bruce. 1981. *The Origins of the Korean War*, Vol. 1. Princeton, NJ: Princeton University Press.

——. 1984. "The Legacy of Japanese Colonialism in Korea," in Ramon H. Myers and Mark R. Peattie (eds). *The Japanese Colonial Empire 1895–1945*, Princeton, NJ: Princeton University Press, pp. 478–496.

——. 1990. *The Origins of the Korean War*. Vol. 2. Princeton: Princeton University Press.

Doe, Jin-soon. 1991. "The Periodization of Modern and Contemporary History in North Korean Academic Circles." *Korea Journal* 31(2): 41–55.

Eckert, Carter. 1991. *Offspring of Empire: The Koch'ang Kims and the Colonial Origins of Korean Capitalism*. Seattle: University of Washington Press.

Gayn, Mark. 1948. *Japan Diary*. New York: William Sloane Associates.

Gragert, Edwin. 1994. *Landownership Under Colonial Rule: Korea's Japanese Experience, 1900–1935*. Honolulu: University of Hawaii Press.

Haggard, Stephen, David Kang, and Chung-in Moon. 1997. "Japanese Colonialism and Korean Development: A Critique." *World Development* 25(6): 867–881.

Hŏ, Chongho. 1965. *Chosŏn ponggŏn malgi ŭi sojakche yŏn'gu* [A Study of the Tenancy System in the Late Chosŏn Dynasty]. P'yŏngyang: Sahoe Kwahagwŏn Press.

Hŏ, Suyŏl. 1989. "Ilcheha Chosŏnin hoesa mit Chosŏnin chungyŏk ŭi punsŏk [A Study of Korean Companies and Korean Executives under Colonial Rule]," in An Pyŏngjik, Yi Dae-kŭn, Nakamura Satoru, and Kajimura Hideki (eds). *Kŭndae Chosŏn ŭi kyŏngje kujo* [Economic Structure of Modern Korea]. Seoul: Pibong Press, pp. 354–388.

Hong, Sŏngch'an. 1981. "Hanmal-Ilcheha ŭi chijuje yŏn'gu – Kangwha Hongssiga ŭi ch'usugi wa changch'aek punsŏk ŭl chungsim ŭiro [A Study of Landlordism in the Late Chosŏn Dynasty and Early Colonial Korea – The Case of the Kangwha Hong Family]." *Han'guksa yŏn'gu* 33: 67–115.

——. 1985. "Hanmal-Ilcheha ŭi chijuje yŏn'gu – Koksŏng Chossiga ŭi chiju roŭi sŏngjang kwa kŭ pyŏndong [A Study of Landlordism in the Late Chosŏn Dynasty and Early Colonial Korea – The Case of the Koksŏng Cho Family]." *Tongbang hakji* 49: 113–164.

——. 1986. "Hanmal-Ilcheha ŭi chijuje yŏn'gu – 50 chŏngbo chiju Posŏng Yissiga ŭi chiju kyŏngyŏng sarye [A Study of Landlordism in the Late Chosŏn Dynasty and Early Colonial Korea – The Case of the Posŏng Yi Family]." *Tongbang hakji* 53: 155–214.

——. 1992. *Han'guk kŭndae nongch'on sahoe pyŏndong kwa chijuch'ŭng* [Social Change and Landlordism in Modern Korea]. Seoul: Chisik sanŏpsa.

Hori, Kazuo. 1994. "East Asia between the Two World Wars – Industrialization of Japan and its Ex-Colonies." *Kyoto University Economic Review* 137: 1–22.

——. 1995. *Chōsen kōgyōka no shiteki bunseki: Nippon shihonshugi to shokuminchi keizai* [Historical Analysis of Korean Industrialization: Japanese Capitalism and Colonial Economy]. Kyōto: Yūkakakū.

Huang, Philip. 1985. *The Peasant Economy and Social Change in North China*. Stanford, CA: Stanford University Press.

Hwang, Hansik. 1985. "Mi kunjŏngha nong'ŏp kwa t'oji chŏngch'aek [Agriculture and Land Reform Policy under the American Military Rule]," in *Haebang chŏnhusa ŭi insik* 2 [Perspectives on Korean History in the Pre- and Post-war Era]. Seoul: Han'gilsa, pp. 251–291.

Jones, Leroy and Il Sakong. 1980. *Government, Business, and Entrepreneurship in Economic Development: The Korean Case*. Cambridge, MA: Harvard University Press.

Kang, Jong-Koo. 1988. "Rethinking South Korean Land Reform: Focusing on U.S. Occupation as a Struggle against History." Ph.D. dissertation, Department of Sociology, University of Wisconsin, Madison.

Kim, Chunyŏp and Ch'angsun Kim. 1986. *Han'guk kongsanjuŭi undongsa* [History of Korean Communist Movements], Vol. 2. Seoul: Ch'ŏnggye yŏn'guso.

Kim, Dongno. 1994. "Peasants, State, and Landlords: National Crisis and the Transformation of Agrarian Society in Pre-Colonial Korea." Ph.D. dissertation, Department of Sociology, University of Chicago.

Kim, Kiwŏn. 1990. *Mi kunjŏng'gi ŭi kyŏngje kujo* [Economic Structure Under American Occupation]. Seoul: P'urŭnsan.

Kim, Yongsŏp. 1960. "Yang'an ŭi yŏn'gu: Chosŏn hugi ŭi nongga kyŏngje [A Study of Land Registers: The Economy of Peasant Households in the Late Yi Dynasty]." *Sahak yŏn'gu* 7: 1–95, 8: 59–119.

——. 1970. *Chosŏn hugi nong'ŏpsa yŏn'gu* [Studies in the Agrarian History of the Late Yi Dynasty]. Seoul: Iljogak.

——. 1972. "Hanmal-Ilcheha ŭi chijuje – Kangwha Kimssiga ŭi ch'usu'gi rŭl t'onghaeso pon chiju kyŏng'yŏng [A Study of Landlordism in the Late Chosŏn

Dynasty and Early Colonial Korea – The Case of the Kangwha Kim Family].” *Tonga munwha* 11: 3–86.

——. 1976. “Hanmal-Ilcheha ŭi chijuje – Naju Yissiga ŭi chijuroŭi sŏngjang kwa kŭ chiju kyŏng’yŏng [A Study of Landlordism in the Late Chosŏn Dynasty and Early Colonial Korea – The Case of the Naju Yi Family].” *Chindan hakpo 42.*

——. 1978. “Hanmal-Ilcheha ŭi chijuje – Kobu Kimssiga ŭi chiju kyŏngyŏng kwa chabon chŏnhwan [A Study of Landlordism in the Late Chosŏn Dynasty and Early Colonial Korea – The Case of the Kobu Kim Family].” *Han’guksa yŏn’gu* 19: 65–135.

——. 1992. *Han’guk kŭn hyŏndae nongŏpsa yŏn’gu* [Studies on the Agrarian History of Twentieth Century Korea]. Seoul: Ilchogak.

Kim, Yunsu. 1988. “8.15 ihu kwisok kiŏpch’e pulha e kwanhan il yŏn’gu [A Study of Sales of Vested Enterprises after August 15].” MA thesis, Seoul National University.

Kohli, Atul. 1994. “Where Do High Growth Political Economies Come From? The Japanese Lineage of Korea’s ‘Developmental State’.” *World Development* 22(9): 1269–1293.

Kong, Cheuk. 1994. *1950 nyŏndae han’guk ŭi chabon’ga yŏn’gu* [A Study of Korean Capitalists of the 1950s]. Seoul: Paeksan sŏdang.

Korea Institute of Rural Economy [Han’guk nongch’on kyŏngje yŏn’guwŏn]. 1989. *Nongji kaehyŏksa yŏn’gu* [A Study of the History of Land Reforms]. Seoul: Korea Institute of Rural Economy.

Langdon, William. 1934. “Tenant Farmer Legislation – Chosen Agricultural Lands Ordinance,” in *Records of the Department of State Relating to Internal Affairs of Korea (1930–39),* 2 rolls. National Archives of the USA (reprinted by Scholarly Resources Inc.).

Lee, Chong-Sik. 1978. *The Korean Worker’s Party.* Stanford, CA: Hoover Institution Press.

Lee, Hoon K. 1936. *Land Utilization and Rural Economy in Korea.* New York: Greenwood Press.

McNamara, Dennis. 1990. *The Colonial Origins of Korean Enterprise, 1910–1945.* Cambridge: Cambridge University Press.

Marsh, O. Gaylord. 1937. “Tenant Arbitration Cases in Chosen,” in *Records of the Department of State Relating to Internal Affairs of Korea (1930–39),* 2 rolls. National Archives of the USA (reprinted by Scholarly Resources Inc.).

Mitchell, C. Clyde. 1951. *Korea: Second Failure in Asia.* Washington, DC: The Public Affairs Institute.

Miyajima, Hiroshi. 1974. “Chōsen Kabo kaikaku igo no shōgyōteki nōgyō [Commercial Agriculture Since the Kabo Reform in Korea].” *Shirin* 57(6).

Moore, Barrington, Jr. 1966. *Social Origins of Dictatorship and Democracy.* Boston, MA: Beacon Press.

Pae, Yŏngsun. 1988. “Hanmal ilche ch’ogi ŭi t’oji chosa wa chise kaejŏng e kwanhan yŏn’gu [A Study of the Cadastral Land Survey and Land Tax Reform in Late Chosŏn and Early Colonial Years].” Ph.D. dissertation, Seoul National University.

Pak, Ch’ŏnu. 1983. “Hanmal-Ilcheha ŭi chijuje yŏn’gu – Amt’aedo Munssiga ŭi chijuro ŭi sŏngjang kwa kŭ pyŏndong [A Study of Landlordism in the Late Chosŏn Dynasty and Early Colonial Korea – The Case of the Amt’aedo Mun Family].” MA thesis, Yonsei University.

Pak, Myŏngnim. 1996. *Han'guk chŏnjaeng ŭi palbal kwa kiwŏn* [The Outbreak and Origins of the Korean War], 2 vols. Seoul: Nanam Press.

Pak, Sangt'ae. 1987. "Chosŏn hugi ŭi ingu-t'oji appak e taehayŏ [Population/Land Pressures in the Late Chosŏn Dynasty]." *Han'guk sahoehak* 21: 101–121.

Pak, Sŏktu. 1988. "Nongji kaehyŏk kwa singmin chijuje ŭi haech'e – Kyŏngju Yi ssiga ŭi t'oji Kyŏngyŏng sarye rŭl chungsim ŭro [Land Reform and Dissolution of Colonial Landlordism – A Case Study of Landlord Yi Family of Kyŏngju]." MA thesis, Department of Agricultural Economics, Korea University.

Pak, Sŏp. 1988. "Singminji Chosŏn e issŏsŏ 1930 nyŏndae ŭi nongŏp chŏngch'aek e kwanhan yŏn'gu [A Study of Agricultural Policy in 1930s Korea]," in Chang Siwŏn (ed.). *Han'guk kŭndae nongch'on sahoewa nongmin undong* [Rural Society and Peasant Movements in Modern Korea]. Seoul: Yŏlŭmsa, pp. 115–150.

Palais, James. 1975. *Politics and Policy in Traditional Korea.* Cambridge, MA: Harvard University Press.

Park, Soon-Won. 1999. *Colonial Industrialization and Labor in Korea: The Onoda Cement Factory.* Cambridge, MA: Harvard University Asia Center.

Postan, Michael. 1972. *The Medieval Economy and Society.* Berkeley: University of California Press.

Shin, Gi-Wook. 1994. "The Historical Making of Collective Action: The Korean Peasant Uprisings of 1946." *American Journal of Sociology* 99: 1596–1624.

——. 1996. *Peasant Protest and Social Change in Colonial Korea.* Seattle: University of Washington Press.

——. 1998. "Agrarian Conflict and the Origins of Korean Capitalism." *American Journal of Sociology* 103: 1309–1351.

—— and Gary Hytrek. 1998. "Conflict Resolution and Regime Formation: The Social Origins of Korean Authoritarianism and Costa Rican Democracy." Paper presented at the annual meetings of the American Sociological Association in San Francisco.

—— and Do-Hyun Han. 1999. "Colonial Corporatism: The Rural Revitalization Campaign of 1932–40 in Korea," in Gi-Wook Shin and Michael Robinson (eds). *Colonial Modernity in Korea.* Cambridge, MA: The Asia Center, Harvard University, pp. 70–96.

Shin, Susan. 1973. "Land Tenure and the Agrarian Economy in Yi Dynasty Korea, 1600–1800." Ph.D. dissertation, Harvard University.

Sin, Yongha. 1997. "'Singminji kŭndaehwaron chae chŏngnip sido e taehan pip'an [A Critique of the Attempt to Reestablish the 'Theory of Colonial Modernization']." *Ch'angjak kwa pip'yŏng* 24(5): 8–38.

Suh, Sang-Chul. 1978. *Growth and Structural Change in the Korean Economy, 1910–1940.* Cambridge, MA: Harvard University Press.

U.S. Army. [1948] 1988. *History of the United States Armed Forces in Korea,* 4 vols (reprint). Seoul: Tobelge.

Yi, Chisu. 1994. "Haebanghu nongji kaehyŏk kwa chijuch'ŭng ŭi chabon chŏnhwan munje [Postwar Land Reform and Capital Conversion of the Landlord Class]." MA thesis, Yonsei University.

Yi, Kyŏngsuk. 1987. "Han'guk nongji kaehyŏk ŭi kyŏljŏng kwajŏng e kwanhan yŏn'gu [A Study of the Decision-making Process of Land Reforms in Korea]." MA thesis, Department of Sociology, Seoul National University.

Yi, Taegŭn. 1987. *Han'guk chŏnjaeng kwa 1950 nyŏndae ŭi chabon ch'ukchŏk* [The Korean War and Capital Accumulation of the 1950s]. Seoul: Kkach'i.

2 Agricultural cooperative development and change

A window on South Korea's agrarian transformation

Larry L. Burmeister

Introduction: The agricultural cooperative and South Korea's agrarian transformation

Aside from land reform, agrarian questions have often been slighted in analyses of South Korea's (hereafter Korea) post-1960 rapid economic growth trajectory. Yet, as Gi-Wook Shin argued in Chapter 1, agriculture has played a critical role in transforming Korean society over the course of the twentieth century. In the post-colonial era, Korean economic growth was intimately tied to agricultural development and state policy. This chapter examines a primary organizational mechanism for Korean intersectoral development linkages, the National Agricultural Cooperative Federation (NACF or *nonghyŏp* in Korean). Burmeister and colleagues (2002) have shown that organizational infrastructure, namely the NACF, played an instrumental role in connecting over two-and-a-half million small farm households to national markets for agricultural commodities, agro-inputs, consumer goods, and labor. Although direct capital transfers from agriculture to industry via taxation or biased terms of trade were less pronounced in the Korean case than in Japan or Taiwan, significant strategic economic ties were created between agriculture and the rest of the economy that supported the country's national development project (see Ban *et al.* 1980: ch. 2; Fei and Ranis 1975; Michell 1988: 31; Oshima 1986: 794–795). Indicators of positive development linkages included higher growth rates for agriculture in Korea than for other middle income oil-importing countries during the period 1960 to 1980 (Hart-Landsberg 1993: 27), and relatively high levels of farm household consumption and educational investment given farm-size constraints (Burmeister 1990: 213–215). A study of NACF organizational development and change thus provides us with a revealing view on major transformations which took place in Korean rural and agricultural society after 1945. This chapter will highlight the relationship between the state and agriculture, and especially the role that the state played in mobilizing rural resources to meet its modernization goals. It will also explore the impact that democratization had on rural institutions, and the challenges faced by farmers and the state in dealing with Korean agriculture in the WTO era.

In the bureaucratic-authoritarian industrialization era (1961–1987), the NACF served as a parastatal implementation organ of government bureaucracy. Organizational growth was conditioned by state-led agricultural development initiatives that prescribed specific organizational functions and activities. From 1988 to the present, the forces of political democratization and market liberalization have continued to reshape the Korean political economy. Organizationally, the NACF has responded with democratic reforms in its governance structure that are congruent with political trends in the wider society. Pressures for NACF business reorganization, a response to current market liberalization initiatives, are being fashioned within this more open, contested political environment. The result is an organization-in-transition. The NACF has become less parastatal and more corporatist associational (see Burmeister 1999), as farmer-member interests must now be reconciled with government policy preferences in fashioning NACF responses to present rural/agricultural development issues.

Using a particular organization, such as the NACF, to explore broader sectoral dynamics makes sense from the open systems perspective within organization theory (see Scott 1992: chs 4, 5). This analytical perspective emphasizes the critical role of the organization/environment relationships for organizational development and change. Organizations depend on their external environments for resources they must secure to insure survival (e.g., people, money, and legitimating ideas). Hence organizational transitions often coincide with dramatic changes in operating environments. Thus we can learn much about the rural/agricultural sector dynamics of the Korean socioeconomic transformation through an analysis of NACF development and change.

The NACF and state/agricultural sector relations

The NACF's organizational development cannot be understood apart from the high degree of state intervention in agriculture that characterized the post-liberation South Korean political economy. The institutional underpinnings of administrative control were responses to agrarian conflicts laid bare in the immediate aftermath of liberation from Japanese colonial rule. Gi-Wook Shin has discussed how disputes over land tenure arrangements during the colonial period and land reform in the early postwar era shaped the subsequent evolution of Korean capitalist modernity (see Shin (Chapter 1, this volume); Ban *et al.* 1980: 283–284; Gragert 1994; Lee 1936). As he and others have noted, immediately following liberation, the communist regime in the north and Provisional Government authorities in the south seized upon land reform as an immediate remedy to past land disputes. After the U.S. military government took control away from indigenous Provisional Government authorities in the South, civil uprisings erupted in the fall of 1946 contesting U.S. military control (Cumings 1981: ch. 10; Shin 1996: 144). Among the most important catalysts was the military government's rollback of land reforms promulgated in the early post-liberation period by local committees of an emergent Provisional Government.

In the wake of South Korea's formal independence in 1948, the political consolidation of a shaky Sygnman Rhee regime required implementation of a comprehensive land-to-the-tiller reform in spite of opposition from powerful landed elites (Cole and Lyman 1971: 21–22; Kuznets 1977: 34; Lie 1998: 11; Zeon 1973). Land reform was completed in the 1950s with provisions for ownership by former tenants and a three-hectare ceiling on landholdings. The political economy effects of land reform were threefold. A conservative landlord class was essentially destroyed as the dominant political and economic force in the countryside. Many former tenants were empowered economically as owner-operator smallholders to the extent that they gained legal control over productive land. However, farmers' collective economic power was limited because state authorities maintained tight controls over the agricultural economy and rural politics (Moore 1985; Wade 1983).

The legal basis for heavy state regulation of agriculture was the 1950 Grain Management Law. This edict gave the government far-reaching budgetary authority to purchase, store, transport, allocate, and establish prices for agricultural commodities. The law evolved from war mobilization measures at the end of the colonial period and in response to immediate postwar economic stabilization problems during the U.S. military government interregnum (1945–1948). In 1942, Japan's Food Control Law instituted a compulsory grain quota delivery and rationing system to insure food provisioning within the Empire. In the immediate post-liberation period, attempts by the U.S. military government in Korea to institute free markets for agricultural products resulted in hoarding, food shortages, and inflationary spirals in food prices, forcing the re-establishment of grain requisitioning and rationing policies similar to the colonial Food Control Law regime (Ban *et al.* 1980: 235–237). While the Grain Management Law adopted in the early days of the Rhee government relaxed food system controls to provide for both government purchase and distribution and private trading, the law retained the Food Control Law principle that made "the government responsible for securing and managing the supply of staple food" (Francks 1999: 122). Ultimate bureaucratic authority for food provisioning resided in the Ministry of Agriculture and Fisheries (MAF).

Momentum for reinvigorated agricultural development initiatives increased with the ascent of General Park Chung Hee to power in the 1961 military coup. Park's rural background and his need to secure a political base in rural areas sparked both rhetorical and policy support for actions aimed at increases in food production and rural revitalization (Whang 1987: 4–8). Park justified the coup in large measure as a response to South Korean economic stagnation and its negative effect on the north–south balance of power on the Korean peninsula. Agricultural productivity had stalled during the later years of the Rhee regime (Michell 1988: 31). With agriculture still the dominant sector in terms of both economic output and employment in the early 1960s, agricultural productivity increases became an important component of a reinvigorated economic growth strategy.

In order to accomplish the military government's economic mobilization and political control objectives, a somewhat fragmented Rhee era agro-bureaucratic structure was consolidated and centralized. The agricultural cooperative was one of the primary organizational components of this bureaucratic reorganization. It was established in 1961 by the merger of the weak village agricultural cooperatives with the relatively successful Korea Agricultural Bank, organizations formed as agricultural development instruments during the Rhee regime (Ban *et al.* 1980: 212–217). These organizations were successors of similar agricultural marketing, technology development and diffusion, and credit organizations established under Japanese colonial rule (Lee *et al.* 1977: 1182–1183; Shin and Han 1999). The merger was promulgated under martial law decree. The agricultural cooperative provided the organizational infrastructure needed to implement agricultural development initiatives and to help secure Park's political base. Other rural development organizations, such as the Office of Rural Development (the national agricultural research and extension organization; see Burmeister 1988) and later the high-profile *Saemaŭl* (New Village) movement (see Brandt and Lee 1979) provided complementary organizational instruments for Park's rural development push.

The legal genesis of the agricultural cooperative (established shortly after the 1961 coup under emergency military government authority), its organizational roots in the colonial agro-bureaucracy, and its establishment at the same time as the abrogation of all local government autonomy signaled how the state intended to bring rural people into the national development project. The term "cooperative," as it is widely understood in the political economy literature (Uphoff 1986: 127–133), does not accurately describe the NACF's organizational structure and operations during the bureaucratic-authoritarian era. Unlike a real cooperative, its formation was not anchored in any grass-roots political action or economic mobilization effort by farmer-members. The agricultural cooperative was established as a de facto implementation arm of other central government agencies, especially the Ministry of Agriculture and Fisheries (MAF). The "federation" was organized as a hierarchical bureaucracy with lower level branch units (primary cooperatives or *tanwi chohap*) under the managerial authority of the central bureau (*chung'anghoe*). Local-level cooperatives (the primary cooperatives) were not involved in establishing an umbrella association (i.e., a real federation) to represent their interests in national political and economic decision-making arenas. In fact, the membership base (i.e., farmer-members) had no role in establishing rules for the formation and dissolution of local-level cooperatives, nor did they have an institutionalized voice in local cooperative affairs.

Land reform freed farm households from onerous tenancy terms and thus provided rural people with an increased measure of self-determination in the sense that households had more control over their production resources. However, the destruction of the landlord class meant that the state had to assume credit supply, technology diffusion, and other functions that landlords and their associations had previously provided. The replacement organizational infrastructure created by the state, as exemplified by the agricultural cooperative, muted much of the emancipatory potential of land reform. Landlords were, in essence, replaced by a supra-landlord, the state agrobureaucracy. In Wade's (1982) cryptic description, state officials reorganized the agricultural sector to facilitate its management as "one farm," thus making it easier to effect economic linkages and political exchanges that were deemed supportive of the national development project. In the post-land reform context, a relatively egalitarian distribution of land plus agro-ecological uniformity (minimal commodity differentiation across farms) generated a potentially unified farm bloc. However, top-down, state-controlled organizations such as the agricultural cooperative were created to insure that a politically docile countryside could be harnessed to the industrialization drive.

Organizational structure and state cooptation

How Korean agriculture was harnessed to the broader development project is quite evident in two key structural dimensions of agricultural cooperative organization: the standardized service areas of the basic, local organizational unit (the primary cooperative), and the multipurpose business activity scope of these units (as well as the federation).

While primary cooperatives were initially organized at the village level during the Rhee era, consolidation was mandated following the establishment of the NACF in 1961, and by the early 1970s all primary cooperatives were reorganized into multi-village service areas coterminous with the lowest level local government unit, the township (*myŏn*). Economic efficiency reasons provided the official justification for this reorganization, and certainly there were problems with economies of scale in the village-based primary cooperatives. But a more important underlying rationale for reorganization rests in the fact that the agricultural cooperatives were now linked directly to the lowest government administrative unit. This meant that it was easy to "second" the staff of the primary cooperatives to work on state rural development initiatives that were directed at the local level from the township administrative offices. These local government units were direct agents of central government authorities (the Ministry of

Home Affairs) – i.e., implementation units rather than governing bodies with autonomous policy-making powers. Not only did this structural arrangement make it easy for the state to appropriate the primary cooperative organizational apparatus for state policy implementation purposes, but it also minimized possibilities for individual primary cooperatives to mobilize collectively in the pursuit of member interests, as the township was not a natural social unit like the village in Korean rural society.

These primary cooperatives were empowered to deal with the entire gamut of agricultural services required of a modernizing agricultural sector: marketing, agro-input supply (fertilizer and machinery), agricultural credit, and other banking services. While the multipurpose structure made sense economically in the context of a homogeneous smallholder agriculture, the fusion of all agricultural service activities under one administrative umbrella configured the organizational field in the rural/agricultural sector in ways that thwarted pluralist social, economic, and political development. One dominant multipurpose organization was more easily manipulated by the state than several specialized organizations catering to somewhat different clientele with different interests. Prospects for a more robust associational network in the South Korean countryside were not enhanced by this centralized approach to the provision of agricultural services.

The inclusion of a "rural guidance" department in the primary cooperative organizational structure reveals the extent to which the agricultural cooperative became a tool for state policy implementation and for ruling party political mobilization in the countryside (Aqua 1974; Steinberg *et al.* 1984). Nominally, guidance personnel were equivalent to extension agents, providing information on cooperative programs and new farming practices to the membership. In reality, these officials often functioned as political operatives in national elections and referendums held for legitimation purposes during the bureaucratic-authoritarian era when rural votes were critical for ruling party victory. They could also be deployed effectively as organizational monitors to keep tabs on villages and farmer-members under their territorial jurisdiction. This monitoring capacity enabled the state to penetrate deeply into the villages to orchestrate compliance with state-initiated rural development campaigns.

Organizational change as development policy response

South Korea's industrialization drive created demands for more robust inter-sectoral linkages. These included the provision of food to the growing urban-industrial sector, the supply of agro-inputs to increase agricultural production, and the supply of consumer goods to farm households. The state harnessed agriculture to meet these needs, and the agricultural cooperative was the center-piece of this effort. An analysis of the organizational evolution of the cooperative thus sheds light on the character of South Korea's industrial development during this era. There were several distinct phases in the history of state policy towards the cooperative. In the 1960s, emphasis was placed on developing physical infrastructure for the agricultural sector, and efforts were made to increase the sector's productive capacity and hence its potential for inter-sectoral transfer of resources. By contrast, the 1970s was a decade of explicit import substitution in agriculture, as protectionist policies combined with new technology development and diffusion were promulgated to effect rice self-sufficiency. A major objective of the rice self-sufficiency drive was to save foreign exchange expenditures that would have been necessary for staple food imports if significant production increases in rice production had not occurred. Foreign exchange savings were channeled into high-priority industrial investments. Since the 1980s, agricultural policy objectives have focused on sectoral restructuring efforts to deal with the increasingly problematic mini-farm structure of Korean agriculture in a more open, globalizing world economy and to try to mitigate socioeconomic marginalization (e.g., decreasing farm household incomes and widespread feelings of social status deprivation) occurring within the rural/agricultural sector (Burmeister 1992; Koh 2001). The periods are discussed in more detail below.

In the 1960s, agricultural sector policy focused on infrastructure improvement projects to increase productive capacity. Improvement of irrigation systems received high priority. In order to make the most of this physical improvement, a complementary increase in fertilizer inputs on improved paddy was required. South Korea was totally reliant on fertilizer imports through the 1950s. U.S. foreign aid was a major funding source for fertilizer imports (Krueger *et al.* 1989: 242). Given the importance of fertilizer for agricultural production at a time when agriculture was still the dominant sector in the south, the fertilizer industry was identified as a priority investment target in economic plans drafted in the immediate post-Korean War reconstruction period (Cole and Lyman 1971: ch. 9). In response, a major import substitution industrialization project was completed in the 1960s with the construction of five fertilizer plants. This industry was established as a public enterprise (the Korean Government Chemical Company) with government agencies holding the controlling interest, but with USAID loans and joint venture investments from Gulf Oil, Skelly, and Dow Chemical playing an important role in industry start-up (Jones 1975: 234; Krueger *et al.* 1989: 242). By the end of the decade, South Korea had become a net exporter of nitrogen fertilizer. Furthermore, the fertilizer industry became the base upon which a much larger petrochemical sector was created in the 1970s (Enos and Park 1988: 60, 91–92).

In its role as majority owner and industry promoter, the government assumed full responsibility for the sale and marketing of domestically produced fertilizer. The NACF, with a countrywide network of outlets able to service Korea's two-and-a-half million farm households, was commissioned as the sole buying agent for all the domestic fertilizer production and the sole distribution outlet for sales of fertilizer to farmers, with all prices fixed by the government. Prices were fixed at levels that insured an agreed upon profit for the joint-venture partners (Kang 1986). This was the quid pro quo for their capital investment and technology transfer contributions to the industry.

Thus fertilizer sales and distribution became a major business priority of the NACF. From an organizational perspective, this arrangement benefited the agricultural cooperative in a most strategic way. Government-delegated responsibilities for handling the fertilizer business gave the agricultural cooperative access to a critical resource that was in chronic short supply throughout the post-liberation period. In order to insure access to this valuable resource, farm households had to join the cooperative. This accounts for the agricultural cooperative's high membership rate. Over 90 percent of all farm households have belonged to the cooperative since its establishment. The downside of this arrangement was that, from its inception, the cooperative became dependent on state-entrusted business and government-supplied resources. This legacy poses an organizational adjustment problem in a liberalized market environment where state intervention in the economy is becoming less pronounced, and the cooperative must rely increasingly on its own entrepreneurial efforts to serve farmer-members and to maintain economic viability in competition with private sector agribusiness and financial services firms.

Important organizational changes in the cooperative occurred in tandem with new state rural development initiatives in the 1970s. The green revolution campaign to achieve rice self-sufficiency (Burmeister 1988) and the *Saemaŭl* movement to promote village infrastructure improvements and income-enhancing farming and non-farm ventures (Brandt and Lee 1979; Turner *et al.* 1993) required much local-level implementation and supervision. Agricultural cooperative personnel doubled during the period 1970 to 1975 when these two high-powered state rural development initiatives were developed and implemented (Burmeister 1999: 117). Personnel increases were concentrated at the primary cooperative level of the organization (a fourfold absolute increase), the unit having direct contact with farmers. Many of these personnel worked closely with local township authorities to insure that new rice variety adoption targets (the green revolution campaign) and *Saemaŭl* project goals were met.

The technology package undergirding the green revolution campaign required increases in purchased inputs (e.g., fertilizer and farm machinery). Increased productivity brought higher farm incomes, as the government increased agricultural product prices in the 1970s to encourage technology adoption. As a result, South Korean farm households became much more integrated into the cash economy for producer and consumer goods during the 1970s. The increased marketization of the rural economy required an improvement in the rural banking system, as demands for financial services increased.

The government addressed the increased marketization of the economy by authorizing an expansion of the cooperative's banking business during the 1970s, strengthening the organization's near monopoly position in the rural banking sector. At the outset of the cooperative's establishment, its banking system consisted of branch banks under federation auspices located in cities, large provincial towns, and county seats. Deposits made in these banks provided capital for agricultural loans. In 1972, the primary cooperatives were legally empowered to establish mutual savings banks to take care of farm household financial needs. Financial services became an increasingly important part of the agricultural cooperative business portfolio. A significant percentage of the increase in primary cooperative personnel during the 1970s was also due to the start-up of this new mutual savings operation.

Consumer linkages between the rural/agricultural sector and the urban/industrial sector were enhanced during this period by the establishment of cooperative chain store outlets throughout the Korean countryside. These stores sold numerous domestically produced everyday necessities that Korean farm households purchased increasingly on a routine basis. Agricultural policies during the 1970s generated an aggregate farm household economic surplus that helped boost domestic demand for Korean-produced consumer goods (E. Lee 1979). The cooperative's dense organizational infrastructure helped to facilitate this important inter-sectoral linkage by connecting millions of small farm households to convenient consumer goods outlets in their localities. Consumer products thus became a routine part of everyday modern life for more and more people living in the rural areas of South Korea.

As in other sectors of the Korean economy, agricultural productivity advances in the 1960s and 1970s were orchestrated through government planning interventions (see Amsden 1989: 79–81; Hart-Landsberg 1993: ch. 2). In order for these plans to bear fruit, implementation instruments such as the NACF were essential mechanisms for the fulfillment of plan objectives. In organization theory terms, the NACF was effective in this role because its local branches, the primary cooperatives, were embedded socially in the localities they served; that is, primary cooperative employees were locals. As a result, they used local knowledge to adjust programs and resource flows to meet perceived and articulated farmer-member needs (to the extent possible in a hierarchical bureaucratic structure). The combination of expansive bureaucratic scope (the NACF was omnipresent in rural Korea) and local social embeddedness (primary cooperative branches were staffed by local people) provided effective organizational support for the implementation of government programs and projects orchestrated by a central planning apparatus (e.g., the Economic Planning Board and the ministries it coordinated). The NACF illustrates how parastatal organizations can be the social linchpins of development-enhancing government/society synergies (see Evans 1996).

Korea's increasing participation in the global economy after the 1970s, and its acceptance of the General Agreement on Trade and Tariffs (GATT) regime had important implications for agricultural policy in the 1980s. In an emergent era of pluralist capitalist modernity (see Lee, Introduction, this volume), agricultural adjustment problems – external market liberalization pressures and domestic economic and sociocultural marginalization – replaced production problems related to foodgrain self-sufficiency as the primary sectoral concerns (Burmeister 1992). Widening income differentials between rural and urban households reappeared as in the late 1960s, causing potential political problems for an increasingly unpopular Chun regime. The uncompetitive position of South Korean agriculture in the global economy became more serious with the institutionalization of trade liberalization rules in the ongoing GATT negotiations and increasing bilateral trade pressure applied by the United States after the US–South Korean trade balance tipped towards South Korea in the mid-1980s. The resolution of these economy-of-size problems requires structural changes in farming that often necessitate large capital outlays (e.g., the expansion of operational farm size; further mechanization; and specialization in high-value, income-elastic agricultural products). On the social side, consumerism and ideas about adequate educational attainment for one's children diffused rapidly from urban to rural areas, enhancing feelings of relative deprivation among rural residents who felt that their socioeconomic situation foreclosed social mobility advances for themselves and their children (KSA 1992: 136–138). Increased infusions of capital were needed to address these economic and social dimensions of rural/agricultural sectoral adjustment.

The agricultural cooperative response is evidenced by relative shifts in the functional allocation of personnel and by changes in the functional composition of business activities. In 1976, agro-input supply and marketing activities accounted for approximately three-quarters of business turnover in the primary cooperatives, an indication of the importance of the production problem at that time. However, by 1988 this percentage had dropped to about one-third. Financial services, on the other hand, rose from approximately one-fifth of business turnover in 1976 to approximately three-fifths in 1988. In addition, the percentage of cooperative employees in banking job classifications increased during the same period (Burmeister 1999: 119–120).

In the agricultural cooperative's credit operations, the mixing of funds provided by the state with funds raised commercially allowed the cooperative to offer loans to farmer-members ("policy loans") at interest rates below those charged by other institutional lenders and well below those charged by private moneylenders. Data from the late 1980s/early 1990s on the loan/deposit ratio of primary cooperatives differentiated by deposit size (aggregate deposits in primary cooperative banks) illustrate the relatively egalitarian distribution of credit through NACF channels, as deposit-poor units received more policy loan funds per deposit base than deposit-rich units (see Park 1993: 159, Table 6.4). Primary cooperatives allocated available loan funds to villages based on number of member households per village. Village councils then parceled out these allotments to members based upon farm size criteria. Since farm size differences remained relatively small in Korea through the early 1990s, this allocation decision rule resulted in widespread farmer-member access to credit. The provision of subsidized loans has been the state's most consistent policy response to the serious economic adjustment problems that faced the South Korean rural/agricultural sector in the 1980s and 1990s, such as decreases in price supports, abrogation of most import controls, farm size constraints, and the lack of off-farm jobs in rural areas. Without these loans as incentives, it is difficult to envision farmer membership in the cooperatives remaining at their present high level.

While cooperative agro-industrial linkages due to expansion of banking business activities in the 1980s and 1990s had less evident direct intersectoral development impact due to the decreasing magnitude of the rural/agricultural sector in the overall Korean economy, it is important to point out that cooperative banking and credit operations financed the education of many rural children who became essential cogs in the industrial workforce. Thus, the cooperative helped to foster human capital formation at the farm household level that has been transferred to the urban-industrial sector (Koo 1991). This underlines the critical linkages between rural and industrial Korea, and the important point made by Shin in Chapter 1 that we need to understand the intersections of agriculture and industry to explain the roots of Korean modernity.

Regime change and organizational adaptation in modern Korea

The post-1987 shift from military to civilian rule set in motion a process of regime transformation in South Korea, with both political democratization and economic liberalization initiatives being implemented. Further impetus for dismantling state/economy relations that privileged big business groups and parastatal public enterprises (such as the NACF) came as the result of Korean entanglement in the Asian financial crisis at the end of 1997. Threats to parastatal organizations such as the NACF that were creatures of the old regime were twofold. First, political legitimacy problems emerged as more participatory and transparent modes of organizational decision-making became normative expectations in the society-wide movement towards a more democratic political culture. Second, questions about economic inefficiencies and political corruption inherent in past state/economy relationships put in jeopardy state-supplied resources (e.g., credit) that were critical economic lubricants of parastatal operations.

In the wake of the post-1987 democratization initiatives and the political and economic reform momentum they created (Han 1989; S. Lee 1993; Lie 1998), the old state/agricultural cooperative relationship came under critical scrutiny from all directions. Powerful agencies within the government, especially the influential Economic Planning Board (now defunct, a result of economic reform), viewed the agricultural cooperative as an outmoded organizational relic of state bureaucratic intervention that needed to be dismantled. Many agricultural cooperative officials were also dissatisfied with the status quo. They resented the fact that important cooperative policy and business decisions were often made over their heads in the government agencies that held oversight powers. Farmer-members also had good reason to complain about the current situation. They had never been privy to institutionalized channels of influence in primary cooperative affairs. While primary cooperatives practiced a "soft authoritarianism" due to local-level staffing practices mentioned earlier (Sorenson 1988: 76–77, 85–88), possibilities for real interest representation for farmer-members were foreclosed by the NACF's subordinate relation to the state administrative hierarchy. Anti-government critics, among them dissident farm groups such as the Catholic Farmers' Organization, complained that the dubious legal foundation of the agricultural cooperative and its past exploitation of farmer-members posed fundamental problems for its continued existence (Center for Research on Rural Society 1989). In this way, with the country ending three decades of military rule, Korean farmers began to articulate their vision of Korean democracy and modernity.

This widespread dissatisfaction with the status quo provided the impetus for an important organizational reform. A revised cooperative law was ratified by the National Assembly in late 1988 following a series of public hearings earlier that summer. Henceforth, primary cooperative presidents would be elected directly by farmer-members, and the federation president would be elected by these elected primary cooperative presidents (NACF 1998: 2–3, 51–54). In addition to electoral reforms, the revised law included provisions that, on paper at least, gave agricultural cooperative officials more power over organizational operations (C. Lee 1991: 263–265; Suh 1989: 71–72). In particular, the system of governmental oversight of agricultural cooperative business activities was changed to a post facto reporting system, where, in principle, the agricultural cooperative did not have to solicit prior government approval of its business and policy decisions. These reforms institutionalized farmer-member voice in cooperative affairs, and provided NACF officials with more policy-making independence vis-à-vis government agencies.

The reforms opened the door for the agricultural cooperative's active involvement in agricultural politics. The election process forced candidates to proclaim publicly policy positions that reflected preferences of their farmer-members (e.g., high rice prices and other protectionist measures). For the first time in its history, the agricultural cooperative began to take policy stances at variance with official government positions.

These actions marked initial efforts by agricultural cooperative officials to transform the organization into a bona fide interest group representing farmer-members, a move that signified an important shift away from its de facto position as a government implementation agency. This transition is a difficult one to effect, given the cooperative's ongoing dependence on resources such as policy loan funds supplied by the government and legal foundations provided by the state that undergird its privileged organizational position within the rural/agricultural sector. The difficulties became clear when the first elected federation president, Han Ho-sun, opposed government stands on such issues as rice market opening, rice price levels, government negotiating strategies in the GATT talks, and the Kim Young Sam administration's "New Agricultural Policy" initiative. In the wake of overt cooperative opposition to state policies and positions orchestrated under Han's leadership, he was charged with corruption during his re-election campaign for the federation presidency (a campaign he was favored to win). While all the particulars in the case are difficult to sort out, many commentators viewed Han's prosecution as a payback for his strident anti-government positions and his attempts to make the agricultural cooperative an independent force in agricultural politics (*Han'guk Ilbo* 1994).

Government officials used the Han corruption case as the backdrop to float legislation for further restructuring of what they perceived to be a flawed agricultural cooperative. In an amendment to the cooperative basic law (the legal foundation for the cooperative), the following organizational changes were proposed: (1) the present agricultural cooperative would be divided into two independent business entities, an agricultural cooperative bank and an economic services (agro-input supply and agricultural marketing) cooperative; (2) a reduction in the power of elected cooperative officials over business operations, with professional managers in charge of many business decisions previously under the formal jurisdiction of elected presidents; (3) indirect election procedures would be instituted for primary cooperative presidents; and (4) existing primary cooperatives would be merged into larger units (*Dong'a Ilbo* 1993).

Agricultural cooperative leaders opposing the reforms outlined above were able to thwart the Kim Young Sam administration's top-down reform attempt, mainly through the exercise of political power in rural areas gained through their new status as elected farmer-member representatives. Renewed challenges to NACF operations appeared after Kim Dae Jung was elected President in 1997. His new Minister of Agriculture, Kim Sung Hoon, was an outspoken dissident university professor who led a nationwide campaign against the Uruguay Round agricultural trade liberalization proposals in the early 1990s and frequently voiced criticisms of the agricultural cooperative. Minister Kim singled out ineffective marketing operations as the prime focus of his attack on agricultural cooperative operations. He charged that cooperative marketing margins were too high, preventing farmer-members from realizing a higher price for their produce. He argued further that the cooperative's quasi-monopoly over the rural banking system gave the organization an easy cash cow, dulling cooperative officials' interest in the improvement of the efficiency of marketing and value-added processing services provided to farmer-members. Once again high government officials started to talk about removing banking from the agricultural cooperative's business portfolio, thus forcing it to concentrate on the provision of income-enhancing services to farmer-members.

A window for significant government-directed organizational change was opened with the prosecution of Han's successor to the NACF presidency, Won Churl-Hee, on embezzlement changes in 1999 (*Korea Herald* 1999a). His conviction was the climax of government investigation and prosecution of a widespread scandal involving scores of cooperative officials charged with accepting bribes in return for loan approvals (K. Lee 1999a). In the scandal's aftermath, a government-directed merger of the NACF with the National Livestock Cooperative Federation and the National Ginseng Cooperative Federation (whose officials were also charged with corruption) was legislated in 2000 (FAS 2001; K. Lee 1999b).

The merger advanced important principles of the cooperative reform agenda laid out in both the Kim Young Sam and Kim Dae Jung administrations. Administrative rationalization and economy-of-scale consolidation are easily justified as farm household numbers plummet even more rapidly due to demographic impact of an aging farm population and the economic impacts of market liberalization are felt on the farm household economy (Bae 2003a). The scandals over kickbacks for loans reinforced the government's arguments for professionalizing management to insulate economic operations from politics. Modest steps in this direction had already been taken with the formal separation of banking and economic services divisions at the federation level, with each division directed by its own CEO (NACF 1998: 52). A recently announced MAF policy requiring that formal farm business plans be filed with policy loan applications exemplifies an ongoing trend of business rationalization within the NACF (Yoo 2002).

Yet resistance to business rationalization and depoliticization measures remains strong among many primary cooperative officials and farmer-members. Farmer-members often express satisfaction with their newly acquired voice in primary cooperative affairs due to electoral reforms. Consolidation of township-level primary cooperatives into much larger, remoter units is generally opposed by farmer-members, who dislike the increased physical and social separation from particular localities that widespread consolidation would entail. Farmer-members and primary cooperative officials fear formal division of the NACF into separate banking and economic service cooperatives. The ability to subsidize economic services from banking profits in a multifunctional cooperative system is viewed as a continuing strength of the present NACF organizational structure in a very turbulent economic restructuring environment. Strong opposition to both primary cooperative consolidation and federation separation into banking and economic service cooperatives accounts for the present "go-slow" approach within the NACF to these big reform issues. Recent pronouncements from NACF Federation President Chŏng Dae-Kŭn suggest a modest primary cooperative consolidation agenda, and do not reveal further measures to increase banking and economic services' organizational separation (Bae 2003b).

In spite of the depoliticization pressures mentioned above, the NACF has maintained an organizational political profile unknown in pre-reform days. NACF political action has been quite evident in international forums including participation in the anti-WTO activities in Seattle, involvement in efforts by food-importing countries to modify the WTO rules in the name of food security and other goals, and as a coalition advocate of "multifunctionality" policy alternatives to current WTO agricultural disciplines in the Doha Round WTO negotiations (Korea *Herald* 1999b; NACF 1999; OECD 2001). Recently the NACF has joined an alliance with grass-roots farm organizations (such as the Catholic Farmers' Organization) to further common agricultural policy agendas in response to Korea's negotiation of a free trade agreement with Chile and to the current Doha Round of WTO negotiations. The negotiations threaten further erosion of agricultural trade barriers that the NACF and other farm groups fear will result in collapse of the Korean farm economy. These high-profile interest group representation activities, which coincide with farmer-member policy preferences and South Korean public opinion, reveal the ongoing struggle of the cooperative to become an "actor-for-itself," taking its place among other interest group organizations that have staked out political representation roles in a more open South Korean polity.

Conclusion: agricultural cooperative adaptation and South Korean agricultural futures

The struggle between the government and the agricultural cooperative over organizational changes highlights ongoing controversy over the future of South Korean agriculture. The top-down reform initiatives that the Kim Young Sam and Kim Dae Jung governments tried to impose on the NACF promoted agribusiness rationalization and the depoliticization of agricultural cooperative operations. These reform initiatives contradicted the democratic cooperative (*minju nonghyŏp*) thrust of the earlier direct election reforms which finally gave farmer-members at least some voice in cooperative affairs. The government still has many powerful cards to play in the tug of war over cooperative restructuring, the most important of which are the financial resources, especially policy loans, that they continue to channel through the organization. On the other hand, the agricultural cooperative, with elected primary cooperative presidents serving in nearly every South Korean township, provides a local organizational base for opposition to government initiatives that threaten the interests of local NACF officials and/or farmer-members.

Increasing differentiation of Korean agriculture (D. Kim 2003), promoted in the 1990s by the government's selection of promising farm enterprises to receive special assistance to increase the economic scale and to upgrade the technical infrastructure of their operations, means that farmers as a group may now be more heterogeneous in terms of policy preferences. Commodity groups (e.g., dairy and livestock farmers) and other farm organizations (e.g., the Farm Successor Association) have formed in recent years to provide support for the interests of particular farmer subgroups. Some of these organizations were formed in the nexus of earlier anti-government social movements in the bureaucratic-authoritarian era; others have emerged in the new era of civil society interest group mobilization. In either case they have often been critical of NACF operations. How these other farm groups relate to the NACF (and vice versa) poses an important organizational adaptation question for the NACF in an era of civil society development.

There are also important intra-organizational conflicts within the NACF that will influence organizational development, as tensions over further organizational restructuring exist between NACF employees located at different levels in the organization. For example, among federation employees working in the banking division, there is sentiment for the formation of a separate agricultural cooperative bank. The agricultural cooperative's banking sector, they argue, must be freed from subsidizing the cooperative's farm business sector if it is to compete in a new world of financial deregulation, a reform goal for the South Korean economy as a whole. In addition, separation would force a specialized farm business cooperative to concentrate on those business activities, thus improving services provided. It is argued that the present multipurpose cooperative structure, while appropriate in an earlier period of national development, mitigates against economic adjustments needed at this point in time. While this line of reasoning focuses on "objective economic" rationales for continued organizational restructuring, it should also be noted that many federation banking employees see significant enhancement of wages and social status in the event of banking separation. As noted earlier, primary cooperative officials are strongly opposed to this separation given that the financial strength of the NACF system currently lies in its banking portfolio.

Such differences in views among farmer-members (due to increasing structural differentiation in agriculture) and within the NACF reflect debates about future directions for the rural/agricultural sector in South Korea that have characterized policy deliberations of the successive governments in the 1990s. An agribusiness model of capital-intensive, larger scale, technologically advanced, highly specialized agricultural production enterprises that can compete in international agricultural commodity markets was the favored mode of adjustment in the highest state policy circles during the Kim Young Sam administration's globalization initiative. The Kim Dae Jung government, by contrast, took a more nuanced view of South Korea's rural/agricultural sector future. Concerns existed about whether economic efficiency rationalization to enhance competitiveness in the global marketplace is a sensible comprehensive policy approach. The view that agriculture should be supported on the basis of wider social goods provision and food security concerns is found in recent legislative initiatives, and in South Korea's position on the codification of revised WTO agricultural policy disciplines. The promulgation of the Sustainable Agriculture Promotion Act and the scheme for environmentally friendly agro-food products marks a significant "green turn" in domestic agricultural policy (Morredu 1999: 65–66; OECD 1999: 130). The South Korean government is actively supporting a multifunctionality option to WTO neoliberal policy reforms. Undoubtedly, the "Sunshine Policy" *rapprochement* initiative of the Kim Dae Jung administration has sensitized many South Korean policy-makers and the general public to the grave agricultural situation in the north, and the demands that will be placed on the peninsular food system in the event of some future north–south accommodation or collapse of the regime in the north. In the eyes of many, the current north–south situation accentuates agricultural sector displacement risks associated with neoliberal, comparative advantage restructuring policies. There is real concern about whether South Korean agriculture could ever compete against the major agro-exporting countries in a truly global "free trade" environment and what would happen to peninsular food supply potential if market-opening measures seriously erode production capacity in the south.

The new Roh Moo Hyun government's approach to these challenges is difficult to discern at this point. The realities of globalization and international trade rules (that Korea formally acknowledges as a WTO member) will make it difficult for the new government to pursue agricultural protectionist policies aggressively. Farm groups have already spoken harshly of Roh's statements promising additional trade liberalization measures in a recent diplomatic visit to the United States (K. Kim 2003; Oh 2003).

The major agricultural cooperative reform issues remain on the table: the separation of banking and economic services, federation and primary cooperative relations, primary cooperative consolidation, and the roles and authority of elected federation and primary cooperative presidents. In line with Roh's promises to foster a "participatory government," it is conjectured that grass-roots farm organizations and other groups in civil society will be invited to provide more substantive input into the agricultural policy-making process than in the past (Cho 2003).

In summary, organizational changes within the agricultural cooperative are occurring in the context of continuing uncertainties and controversies over what the future holds for South Korean agriculture. What is happening also reflects contradictions embedded in cooperative enterprises in a globalizing world capitalist economy that threatens organizational forms which were institutionalized in an earlier, more nationally focused capitalist epoch (Mooney *et al.* 1996). The transformation of the NACF into an agricultural cooperative where both political representation and collective economic self-help attributes are brought together under one organizational roof may ultimately depend upon the extent to which globalization forces generate counter-responses within Korean society (as happened in previous capitalist eras when the social costs of unfettered capitalist development reached unacceptable political levels). Two possible counter-response catalysts are now on the horizon in contemporary South Korea (e.g., social movements that coalesce around social amenities produced by agriculture that would be lost in the event of South Korean agricultural sector displacement by cheap imports and/or social movements that focus on food security (and perhaps related cultural identity) issues associated with north–south *rapprochement* on the Korean peninsula).

Acknowledgments

This chapter is based on fieldwork in the 1990s supported by awards from the Kyungnam University Institute of Far Eastern Studies, the Korean-American Educational Commission (Fulbright Program in Korea), the Northeast Area Council (NEAC) of the Association for Asian Studies, and the Social Science Research Council. The author gratefully acknowledges this program assistance. Many thanks are also due to personnel (too numerous to mention) of the National Agricultural Cooperative Federation who kindly provided interview access at critical points in the research process throughout the decade of the 1990s. An anonymous reviewer and my current research assistant, Mr. Choi Yong-Ju, have provided helpful comments that guided revisions of an earlier draft.

References

Amsden, Alice. 1989. *Asia's Next Giant: South Korea and Late Industrialization.* New York: Oxford University Press.

Anderson, Kim. 1983. "Fertilizer Policy in Korea." *Journal of Rural Development* 6: 43–57.

Aqua, Ronald. 1974. *Local Institutions and Rural Development*. Ithaca, NY: Cornell University, Rural Development Committee, Center for International Studies.

Bae, Keun-min. 2003a. "Farming Population Drops by 37% in Decade." *The Korea Times* (March 26).

——. 2003b. "NACF to Open More Domestic Distribution Outlets." *The Korea Times* (April 21).

Ban, Sung Hwan, Pal Yong Moon, and Dwight H. Perkins. 1980. *Rural Development: Studies in the Modernization of the Republic of Korea, 1948–1975*. Cambridge, MA: Harvard University Press.

Brandt, Vincent S.R. and Man-gap Lee. 1979. "Community Development in the Republic of Korea," in Ronald Dore and Zoe Mars (eds). *Community Development: Case Studies in India, the Republic of Korea, Mexico and Tanzania*. London: Croom Helm, pp. 49–136.

Burmeister, Larry L. 1988. *Research, Realpolitik, and Development in Korea: The State and the Green Revolution*. Boulder, CO: Westview Press.

——. 1990. "State, Industrialization and Agricultural Policy in Korea." *Development and Change* 21: 197–223.

——. 1992. "Korean Minifarm Agriculture: From Articulation to Disarticulation." *The Journal of Developing Areas* 26(2): 145–167.

——. 1999. "From Parastatal Control to Corporatist Intermediation: The Korean Agricultural Cooperative in Transition," in Dennis L. McNamara (ed.). *Corporatism and Korean Capitalism*. London and New York: Routledge, pp. 110–138.

Burmeister, Larry L., Gustav Ranis, and Michael Wang. 2002. "Group Behaviour and Development: A Comparison of Farmers' Organizations in South Korea and Taiwan," in Judith Heyer, Frances Stewart, and Rosemary Thorp (eds). *Group Behaviour and Development: Is the Market Destroying Competition?* New York: Oxford Unversity Press, pp. 125–143 .

Center for Research on Rural Society. 1989. *The Meaning and Limitations of the Amended Cooperative Law* (in Korean). Seoul: Center for Research on Rural Society.

Cho, Hyo-je. 2003. "Rising Influence of Civil Society." *The Korea Times* (March 5).

Cole, David C. and Princeton N. Lyman. 1971. *Korean Development: The Interplay of Politics and Economics*. Cambridge, MA: Harvard University Press.

Cumings, Bruce. 1981. *The Origins of the Korean War*, Vol. 1. Princeton, NJ: Princeton University Press.

Dong'a Ilbo. 1993. "Plans for Consolidation of Agricultural, Fisheries, and Livestock Cooperative Banking Operations" (in Korean) (April 15).

Enos, J.L. and W.-H. Park. 1988. *The Adoption and Diffusion of Imported Technology: The Case of Korea*. London: Croom Helm.

Evans, Peter. 1996. "Government Action, Social Capital and Development: Reviewing the Evidence on Synergy." *World Development* 24: 1119–1132.

FAS (Foreign Agricultural Service-USDA). 2001. *Merger of Agricultural, Livestock, and Ginseng Cooperative Federations*. GAIN Report No. KS0086. Seoul, Korea: U.S. Embassy.

Fei, John C.H. and Gustav Ranis. 1975. "A Model of Growth and Employment in the Open Dualistic Economy: The Case of Korea and Taiwan." *Journal of Development Studies* 11: 32–63.

Francks, Penelope, with Johanna Boestel and Choo Hyop Kim. 1999. *Agriculture and Economic Development in East Asia: From Growth to Protectionism in Japan, Korea, and Taiwan*. London: Routledge.

Gragert, Edwin H. 1994. *Landownership Under Colonial Rule: Korea's Japanese Experience.* Honolulu: University of Hawaii Press.

Han, Sung Joo. 1989. "South Korea: Politics in Transition," in Larry Diamond, Juan Linz, and Seymour Martin Lipset (eds). *Democracy in Developing Countries: Asia,* Vol. 3. Boulder, CO: Lynne Rienner, pp. 267–303.

Han'guk Ilbo. 1994. "Reduction of NACF Federation President's Authority" (in Korean) (May 2).

Hart-Landsberg, Martin. 1993. *The Rush to Development: Economic Change and Political Struggle in South Korea.* New York: Monthly Review.

Jones, Leroy P. 1975. *Public Enterprise and Economic Development: The Korean Case.* Seoul, Korea: Korea Development Institute.

Kang, Jung-Il. 1986. "Supply, Demand and Marketing of Fertilizer in the Republic of Korea." *Journal of Rural Development* 9: 145–170.

Kim, Deok-hyun. 2003. "Income Gap Widens in Farmers." *The Korea Times* (February 2).

Kim, Ki-tae. 2003. "Roh's Liberalization Plan Irks Farmers." *The Korea Times* (May 15).

Kim, Mi-hui. 1999. "NACF Reform Plan Under Criticism." Korea *Herald* (March 9).

Kim, Sung-jin. 2003. "Cabinet Ministers Alarm Trading Partners." *The Korea Times* (February 28).

Koh, Seung-Hahn. 2001. "The Social Reproduction Crisis of Farm Succession in South Korea: A Riverside Village Case Study." *Journal of Rural Development* 24: 31–63.

Koo, Hagen. 1991. "From Farm to Factory: Proletarianization of Korea." *American Sociological Review* 55: 669–681.

Korea *Herald.* 1999a. "Prosecutors to Question NACF Executives on Widespread Allegations." (March 3).

——. 1999b. "Farmers' Co-op Opposes Rice Import Liberalization." (August 14).

——. 1999c. "NACF Reforms to Provide More Efficient Services to Farmers." (September 27).

Krueger, Anne O., Constantine Michalopoulos, and Vernon W. Ruttan. 1989. *Aid and Development.* Baltimore, MD: The Johns Hopkins University Press.

KSA (Korea Statistical Association). 1992. *Social Indicators in Korea 1992.* Seoul, Korea: The National Statistical Office.

Kuznets, Paul W. 1977. *Economic Growth and Structure in the Republic of Korea.* New Haven, CT and London: Yale University Press.

Lee, Chang-Woo. 1991. "Republic of Korea (2)," in Asian Productivity Organization (ed.). *Agricultural Cooperatives in Asia and the Pacific.* Tokyo: APO, pp. 253–269.

Lee, Eddy. 1979. "Egalitarian Peasant Farming and Rural Development: The Case of South Korea," in D. Ghai, A. Khan, E. Lee, and S. Radwan (eds). *Agrarian Systems and Rural Development.* New York: Holmes & Meier, pp. 24–71.

Lee, Hoon K. 1936. *Land Utilization and Rural Economy in Korea.* Chicago, IL: University of Chicago Press.

Lee, Kap-soo. 1999a. "Structural Problems Blamed for NACF Irregularities." Korea *Herald* (March 3).

——. 1999b. "NACF, Three Other Cooperative Federations to be Merged by 2001." Korea *Herald* (March 9).

Lee, Su-Hoon. 1993. "Transitional Politics of Korea: 1987–1992." *Pacific Affairs* 66(3): 351–367.

Lee, Tae Young, Dong Hi Kim, and Dale W. Adams. 1977. "Savings Deposits and Agricultural Cooperatives in Korea." *Asian Survey* 17: 1182–1194.

Lie, John. 1998. *Han Unbound: The Political Economy of South Korea.* Stanford, CA: Stanford University Press.

Michell, Tony. 1988. *From a Developing to a Newly Industrialized Country: The Republic of Korea, 1961–82.* Geneva: International Labour Organisation.

Mooney, Patrick H., Jerry Roahrig, and Thomas W. Gray. 1996. "The De/repoliticization of Cooperation and the Discourse of Conversion." *Rural Sociology* 61: 559–576.

Moore, Mick. 1985. "Mobilization and Disillusion in Rural Korea: The *Saemaŭl* Movement in Retrospect." *Pacific Affairs* 57: 487–508.

Morredu, Catherine. 1999. *Review of Agricultural Policies in Korea.* Paris: OECD.

NACF. 1998. *Agricultural Cooperatives in Korea.* Seoul: NACF.

——. 1999. *Position of Korean Farmers on the WTO Negotiations in Agriculture.* Seoul: NACF.

OECD. 1999. *Agricultural Policies in OECD Countries: Monitoring and Evaluation 1999.* Paris: OECD.

——. 2001. *Multifunctionality: Toward an Analytical Framework.* Paris: OECD.

Oh, Young-jin. 2003. "[Korea–US Summit] Roh Pledges Full Opening of Agricultural Sector." *The Korea Times* (May 14).

Oshima, Harry T. 1986. "The Transition from an Agricultural to an Industrial Economy in East Asia." *Economic Development and Cultural Change* 34: 783–809.

Park, Seong Jae. 1993. *A Study of the Banking Production Efficiency of the Primary Cooperatives in Korea: A Cost Function Approach.* Ph.D. dissertation, The Ohio State University.

Scott, W. Richard. 1992. *Organizations: Rational, Natural, and Open Systems* (3rd edn). Englewood Cliffs, NJ: Prentice Hall.

Shin, Gi-Wook. 1996. *Peasant Protest and Social Change in Colonial Korea.* Seattle: University of Washington Press.

Shin, Gi-Wook and Do-Hyun Han. 1999. "Colonial Corporatism: The Rural Revitalization Campaign, 1932–1940," in Gi-Wook Shin and Michael Robinson (eds). *Colonial Modernity in Korea.* Cambridge, MA: Harvard University Asia Center and Harvard University Press, pp. 70–96.

Sorenson, Clark W. 1988. *Over the Mountains are Mountains: Korean Peasant Households and Their Adaptation to Rapid Industrialization.* Seattle: University of Washington Press.

Steinberg, David I., Sung Hwan Ban, W. Donald Bowles, and Maureen A. Lewis. 1984. *Korean Agricultural Services: The Invisible Hand in the Iron Glove, Market and Nonmarket Forces in Korean Rural Development.* AID Project Evaluation Report No. 52. Washington, DC: Agency for International Development.

Suh, Won Ho. 1989. "The Agricultural Co-operative Movement in Korea." *Review of International Co-operation* 82: 65–74.

Turner, John E., Vicki L. Hesli, Dong Suh Bark, and Hoon Yu. 1993. *Villages Astir: Community Development, Tradition, and Change in Korea.* Westport, CN: Praeger.

Uphoff, Norman. 1986. *Local Institutional Development: An Analytical Sourcebook with Cases.* West Hartford, CN: Kumarian Press.

Wade, Robert. 1982. *Irrigation and Agricultural Politics in South Korea.* Boulder, CO: Westview Press.

——. 1983. "South Korea's Agricultural Development: The Myth of the Passive State." *Pacific Viewpoint* 24: 11–28.

Whang, In-Joung. 1987. *The Role of Government in Agricultural and Rural Development in Korea, 1970–1985*. KDI Working Paper No. 8712. Seoul, Korea: Korea Development Institute.

Yoo, C.M. 2002. "Debt-workout Eyed for Agricultural Sector." Korea *Herald* (April 26).

Zeon, Young-cheol. 1973. *The Politics of Land Reform in South Korea*. Ph.D. dissertation, University of Missouri.

Part II

Business and industrial transformations

3 Causes, consequences, relevance

Korea's industrialization

Paul W. Kuznets

A major feature of the post-World War II era has been the transformation of colonies into autonomous states, each free to establish its own course of development. Economic development in South Korea, a former Japanese colony, has been distinguished since the mid-1960s by unusually rapid industrialization and, more broadly, by especially rapid economic growth. Such growth has attracted widespread attention in recent decades, generated a substantial English-language literature on Korea's economic performance, and raised a host of issues that have yet to be resolved. Among these are issues of what has been responsible for rapid growth, how this growth has affected people's lives, and the extent to which the Korean experience is relevant for Korea's future or for other countries.

Such issues are too complex to be wholly resolved, so the goal here is more modest: to examine the questions that inevitably arise when exploring issues of causes, consequences, and relevance. We know that industrialization is shaped by institutional, political, and social factors as well as by economic factors. This raises a first question of how to weigh non-economic factors in explaining economic processes. Answers will depend upon one's field or comparative advantage and will vary according to the importance attached to ultimate as opposed to proximate influences. Emphasis here is on the proximate or economic causes.

Before examining this and other questions, however, there is a prior question of what has happened in Korea. The following section therefore deals with macroeconomic indicators of output growth, production structure, and expenditure allocation. As quantitative, summary measures, these necessarily abstract from the detail, the variation, and the institutions that mold economic affairs. They are used, nevertheless, because they permit generalization, allow comparison with experience elsewhere, and have independent explanatory power.

The economic record

Consistent, reliable economic data, available only since 1953, show slow GDP growth following the Korean War until the mid-1960s, then much more rapid growth afterward. This growth increased real per capita GDP over sixfold after 1970, almost thirteenfold since 1953 (see Table 3.1). Such growth is rare. Recent World Bank World Development Reports show, for instance, that of the 112 countries whose GDP growth rates are given for 1980 to 1990, only China's growth was faster. Korea's growth was still in the top 10 percent of the 133 countries shown for 1990 to 2000. Such growth, combined with declining rates of population increase, has raised incomes so that the average, adjusted to reflect differences in purchasing power, was over $17,000 by 2000. (The comparable figure for a developed country such as Canada was $27,000.) Unlike averages in many countries, this one does not conceal a highly unequal income distribution. Inequality has increased, which is not surprising, and distribution is not as egalitarian as is popularly believed, but inequality has been relatively low by international standards (Yoo 1990: 381).

Rapid industrialization not only brought high rates of growth in output and incomes but also created major changes in economic structure and population distribution. Data on GDP by sector of origin show a sharp decline in agriculture's share, a sharp increase in industry's share, and a moderate increase in services' share (see Table 3.2). These output changes have a counterpart in employment with a major decline in agricultural employment after 1963 and a sharp expansion of the industry and service shares of total employment (Table 3.2). In addition, since changes in output and employment shares have been associated with rapidly rising totals, they have been responsible for much of Korea's urbanization and population redistribution.[1] Census estimates show, for instance, that in 1955 only a quarter of the population lived in urban areas; by 2000 the figure was 88 percent.

These indicators reveal the rapidity of growth and the large size of

Table 3.1 Gross domestic product, 1953 to 2000

	GDP in 1990 prices (billion Won)	*Average annual growth rate (%)*	*Population (thousands)*	*GDP/capita (thousand Won)*
2000	326,140		47,008	6,938
		6.2		
1990	179,539		42,869	4,188
		9.4		
1980	73,311		38,124	1,923
		8.1		
1970	33,693		32,241	1,045
		8.4		
1960	15,036		25,012	601
		3.8		
1953	11,573		21,526	538

Sources: Bank of Korea, *Economic Statistics Yearbooks*, National Statistical Office, *Korea Statistical Yearbooks*.

Table 3.2 Structure: output, employment, expenditure, 1953 to 2000

A. Output and employment

Year	*% of GDP*			*% of total employment*		
	Ag.	*Ind.*	*Serv.*	*Ag.*	*Ind.*	*Serv.*
2000	5	31	64	11	20	69
1990	9	30	61	18	28	54
1980	15	40	45	34	29	37
1970	26	29	45	50	17	33
1960	40	19	41	63[a]	11[a]	26[a]
1953	49	12	39	–	–	–

B. Expenditures (% of GDP)

	Govt	*Gross Dom. I*	*Export*
2000	10.1	28.2	44.8
1990	6.6	36.9	30.0
1980	8.0	30.1	36.6
1970	10.5	26.9	14.3
1960	14.6	11.0	3.4
1953	8.0	15.6	2.0

Sources: Bank of Korea, *National Income in Korea*; *Economic Planning Board, Korea Statistical Yearbooks*; National Statistical Office, *Korea Statistical Yearbooks.*

Note
a = 1963.

structural changes. Korea is also distinguished by its pattern of expenditures or demand structure. In particular, the public sector has been relatively small. Government consumption has averaged 8 to 10 percent of GDP in recent years, which is well below World Bank averages. While there is conflicting evidence on the relation between growth and government size, the reason for Korea's small public sector is clear: less is spent on health, housing, social security, and welfare than in most countries (see Kuznets 1994).

Table 3.2 also shows Korea's high investment ratios. Large outlays for factories, equipment, inventories, and infrastructure are required to expand the capacity needed to increase output. This is confirmed by the ubiquity and clangor of construction in Seoul and elsewhere in Korea. If there is a real supply-side economics, it is this investment–capacity–output nexus that was a staple of development economics well before the Reagan presidency.[2] Heavy investment has important implications for saving, efficiency, and profitability. It means, in particular, that interest paid and income increases are both high enough to encourage private saving. Conservative fiscal policy has also generated government surpluses rather than deficits. Investment must have been sufficiently profitable to attract investors or, alternatively, efficient enough to generate worthwhile returns.

The export ratios (exports/GDP) shown in Table 3.2 illustrate a third way that Korea's demand structure is unusual. Although Korea is a large country in terms of population and GDP, and large countries have low export ratios, Korea's ratios are well above the norm. The multiple expansions of exports, from less than $100 million in 1963 to over $172 billion in 2000, have played important roles in Korea's industrialization. One such is to pay for the imported machinery and materials needed to expand capacity and output. Another has been to raise efficiency by increasing output in areas of comparative advantage and exchanging their product for other products which cannot be produced domestically or produced only at great cost. Yet another role has been to assure foreign lenders that the foreign exchange needed to repay them would be forthcoming. Foreign loans were particularly important in financing investment prior to the mid-1970s and in coping with oil shocks.

Causes

Korea's pattern of slow growth prior to the mid-1960s and subsequent fast growth raises questions of why growth was slow at first, what accelerated growth, and why rapid growth was possible in recent decades. The first two questions may be answered simply by examining events following liberation in 1945 and the new policy set adopted from 1963 to 1966. The third and most important question cannot be answered simply, however, and so the discussion below concentrates on causes of Korea's recent high-speed growth.

South Korea, as part of a formerly unified country that had played a specialized role in Japan's colonial empire, suffered from severe economic dislocation in 1945. Separation from the north left the south with little heavy industry and insufficient electric power. Dissolution of the empire and departure of the Japanese cut off export markets and input sources, and drained the country of technicians and high-level manpower. The situation was so bad that the American military government which ran the country had to concentrate on relief rather than development. An independent Republic of Korea was established under Syngman Rhee in 1948 but the Korean War began less than two years after Rhee's inauguration and devastated most of the Korean peninsula. The war's legacy was not only death and destruction but also a pre-eminent army.

Dislocation and war are not the stuff of economic development and neither, ultimately, were Rhee's economic policies. These were designed to maximize the inflow of American assistance and thus made it impossible to devalue the overvalued currency. Rhee also tried to industrialize through import substitution. Import substituting industrialization (ISI) was widely accepted in newly independent countries and worked well as long as the new industries supplied established demand, suited domestic factor endowments, and employed existing technology. ISI in Korea was also motivated by a desire to end continued dependence on Japan (see Woo 1991: ch. 3).

One problem with ISI is that once easy substitution for consumer nondurables gives way to substitution for intermediates (such as the "three whites": cement, sugar, and flour), it absorbs scarce capital and typically creates excess capacity. Another problem is that substitution requires protection for infant industries, which raises domestic prices. Price increases serve to overvalue the currency, while the exchange controls needed to protect the overvalued currency warp economic incentives. Profits are made by avoiding controls rather than by increasing output, improving quality, or lowering costs. These problems were compounded in Korea by the regime's absorption with survival, at the expense of economic policy, and by political turmoil which culminated in the student revolt of 1960 that overthrew Rhee, and the military coup in 1961 that deposed the successor Chang government.

The new military regime under Park Chung Hee inherited a stagnant economy, a public demanding better economic performance, and a failed economic strategy that depended on American economic aid to cover fiscal and trade deficits. When the U.S. announced that aid would be reduced and then ended, a new strategy was clearly needed. This began with a stabilization program that ended government deficits (1963–1964), devalued the won (1964), reformed (raised) interest rates (1965), and improved tax collection (1966).[3] Export promotion also intensified. Park and his successor, Chun Doo Hwan, both stressed economic performance and adopted "growth-first" strategies. They did this to satisfy public demand, to claim legitimacy for their governance since both had seized power by coup, and because they recognized the political and strategic benefits of good economic performance.

While the stabilization program was the proximate cause of growth acceleration, it cannot explain why rapid growth continued for the following three decades. Any explanation for this is multivariate and might include Korea's political situation, the role of the state and bureaucratic discipline, the institutional inheritance, the effects of a Confucian tradition, and external developments. Other factors to consider include resource possession, existence of excess capacity, productivity-raising variables such as technical expertise, scale economies, and advances in knowledge, and economic policy choice.

Some of these, particularly technical expertise, advances in knowledge, and policy choice, are associated with education and training. A combination of literacy campaigns after liberation, early expansion of primary schooling, and an unusually high proportion of graduates going on to higher levels gave Korea an education profile by the early 1960s that resembled those of rich countries rather than similarly poor ones (see McGinn *et al.* 1980: 60). One cause of rapid industrialization was undoubtedly this early investment in education and its subsequent pay-off in productive skills and in the capacity "to judge opportunities correctly . . . and to act vigorously" (Lim 1978: 191).

Political instability, social turmoil, and war have all slowed down economic development. The Korean War was a prime example, but there have been other, less extreme examples in Korea. One was the shift in ruling party policy and leadership in 1958, reflected in the new National Security Law that was followed by recession in 1959 to 1960; another was the riots and the President's assassination in 1979 which contributed to the economic reversal of 1980; more recently, demonstrations and strikes in 1987 to 1989 significantly reduced output and exports. Unlike many coup-prone Latin American countries, however, Korea has benefited economically from long periods of political stability under authoritarian rule (1963–1987) and, since 1987, democratic governance.

Two notable features of Korea's economic development have been the state's economic leadership and, since the 1970s, the rise of giant conglomerates or *chaebŏl*. State leadership is part of Korea's colonial inheritance since the 1930s when the Japanese colonial administration used private banks and the Industrial Bank to direct resources toward heavy industry with war potential, particularly in the north under the new *zaibatsu* (Woo 1991: 24–25, 31–33). The *chaebŏl* are today's *zaibatsu* analog while the colonial state's use of finance to direct industrialization reappeared in the 1970s when the Park regime employed "priority" loans to establish heavy and chemical industries with war potential.

State leadership cannot be taken for granted, even in authoritarian states, and so something more than colonial precedent must be invoked to explain the phenomenon. Leadership follows from a desire to catch up with Japan and other advanced industrial countries, from the success of tightly focused industrial policy, and from a culture that allows the government to impose policies which provide future as opposed to present benefits. It also follows from particularly strong policy implementation, a product of leaders' military training, and of a hierarchical command system where "officials can seldom afford to act in a manner that seriously obstructs . . . leadership commitment to growth" (Jones and SaKong 1990: 139).

In addition, though the *zaibatsu* provide a precedent for the *chaebŏl*, they were Japanese, not Korean enterprises. There were, however, prominent Korean enterprises during the colonial era whose close ties with the state, concentrated family ownership and management, and mutual participation in joint ventures and other networks are strongly reminiscent of the present *chaebŏl*.[4] And large conglomerates, whether *zaibtsu* or *chaebŏl*, possess features that have contributed to their longevity and inspired governments to use them as instruments of economic policy. One is that large size and a proven track record go together. Conglomeration also reduces the risk of entering new, and therefore risky industries. Large firms have advantages unavailable to small ones as well. They benefit from scale economies, particularly in management, as Kwon and Suh make clear in Chapter 4; they can benefit from economic use of the rare entrepreneurial talent needed to initiate new industries and production processes; and they have workers who are sufficiently motivated, because of relatively high pay, to master new and unfamiliar production processes (see Amsden 1989: 209).

Political stability, state economic leadership, and emergence of the *chaebŏl* are not the only features of the Korean scene associated with rapid growth. For instance, Korea's ethnic homogeneity, compact geography, and intermediate population size all favor growth because these factors tend to reduce potential social conflict, ease transport and communication, and permit scale economies. The country's lack of natural resources, paradoxically, has a similar impact. Demand for resources and resource-based goods is inelastic, it is argued, and therefore their export is subject to wide, destabilizing price fluctuations. More importantly, economic rents from producing such goods encourages rent seeking rather than output expansion and production for export (Lee and Naya 1986; Ranis and Fei 1988: 106–111). In addition, resource possession, like access to foreign assistance, allows policy-makers to postpone the reforms needed to accelerate development.

Two other possible reasons for growth can be dismissed. One is the large-scale U.S. economic and military assistance that Korea has received. Although economic aid had long-term positive economic benefits to Korea, when growth accelerated in the mid-1960s, economic assistance was already being phased out. And, despite continued military assistance, defense expenditure has been well above international norms so that assistance has not simply substituted for Korea's own outlays. If the U.S. contributed to Korea's economic success, it was mainly by providing major markets for Korean exports.

The other reason is that favorable initial conditions, especially the accelerated increase in global trade in the 1960s, allowed the export expansion that was critical for Korea's rapid growth. If acceleration had occurred in the 1970s or 1980s, some have argued, growth would have been hampered by the slowdown in world trade and the protectionism triggered by earlier floods of exports from countries such as Korea (Cline 1982). While world export volume more than doubled in the decade prior to the first oil shock in 1973, and rose only 3 percent a year during the following decade, Korea's exports increased eighteenfold between 1963 and 1973, and more than tripled from 1973 to 1983. Success was evidently less a matter of demand expansion than of rising market shares. In addition, the earlier success of countries such as Korea did not spoil markets for those who followed. Export growth of a dozen "newly exporting countries" in the 1970s surpassed that of Korea and their other immediate predecessors (Havryshin and Alikhani 1982).

A major source of Korea's swift industrialization has undoubtedly been a set of Confucian cultural values that contribute directly by emphasizing perseverance, thrift, and the legitimacy of hierarchy. They contribute indirectly by allowing policy-makers to employ growth-oriented policies which sacrifice present for future consumption (see Gray 1996). Other, traditional elements of Confucianism such as the distaste for commerce or excessive spending on ceremonies detract from rather than contribute to industrialization. However, these have been displaced over time in countries like Korea so that they no longer slow down modernization and economic development.[5]

While culture can influence economic performance in many ways, of particular interest in Korea are the cultural roots of state economic leadership, the *chaebŏl*, and the relationships between government and big business. An ethic that promotes responsibility and loyalty should limit opportunistic behavior and encourage identification with large organizations such as government and the *chaebŏl*. For instance, emphasis on harmony and management identification of national welfare with *chaebŏl* interests is used to promote public support and instill discipline among employees (Jannelli with Yim 1993: ch. 3).

State leadership, as noted earlier, has been facilitated by bureaucratic discipline within a hierarchical structure. It also stemmed from Confucian tradition in which the government was the senior, and business, the junior, partner. This partnership requires direct relations between the *chaebŏl* and economic ministries through discussion groups and other organized meetings. These relations substitute for policy implemented at arm's length through the market mechanism and so are sometimes seen as suspect on efficiency grounds. Government–*chaebŏl* relations constitute a form of "quasi-internal" organization, however, and this form "favored by Confucian culture . . . can be efficient because it reduces information costs and increases specialization in decision making" (Cho and Lee 1989: 462–464).

Economic causes of Korea's high-speed industrialization might include high investment levels, export expansion, competition in labor markets, and a "developmental" state. The list is not meant to be exhaustive. Since I have dealt with these causes at length elsewhere, what follows will be brief (see Kuznets 1994).

The importance of investment for the added capacity needed to increase output was mentioned above, as were the supply-and-demand factors that have contributed to Korea's unusually high investment ratios. Similarly, we have discussed the significance of the multiple expansion of exports and the different roles exports have played in paying for capital-goods imports and increasing efficiency. Another feature noted earlier was the radical change in employment structure and its correlate, urbanization. These changes, and increased labor absorption as employment grew half again as fast as the working-age population, are evidence that labor markets have been competitive and have functioned efficiently.

Competition and efficiency cannot be taken for granted because wage-setting institutions, such as minimum wage laws, public-sector wage leadership, labor unions, and protective legislation, have often pushed wages above market-clearing levels and restricted absorption (Fields and Wan, Jr. 1989). Both increase in labor inputs and better labor utilization have been major sources of Korea's industrialization (see Kim and Park 1985: 60–66). This is no surprise because post-liberation Korea was the epitome of Arthur Lewis's celebrated model of economic development with unlimited supplies of labor. In this model, development depends upon shifting workers from traditional work, where they suffer from "disguised unemployment" or low productivity, to high-productivity, modern-sector jobs.

The impetus for heavy investment, export expansion, and labor market competition has come from Korea's developmental state. "Developmental" because economic development gets top priority and is achieved by implementing "growth-first" policies where the state leads and private enterprise follows. This statement must be qualified because there is more – and less – to developmentalism and because it has changed over time.

Monetary, fiscal, and exchange-rate measures are universal instruments of macroeconomic policy, so developmentalism requires more than the use of such measures. What is developmental about the Korean state, rather, has been a set of five-year plans that established an industrial policy. This policy typically targeted a few new industries which would be developed by one or two of the *chaebŏl*. The conglomerates were given access to cheap credit while the government licensed the necessary technology imports to improve *chaebŏl* bargaining power, supervised construction to insure that design standards were met, and then pushed for cost reduction. The latter allowed the government to end protection for the infant industry and, eventually, made the industry sufficiently competitive to export its products.

Three aspects of the state's industrial policy are noteworthy. One is that intervention has been justified on grounds that technology markets are imperfect (because information is asymmetric), infant industries require protection, and even the *chaebŏl* sometimes lack the resources needed to produce new products and/or master new technologies. Another is that much of what Korea now exports was either imported or only started production fifteen to twenty years ago. Finally, industrial policy reached its apogee in the 1970s with the drive to establish the heavy and chemical industries. It is now less significant because the HCI drive violated the need for a tight focus and sparked disruptive inflation, because costs were found eventually to outweigh benefits, and because the pendulum of economic fashion has swung from interventionism to increased reliance on market mechanisms.

Consequences

The high-speed growth shown in Tables 3.1 and 3.2 has had a measurable impact upon Korea's GDP, per capita GDP, and economic structure. It has also redistributed the population, altered economic welfare, and affected the quality of life. The latter two are multivariate and difficult to measure but are in many ways the real counterparts of the economic aggregates. Poverty estimates, where poverty is defined in absolute terms to include any income below that corresponding to the minimum necessary food consumption level, show that in 1965 41 percent of all Koreans were living in poverty. By 1982 the figure was less than 8 percent (see Suh 1985). Life expectancy, often used as an indicator of the physical quality of life, increased by twenty years from age fifty-three in 1960. Consumption patterns have also changed for the better. In 1972 urban families spent about two-thirds of their income on basic needs like housing and food; by 2000 this figure had dropped below 40 percent.

Since development should reduce poverty and increase longevity, Korea is not unique. A study of how per capita income relates to poverty and life expectancy for thirty-four countries in the 1970s shows, however, that Korea was one of the countries that performed best in reducing poverty (both absolutely and relative to per capita income) but was not among the best in increasing longevity (Sen 1980). These results are consistent with the state's growth-first policies, relatively low government expenditure on health, housing, social security, and welfare, and the Confucian emphasis upon the family's responsibility for its members' welfare.

Other features of rapid growth have not been so favorable. A combination of heavy rural-to-urban migration, the consequent rapid urbanization, and government policies that discriminate against residential construction has created housing shortages. These inspired the sixth five-year plan (1987–1991) to include a housing target of 1.7 million new units for low-income families. This would have raised the housing–supply ratio (units/households) from 58 percent in 1985 to 72 percent by 1991, but a burst of construction-sparked inflation eventually forced the government to restrict all construction in late 1991.

Housing shortages have been coupled with traffic congestion and rising levels of pollution in Korean cities. These latter are by now classic common property problems where markets impute too little cost to private sources of the problem and therefore generate excess social costs. Such failure justifies intervention, but intervention has so far been ineffective without draconian measures. Maoist China, which achieved rare success in curbing congestion (if not pollution), did this only by requiring residence permits, food-ration coupons, and "rustification" where urban school-leavers were banished to the countryside.

Rapid industrialization has not only influenced economic welfare and the quality of life but has also changed the course of economic development. Cases in point include the economic causes of high-speed growth that were discussed earlier: high investment ratios, export expansion, labor market competition, and state leadership. These changes, though incomplete, are as much a consequence of the Korean experience as any change in welfare or quality of life.

The enormous increase in investment in recent decades, both absolute and relative to GDP, has reached levels where further increase is unlikely. There are other reasons to expect this besides the difficulty of maintaining increments on ever larger bases. One is a long-term increase in the investment share of residential construction. This investment has an unusually long stream of returns and therefore a less immediate impact upon GDP than most investment. Another reason has been a sharp increase from 1989 in direct foreign investment by Korean firms, mainly to move production of labor-intensive manufactures offshore and to establish trade outlets in EC and U.S. markets. Like housing, these investments have a less immediate impact on GDP than most. Finally, recent five-year plans call for increasing expenditure on research and development, establishment of science parks, and "reinforcing education ... in basic sciences" (Government of the Republic of Korea 1986: 59). Although outlays for education, research, and development are as much "investment" as outlays for physical capital, they are excluded from investment by national-accounting convention.

Like high investment, export expansion is subject to the difficulty of maintaining growth in ever larger totals. Except where trade is restricted for political or strategic reasons, exporting is a function of comparative advantage and the commercial policies of trading partners. Rapid industrialization and development have shifted Korea's comparative advantage from labor-intensive manufactures to capital-intensive goods, and more recently to more technology-intensive products. These bring Korea into competition with firms in advanced industrial countries which, because they fear boomerang effects, have proven unwilling to share proprietary technology with their Korean rivals. Such unwillingness, in turn, is one reason for the increased emphasis upon research, development, and the basic sciences in Korea itself.

A major threat to continued export expansion has been rising protectionism, Korea's greater visibility in export markets, and the emergence of regional trading blocs such as the European Community and NAFTA. U.S. protectionism has been particularly troublesome because America took one-third of Korean exports as late as the mid-1980s. By 2000 the collapse of the Soviet Union, further opening up of China's trade, and efforts to diversify had reduced the U.S. share to less than 20 percent. The combination of growing protectionism and difficulties in shifting comparative advantage has led to a new export pessimism, as revealed in the sixth plan's goal of reducing "dependence on exports for growth" and "expanding the domestic economy" (Government of the Republic of Korea 1986: 38).

Labor–market competition, particularly prior to 1975 when labor was abundant and underutilized, undoubtedly provided more jobs and more productive work than would have been the case without competition.[6] Competition was achieved, unfortunately, by repressing unions during the Park and Chun presidencies (see Choi 1989). Repression ended in early 1987 when Chun needed labor votes to elect his chosen successor, Roh Tae Woo. Two years of strikes and rapid wage escalation followed. These demonstrated the need for a new labor-management system and encouraged producers of labor-intensive goods to invest in countries where labor is cheaper and more docile.

The developmental state's economic leadership has been challenged by two features of industrial policy, and, from 1987, by democratization. One challenge emerged from the allocation of loans to "priority" investments, and the other was allocation that favored the *chaebŏl*. The first burdened the banking system with non-performing loans. These slowed down financial reform so that finance has become a bottleneck in Korea's development. Non-performing loans – and inadequate prudential regulation – combined in spectacular fashion to undo the Korean economy during the Asian financial crisis of 1997 to 1998. The second concentrated resources in the *chaebŏl*. This increased their monopoly power while the benefits of this organizational form were eventually outweighed by debt-heavy capitalization which, when combined with overexpansion, resulted in bankruptcy or near bankruptcy.[7]

Although democratization, unlike weak banks or the *chaebŏl*, cannot be attributed directly to industrialization, it is tempting to argue that economic success increased the desire for political reform and so contributed to democratization. Whatever the relation between the two, state developmentalism and economic leadership have diminished since 1987. One reason for this is that elected officials are hostage to previously disenfranchised economic interest groups, as witnessed by the wave of strikes that began in 1987. Another is that the state can no longer limit *chaebŏl* power by dropping financial support because the cost in unemployment and market disruption would be too great.[8] In addition, economic policymakers are less insulated from executive and legislative influence or public pressure than they were earlier under authoritarian governments.[9] This is particularly undesirable because Korea's economic policies, crafted by highly trained technocrats, have been better than economic policies in most countries.[10]

Relevance

The discussion thus far has left issues of the relevance of Korea's industrialization unanswered: to what extent is the experience of rapid industrialization relevant for Korea's future economic development? Is Korea's experience relevant for other countries? Although the Korean experience has distinctive features, and it is no "model for total emulation," it can be instructive about what to do or not to do in pursuing development in Korea's future or elsewhere (see Steinberg 1982: 103).

The past is usually invoked when trying to predict the future. Or, to put the point differently, expectations are typically regressive. This fits well with the view that much is to be learned from the past and that history is marked by continuity, but Korea's experience since the mid-1960s makes extrapolation particularly hazardous. One reason for this is that changes in Korea's economic structure and performance have been so large that projecting them into the future produces nonsensical results. Another is that industrialization has itself brought changes so that causal variables such as investment, exports, labor markets, and state leadership no longer operate as they once did. Nevertheless, the past, particularly the problems that have been recognized in public documents such as the seventh five-year plan (1993–1997) and President Kim's New Economy Plan (NEP), should be relevant for the future.

The unusually high levels of investment and export growth that supported rapid industrialization are, as noted earlier, likely to decline. This suggests that GDP growth is likely to drop too. Democratization, which ended labor repression, has brought higher wages, a shift in labor-intensive manufactures offshore, and the NEP's call for labor–management cooperation (see Cha 1994). One consequence of wage escalation, though not apparent at the time, was that it hastened the substitution of capital for labor and thus raised labor productivity.

Productivity is particularly important because future economic performance will depend more on increasing total factor productivity (which includes capital as well as labor productivity) than it has in the past. Growth in Korea and other East Asian countries (Taiwan, Singapore, and Hong Kong) has been driven much more by a dramatic increase in factor inputs than by productivity increase, which has been no higher than in OECD and Latin American countries (Young 1995). Since high rates of absorption have eliminated surplus labor in Korea, future growth will have to come mainly from capital deepening and productivity increases. This has been recognized since the early 1980s when the revised fifth plan (1984–1986) proposed to raise outlays for research and development and expand the supply of scientists and engineers, both of which promote productivity increases.

Challenges to state economic leadership from the *chaebŏl* and other economic interest groups are likely to continue. In the 1980s, governments responded with statements on the proper economic role of the state in the fifth plan (1982–1986), which said that the government would reduce its intervention in the market mechanism, and a sixth plan (1987–1991) assertion that governmental economic management was to be conducted so as to promote private-sector initiative. In the seventh plan (1992–1996), the emphasis was upon indicative rather than directive planning, while the NEP (June 1993) promised to reduce regulation and intervention so that the private sector would propel development while the government played "only a supplementary role" (Young 1995: 519). However, the government still wanted to encourage investment in industries expected to gain comparative advantage (fifth plan), build housing for low-income households (sixth and revised sixth plan (1988–1991)), and restrict borrowing to encourage *chaebŏl* specialization (NEP). Such contradictions between word and deed are consistent with Korea's tradition of government leadership. It also indicates that despite challenges, the tradition lives on.

The relevance of the Korean experience for other countries depends on whether causal factors exist or can be reproduced elsewhere. Among those mentioned earlier are political stability, state economic leadership, strong policy implementation, and national characteristics such as ethnic homogeneity, compact geography, lack of natural resources, and a Confucian cultural heritage. These are either not reproducible or not easily reproducible. Also included were the state's priorities (economic growth first), and its focus on industrial policy in a basically market setting. These latter distinguish South Korea from North Korea, which shares the south's non-reproducible attributes, and shows that neither the south's success nor the north's failure are historically or regionally specific.[11]

If any causes of Korea's rapid industrialization can be reproduced or generalized, it is the policy causes. Export expansion, high investment ratios, and labor market competition have been achieved by adopting policies to promote exports, assist investors, and encourage market wage determination. Establishing a developmental state, or state economic leadership focused on industrial policy, is another matter. This requires that economic growth be given top priority, that it have political backing, and that public servants be sufficiently capable and disciplined to implement economic policies. If anything reduces the relevance of the Korean experience for other countries, it is that they do not meet these requirements.

The World Bank makes the same point in *The East Asian Miracle* when it says that many countries lack "the high level of institutional capacity" needed for "highly directed interventions" (World Bank 1994: 25). Industrial policy has been the main "highly directed intervention" in Korea but the World Bank is skeptical of intervention because it violates the accepted view that because intervention cannot be incentive-neutral it must be inefficient. The success of East Asian economies like Korea contradicts this view, so the Bank argues that success occurred despite intervention, or because intervention has been "market-friendly" since it has been selective (i.e., highly directed) and designed to correct market failures or enhance competition (World Bank 1994: 84–86).

The controversy over industrial policy should not obscure the fact that the World Bank's developmental states have built the institutions and adopted the policies needed to implement rapid industrialization. "The East Asian Miracle" is mistitled because there is nothing miraculous about rapid industrialization in East Asian countries like Korea. What is relevant is their long-term commitment to economic growth, generally consistent and correct policy choices, and capacity to focus on and solve economic problems. Korea has met these requirements, which is all too rare, and has done so by hard work and foresight without the aid of any miracles.

Notes

1 There is relatively little industry or service activity in rural areas. See Ho (1982: 973–990).
2 For instance, United Nations (1960: ch. 2).
3 For more details see Kanesa-Thasan (1969: 257–276).
4 McNamara provides case studies of leading Korean entrepreneurs during the colonial era which illustrate these points (see McNamara 1990). Note that parallels between today's *chaebŏl* and Korean colonial enterprise are not simply a matter of inheritance. Only three of the twenty largest *chaebŏl* in 1986 were founded under the Japanese (see Fields 1995: 33).
5 These points are made in more detail by Metzger to explain Taiwan's industrialization, but apply to Korea as well (see Metzger 1989: 141–195).
6 The "turning point" from surplus to shortage probably occurred in 1975 (see Bai 1982: 117–140).
7 For more on the financial bottleneck and Korea's experience during the Asian financial crisis, see "Symposium on the Korean Financial Crisis: Causes and Challenges" (1998: 609–670). It is concentration, or domination of particular markets, not size, which allows exercise of monopoly power. In addition, estimates to show size exaggerate when they use sales rather than value-added. Sales of one affiliate to another are counted twice while the contribution of non-affiliated suppliers is included in *chaebŏl* sales when it should not be, and differences between sales and value-added can be substantial. In 1978, for example, combined sales of the top ten *chaebŏl* equaled 30.1 percent of GNP (see Fields 1995: 37). Value-added by the top ten equaled only 10.9 percent (see Jones 1987: 98).
8 This poses a "moral hazard" faced by any large debtor, namely that if bankruptcy is no threat, there is little incentive to undertake the difficult steps needed to avoid the problem.
9 For further discussion of this point, see Haggard and Moon 1996: 210–237, esp. pp. 230–237.
10 The results have certainly been better, which may be attributed to bureaucratic discipline, strong implementation, and better training as well as to insulation. Although mistakes have been made (see Kuznets 1982: Supplement), insulation has allowed a particularly able group of technocrats to advance good policies and avoid bad ones. They do not deserve to be labeled "eremites in ivory towers" (Woo 1991: 191) or "A-TKEs" (American-trained Korean economists) who have swallowed free-market theory and are applying it uncritically to Korean circumstances (see Amsden 1994: 87–125).
11 This point contradicts the view that "the development 'successes' of Taiwan and Korea are historically and regionally specific, and therefore provide no readily adaptable models for other developing countries" (Cumings 1987: 81).

References

Amsden, Alice H. 1989. *Asia's New Giant: South Korea and Late Industrialization.* New York: Oxford University Press.

Amsden, Alice H. 1994. "The Specter of Anglo-Saxonization is Haunting South Korea," in Lee-Jay Cho and Yoon Hyung Kim (eds). *Korea's Political Economy: An Institutional Perspective.* Boulder, CO: Westview Press, pp. 87–125.

Bai, Moo Ki. 1982. "The Turning Point in the Korean Economy." *The Developing Economies* 20 (June): 117–140.

Cha, Dong-Se. 1994. "Korea's New Economy Plan and Recent Economic Reforms." *Journal of Asian Economics* 5: 514–523.

Choi, Jang Jip. 1989. *Labor and the Authoritarian State: Labor Unions in South Korean Manufacturing Industries, 1961–1980.* Seoul: Korea University Press.

Cho, Lee Jay and Chung Hoon Lee. 1989. "The Government–Business Relationship in Korea: Cultural Dimensions," in *Conference on Confucianism and Economic Development in East Asia,* Conference Series No. 13. Taipei: Chung-Hua Institution for Economic Research, pp. 451–471.

Cline, William R. 1982. "Can the East Asian Model of Development Be Generalized?" *World Development* 10: 81–90.

Cumings, Bruce. 1987. "The Origins and Development of the Northeast Asian Political Economy: Industrial Sectors, Product Cycles, and Political Consequences," in F.C. Deyo (ed.). *The Political Economy of the New Asian Industrialization.* Ithaca, NY: Cornell University Press, pp. 44–83.

Fields, Gary S. and Henry Wan, Jr. 1989. "Wage-setting Institutions and Economic Growth." *World Development* 17: 1471–1483.

Fields, Karl J. 1995. *Enterprise and the State in Korea and Taiwan.* Ithaca, NY: Cornell University Press.

Government of the Republic of Korea. 1986. *The Sixth Five-Year Economic and Social Development Plan: 1987–1991.* English version. Seoul: Government of the Republic of Korea.

Gray, H. Peter. 1996. "Culture and Economic Performance: Policy as an Intervening Variable." *Journal of Comparative Economics* 20: 278–291.

Haggard, Stephan and Chung-In Moon. 1996. "Institutions and Economic Policy: Theory and a Korean Case Study." *World Politics* 42: 210–237.

Havrylyshin, Oli and Iradj Alikhani. 1982. "Is There Cause for Export Optimism? An Inquiry into the Existence of a Second Generation of Successful Exporters." *Weltwirtschaftliches Archiv* 118: 651–662.

Ho, Samuel P.S. 1982. "Economic Development and Rural Industry in South Korea and Taiwan." *World Development* S: 973–990.

Janelli, Roger L. with Dawnhee Yim. 1993. *Making Capitalism: The Social and Cultural Construction of a South Korean Conglomerate.* Stanford, CA: Stanford University Press.

Jones, Leroy. 1987. "Jaebul and the Concentration of Economic Power in Korean Development," in Il SaKong (ed.). *Macroeconomic Policy and Industrial Development Issues.* Seoul: Korea Development Institute.

Jones, Leroy and Il SaKong. 1990. *Government, Business, and Entrepreneurship in Economic Growth: The Korean Case.* Cambridge, MA: Harvard University Press, Korea Development Institute.

Kanesa-Thasan, S. 1969. "Stabilizing an Economy: The Korean Experience," in

Irma Adelman (ed.). *Practical Approaches to Development Planning: Korea's Second Five Year Plan*. Baltimore, MD: The Johns Hopkins University Press, pp. 257–276.

Kim, Kwang Suk and Joon Kyung Park. 1985. *Sources of Economic Growth in Korea, 1963–1982.* Seoul: Korea Development Institute.

Kuznets, Paul. 1982. "The Dramatic Reversal of 1979–80." *Journal of Northeast Asian Studies* 1: 71–87.

Kuznets, Paul. 1994. *Korean Economic Development: An Interpretive Model.* Westport, CT: Praeger.

Lee, Chung H. and Seiji Naya. 1986. "Trade in East Asian Development with Comparative Reference to Southeast Asian Experience." *Economic Development and Cultural Change* 36: Supplement.

Lim, Youngil. 1978. "Review Article: What is Pushing Korean Industrialization?" (Center for Korean Studies, University of Hawaii). *Korean Studies* 2: 191.

McGinn, Noel, D.R. Snodgrass, Y.B. Kim, S.B. Kim, and Q.Y. Kim. 1980. *Education and Development in Korea.* Cambridge, MA: Harvard University Press, Korea Development Institute.

McNamara, Dennis. 1990. *The Colonial Origins of Korean Enterprise, 1910–1945.* Cambridge: Cambridge University Press.

Metzger, Thomas A. 1989. "Confucian Culture and Economic Modernization: An Historical Approach," in *Conference on Confucianism and Economic Development in East Asia*, Conference Series No. 13. Taipei: Chung-Hua Institution for Economic Research, pp. 141–195.

Ranis, Gustav and John C.H. Fei. 1988. "Development Economics: What Next?," in Gustav Ranis and T. Paul Schultz (eds). *The State of Development Economics: Progress and Perspectives.* Oxford: Blackwell, pp. 106–111.

Sen, A.K. 1980. *Levels of Poverty: Policy and Change.* Staff Working Paper No. 401. Washington, DC: World Bank.

Steinberg, David I. 1982. "Development Lessons from the Korean Experience – A Review Article." *Journal of Asian Studies* 42: 91–104.

Suh, Sang Mok. 1985. *Economic Growth and Change in Income Distribution: The Korean Case.* Working Paper Series No. 8508. Seoul: Korea Development Institute.

"Symposium on the Korean Financial Crisis: Causes and Challenges." 1998. *Journal of Asian Economics* 9: 609–670.

United Nations. 1960. *Programming Techniques for Economic Development.* Bangkok: Economic Commission for Asia and the Far East.

Woo, Jung En. 1991. *Race to the Swift: State and Finance in Korean Industrialization.* New York: Columbia University Press.

World Bank. 1994. *The East Asian Miracle: Growth and Public Policy.* New York: Oxford University Press.

Yoo, Jong Goo. 1990. "Income Distribution in Korea," in Jene K. Kwon (ed.). *Korean Economic Development.* New York: Greenwood Press pp. 373–391.

Young, Allwyn. 1995. "The Tyranny of Numbers: Confronting the Statistical Realities of the East Asian Growth Experience." *Quarterly Journal of Economics* 110: 641–680.

4 Transformations in Korean capitalism

A case study of the Hyundai Business Group

Seung-Ho Kwon and Chung-Sok Suh[1]

Chaebŏl managerial capitalism in comparative perspective

The historical evolution of large-scale capitalist business entities is a frequently canvassed topic of research across a variety of related disciplines, including economics, business history, and management. Most research, however, has focused on multinational enterprises in the West and Japan.[2] Relatively little attention has been paid to these enterprises in the newly emergent capitalist economies of Eastern Asia, especially South Korea.[3] This is surprising, given the dominant role of family-controlled conglomerates, the *chaebŏl*, in the course of Korea's rapid industrialization, and the position of Korea in the world economy.[4] In Chapter 3, Paul Kuznets highlighted the *chaebŏl* as one of the significant institutions of Korean capitalism which helped propel the country's economic and societal transformation. The *chaebŏl* are also integral to our effort to uncover the dynamics of capitalist modernity in contemporary Korea. In this chapter we take a case study approach to understanding the historical trajectory of a large Korean conglomerate, the Hyundai Business Group, focusing in particular upon its relationship to the Korean state, and the unique character of its managerial organization within the capitalist world after 1945.

One of the prevalent themes in the study of large corporations is the evolutionary nature of capitalism. Many scholars have sought to understand the relationship between the emergence and development of multinational enterprises and the logic of the capitalist transformation. Pioneering work in the field came from Alfred Chandler, who published *Strategy and Structure* in 1962 and *The Visible Hand: The Managerial Evolution in American Business* in 1977. Chandler charted the transformation of American capitalism from the period when it was dominated by single entrepreneur-owned and controlled enterprises to the era of stock-exchange listed companies governed by professional managers.[5] He contended that in response to increasingly complicated and expanding business systems and highly competitive market forces, single family-owned controlled firms developed professional management systems to run their companies. This critical strategic innovation laid the foundations for growth of large-scale, multi-divisional industrial corporations. In the process, ownership and management of the company became separated. While the owners were listed on the stock-exchange, managerial control of the company was taken over by the professionals. Chandler applied the term 'managerial capitalism', to describe this development in American capitalism (Chandler, 1990a, 1992; Chandler and Daems, 1980).

Over time, the traditional nature of business activities regulated by free market forces was replaced by oligopolistic enterprises which had grown to economies of scale and scope and were thus able to take advantage of reduced transaction costs. This resulted in increased productivity and a stable supply of resources for production. In the course of developing such enterprises, the levels of strategic activity and the structural units themselves became more diversified. Chandler (1990a) argued that in order to achieve economies of scale and scope, managers pursued diversification strategies which led to the creation of horizontally combined and vertically integrated companies. To control complicated managerial activities, the corporations established a centralized managerial control unit, what Chandler termed 'the M-Form structure' (Chandler, 1982).

Chandler's studies have been a major force behind the rise of the study of large-scale industrial enterprises in other advanced countries. Some analyses focusing on European capitalism have provoked controversy by asserting that variations in the timing, degree, and forms of growth between European and American firms gave rise to somewhat disparate enterprise and country-specific paths of capitalist transformation (Schmitz, 1993: 28–48). However, other scholars have shown that the American pattern was not unique, and that somewhat similar patterns of capital transformation have occurred in Europe.[6]

By contrast, social scientists have emphasized the unique character of the historical transformation of industrial capitalism in Japan. Most have pointed to the distinctive role of the state in Japanese capitalism. In the pre-1945 era, the imperial state played a fundamental role in developing a brand of family-controlled oligopolistic industrial capitalism within the empire. In the postwar era, however, the American military government forced the restructuring of the *zaibatsu* (Chandler, 1982: 21–22). Lazonick (1991) identified a pattern whereby 'collective capitalism' eventually superseded the family-controlled *zaibatsu*. He argued that ultimate control by family members of the business was lost to the top management of the core companies in the conglomerate. These managers then established vertically integrated business systems across the core and satellite companies of the former *zaibatsu* in order to obtain competitive advantages for business activities (Lazonick, 1991: 36–43).[7] Japanese conglomerates diversified their companies through further expansion and by founding more satellite companies. In the US and Europe, on the other hand, diversification occurred more often through merger or acquisition (Church, 1993: 36).

Three propositions from the literature on big business and global capitalism provide signposts for the chapter. Our first marker relates to the nature of the external environment which shapes the pattern of the transformation. As we have seen above, different external forces produce variations in the characteristics of local capitalist development. How, then, did Korea's external environment shape the evolution of the *chaebŏl* and what implications does this have for our study of the Hyundai group? Specifically, what role did the Korean state play in shaping the evolution of the *chaebŏl*? Our second proposition arises from Chandler's thesis about the strategy, structure, and evolution of American firms. Chandler noted that the long-term economic and managerial strategies of firms led to significant structural changes in the firm's organization and business, and that these changes provided companies with additional leverage and competitiveness in domestic and international markets. We therefore ask the question: In what ways has the Hyundai group organized its business enterprise to deal with the increasing complexity and range of products and services offered by its companies? Our third proposition relates to the role of professional managers as agents in the transformation of enterprises from small family businesses to large-scale industrial corporations. In American and Japanese firms, the initiative of managers stands out as one of the distinctive features of modern capitalism. 'Managerial capitalism' distinguishes modern corporations from family businesses of the past, and the use of professional management results in a separation between the ownership and managerial control over the large industrial enterprises. To what extent did Hyundai follow the path which led to professional management of the company?

The following three sections examine the historical transformation of the Hyundai Business Group, focusing on its three major subsidiaries, Hyundai Engineering and Construction Company (HECC), Hyundai Motor Company (HMC), and Hyundai Heavy Industries (HHI). The analysis is divided into three chronological periods which follow the distinctive stages of growth patterns of the Hyundai conglomerate. These eras are the mid-1940s through to the late 1960s and early 1970s, the decade from 1972 to 1982, and 1982 to the 1997 economic crisis. We also compare the evolution of Hyundai with that of other Korean *chaebŏl* in order to identify distinguishing characteristics of Korean capitalism. The concluding section discusses the implications of the findings in this chapter for our understanding of ongoing changes in the structure of *chaebŏl* following the 1997 economic crisis.

Family business and patriarchal control at Hyundai: 1946 to the 1960s

Hyundai had its origins in a rice wholesale business established by its founder Chung Ju Yung in the 1930s and in an automobile repair shop established in the early 1940s. The Hyundai Engineering and Construction Company was founded in 1947, but its business was negligible until the mid-1950s. Until that time it operated mainly as a small civil engineering subcontractor, and undertook mostly simple maintenance and repair work (Park, 1982: 68–69). In the decade following the mid-1950s, the small family business was transformed into a modern industrial enterprise engaged principally in construction activities. This section will explain some of the underlying reasons for the company's success in the late 1950s and 1960s. To do this, we should have a better understanding of the role of the state in South Korea's post-1945 economic development.

The dominant theme running through most literature on Korean capitalism is the role of the state. The Korean government's 'developmentalist' (Amsden, 1989) and 'interventionist' (Wade, 1990) approach to the economy has been a major factor in the country's rapid industrialization in the latter half of the twentieth century. State-guided economic policies, such as the five-year plan described by Kuznets, influenced the growth strategy and structure of the *chaebŏl* in such a way as to help them obtain oligopolistic or monopolistic conditions in the domestic market. This was done to sharpen their competitive edge in domestic and international markets. In this way, the Korean government played a vital role in the transformation of Korean companies from originally small, family capitalist enterprises in the late 1940s, to large-scale industrial conglomerates of today. But because of their similarities with Japanese companies in the areas of state–business relations, family ownership, managerial control, and the oligopolistic nature of business practices, the *chaebŏl* are often compared with the pre-war Japanese corporation (Jones and SaKong, 1980; Kang, 1990; Kim, 1997; Kuk, 1988; Rhee, 1994; Yang, 1991).[8] As Paul Kuznets pointed out, the *chaebŏl* are a Korean variant of the colonial *zaibatsu*. The evolution of Korean conglomerates has often therefore been interpreted as a permutation of the Japanese model of corporate capitalism. We agree with some elements of this argument, but also place emphasis upon the distinctive features of the Korean *chaebŏl*. In particular, a dominant and singular aspect of the Hyundai Business Group is that the *chaebŏl*'s business operations and governance have remained under the direct control of family owners since its inception. Given that this tendency exists in other *chaebŏl*, we conclude that Korean capitalist modernity has evolved in the broader context of a state-sponsored family corporatism.

The close ties that Hyundai's founder developed with the state were a major factor in the *chaebŏl*'s transformation in the 1950s and 1960s. HECC, for example, obtained a series of contracts with the American Military Forces in Korea (AMFK) during the Korean War (1950–1953), and emerged after the conflict with well-established political ties and as one of Korea's leading construction companies. It joined a construction cartel, whose members were awarded the government's major war recovery construction projects which were implemented under foreign aid schemes.[9] The government awarded HECC with the First Han River Bridge Reconstruction Project in 1957. Worth 32 million won, it was one of the largest national projects, and HECC soon became Korea's sixth largest construction company (Kong, 1994: 221–222, 236; Lee, 1985: 102–107; Lee, 1994: 107–109, 127–138).

Despite engaging with other leading *chaebŏl* in corrupt business activities during the 1950s, HECC was treated as a favoured construction company by the Park Chung Hee military government (1961–1979).[10] Other large construction companies, such as *Daedong* and *Chungang*, had a less favourable relationship with the government. HECC's privileged position allowed it to secure a position of market leadership. During the first (1962–1966) and second (1967–1971) five-year plans, the company succeeded in obtaining a series of large national infrastructure construction projects, such as highways, dams, power plants, and factories, thus creating a framework for rapid expansion. The vital role of the state is readily apparent in an analysis of the contribution that government projects made to the total value of contracts obtained by HECC. Their contribution to HECC earnings grew from 41 per cent (732 million won) between 1953 and 1961 under the Rhee government to 88 per cent (44,555 million won) between 1963 and 1971 (HECC, 1982: 579, 638–639, 1096–1143). This enabled Hyundai aggressively to diversify its businesses and to achieve economies of scale and scope in production and market share in the heavy and machinery industries from the 1970s onward. In the process, the managerial structure of the company was formalized to underpin the founder's continuing control over business and managerial activities.

Once it was well established at home, HECC entered the overseas construction market with the Pattani Narathiwat Highway project (1966–1968) in Thailand. The company then went on to projects in Vietnam, Guam, Papua New Guinea and Australia. Its participation in the economic boom associated with the Vietnam War contributed much to the growth of the corporation. The annual earnings of HECC grew from 1,500 won in 1947 to 200 million won in 1959, and then to 19,000 million won in 1969 (HECC, 1982: 588–590, 614). The international experience and profits provided by the war accelerated the company's expansion into the Middle East construction market in the 1970s, and resulted in HECC becoming Korea's leading construction exporter.[11]

Vertical integration of Hyundai's construction businesses

During the late 1950s and 1960s, Hyundai's growth strategy was premised on a 'one set' approach. This constituted a typical diversification strategy for Korean *chaebŏl*, the objective of which was to vertically integrate related businesses in order to obtain a combined competitive advantage. In the case of Hyundai, the core company, HECC, generated a sizeable demand for building materials in connection with the large-scale construction contracts it obtained. Hyundai met this demand internally by establishing seven subsidiaries in the 1960s, six of which were dedicated to the production, for internal use, of various construction materials such as slate, cement and concrete. These subsidiaries supplied construction materials to HECC at a lower cost than those obtainable from external suppliers. Hyundai Motor Company (HMC), established in 1968, was also incorporated into the 'one set' system to augment the heavy construction equipment capacity of HECC, and to meet the construction needs associated with greater use of complicated heavy construction equipment. Although this 'one set' approach to construction had certain built-in structural rigidities, it was vital to sustaining the leading position of HECC in the construction market.

Formal patriarchal control

Until the mid-1950s, the management of Hyundai was typical of a small-scale single-family business employing less than 100 workers. Its managerial structure was informal, organized around Chung Ju Yung's kin, his friends, business associates and engineering experts. Chung was intimately involved in daily management decisions, and managers were assigned tasks by him directly (Chŏn, 1984: 62–85; HECC, 1982: 141, 539–551, 561; Kim, 1991: 259).

This protean, idiosyncratic managerial style yielded to a more formal managerial structure, but one also largely based on kinship. Thus, when the company adopted a professional managerial system in 1950, Chung's two younger brothers and one brother-in-law were placed on the management board, along with four of Chung's friends. This formalization of management paralleled the growth in the scope and size of the business. By the mid-1960s, the sectional organization of HECC had largely been converted to a department-oriented one.[12]

The continued expansion of the business was the major factor which contributed to the continued evolution of HECC's organizational structure (HECC, 1982: 544–550, 573–574, 627–628; *Monthly Chŏngkyŏng Munhwa*, December 1984: 150–151). The number of top executives increased from a single person, President Chung, in 1950, to eleven in 1964, and to seventeen in 1968 (see Table 4.1). The expansion of hierarchical positions at the top management board level was accompanied by the adoption of a chairperson system. Chung appointed a member of his family to manage each of Hyundai's subsidiaries.[13] This kinship strategy was instrumental in allowing him to maintain effective and efficient control over the increasing number of subsidiaries in the various areas of the business of Hyundai and HECC (Chŏn, 1984: 91; HECC, 1982: 623–625).[14]

The executives selected for the data were based on employment conditions. Those who were appointed by the shareholders' meeting were

Table 4.1 Changes in managerial structure of HECC by number of position holders, 1950s to 1960s

Year	*1950*	*Late 1950s*	*1964*	*January 1968*	*1970*
Chairman	–	–	–	–	1
President	1	1	1	1	1
Vice-president	–	1	1	1	5
Chunmu	–	3	2	4	2
Sangmu	–	4	7	11	6
Yisa[a]	6	n/a	n/a	n/a	7
Total	1	9	11	17	15

Note

a *Yisa* was excluded in the total number due to its inconsistent data.

selected here, and other managers whose employment conditions were determined by company regulations were excluded (HECC, 1982: 549–550, 572–573, 623–625).

The emergence of a cadre of professional managers within a structure dominated by the family hierarchy was a significant development. Of twenty-two managerial executives hired in 1970, eleven were products of the so-called 'Open Recruitment System' (ORS), begun in 1958 for four-year university graduates. These recruits were internally promoted from their entry point at the bottom rung of the white-collar employees' ladder. They were supervised by the founder's kin and personal associates. The professionalization of management effected a significant advance in the scope and quality of decision-making. A typical example was the evolution of planning functions. The first formal planning body emerged in the form of a section in 1965. To support the strategic decisions of the top managers, it evolved into a HECC department in 1967. In conformity with the rapid growth of HECC and Hyundai, the department became a planning management office organized with four sections in 1969, while its function and size further expanded to cover various policy developments in business planning, personnel and finance (HECC, 1982: 627). This allowed Hyundai management to maintain more effective and senior levels of control over its rapidly diversifying businesses. Hence, direct supervision of operational workplace matters by top management was gradually transferred to a professional management class. As a result, various aspects of Hyundai's business activities, including work methods, employment and union relations, were gradually rationalized. Although there were problems in company managerial strategy, restructuring and rigid subordination of businesses within the conglomerate, the management structure and business practices employed by Hyundai during this period functioned sufficiently well to allow the company virtually to monopolize key products of the construction industry by the 1970s.

Oligopolistic capitalism: patriarchal and managerial hierarchy at Hyundai, 1972 to 1982

In the 1970s and early 1980s the state continued to play a critical role in the evolution of the company. David Kang (Chapter 7, this volume) notes that during the Fourth Republic, Park Chung Hee used his executive authority to promote big chemical and heavy industries. His government designed a strategy to prompt *chaebŏl* to diversify aggressively into these fields. Hyundai expanded the operations of its car company and moved into the shipbuilding industry in 1974 by establishing Hyundai Heavy Industries. The diversification strategy built upon the successful construction business of HECC, which took on projects requiring heavy and industrial machinery, thereby creating an internal market for such equipment. To this end, the existing 'one set' approach, which had been created for low-cost market competition, was revised to suit the various heavy and machinery industries in which Hyundai was now engaged. The heavy construction works of HECC, the automobile production of HMC and the shipbuilding of HHI became the dominant businesses of Hyundai, and the conglomerate soon developed an oligopolistic production and market position in certain key products of the Korean economy. To this extent, the 'capitalist pluralism' of this period was one characterized by the near monopoly of *chaebŏl*-produced heavy industrial goods. The 'pluralism' was thus an externally oriented one; domestic markets were heavily regulated, not only from external competition, but from potential internal challenges as well.

Although HECC faced financial insolvency at the end of the Vietnam War, the decline in overseas contracts was compensated for by obtaining a series of large-scale government construction projects which were part of the third and fourth five-year economic development plans in the 1970s.[15] HECC's most important new business, however, was in the Middle Eastern construction market. The Arab Shipbuilding and Repair Yard project in Bahrain was a critical contract for the company. Worth US$114 million, it lasted from 1975 to 1978. With its success in this benchmark project, HECC soon expanded its market position in the region, winning various large and heavy industrial contracts, including the Jubail Industrial Harbour project in Saudi Arabia (1976–1982), which was worth US$940 million. This entry into the Middle East construction market had important implications for the growth of HECC and Hyundai. This market expansion enabled HECC to become an international construction company no longer dependent on its domestic market, which had up until 1975 accounted for over 80 per cent of the corporation's projects. Between 1976 and 1981 the Korean market accounted for less than 30 per cent of company projects. Even so, Korean contracts remained important for the overall well-being of the company.[16] Given the *chaebŏl*'s internal vertical structure, the significant expansion of Hyundai's heavy industry companies created a large internal demand for materials. This, in turn, enabled the conglomerate to enhance its monopolistic position in the local construction scene during the 1970s (HECC, 1982: 706, 735, 913, 1088–1089).

The evolution of Hyundai's car and shipbuilding industries

In 1968, HMC, like existing Korean automobile companies, began to operate as a completely knocked down (CKD) assembler. Under assembly and technological cooperation agreements with the Ford Motor Company, car parts were imported and assembled, but not produced in Korea. In early 1973, the partnership between HMC and Ford ended over disagreements regarding managerial control of HMC.[17] In 1974, the company developed and produced the 'Pony', a low-cost, small-sized passenger car. Technological support and 10 per cent of the capital for the project came from Mitsubishi Motors of Japan. Based on the success of the first model, the initial stage of a mass production system was established in 1979. It was designed to produce 100,000 passenger cars annually (HMC, 1987: 34–38, 1992: 362–547; *Monthly Chungkyeong Munhwa*, February 1986: 166–167).

But Hyundai's expansion was hit by the second oil price hike, a crisis from which it recovered with the assistance of the industrial restructuring policies of the new Chun Doo Hwan military government (1981–1988), which granted a monopoly to the company for the production of small-sized passenger cars. Internally, HMC changed its production strategy from a focus on the domestic market to an emphasis on export. A good example of this new era of thinking was the company's decision in 1983 to produce cars in Canada. As a result of the success of the company's mass production system, overall sales increased sharply from 528 million won in 1968 to 26,092 million won in 1976 and to 430,149 million won in 1982 (HMC, 1992: 418, 548–628, 1084, 1099; Lee Ho, 1993: 121).

The establishment of Hyundai Heavy Industries in 1974 was a significant milestone in the history of the Korean economy and the turning point for the company's entry into large-scale shipbuilding. The industry was a critical target of the government's economic strategies in the 1970s. Thereafter, whenever the shipbuilding industry was in crisis, the state intervened to protect it.[18] In the years following the 1974 oil shock, for example, HHI received more state assistance than any of the other shipbuilding companies, gaining 67.2 per cent of all government-backed orders between 1975 and 1980. The growth of HHI was also associated with the expansion of HECC into the Middle East construction market. HECC functioned as a supportive base for the shipping industry because of its requirements for various heavy industrial products, including offshore steel structures and barges. HHI sales increased rapidly from 58,840 million won in 1974 to 992,876 million won in 1983. In that year the company became the world's largest shipbuilder (HHI, 1992: 391–392, 459, 461–463, 547, 1487).

Overall, the total sales of the Hyundai conglomerate increased more than one hundredfold in the period from 1973 to 1984, from 5,200 million won to 69,792 hundred million won. Between 1978 and 1980 its contribution to the national economy increased from 8.56 per cent to 9.5 per cent of South Korea's Gross National Product (Kuk, 1988: 67; Lee, 1990: 16; Park, 1979: 364). Table 4.2 shows the rapid expansion of Hyundai and the leading roles played by HECC, HMC and HHI. Owing to the intensive diversification practices of Hyundai away from a base dominated by the construction business and into large-scale heavy industries (see Table 4.2), the role of the three main companies in Hyundai's total sales actually declined in the mid-1970s and early 1980s. This does not imply that the role of the three companies had been replaced by others. Rather, it shows the increased role of Hyundai's other subsidiaries, which developed as a result of the systematic organization of monopolistic production and market strategies in the heavy and machinery industries from the late 1970s onward. It is to this latter point that we shall now turn our attention.

Vertical and horizontal integration of Hyundai's heavy and machine industries

In the 1970s and 1980s Hyundai revised its vertically integrated 'one set' managerial approach in order to permit the *chaebŏl*'s heavy machine industries to benefit from economies of scale. The strategy entailed the establishment of new companies to supply common materials and parts. By 1985, a total of eleven such support businesses had been set up. Inchon Steel, for example, supplied steel at low internal prices for heavy industrial

Table 4.2 Total annual sales of Hyundai, HECC, HMC, and HHI, selective years from 1968 to 1980 (Unit: 100 million won)

Year	*1968*	*1973*	*1977*	*1978*	*1979*	*1980*
Group total (A)	129	520	14,799	19,049	22,428	32,620
HECC	124	315	5,360	6,353	6,173	10,517
HMC	5	179	930	2,158	2,690	2,249
HHI	n/a	n/a	4,309	4,013	2,051	3,751
Total (B)	129	484	10,500	12,424	10,914	15,751
Ratio (%: B/A)	100.00	93.07	70.95	65.22	48.66	51.35

Source: Derived from You (1991: 67); Park (1979: 364); Lee (1989: 19); HECC (1982: 1088–1089); HHI (1992: 1487); HMC (1992: 1084); *Maeil Economic Newspaper* (1985: 802).

Note

Total sales amount in 1968 is calculated by only those of HECC and HMC due to absence of other data.

structures made by HECC, ships constructed by HHI and automobiles manufactured by HMC. Integration, however, extended beyond the support and core companies. Among the top three companies, businesses were closely managed and tightly integrated under the direct control of top management. Table 4.3 shows changes in the sourcing of HECC projects over a twenty-year period and the increasing internal business cooperation between HECC and other Hyundai companies, especially in the latter part of the 1970s.

The 'one set' approach played an important role in helping the three major companies secure a sizeable, often dominant, share of domestic and international product markets. In 1977, for example, Hyundai produced sixteen products which had monopoly or semi-monopoly status in the domestic market, including automobiles, slate, steel, pipes and ships (Cho, 1991: 193). Between 1977 and 1981, HECC obtained over 20 per cent of the total value of projects undertaken by Korean construction companies in overseas markets (HECC, 1982: 659, 836). HMC's share of the domestic motor vehicle market increased from 19.4 per cent in 1970 to 62 per cent in the second half of the 1970s (HMC, 1992: 116).[19] HHI held 77.4 per cent of the domestic ship construction market between 1976 and 1978, and its share of the international shipbuilding industry almost doubled from 1.7 per cent in 1973 to 3 per cent in 1974.

As a result of this rapid growth, by the late 1970s Hyundai had become the leading *chaebŏl* in Korea. Its annual average growth rate, as measured by total sales, was over 11 per cent between 1980 and 1984. Samsung and Daewoo grew at less than 9 per cent (Kim, 1986: 175). The expansion of Hyundai's heavy and machinery industry businesses resulted in a substantial increase in its workforce, and a regional concentration of its production also occurred, particularly in the Ulsan industrial area of South Kyongsang province where by 1982 50,695 workers were employed in eighteen Hyundai companies (Lee, 1989: 15, 35).

Table 4.3 Changes in the internal sourcing of HECC industrial projects, 1961 to 1981 (Unit: million won, %)

Period	*1961–1970*	*1971–1975*	*1976–1981*	*Total*
Projects				
Total number	15	15	27	57
Internal source	1	6	21	28
Contract amount				
Total (A)	4,042	633,635	84,233	151,910
Internal source (B)	1,780	2,132	56,438	60,342
B/A (%)	44.0	33.0	66.9	47.9

Source: Derived from the construction lists of HECC in HECC (1982: 1096–1165).

Combining patriarchal and managerial hierarchies

In response to the sustained growth of the corporation, and as part of a strategy to maintain and consolidate the central authority of Chung Ju Yung, his kin and his associates, the company restructured its management. Professional management groups, especially those in HECC, were reorganized to form a second-tier position in a revised hierarchical structure which underpinned the central control of top managers. Unlike American or Japanese companies, Hyundai developed a unique style of 'managerial capitalism'. In particular, the *chaebŏl* combined a managerial hierarchy with its older patriarchal authority, but in a way that strengthened the power of Chung and his associates. Moreover, the unique character of management–ownership relations at Hyundai evolved at a time when one might expect, based on Japanese and American case studies, that management would gain a stronger controlling hand in the everyday running of the company. That this did not happen was a function of the determination of the Chung to maintain his influence over the corporation and to the willingness of a new generation of his family to take on leadership positions in the business.

The first major structural change began in the latter part of the 1970s, and involved the replacement of the existing department system with divisions. The size of departments had rapidly increased over the course of the decade. This forced a new division of responsibilities within larger managerial units. For example, the number of executives in HECC rose from twenty-six in 1975 to ninety-five in 1982. Similarly, there were twenty executives in HHI in 1976 and forty-eight in 1982 (Kwon, 1997: 91). All in all, the introduction of a division structure constituted a formal bureaucratization of the large-scale division system. Figure 4.1 simplifies the managerial structure of Hyundai which developed from this time.

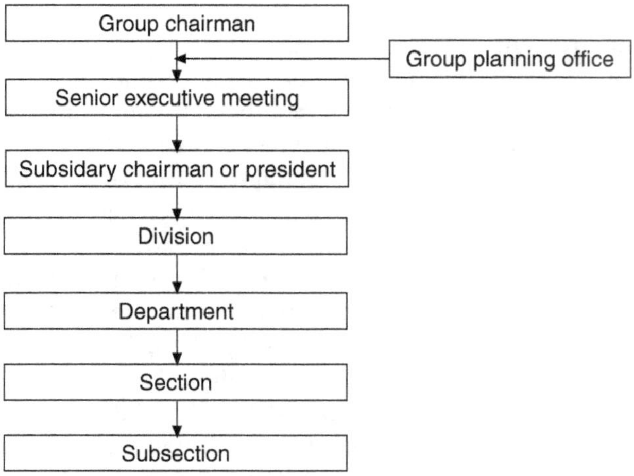

Figure 4.1 Formal managerial structure of Hyundai since 1979 (source: drawn from the analysis by the authors).

Important changes also occurred at the top decision-making level. A chairperson system and a Group Planning Office were established in 1979. Three years later, all chairperson positions with the exception of the chair of HHI were held by the founder. This enabled Chung to be formally involved in every aspect of the business and management of the *chaebŏl*'s three biggest companies in its subsidiaries. The Group Planning Office grew out of the planning office which had been set up in HECC in the 1960s to develop a management science capability, and to support top management in the creation, implementation and monitoring of long-term business plans (HECC, 1982: 627, 776, 786; HHI, 1992: 533). The role of the new Group Planning Office was critical to Hyundai's ability to derive benefits from economies of scale and scope and from the systematic integration of its businesses, or what Ansoff describes as the 'synergy effect' (Ansoff, 1969).[20] From his position in the Group Planning Office, Chung was able to maintain oversight and control of Hyundai's businesses.[21]

In addition to creating a centrally controlled managerial structure, Chung continued to place his kin in top managerial positions. In the 1970s, his brothers were given high-ranking posts in strategic subsidiaries. The organizational chart of Hyundai for 1979 reveals that four of Chung's brothers were appointed presidents of subsidiary positions, and that a brother-in-law was appointed Chairman of HHI (Kim, 1985: 269–270; Park, 1979: 360). While the major companies presided over by Chung's four brothers were legally separate from Hyundai, they nevertheless functioned as satellite *chaebŏl* through an interconnected business structure and exchange of senior executives. Hyundai products were supplied to the satellite *chaebŏl*; and Mando Machinery Company, a subsidiary of the Hanra Group, which itself had close ties with Hyundai, supplied auto parts to HMC.

The kinship structure, which was unique to global multinational companies, expanded further with the emergence of a second generation of the founder's family in the early 1980s. Younger members of Chung Ju Yung's family who had been employed as middle or senior managers in the 1970s gradually took over key positions in the managerial structure. In the context of a Confucian socio-cultural tradition in which the father and the eldest son are given authority in decision-making, a strong patriarchal kinship system was effective in securing the authority of Chung's power in Hyundai. In this sense, cultural values favoured Chung, the eldest brother and father, in managerial decision-making (Chang, 1988: 51–57; Chŏn, 1984: 436–444; Chŏng, 1989: 291; HECC, 1982: 1081; Kim, 1985: 269–270, 290–291; Kim and Kim, 1989: 27–46; *Monthly Chosŏn*, September 1980: 281–283).[22]

But kinship alone was not enough to guarantee Chung's power. Many professional managers who had been loyal to the family for decades, especially those from HECC, were also promoted. The initial diffusion of professional managers into management positions during the 1960s was accelerated in the 1970s with the rapid expansion of Hyundai as a whole. In the organizational chart for 1981, of sixty-one top managerial executives in sixteen Hyundai subsidiaries, twenty-eight executives came from those who had been hired in the late 1960s under the formal recruitment system and who had served for over ten years in HECC.[23] With such service, they in effect supported the kinship structure and central authority of top management (HECC, 1982: 1081–1082).

Several factors contributed to the emergence of HECC-backed professional executives at Hyundai. Historically, HECC had functioned as the parent company in executing the corporation's overall growth strategy. The diffusion of HECC-backed managers to other companies was necessary due to the growth in interrelated business operations between HECC and other branch companies. These executives were mostly middle managers who had worked for a long time under the direct supervision of the founder in the 1960s, a relationship which was crucial for the continued implementation of the founder's managerial decisions. The experience of the founder in construction work led him to prefer HECC-backed managers, but these executives also helped to extend the patriarchal aspects of managerial control during these years. As the professional management class was regarded as a means of enforcing the central authority of top management, so employment conditions extended to control the mass of production workers. In this way, central control by the founder combined with a kinship structure in the family hierarchy and the diffusion of HECC-backed executives. The founder was thus able to maintain managerial control of a large, rapidly expanding conglomerate.

Crisis at Hyundai: managerial strategies, 1982 to 1992

The increasing dependence of Hyundai upon large-scale heavy and machinery exports made the company vulnerable to changes in the international supply and price levels of natural resources. A series of crises beset the company in the 1980s, and these were exacerbated by the emergence, from the mid-1980s onwards, of a mass, independent trade union movement.[24] These developments undermined the conglomerate's low-cost market approach and competitiveness. Politically and economically, the state also became less well disposed towards the monopolistic capitalism of the *chaebŏl*. Yet, as David Kang discusses,[25] *chaebŏl* successfully fended off state efforts to 'rationalize' the car and power industries. From the mid-1980s, Hyundai redirected its investment from heavy and machinery industries to technologically intensive, high value-added industries such as microelectronics and services. The three major companies, HECC, HMC and HHI, reorganized their business strategies to accommodate these changes.

In the early 1980s, HECC faced a number of political and economic challenges. It suffered a sharp decline in its Middle East construction contracts as a result of adverse political and economic developments in the region. Outdated construction technologies limited its potential expansion into more advanced construction projects, such as nuclear power plants. Consequently, from 1982, the company adopted a new long-term growth strategy, focusing on high value-added engineering designs and the development of advanced construction technologies. To overcome its regional concentration in the Middle East, especially Saudi Arabia, HECC made a concerted effort to increase its market penetration in the Middle East, Asia, Africa, and Central and South America (HECC, 1982: 882–883, 913–916).[26] This new strategy led to additional construction contracts overseas, including a hydro power plant in 1988 in Pakistan worth US$680 million, and a polythene factory in 1990 in Libya valued at US$330 million. At the same time, to maintain low labour costs, HECC's Korean construction workers were replaced by those from other developing world countries. Non-Koreans increased from 30 per cent of overseas project workforce projects in the early 1980s to between 70 and 80 per cent in the late 1980s (*Chungang Economic Newspaper*, 7 June, 10 July 1990, 6 July, 18 May, 24 October 1993, 28 February 1994; *Korea Economy Newspaper*, 24 March 1992; *Monthly Chungang*, October 1988: 378–381; *Monthly Chungkyŏng Munhwa*, April 1983: 346).

At the time of HMC's entry into mass production in the late 1970s, the Korean automobile industry experienced a recession caused by a domestic political crisis and the second oil price shock. To enable it to recover, the new Chun Doo Hwan government (1981–1989) granted HMC a monopoly on small-sized passenger cars. Into the late 1980s, then, the military government continued to provide significant favours to Hyundai. Following a recovery, HMC expanded its mass-production capacities with the goal of dramatically increasing sales in the international market. Production grew from 110,000 cars in 1979, to 300,000 in 1985, and to 890,000 in 1990. HMC also developed various models in the small (under 1,500cc) and medium (under 2,500cc) classes of passenger cars through continued technological cooperation with Mitsubishi. The success of its first effort to export overseas – to Canada – enabled the company more easily to extend its operations into the United States, which it did in 1986 with its competitively priced Excel.[27] This expansion into foreign markets, however, was constrained by barriers of entry and rising production costs at home.

In the domestic market, HMC's monopoly of small sized cars was broken by Daewoo and Kia Motors in 1986. Domestic competition further intensified with the entry into the car-manufacturing business of two other *chaebŏl*, Ssangyong and Samsung. In response to these events, by 1993 HMC had developed a long-term business strategy known as the 'Global Top 10'. This aimed to make HMC, the twentieth largest car manufacturer in the world in 1992, one of the ten largest global car-makers by 2000. To achieve this goal, HMC accelerated its effort to increase export markets, and further decentralized and localized production. Plants in

Korea were to produce 800,000 cars annually; in Southeast Asia and South America new and existing plants would build 320,000 units. HMC also regionally diversified its exports in order to reduce its dependence on the US market. In 1986 Hyundai Motors exported to sixty-five countries, but by 1994 the number had risen to 141. This represented a dramatic increase in the scope of the globalization of the company's activities since the 1970s (HMC, 1992: 592–754; *Chosŏn Ilbo*, 21 July 1993, 4 January, 6, 7, 9, 15 December, 1994; *Chungang Ilbo*, 18 July 1995; *Dong'a Ilbo*, 24 November 1995; *Monthly Observer*, November 1991: 292–304).[28]

Among the three largest Hyundai corporations, HHI suffered most seriously from the 1979 worldwide recession. The Korean government, however, once again used its power to help the *chaebŏl*. This time Chun's regime provided HHI with additional financial support and a monopoly over the production of marine engines in excess of 6,000 horsepower. To gain additional orders, HHI also adopted a low-cost market approach, and in 1986 the company received contracts for twenty tankers and nine very large crude carriers (VLCCs) out of a total of fifteen new VLCCs offered on the international market. The impact of the recession was thus short-lived, and HHI's international market share increased from 3 per cent in 1974 to 18 per cent by 1986 (HHI, 1992: 514–535, 686–690; Korean Shipbuilding Industries Association, 1991).

Even so, HHI's shipbuilding business had inherent structural deficiencies related to its new low-cost market practices and its labour-intensive mode of production. These features of its business also contradicted industry trends. From the late 1970s, competitors had gradually moved from large-scale, bulk carrier ship construction to micro- and technologically intensive product carriers. In addition, after the mid-1980s HHI's new mass trade unions demanded higher wages, and this ran counter to the company's low-cost market advantage. This problem was aggravated by the emergence of shipbuilding in other developing countries such as Brazil and China which had low labour costs. HHI's market position declined in the mid- to late 1980s. From 1986 to 1989 its domestic market share went from 74.4 per cent to 31.4 per cent, and in the international market its share went from 18 per cent to 10 per cent (HHI, 1992: 532–535, 544–547, 617–624, 730–735; *Monthly Economic Review*, September 1987: 73–86).

By the late 1980s, therefore, HHI was under pressure to abandon outdated production methods and to adopt a growth strategy based on the production of high value-added ships that required an advanced level of marine engineering. With assistance from the government and Hyundai research and development institutes, the company automated production lines and introduced new shipbuilding technologies. These efforts helped boost the average value of ships constructed from US$30 million in 1981 to US$60.5 million in 1990. By 1993, production included the most technologically advanced ships, the liquefied natural gas carriers (LNG). In order to reduce its dependency upon the shipbuilding industry, HHI also diversified into other heavy industrial goods, including marine products, industrial plant and industrial robots. In the process of diversification, Hyundai Steel Tower (1987), Hyundai Industrial Robots (1987) and Hyundai Heavy Machinery and Equipment (1988) became independent subsidiaries of HHI (HHI, 1992: 594, 659–665, 786, 961, 984–985; *Chungang Ilbo*, 21 July 1995).

Product diversification: 1980s to early 1990s

In response to the structural problems resulting from its overdependence upon heavy and machinery industries, Hyundai began to diversify into higher value-added industries such as microelectronics and services. Of the corporation's fifty-four subsidiaries in 1994, twenty-five were established after the mid-1980s as part of this strategy (Hyundai Group Public Relations Office, 1994: 80–81). A typical example of the new companies was Hyundai Electronic Industries (HEI), founded in 1983 to produce semi-conductors and various microelectronic products such as computers, automotive electronic products and telecommunications systems. Once again, the switch into these fields was encouraged by the government. In its economic policies that favoured technologically intensive industries, the government gave special attention to helping companies produce the semi-conductor.

Using market demand in Korea – in designing automotive electronics for HMC, for example – HEI started on a path designed to make the company a leading international electronics firm. To that end, HEI succeeded in developing the 4M Dynamic Random Access Memory (DRAM) in 1989, the 16M DRAM in 1991, and the 64M DRAM in 1993. These were collaborative research and development projects involving the Korean government and other semi-conductor companies, including Samsung and Lucky Goldstar. These and other inventions helped increase HEI sales from three million wŏn in 1984 to two trillion (2,075,000 million) wŏn in 1994 (Hyundai Electronics Industries, 1994; *Chosŏn Ilbo*, 24 July 1994; *Shin Dong-Ah*, February 1987: 340–348). During this period, the relative importance of HECC, HMC and HHI for Hyundai's profits declined (Table 4.4). While the total sales of Hyundai products grew, the dependence of the conglomerate upon the profits made from its three core companies decreased. In 1977 the 'big three' accounted for over 70 per cent of earnings, while in 1993 they accounted for only 31 per cent. Figure 4.2 also shows the burgeoning structure of Hyundai in 1994. It outlines the expansion of a wide range of business areas, from the production of resources, to manufacturing, the retail sector, mass media, banking, and the knowledge-based service industries.

A significant change also occurred in Hyundai's globalization strategy, which now called for the transplanting of production systems in Southeast

Table 4.4 Changes in total sales of Hyundai and contribution of HECC, HMC, and HHI, 1977 to 1993 (Unit: 1,000 million won)

Year	*1977*	*1980*	*1983*	*1985*	*1987*	*1989*	*1990*	*1993*
Group (A)	1,479	3,262	6,879	13,594	14,648	17,284	31,939	39,742
HECC	536	1,075	1,764	1,988	1,521	1,372	1,978	2,774
HMC	93	224	577	1,047	2,840	3,806	4,655	7,181
HHI	430	375	922	1,164	955	978	1,480	2,568
Total (B)	1,059	1,674	3,333	4,119	5,316	6,156	8,113	12,523
B/A(%)	70.95	51.35	49.09	30.29	36.29	35.61	25.40	31.51

Source: Kwon (1997: 108).

Note
The total sales of Hyundai may be changed according to one's use of the definition 'subsidiary'. The amounts listed above were chosen to ensure consistency: total sales are only for those subsidiary companies of Hyundai for which Chung Juy-ung and his family have owned over 50 percent of total shares.

Asia, Europe, and North and Central America. This new strategy was a function of an effort to overcome market protection and to maintain low-cost production. These considerations led HEI to establish a US$1,300 million electronics plant in the USA in 1996. In the same year HHI set up a number of heavy construction machinery factories in China. Labour-intensive industries were prime targets for relocation to developing countries such as Vietnam, China and India (Kong, 1994: 46–47; *Chungang Economic Newspaper*, 25 May 1994; *Chosŏn Ilbo*, 29 September 1995; *Maeil Economic Newspaper*, 29 July, 19 August 1991, 19 January 1993).

From patriarchal to patrimonial hierarchy

In contrast with the phase of rapid expansion in the 1970s, the managerial structure of Hyundai in the 1980s reflected a more stable period of growth for the three core companies (Table 4.5). In the 1980s and early 1990s, however, there were significant changes in the role of the Group

Table 4.5 Annual changes in the total number of executives

Year	*1983*	*1984*	*1985*	*1986*	*1987*	*1988*	*1989*	*1990*	*1991*	*1992*	*1993*
HECC	84	86	99	102	90	102	89	85	n/a	86	101
HMC	21	29	33	38	44	46	52	54	51	35	73
HHI	52	67	69	84	91	92	93	108	76	79	81

Source: Derived from Maeil Economic Newspaper Company, selective years (1983–1993).

Note
The executives selected for the data were based on employment conditions. Only those executives who were appointed by the shareholders' meeting were selected for the data.

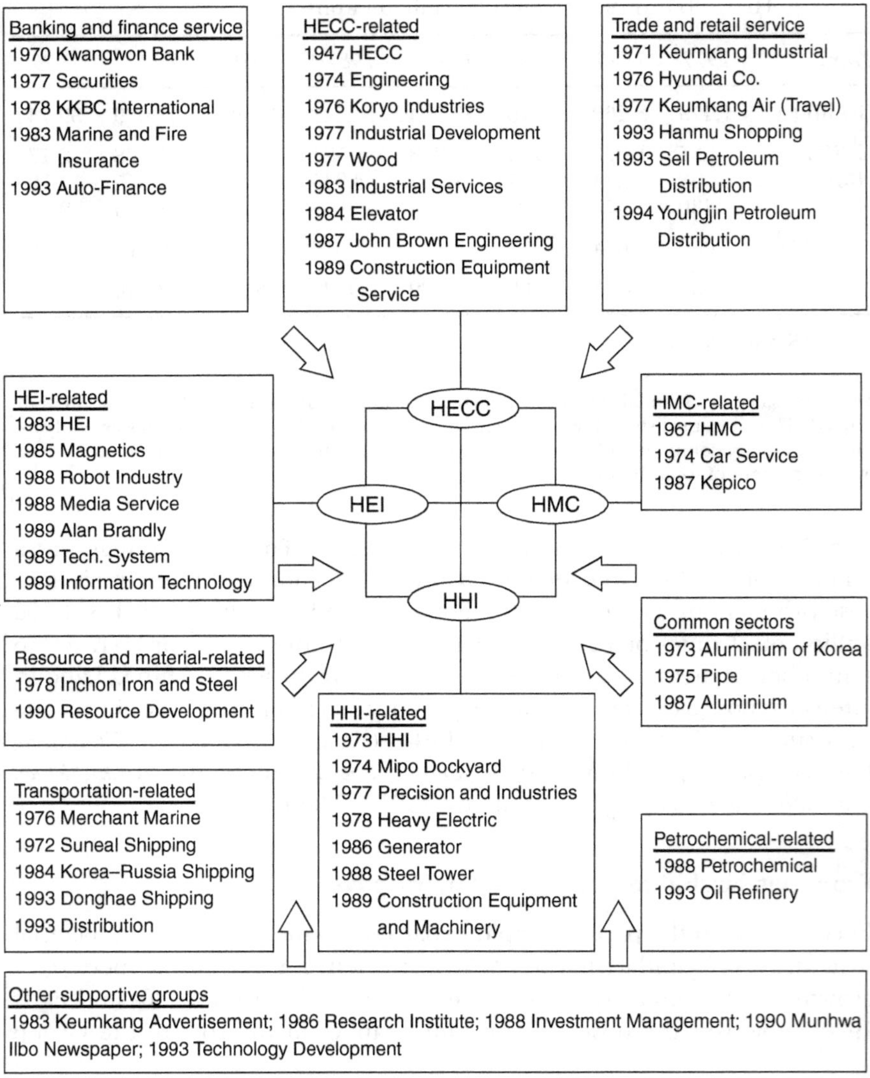

Figure 4.2 Growth structure of Hyundai in 1994 by type of business with foundation year (source: Kwon and O'Donnell 2001: 109).

Planning Office in providing support to top management at the company. The Office's operations have been extended to encompass long-term managerial policies of the diversified, conglomerate business at Group level. Between 1982 and 1990, the Group Planning Office was expanded from twenty-five employees and a vice-presidentship to forty employees and a presidentship.[29] The managerial hierarchy of Hyundai which was established in the 1970s and 1980s did not change during this period. The upgraded service functions of the office continued to support the central authority of the corporation's top management. For example, the Group Planning Office has been involved in a revision and consolidation of personnel and labour management policies and practices at Group level in close liaison with the personnel and labour sections of the subsidiaries (HECC, 1982: 627, 766, 786; HHI, 1992: 533; *Monthly Observer*, July 1990: 175–176; *Shin Dong-A*, September 1991: 257).

Important changes also occurred in the character of the kinship and HECC-dominated structure of Hyundai top management. As we saw earlier, the conglomerate's patriarchal leadership structure had been formed in part through the promotion of Chung Ju Yung's sons to key decision-making positions in various subsidiaries. Their positions were strengthened with the official retirement by the founder from the group chairmanship in 1987. Hyundai remained subject to his indirect control through his kinship networks and his links to professional executives with HECC backgrounds. In effect, Chung's retirement meant that the company moved from a patriarchal dominated hierarchy to a patrimonial one. Although the number of non-HECC-backed professional managers gradually increased, by 1994 managers with HECC backgrounds were still dominant in the Hyundai hierarchy.[30] The centralized authority of Hyundai's top management, many of whom were related, remained a key institution of control. In 1994, ten of the seventeen chairmen in the company had kinship ties.

Family proprietary and managerial capitalism in the Korean *chaebŏl*

So far, this chapter has sought to identify and explain the three developmental stages of Hyundai from its inception in the 1940s to that of a large-scale conglomerate in the 1990s. We have explored three distinctive features of Hyundai's transformation. First, government support for the *chaebŏl*, as part of rapid industrialization strategies, underpinned and facilitated the expansion and diversification of Hyundai businesses. Second, through the 'one set' growth strategy, the *chaebŏl* achieved vertical and horizontal integration of its diversified businesses in the construction industry (1950s to 1960s), heavy and machinery industries (1970s to early 1980s), and the electronics and service industries (the mid-1980s onwards). The most critical goal behind the deployment of this 'one set' strategy was to reinforce market competitive advantages obtained from economies of scale and scope. Third, in spite of Hyundai's transformation and growth, there was no separation between managerial control and ownership, which remained under the leadership of the owner-founder, Chung Ju Yung and his family members. To retain central authority within the family, the governing structure of Hyundai businesses was modified over time from informal patriarchal control of the founder, to a combined hierarchy of patriarchal and managerial control. With the emergence of a second generation of family members and the retirement of Chung, the *chaebŏl* developed a patrimonial structure with a subordinated managerial hierarchy. This does not deny the significant role of professional managers, who have played a critical role in sustaining the company's evolution and growth. The three aspects of the company's transformation are summarized in Figure 4.3, which highlights the main characteristics distinguishing each developmental stage.

Given that Hyundai has emerged as one of Korea's leading *chaebŏls*, it is not unreasonable to make the assumption that its historical development provides a model for understanding a number of aspects of Korea's capitalist transformation. Indeed, such evidence as is available suggests that other *chaebŏl* have followed a somewhat similar path of development. As mentioned earlier, existing work argues that the state was a major factor in leading Korea's industrialization and shaping the strategic decisions of the large corporation.[31] The main characteristics of the diversification strategy of the conglomerates were, to a greater or lesser degree, similar to the one set systems of Hyundai. For example, into the late 1990s the businesses of Samsung or Daewoo included textiles, electronics, automobiles and shipbuilding industries. Furthermore, other *chaebŏl* have evolved similar central governing systems as Hyundai. The company's Group Planning Office, which implements strategic decisions of the family and top management, is typically characteristic of other big businesses in

Period	1946–1960s	1970s–early 1980s	1980s–1990s
Political economy	Liberation and war economy Initial industrialization	State-guided economy Rapid industrialization	Transition to less regulated market economy
Growth pattern	Family to industrial economy >One-set = system in construction industry	Monopoly capitalism >One-set = system in heavy and machinery industries	Transition >One set = system in diverse industries
Growth structure	Single company Section/department system	Conglomerate structure Division system	Transitional character Small business groups
Managerial pattern	Formalization of patriarchal control	Development of patriarchal and managerial heirarchy	Development of patrimonal and managerial hierarchy

Figure 4.3 Developmental patterns of Hyundai since its inception in 1946 (source: drawn from the analysis by the authors).

Korea.[32] In relation to changes in the dimensions of family ownership, in 1990 among the forty-nine top *chaebŏl*, the second generation of twenty-one succeeded the managerial control of the founder, while twenty-eight *chaebŏl* were still controlled by the founder's family members (*Monthly Chosŏn*, February 1990).

Hyundai in comparative perspective

In a number of ways, the growth strategy employed by Hyundai to diversify and expand was similar to American, European and Japanese industrial enterprises, as it aimed to achieve economies of scale and scope for competitive market advantages. Yet there were also important differences between Korean, American, European and Japanese corporations. Our point is that the post-1945 development of Korean *chaebŏl*, or at least that of Hyundai, in many ways constitutes a distinctive element in the history of global capitalism.

In association with the development of its large-scale conglomerate businesses, Hyundai devised a central governing system, the Group Planning Office, which enabled top management to maintain control over their interlinked businesses. This is similar to what occurred in comparable American firms, which functioned under a central administration designed to obtain the profit advantages associated with the horizontal and vertical integration of diversified businesses (Chandler, 1982). Although the Group Planning Office is similar to the central administrative unit of Western companies and Japanese holding companies, its organizational character is substantially different. The Group Planning Office is neither a unit in the managerial structure of a company, nor an independent holding company. As each subsidiary of Hyundai has operated with independent legal status, the *ad hoc* unit, the Group Planning Office, was designed by Chung and his kin centrally to control all aspects of the management of subsidiaries.

In relation to the external environment, unlike Western capitalist states, the Korean government provided critical incentives and rewards to those companies in its favour. The role of the state in Korea was thus unique compared to the state's role in Western capitalism, yet it was similar to other developmental state models, particularly Japan's. In the West, the continued growth of enterprises depended upon how they utilized advanced technologies, capital, distribution channels, natural resources and production capacity. Given the limited resources in these fields in Korea, the state played a leading role in controlling resources for the rapid industrialization of the economy. The state–business relationship, and not market forces, has historically been the most critical external source for the growth of the large industrial conglomerates. This has been a defining feature of Korea's capitalist modernity.

The growth strategy and structure of Korean *chaebŏl* are distinctive from those which evolved in the West and Japan. Korean conglomerates are unique in the extent to which they collectively dominate a wide range of product lines. The *chaebŏl* has been described as an octopus' arm which operates across industrial boundaries (Kim, 1991: 16–25). Hyundai's own businesses range from shipbuilding to mass media, finance, and chemicals. Similarly, the Lucky Goldstar Business Group produces a wide range of goods, including toothpaste, clothes, semi-conductors and heavy machinery. In 1997, the top thirty *chaebŏl* owned an average of 27.3 subsidiaries in 19.8 unrelated industries (*Chosŏn Ilbo*, 23 January 1998).

Korean companies have also been unique in the sense that their transformation from family-based corporations to more impersonal institutions of managerial capitalism has not yet taken place. Family capitalism remains a dominant feature of Korean *chaebŏl* and Chung Ju Yung's family members have maintained close control over the Hyundai conglomerate's business activities. This is not to say that we should underestimate the role professional managers played in the historical transformation of the *chaebŏl*. These managers underpinned the hierarchical managerial structure, which in turn enabled the Chung family to retain central control of increasingly extensive and complex businesses (Kwon, 1997: 25–26).

These conclusions should be understood in conjunction with one another, as they are interrelated and interdependent. External conditions influence the dynamics of strategy and structure. Policies adopted by the Korean government changed the strategies and structures of Korean *chaebŏl*. The fact that a separation of power between owners and managers has not taken place may reflect the relatively short history of Korean capitalism, but this is also a function of government policy.

A new era for Korean capitalism?

The extent to which the future of Korean capitalism will continue to be dominated by the *chaebŏl* is uncertain. Questions also surround issues concerning ownership and control, and whether there will be a degree of convergence with the model of managerial capitalism predominant in Western countries. To help understand possible directions for Korean capitalism, this concluding section will discuss structural changes in Korean *chaebŏl* and capitalism since the 1997 economic crisis.

The Korean economy was severely affected by the 1997 financial crisis. The banking system was unable to repay its large external debt or to maintain the stability of the currency. The causes and implications of this crisis may be understood within the context of the distinctive features of Korean capitalism summarized in this chapter.

The origin of the crisis lay in the close relationship between the *chaebŏl* and the state, which controlled the banking sector. The ties between the two resulted in widespread corruption, and provided the *chaebŏl* with ready access to state support during difficult times. To rescue strategic industries, the government created market demands or provided generous financial options for companies which took over financially insolvent firms.[33] The government–*chaebŏl* relationship also influenced the dynamics of strategy and structure within firms. The non-performing debts held by Korean banks and conglomerates increased considerably. The average debt ratio of the top thirty corporations (excluding the finance and banking sectors) reached 4.5 times (247.6 trillion won) their capital size (55.1 trillion won) by December 1997 (*Hankyorae Shinmun*, 24 March 1998). The four largest companies, Hyundai, LG, Samsung and Daewoo, accounted for more than half of Korea's debt. In addition, while they were pursuing the 'one set' growth strategy, firms within each *chaebŏl* cross-guaranteed the debts of other firms. These debts totalled about 33 trillion won among the top thirty *chaebŏl* (*Korea Herald*, 13 February 1998). This debt-driven growth strategy was workable during the period of rapid growth.[34] The expansionist strategy by all *chaebŏl* across the board was indeed possible due to the tight control of the owner managers over the entire group through their group planning offices. However, when the economy turned to crisis and experienced decreases in sales and increases in interest rates, this growth approach was confronted with serious financial problems (*Business Review Weekly*, 6 April 1998).

The inability of the *chaebŏl* to handle their debts caused a crisis in the Korean banks and the Korean economy. In this context, former President Kim Young Sam requested urgent financial support from the International Monetary Fund (IMF). In return for financial assistance, the IMF demanded that the Korean economy be opened up to increased foreign competition, that the *chaebŏl* be pressured to restructure and that the Korean labour market be deregulated to increase flexibility (*Chosŏn Ilbo*, 13–18 November, 1–9 December 1997).

As a result of the crisis, the growth rate of the Korean economy decreased from 7 per cent in 1997 to almost −7 per cent in 1998. This was accompanied by an unemployment rate of over 7 per cent, high for Korea. However, the restructuring process was more important than the short-term effects of the crisis. The economic situation called for radical changes both in the government and in the Korean corporate sector. The ramifications of these structural changes may be summarized as follows.

There has been a critical change in the role of the state since the 1997 presidential election. The long-repressed opposition leader, Kim Dae Jung, was elected and his government aimed to achieve 'harmony of democracy and market economy' (*Korea Economic Weekly*, 2 March 1998). The emergence of the Kim government inaugurated the end of state authoritarian practices and the growth of a more genuinely democratic approach to governance. Hence, the authoritarian state-guided economy was targeted for change and the removal of other corrupt business practices became a focus of policy-makers.

The new government pressured the *chaebŏl* to restructure their 'octopus arm' business practices. They were forced to focus upon a small number of key subsidiaries which possessed competitive advantages. Other subsidiaries were then required to be sold off in order to meet the government's control programme of reducing total *chaebŏl* debt from 450 per cent to 200 per cent by the end of 2002. In addition, consolidated financial statements became compulsory, and accounting practices have been revised to secure more transparent managerial operations of the conglomerates. To minimize economic and ownership concentration, the government also banned the cross-guaranteeing system and capital investments among *chaebŏl* subsidiaries by revising the Fair Trade Act in February 1998. It also levied higher tax rates on inheritance income, a policy which was designed in part to target the owners of the *chaebŏl*.

In response to this unfavourable politico-economic environment, the *chaebŏl* strove to modify the state's new economic policies through their collective organization, the Federation of Korean Industries (FKI). This effort resulted in some moderation of the aggressive government approach to the *chaebŏl* – an example of the 'mutual hostage' scenario described by David Kang (see Chapter 7, this volume) – but it was accompanied by public criticism of the *chaebŏl* for their responsibility for the economic crisis. To rebuild or enhance their competitiveness, the Korean conglomerates began to slim down their excessively diversified and vast business enterprise to a few strategic businesses. For example, the Hyosung Business Group, the seventeenth largest *chaebŏl* ranked by sales in 1997, massively reorganized its twenty-four businesses into six sectors with five major subsidiaries. Hyundai's newspaper corporation, the *Muhwa Ilbo*, was the first to be separated from the business conglomerate due to its financial debt and unrelated business nature. Ssangyong, the sixth largest *chaebŏl* in 1997, sold its automobile company, Ssangyong Motor, to Daewoo Motors in 1998 (*Hankyore Sinmun*, 10–19 January 1998). Daewoo Motors went bankrupt in 2000 and was bought out by General Motors, which now has a controlling interest of just over 42 per cent of the company.

Globalization of business was one of the characteristics of the *chaebŏl*'s growth strategy in the 1990s. Among others, Daewoo's internationalization strategy was noticeable. The company's international operations, before Daewoo Motors went bankrupt, included thirty-two domestic subsidiaries, and 590 overseas business sites. They employed 320,000 people in 110 countries with revenues which reached US$80 billion in 1997 (*Hankyorae Shinmun*, 28 December 1997; *Business Review Weekly*, 6 April 1998). The globalization drive of the Korean *chaebŏl* initially slowed down somewhat as a result of the 1997 economic crisis, but globalization remains an indispensable option for the Korean corporations as a way of overcoming increasing domestic production costs, global competition, and the market protection of OECD and Asian economies.

As a consequence of state pressure to change managerial structures, restructuring of central administration units has occurred. In some cases, the work of the various planning offices has been divided up and taken over by the mother company of the *chaebŏl*. At Hyundai, the major functions of the Group Planning Office have been transferred to HECC. The work of Samsung's planning office is now shared between Samsung Company and Samsung Electronics. In line with these changes, family owners and their immediate family members have been appointed to key executive positions in the major subsidiaries of their *chaebŏl* group. Before Chung Ju Yung passed away, his eldest son, Chung Mongku, was appointed to senior managerial positions in six of Hyundai's key subsidiaries (*Chosŏn Ilbo*, 24 January and 8, 16, 27 February 1998; *Hankyorae Shinmun*, 19, 26 February 1998; *Korea Economy Weekly*, 23 February 1998; *Sisa Journal*, 19 February 1998).

In the process of restructuring their businesses, the *chaebŏl* have been decentralized into a number of smaller business groups managed by founders' sons.[35] These smaller business groups are likely to function as satellite groups cooperatively, as looser versions of the 'one set' system, in order to continue to promote collective growth in uncertain politico-economic environments. In the increasingly competitive, globalized business environment, professional managers will likely play an expanding role in governing the *chaebŏl*, though they will probably still be subject to contingent managerial oversight and the dominance of family ownership. In all, the structural changes in the *chaebŏl* since 1997 imply that the large-scale conglomerates are likely to be further decentralized and reconfigured to some indeterminate extent within a patrimonial mode of managerial capitalism.

The impact of the 1997 crisis required a substantial realignment of strategies by both the government and the business sector. Accordingly, the business sector has redefined its policies and established new internal structures befitting its revised goals and external constraints. As the role of owner-managers decreases, the role of professional managers will become increasingly important. The Korean business sector is thus at an important crossroads.

The evolution of the Hyundai *chaebŏl* provides significant insight into the evolution and structure of Korean capitalism in the postcolonial era. The complex corporate networks of power that emerged out of the close state–*chaebŏl* relationship and the continued control over the company structure by Chung Ju Yung and his family have been defining elements of Korea's corporate modernity. It is also important to underline the tensions and conflict which accompanied modernization in industry. Labour unrest took the form of strikes, as in September 1974 when shipyard workers went on strike for three days to protest against the hiring of contract workers. In Saudi Arabia in 1977 another strike revolved around poor benefits, low wages and accelerated production schedules (Kwon and O'Donnell, 2001: 94–95). These strikes were generally unsuccessful, and the Korean state strengthened its restrictive labour laws and intervened to weaken the union movement. It was not until 1987 that an independent union movement appeared at Hyundai, and it succeeded, unlike its predecessors, in achieving important concessions and wage increases from the company. Between the early 1980s and the mid-1990s workers' wages increased five times. However, as Kuznets noted, the success of the democracy movement has also resulted in a shift of jobs offshore, to other areas of the developing world where Korean companies could regain some of the competitive advantages lost at home. Such is the character of the dialectic of power in an era of 'flexible capitalism'. It is thus clear that the complexities of Korea's capitalist modernity will continue to challenge Korea's new democratic polity. The state's role may no longer be to serve the interests of the *chaebŏl*, but to serve the interests of society, and to try to forge a more egalitarian regime, based on the pluralist civil society that transformed so much of the country since the 1980s.

Notes

1 This is a modified version of a paper previously published; see Seung-Ho Kwon and Chung-Sok Suh (2003) 'The *Chaebŏl* and Korean Capitalism: the Hyundai Business Group,' in Moonjoong Tcha and Chung-Sok Suh (eds). *The Economic Crisis and The Korean Economy at the Crossroads.* London: RoutledgeCurzon, pp. 127–152.

2 See, e.g., Chandler, 1962, 1990a; Fligstein, 1990; Lazonick, 1991; Prais, 1976; Schmitz, 1993.

3 For a sampling of some of the literature see Kim, 1997; Kwon and O'Donnell, 2001; Steers, 1999.

4 The top thirty *chaebŏl* contributed over 90 per cent of Korea's gross national product (GNP) in 1991 (Bank of Korea, 1990) and employed about 18 per cent of the total Korean workforce in 1987. Total trading volume of Korea reached U$153.4 billion in 1991 and by the early 1990s, Korea had become the eleventh largest exporter in the world economy (SaKong, 1993: 248). In 2002, according to the World Trade Organization, Korea was the twelfth largest exporter in world merchandise trade. http://www.wto.org/english/res_e/statis_e/its2003_e/its03_overview_e.htm.

5 For a further definition of entrepreneur capitalism, see 'family' capitalism, in Church (1993: 1), and 'proprietary' capitalism, in Lazonick (1991: 25–27).

6 For arguments of variations in the historical transformation, see British case studies in Elbaum and Lazonick (1986), and of similarities, Chandler (1990a); Chandler and Daems (1980); Lazonick (1986); Schmitz (1993).

7 For further details of strategy and structure developments of *zaibatsu* in the pre- and post-Second World War period, see Nikagawa (1976), esp. Part I.

8 See, e.g., Tamio (1986). In this chapter, Korean surnames precede given names. However, in the case of Korean authors writing in English, I use Western name order.

9 This is the so-called '*Chayudang* (the Liberal Party) Five Main Contractors', which was initiated by Daedong Manufacturing Co., whose owner was chief officer in the party's political finance department. Usually 10 per cent of the total amount of the contract was donated as political funds to the Rhee government (1948–1960) (Lee, 1994: 107–109, 127–138).

10 The *Kyŏngbu* Highway Construction project (428km in length, 1968–1970) constitutes a classic example of HECC and government links and their style of doing business in this period. President Park Chung Hee personally asked Chung Ju Yung to provide the government with a fully budgeted plan of the construction project before the government called for tenders. The project, as awarded to HECC, was worth 9,442 million won, and was the largest in the history of Korean construction at that time (HECC, 1982: 655–656, 1410).

11 For example, between 1966 and 1973, 43 per cent or US$281.9 million of total overseas construction sales by the fifteen largest Korean companies went to HECC (HECC, 1982: 588–590).

12 The 'section' stands for an organizational unit located hierarchically between a department (*Pu*) and subsection (*Kae*). It is usually organized by five to eight members including a manager.

13 Chung In Yung, the first brother, was appointed President of HECC in 1968; Chung Se Yung, the third brother, was appointed President of HMC in 1968; Chung Sun Yung, and the second brother, as President of Hyundai Cement in 1970.

14 For example, Chung Sun Yung (Vice-President, management), Chung Heeyung (Leesa, a younger sister, Tokyo Branch) and her husband, Kim Young-ju (Vice-President, heavy machinery, 1970). This kinship pattern has remained to this day. Hence, the term 'top management' or 'Hyundai top management' implies the founder, Chung Ju Yung, and his family appointees.

15 In the 1970s, construction projects from government included an iron and steel mill for Pohang Steel Corporation (1970–1980), a series of Kori Nuclear Power Plants (1971–1978), subway projects (1972–1980), and chemical industrial plants in Ulsan Industrial Park (1972–1974).

16 It increased from 54,540 million won in 1975 to 135,048 million won in 1976 and to 1,659,215 million won in 1981.

17 This was an inherent conflict with Ford, which cooperated with HMC under its international market strategy to confine HMC to its regional domestic market as a distributor.

18 For this aspect of government assistance, see Amsden, 1989.

19 The market share of HMC is calculated by the total amount of domestic sales of passenger cars of four major Korean passenger car companies, Hyundai, Daewoo, Kia and Ssangyoung.

20 This kind of internal structure was defined as an M-form industrial group by Chandler (1982: 3–23).

21 A distinctive feature of the pre-eminent managerial position of the Group Chairman and Hyundai's Group Planning Office was that they had no formal legal status *vis-à-vis* the legally independent subsidiary companies of Hyundai. Their *de facto* existence as managerial control mechanisms was a consequence of the kin ownership concentration (i.e. 40 to 50 per cent of the total capital of subsidiary companies was held by Chung Ju Yung and his family). Their total shareholdings of some companies was less than 50 per cent, but other subsidiary companies owned the rest, leaving Chung Ju Yung in control. This concentration of ownership allowed Chung Ju Yung – on a *de facto* if not a *de jure* basis – to be involved in every aspect of the management of Hyundai subsidiaries. Thus, notwithstanding the legally independent status of the subsidiaries, the Group Chairman and Group Planning Office systems were developed to control centrally a large-scale and complex conglomerate which utilized the 'one set' approach.

22 For the principles of Confucian values and implications in managerial activities in Korea and other NICs countries, see Hofstede and Bond (1988: 5–21), Chang (1988) and Kim and Kim (1989).

23 Here, top managerial executives refer to those held over the *Sangmu* position, which is equivalent to the position of a president in a Western company.
24 For details of the independent trade union movement at Hyundai workplaces and its impact upon the conglomerate's businesses, see Kwon (1997) and Kwon and O'Donnell (2001).
25 See Chapter 7, this volume.
26 Changes in the number of HECC's overseas branches, in part, showed its efforts in HECC's regional diversification in the 1980s. These increased from thirty-four in 1982 to fifty-three in 1988, covering from Asia to North America (Maeil Economic Newspaper, 1982, 1986, 1988).
27 With the Pony, HMC sold 79,072 cars, or 7 per cent of the Canadian small passenger car market in 1985. With its second model, the Excel, HMC sold 168,882 cars, the third largest number of sales in the small-sized and imported passenger category in the USA in 1986 and in 1987.
28 In 1988, 88 per cent of its total export sales were to the USA (HMC, 1992: 751).
29 In the course of implementing the new growth strategy, its previous public relations and research functions were transferred to the Keumkang Advertising Agency and Hyundai Research Institute which had been established in 1983 and 1984 respectively to enhance the provision of such professional services to the subsidiaries.
30 In 1994, out of a total forty-four presidents in Hyundai, twenty-five came from non-HECC backgrounds (Hyundai Group Public Relations Office, 1994: 80–81). This implies a gradual evolution in the second level of top management away from dominance by Chung Ju Yung and his subordinates.
31 See, e.g., Amsden (1989); Jones and SaKong (1980); Kang (1990); Kuk (1988).
32 For further details of the Group Planning Office systems in the Korean *chaebŏl*, see Park (1992).
33 In 1974, Park's 'New Policy for Heavy and Chemical Industries' was meant to offset the loss of exports through generous loans and tax policies. Government-backed shipbuilding orders also helped to overcome the first oil shock crisis of Hyundai shipbuilding business. In 1981, the Kukjae Business Group, which was the sixth largest *chaebŏl*, was bankrupted by the Chun government because the group failed to gain political preference from the Chun government and thus to obtain financial support when it was in crisis. Its subsidiaries were taken over by other *chaebŏl* on very generous financial terms: ten years' delay on the outstanding debts of the firm with no interest (*Monthly Chosŏn*, December 1988: 312–315).
34 In 1996, the top fifty *chaebŏl* had profits of only US$32 million on sales of US$274 billion (*Business Review Weekly*, 6 April 1998).
35 In August 2003, Chung Mong-hŏn committed suicide. Hyŏn Chŏng-ŏn, his wife, replaced him as chairperson of the Hyundai group.

References

Ansoff, H. 1969. *Business Strategy*, London: Penguin.

Amsden, A. 1989. *Asia's Next Giant: South Korea and Late Industrialisation*, New York: Oxford University Press.

Bank of Korea. 1990. *Annual Reports on Economic Statistics*, Seoul: BOA.

Chandler, A. 1962. *Strategy and Structure*, Cambridge: MIT Press.

——. 1977. *The Visible Hand: The Managerial Revolution in American Business*, London: Belknap Press.

——. 1982. 'The M-Form: Industrial Groups, American Style', *European Economic Review*, 19: 3–23.

——. 1990a. *Scale and Scope: The Dynamics of Industrial Capitalism*, Cambridge: Belknap Press.

——. 1990b. 'The Enduring Logic of Industrial Success', *Harvard Business Review*, 68(2), March–April: 130–140.

——. 1992. 'Managerial Enterprises and Competitive Capabilities', *Business History*, 34(1), January: 11–41.

Chandler, A. and H. Daems (eds). 1980. *Managerial Hierarchies: Comparative Perspective on the Rise of the Modern Industrial Enterprise*, Cambridge, MA: Harvard University Press.

Chang, C.S. 1988. '*Chaebŏl*: The South Korean Conglomerates', *Business Horizons*, 31, March and April: 51–57.

Chŏn Pom-sŏng. 1984. *Chung Ju Yung*, Seoul: Seomundang.

Cho, Dong-sŏng. 1991. *Han'guk Chaebŏl Yŏn'gu* (A Study of Korean *Chaebŏl*), Seoul: Maeil Economic Newspaper.

Chŏng, Ku-hyŏn. 1989. *Han'guk Kiyŏpui Sŏngjang Chŏllackkwa Kyŏngyŏnggujo* (Growth Strategy and Managerial Structure of Korean Companies), Seoul: Korean Commercial Industry.

Church, R. 1993. 'The Family Firm in Industrial Capitalism: International Perspectives on Hypotheses and History', *Business History*, 35(4), October: 17–43.

Elbaum, B. and W. Lazonic (eds). 1986. *The Decline of the British Economy*, Oxford: Clarendon Press.

Fligstein, N. 1990. *The Transformation of Corporate Control*, Cambridge, MA: Harvard University Press.

Gospel, H. 1983. 'New Approaches to Industrial Relations: Major Paradigms and Historical Perspective', *The Journal of Industrial Relations*, June: 162–176.

Hofstede, G. and M. Bond. 1988. 'The Confucius Connection: From Cultural Roots to Economic Growth', *Organizational Dynamics*, 16(4): 5–21.

Hong, Dŏk-nul. 1985. *Han'guk Chaebŏl ui Hwan'gyŏng T'onjae Kijae e Kwanhan Yŏn'gu* (Environment Control Systems of the *Chaebŏl*), Master's Thesis, Seoul: Seoul National University.

Hyundai Electronics Industries (HEI). 1994. *Hyundai Chŏnja 10 nyŏnsa* (A Ten-Year History of Hyundai Electronics Industries), Seoul: HEI.

Hyundai Engineering and Construction Corporation (HECC). 1982. *Hyundai Kŏnsŏl 35 nyŏnsa* (A Thirty-five Year History of Hyundai Engineering and Construction), Seoul: HECC.

Hyundai Group Public Relations Office (HGPRO). 1994. *Hyundai*, Seoul: HGPRO.

Hyundai Group Trade Union Association (HGTUA). 1994. *Hyŏnchongnyŏn Tanhyŏp Charyojip* (Data for Collective Bargaining of the Hyundai Trade Union Association), Seoul: HGTUA.

Hyundai Heavy Industries (HHI). 1992. *Hyundai Chung'gongŏpsa* (History of Hyundai Heavy Industries), Seoul: HHI.

Hyundai Motor Company (HMC). 1987. *Hyundai Chadongch'a 20 nyŏnsa* (A Twenty-Year History of Hyundai Motor Company), Seoul: HMC.

——. 1992. *Hyundai Chadongch'a* (The History of Hyundai Motor Company), Seoul: HMC.

——. 1997. *Hyundai Chadongch'asa 35 sa* (The 35-year History of Hyundai Motor Company), Seoul: HMC.

Jones, L. and Il SaKong. 1980. *Government, Business and Entrepreneurship in Economic*

Development: The Korean Case, Cambridge, MA: Council on East Asian Studies, Harvard University Press.

Kang, Y.G. 1990. *The Rise of Korean* Chaebŏls *from the Perspective of Organisation Theory*, Ph.D. thesis, Arizona: University of Arizona.

Kim, Pyŏng-ha. 1991. *Chaebŏl Hyŏng kwa Kiŏpka Hwaldong* (Formation of *Chaebŏl* and their Entrepreneurs), Seoul: Hankuk Neungyeulhyeobhoe.

Kim, Eun-Mee. 1997. *Big Business, Strong State: Collusion and Conflict in South Korean Development, 1960–1980*, New York: State University of New York Press.

Kim, Hyo-gun. 1986. *Han'guk Chaebŏl ŭi Sŏngjang Paljŏn e Kwanhan Yŏn'gu* (The Developmental Factors for the Growth of the *Chaebŏl*), Master's thesis, Seoul: Seoul National University.

Kim, K.C. and S. Kim. 1989. 'Kinship Group and Patrimonial Executives in a Developing Nation: A Case Study of Korea', *The Journal of Developing Areas*, 24, October: 27–46.

Kim, Young-ho 1985. *Kyŏnje ui Hyŏnjang* (Reality of Economy in Korea), Seoul: Dongcheonsa.

Kong, Byŏng-ho 1992. *Chaebŏl Pinan Padaya Hannŭn'ga?* (Why Should The *Chaebŏl* Be Criticized?), Seoul: Yeyŭmsa.

Kong, Jae-uk. 1994. *1950 nyŏnda ŭi Han'guk ŭi Chabon'ga Yŏn'gu* (Korean Capitalists in the 1950s), Seoul: Baeksan.

Korean Shipbuilding Industries Association (KSIA). 1992. *Annual Reports on Shipbuilding Industries*, Seoul: KSIA.

Kuk, M.H. 1988. *The Relationship between Government and Private Companies in the Industrial Development of South Korea*, Ph.D. thesis, Urbana: University of Illinois.

Kwon, S.H. 1997. *Control and Conflict: The Historical Development of Labour Management within the Hyundai Business Group, 1946–1995*, Ph.D. thesis, Sydney: University of New South Wales.

Kwon, S.H. and C. Leggett. 1994. *Industrial Relations and the South Korean Chaebŏl*, A Proceeding of the 8th AIRAANZ Conference, February, Sydney.

Kwon, S.H. and M. O'Donnell. 2001. *The Chaebŏl and Labour in Korea: The Development of Management Strategy in Hyundai*, New York: Routledge.

Lazonick, W. 1986. 'Strategy, Structure and Management Development in the United States and Britain', in Kobayashi, K. and H. Morikawa (eds) *Development of Managerial Enterprise*, Tokyo: University of Tokyo, pp. 101–146.

——. 1991. *Business Organisation and the Myth of the Market Economy*, Cambridge: Cambridge University Press.

Lee, Ho. 1993. *Chŏngsangŭn Uyŏnhi Ojiannunda: Chŏng Seyŏng kwa Hyundai Chadongch'a* (Chung Seyung and Hyundai Motor Company), Seoul: Usŏk.

Lee, Jong-nam. 1985. *Chaebŏl*, Seoul: Hyŏnjae.

Lee, Jong-sŏn. 1989. *Chunggong'ŏp Kodaedokchomkiŏp esŏ ŭi Nodong undong e Kwanhan Yŏn'gu* (The Labour Movements in Large Scale and Monopolistic Heavy Industries), Master's thesis, Seoul: Korea University.

Lee, Jong-jae. 1994. *Chaebŏl Iryŏksŏ* (The *Chaebŏl* and its Status), Seoul: Hankuk Newspaper.

Lee, Sung-tae. 1990. *Kamchuŏjin Tokchŏmchaebŏl ŭi Yŏksa* (Hidden History of Monopolistic *Chaebŏl*), Seoul: Nokdu.

Maeil Economic Newspaper (MEN). 1975–1994. *Annual Corporation Reports*, Seoul: MEN.

Nakagawa, K. (ed.) 1976. *Strategy and Structure of Big Business, Proceedings of the First Fuji Conference*, Tokyo: University of Tokyo.

Park, Byung-yun. 1982. *Chaebŏl kwa Chŏngji* (The *Chaebŏl* and Politics), Seoul: Hankuk Yangseo.

Park, Dong-sun. 1979. *Chaebŏl ui Ppuri* (Roots of the *Chaebŏl*), Seoul: Taechang.

Park, Hee. 1992. *Han'guk Taegiŏp ui Chojik Kwalli wa Nosagwangye ŭi Kwanhan Yŏn'gu* (Organizational Operation and Labour Relations in Big Corporations), Ph.D. thesis, Seoul: Yonsei University.

Park, Moon-Kyu. 1987. 'Interest Representation in South Korea', *Asian Survey*, 27(8): 904–919.

Prais, S. 1976. *The Evolution of Giant Firms in Britain*, Cambridge: Cambridge University Press.

Rhee, J.C. 1994. *The State and Industry in South Korea: The Limits of the Authoritarian State*, London: Routledge.

SaKong, I. 1993. *Korea in the World Economy*, Washington, DC: Institute for International Economics.

Schmitz, C. 1993. *The Growth of Big Business in the United States and Western Europe*, London: Macmillan.

Steers, R. 1999. *Made in Korea: Chung Gu Yung and the Rise of Hyundai*, London: Routledge.

Steers, R., Y.K. Shin and G. Ungson. 1989. *The Chaebŏl: Korean's New Industrial Might*, New York: HarperCollins.

Tamio, H. 1986. *Han'guk Kiop ui Kujo wa Chŏllak* (Strategy and Structure of Korean Firms), Seoul: Beobmun.

Wade, R. 1990. *Governing the Market: Economic Theory and the Role of Government in East Asian Industrialisation*, New York: Princeton University Press.

Yang, Yoo-jin. 1991. *Han'guk Chabonjuŭi Punsŏk* (Analysis of Korean Capitalism), Seoul: Ilbit.

You, Inhak. 1991. *Han'guk chaebŏl ui Haebu* (Analysis of the Korean *Chaebŏl*), Seoul: Ilbit.

5 What makes us great

Chaebŏl development, labor practices, and managerial ideology

John Lie

Faced with the phenomenal growth of the South Korean economy, many observers pointed to the large business conglomerates – *chaebŏl* – as the principal engine of economic growth. William Overhold, an American businessman, stated that *chaebŏl* constitute "the most efficient economic machine the world has ever seen" (Stephens 1998: 193). Most scholars are more circumspect in singing their praises but many nonetheless equate *chaebŏl* growth and economic dynamism (Amsden 1989; Steers *et al.* 1989). In this view, Samsung, Hyundai, and other business conglomerates embody the spirit of entrepreneurship and efficiency.

In this chapter I challenge the celebratory accounts of *chaebŏl* that dominated the scholarly discussion in the 1980s and 1990s. I begin by presenting a brief overview of *chaebŏl* development which underplays the significance of private entrepreneurship and instead highlights the role of state patronage in propelling conglomerate growth. Next, I criticize the received view that portrays large South Korean corporations as highly efficient. I use ethnographic examples, drawing on my work experience in a large South Korean conglomerate in the late 1980s, to suggest that, at least for some white-collar workers, there was very little of the fabled Confucian work ethic in evidence. However, a distinct labor regime existed for blue-collar workers, which was shaped more by the military rather than by Confucianism. *Chaebŏl* managerial ideology is Confucian and familial but it serves principally to justify managerial interests.

State patronage and *chaebŏl* development

In order to promote rapid industrialization the South Korean state accentuated capital concentration, and in so doing caused *chaebŏl* to become a commanding presence in the South Korean economy. Given the omnipresent character of *chaebŏl* in South Korean life, some writers have argued that they are unique to South Korea, if not to East Asia (e.g. Kirk 1994: 32–35). However, large family-owned corporations are prevalent in other countries, whether overdeveloped or underdeveloped. In the early 1990s, for example, the Salim Group accounted for 5 percent of Indonesian GNP. More importantly for our purposes, many observers depict *chaebŏl* as bastions of entrepreneurship: "The success of the chaebŏl can largely be attributed to aggressive and ambitious entrepreneurship" (Koo 1994: 157). Indeed, in the mid-1980s, the founders of Samsung, Hyundai, and Daewoo wrote bestselling narratives of their rags-to-riches trajectories. The retrospective celebration of the hero-entrepreneur is well-nigh universal among capitalist societies. But the individualistic and hagiographic perspective misses the salient and unifying characteristic of all the major *chaebŏl*: the crucial role of state patronage and social networks. *Chaebŏl* were followers rather than leaders, at least until the late 1980s; they largely executed the industrial policy conceived by the state. Furthermore, personal connections often framed the flow of state-controlled resources.

State patronage

State patronage was crucial for corporate success. As Chapters 3 and 4 have shown, the state shaped the very possibility and contours of corporate growth and formed the institutional framework of corporate opportunities. "Investment licenses" granted monopolistic privileges over selected commodities to favored corporations. In 1972, for example, each of the ten largest conglomerates had one or more exclusive investment licenses (Kim 1987: 111–117). International opportunities were also meted out by the state. In the very profitable Middle East construction boom of the 1970s, for example, the top ten businesses garnered 16 percent of aggregate sale (Kim 1987: 196–201). The state designated ten General Trading Companies (in effect, the ten largest *chaebŏl*), which were given special privileges and loans in conducting foreign investment and trade. It also offered significant financial incentives to corporations operating in the targeted import-substitution industries (Suh 1975: 214).

Suh and Kwon's findings regarding Hyundai's strategies for building subsidiary companies hold true for *chaebŏl* in general: corporate diversification followed the state-shaped structure of opportunities. Given the privileged position afforded to select corporate groups, it was in their interest to expand into as many monopolistic spheres as possible. Riding on the wave of South Korean economic growth, corporate diversification, in other words, was the most effective way to achieve growth and to accumulate wealth. The state in this regard sold state-owned enterprises (Chŏng 1989: 183–184), and facilitated the acquisition of small and medium-sized firms (Koo and Kim 1992: 135–136). The result was corporate diversification and development. While only thirty-four subsidiary companies were founded or incorporated by the top ten conglomerates in the 1960s, the number rose to 114 in the 1970s (Kuk 1988: 116).

State financial control was an especially powerful instrument to promote – and in some cases to demote (see Kang, Chapter 7, this volume) – corporate ascent in the domestic and international markets

(Woo 1991: 159–169). The state turned on and off the spigot of capital and credit. It controlled foreign loans, and other sources of credit, such as the National Investment Fund. In times of capital shortage, access to credit determined the difference between expansion and stagnation. There was a high correlation between the amount of debt a corporation could generate and its corporate success (Kuk 1988: 120–121). *Chaebŏl* in South Korea were heavily leveraged. Given the corporate dependence on loans, state disfavor could lead to decline or even bankruptcy.

The primacy of social networks

The play of social networks shaped the beneficiaries of state patronage. The most crucial ties were those forged between the president and *chaebŏl* owners. Personal connections to Park Chung Hee in the 1960s and 1970s and to Chun Doo Hwan and Roh Tae Woo in the 1980s provided businesspeople with the royal road to corporate success in South Korea. Personal networks between the successive presidents of South Korea and *chaebŏl* owners provided access to capital and credit on the one hand and monopolistic privileges on the other hand. The former Deputy Prime Minister Lee Hahn-Been remarked:

> You name one hundred [of the] largest or most conspicuous projects or plants in the sixties and seventies. Whatever they may be, the final decisions were made . . . at the top of the regime. . . . The primary job of the bureaucrats was to prepare justifiable rationale for the decisions made . . . at the top of the regime, and to implement these decisions.
>
> (Kim 1987: 109)

Beyond the "top of the regime," ties to relevant officials, whether in the Ministry of Construction or the Ministry of Finance, generated business favors and, equally important, prevented bureaucratic obstacles.

The visible hand uniting political and business elites spawned a torrent of social criticism. Kim's (1973: 222) complaint is exemplary:

> The vicious circle continues in which the entrepreneur must obtain government support to start a business; to obtain this he begins by buying the goodwill of officials and ends with a substantial "token" of his appreciation for favors rendered. Entertainment must be offered only at first-rate restaurants.

Critical writings on *chaebŏl* focus on the pervasive personalistic ties that constituted the political–business nexus (Janelli with Yim 1993: 82–88).

Family, military, school, and regional ties favored some individuals over others in gaining Park's or bureacrats' favor. In particular, former military and government officials often joined *chaebŏl* management and forged ties between corporations and the state (Hattori 1984: 183–184). Regional affiliation became significant, as those from the Kyŏngsang provinces (where Park, Chun, and Roh all grew up) were disproportionately represented among the successful military, state, and business elite, while the neighboring Chŏlla provinces became underdeveloped (Chon 1992: 155–158). Prized above all was the TK mark (referring to the city of Taegu and Kyŏngbuk High School), which became a royal road for the political, military, and business elite. Both Chun Doo Hwan and Roh Tae Woo belonged to the TK tribe. Traditionally more powerful were graduates of elite schools such as Kyŏnggi High School or Seoul National University, who also populated the government and business elite in South Korea.

In stressing the significance of state patronage and social networks, I do not mean to dismiss the significance of personal initiatives altogether. There was a cultural and social foundation for entrepreneurship in the post-Korean War South Korea when the traditional Confucian disdain for commercial activities declined. The disappearance of the landed oligarchs created a pool of overeducated elites seeking new sources of wealth and power (Hattori 1988: 153–156). The new structure of business opportunities was seized by the ambitious – not only the scions of the landed gentry, but also some who raised themselves by dint of their talent and diligence. There was a meritocratic moment in South Korea from the end of the Korean War to the consolidation of *chaebŏl* in the 1970s when enterprising individuals could make a fortune. Like the fictional protagonist of the Horatio Alger novels, however, it was not just sheer hard work but connections to the powerful that ensured success.

Chaebŏl *development*

The four crucial modes of *chaebŏl* growth were: (1) taking over Japanese-owned plants; (2) processing the "three whites" (cotton, flour, and cement) in the 1950s; (3) riding on the Vietnam War-generated boom; and (4) following Park's industrialization plan. In all four ways, state support was crucial. Essentially, successful *chaebŏl* ascended the ladder of high value-added production – a microcosm of the South Korean economy's rise toward higher value-added production. It was in the 1970s, however, that the most dramatic growth occurred. Consider in this regard that by 1973 less than 10 percent of the total industrial capital stock was from before the Korean War (Hong 1976: 22). The recent provenance of contemporary large conglomerates should be clear from comparing the seven largest *chaebŏl* in 1966 with those in 1985. In 1966, the largest corporations were Samsung, Samsang, Samyang, Kaetong, Tong'a, Lucky, and Taehan; by 1985 they were Samsung (established in 1952), Hyundai (1947), Lucky Goldstar (1947), Daewoo (1967), Sunkyung (1953), and

Ssangyong (1948). Samsang, Samyang, Kaetong, Tong'a, and Taehan declined or had disappeared by the 1980s. By the mid-1980s, only two major corporations (Ssangyong and Daelim) could trace their lineage to the colonial period. Furthermore, only two of the ten largest corporations in the mid-1980s were targets of the 1961 Illicit Accumulation Law. State-led development and *chaebŏl* growth cannot be separated.

Case studies of *chaebŏl* highlight the significance of state patronage and social networks. Ssangyong's founder Kim Sŏng-gŏn's first business venture was to make soap in 1940, but his first large enterprise, Kŏmsŏng Textiles, was taken over from a Japanese textile factory in 1948. Its flagship cement company, which was established after Kim sold his textile company in 1967, proved to be profitable. Ssangyong's inclusion in the ranks of the largest corporations came about as Kim and his successor entered oil, construction, and other heavy industries. Ssangyong's growth may be traced to Kim's intimate personal ties with Park Chung Hee and its role in fulfilling the demands of South Korean state-led growth (Lie 1988).

Samsung's initial economic success after its founding in 1953 was inextricable from the founder Lee Byung-chull's close tie to Rhee. Samsung expanded rapidly by processing the "three whites." Although sheared of its vast banking concerns in the early phase of Park's rule, Samsung managed to regain close ties to the governing elite (Hattori 1988: 244–245). Its continued well-being relied on Lee's successful effort to follow the state-led trajectory of South Korean industrialization, especially during the period of the Vietnam War-related economic boom (Pak 1993: 131–134).

Although founded in 1948 by Chung Ju Yung, Hyundai only began to distinguish itself in the 1960s as a construction company by gaining U.S. military contracts and by undertaking major state projects, including the 1970 completion of Kyŏngbu Highway (see Chapter 4, this volume). Hyundai's growth continued through its heavy involvement in Vietnam-related businesses, the Middle East construction boom, and Park's heavy industrialization plan, which included highway construction and shipbuilding. Hyundai created thirteen companies during the Third Five-Year Plan, following the contours of state economic priorities. The founder-entrepreneur was close to Park, leading the media to dub Hyundai a *Yusin chaebŏl.*

As these examples suggest, state patronage propelled corporate growth. Exceptions prove the rule. Major corporations, such as Lotte and Kolon, that did not rely initially on close state ties, were founded by Korean–Japanese entrepreneurs. More significantly, opposing the state was often disastrous. Consider the example of Samhak, a major distillery and one of the largest conglomerates in the late 1960s. The owner backed Kim Dae Jung in the 1971 presidential election. Several months later, tax inspectors convicted Samhak of tax evasion and the corporation was forced into bankruptcy (Shim and Sherry 1995: 71). As the later examples of Yulsan and Kukje suggest, the state penalized not just poor performers, but also those that defied it (Clifford 1994: 219–226).

In summary, state patronage and social networks shaped *chaebŏl* growth. It would be misleading to highlight the individual initiative of the founder-entrepreneurs of major South Korea *chaebŏl* in explaining conglomerate growth. They were undoubtedly bright and diligent, but their entrance to the ranks of the *chaebŏl* during the 1960s and 1970s depended on their ability to cultivate political favors.

Chaebŏl labor practices

In explicating *chaebŏl* labor practices, it is important to distinguish between office, or white-collar, workers, and factory, or blue-collar, workers. Needless to say, these two strata of workers experienced significant wage differentials. Equally important, however, was the qualitative difference in working conditions.

White-collar workers

When I worked at a *chaebŏl* in the late 1980s, I was struck by how many people went around saying "I am busy" in lieu of ordinary greetings. Although they were busily pacing to and fro or conspicuously shuffling papers at their desk, I noticed over time that their punctuality and overt expressions of diligence masked a variety of efforts to avoid work. Managerial gaze targeted discernible features, such as tardiness, early departure, or relaxed demeanor. The constant refrain of "I am busy" not only reminded superiors and colleagues about their busy-ness (and therefore their excellence) but also warded off additional business that would otherwise be foisted upon them.

Although many office workers claimed repeatedly to work very hard, their concrete actions often belied their rhetoric. For example, it was not uncommon to find employees taking several hours off during the day to go to movie theaters or to relax in a sauna. Many male employees were groggy as they sought to recover from their hangovers – a consequence of a drinking binge from the previous evening. The nocturnal carousing was expressed as part of their all-important work, but they in fact offered very little in the way of promoting business. Participation was either mandated by a superior or the desire to avoid group ostracism.

My year-long work experience, in short, yielded very little evidence in the way of hard work. To be sure, some employees, especially women who did a great deal of substantive tasks, worked long and hard. However, given the long hours mandated by the company, hard work was a product more of impression management than actual exertion (cf. Janelli with Janelli 1993: 9–10). Ironically, the most "diligent" person in my office was the vice-president who spent much of his time reading the Confucian classics. This latter-day literati spent much of the day musing on the Confucian character of South Korea while being oblivious to corporate goings-on. In the early 1970s, Donald Christie (1972: 142) found that "the men in our section were not working but were reading English novels or a newspaper or just chatting with one another."

In spite of the generally lax pace in the white-collar workplace, the nature of managerial authority was strikingly authoritarian and demanded unquestioned obedience. One-man, top-down managerial style was the norm (Lie 1990). There were very few overt cases of rebellion against the hierarchy and the rare offender was frequently forced to resign or to be demoted. In other instances, harsh scolding – screaming and threats of physical violence – ensued.

Nonetheless, it is important to contextualize the nature of managerial authoritarianism, which was despotic in character, but without effective infrastructural power. Michael Mann (1986), in another context, draws a distinction between despotic and infrastructural power. Translated into the workplace context, a manager with despotic power may be able to fire a worker at will, just as a sovereign may be able to execute a rebel. Yet the same despotic manager and sovereign may lack the infrastructural power to elicit effective and efficient work from their subordinates. The manager may not be able to generate much work when workers are beyond his gaze, just as the sovereign may not be able to collect taxes.

Indeed, hierarchical control and symbolic dominance characterized direct encounters in the workplace. The very ability to go home was dictated by a department or section chief (cf. Janelli with Janelli 1993: 203–210). Numerous rules and regulations sought to govern employees. The company I worked for mandated, for example, that every male employee wear long-sleeved shirts, even in the hot and humid summer that characterizes Seoul.

The general recitation of the "busy-ness" discussed above is generated by a condition of high despotic but low infrastructural managerial power. In instances of face-to-face encounters, absolute power reigned. Outside the narrow perimeter, however, form, not substance, denoted largely nominal or rhetorical obedience to managerial authority. It was not rare for employees to mutter angry invectives about their superiors or to engage in "silent" resistance by going off to the movies or the sauna. In other words, South Korean managers did not exercise hegemony over white-collar workers. The very lack of control accounts in part for the explicit emphasis on employee training, which sought to promote obedience and loyalty (cf. Janelli with Janelli 1993: 140–144).

The authoritarian managerial style accounts for the problematic information flow in the South Korean corporate hierarchy. Many routine decisions required top management's consent. To decide on a cover of a publication, for example, all the division and section chiefs were called upon to deliberate for several hours. In another instance, I found out to my horror that none of the mail that I had entrusted to the man in charge of office mail had been delivered. I came to realize that I had, because of my foreign correspondence, exceeded the mail budget for my section. Because I was ranked higher than he, however, he did not want to inform me of this "bad" news or to requisition more money from his immediate supervisor. In order to ensure the status quo, he simply hid my mail in his drawer!

A particularly memorable experience was symptomatic of the way in which managerial inefficiency overlapped with managerial authoritarianism. One day my boss asked me to write a report for the president. Although I had finished a draft soon thereafter, it was ignored for weeks until the night before it was due. Just before I was about to head home, the boss asked me, as well as about a dozen others, to stay behind to work on it. After strenuous hours of rewriting we finished our task at around 3 a.m., at which point the boss insisted we go out to celebrate. After a few rounds of drinks he put his arm around me and asked, "Dr. Lie, do you know why we [South Koreans] developed so quickly?" Without waiting for my reply, he exclaimed triumphantly: "Because we work so hard! Because of our Confucian heritage!"

I do not want to insist that no one worked hard. The desire for upward mobility prompted some to work efficiently and effectively. Many women employees, as I mentioned, were diligent. However, it would be problematic to equate white-collar workplaces as the site of the fabled Confucian work ethic in action.

Blue-collar workers

The nature of *chaebŏl* labor management practice was qualitatively distinct for factory workers.[1] The dominant mode of labor control was not only despotic but it also relied on systematic surveillance. Although managers often claimed that a corporation was like a family, it in fact operated more like a platoon or a prison. Blue-collar workers were monitored more closely and extensively than their white-collar counterparts.

The fundamental reason for disciplining factory workers was the imperative of export-oriented industrialization. In order to undercut global competition, *chaebŏl* firms needed to maximize on their comparative advantage, low labor costs. Hence, the state and corporations pursued a strikingly anti-labor policy. The state curtailed the right of workers to organize, and corporations sought to quell dissent and to maximize labor exploitation (Choi 1989; Lie 1998).

Nonetheless, it would be misleading to stress simply the condition of cheap labor. An effective factory requires adequately trained and motivated workers, which is lacking in most non-industrial societies. As Alexander Gerschenkron (1962: 9) argued:

> [The] overriding fact to consider is that industrial labor in the sense of a stable, reliable, and disciplined group that has cut the umbilical cord connecting it with the land and has become suitable for utilization in factories, is not abundant but extremely scarce in a backward country. Creation of an industrial labor force that really deserves its name is a more difficult and protracted process.

As E.P. Thompson (1991) argued, the disciplined workers must acquiesce to the mandates of modern industrial production. They must be able to execute commands, deal with the new machinery, and cooperate with other workers. In other words, it is not adequate to have low-paid labor; managers must seek a trained labor force. This insight has been clear to management scholars: "Management is the principal factor determining the productivity of labor if we assume that capital and raw material inputs are the same" (Harbison and Myers 1959: 27).[2]

In South Korea, a literate and disciplined labor force was in large part a product of the post-liberation education system and the military. In particular, the military played a crucial role in transmogrifying South Korean men into industrial workers. The military literally disciplined the entire male population, since nearly every man spent three years in the service. By imposing homogeneous training on South Koreans from every status and regional background, the military contributed to national integration and cultural homogeneity. The life in the military became a common cultural and organizational reference point. The military drilled the skills and habits of modern industries (Clark 1954: 172). It forced every soldier to meet the dictates of modern institutions:

> hierarchical regimentation, punctuality, and so on. The quasi-natural rhythm of agrarian life was replaced by the mechanical exactitude of modern life. No single institution was as crucial as the military in delivering the modern to South Korea. We cannot come to an adequate understanding of contemporary South Korean society without grasping the centrality of the military in forging a virtual cultural revolution. Although there were some colonial-period continuities, the U.S. military influence was paramount (Martin 1973). The U.S. military entrenched its administrative management ideas and practices through military contacts as well as through shaping academic curricula.
>
> (Bark 1984: 274–275)

The pervasive military influence contributed to managerial authoritarianism; there was a smooth transition from the barracks to the factories. Corporations imitated the military by institutionalizing managerial hierarchy and discipline. The isomorphism of the military and the factory was ensured by the transfer of military officers as corporate managers and by the reference of military conscripts as factory workers. Hyundai, for example, systematically preferred workers with ROTC training (Kearney 1991: 156). The South Korean sociologist Kyuhan Bae (1987: 37) relayed the following impression of Hyundai's Ulsan factory: "When I visited the factory, many things reminded me of my experiences in the military service." The reminders included the mandatory uniform and name tag, regulations that pervaded every sphere of life, and the predominance of young males. Given that many manufacturing workers lived in company dormitories, factories resembled hyper-disciplined barracks (Bae 1987: 37–8).

The militarization of factory life manifested itself in stern discipline, often degenerating into violence. However, it is important to note that the U.S. influence was not unremittingly negative. A sociological survey of heavy-industry workers found that many workers had "American" or "materialistic" orientation (Bae and Form 1986). Quite clearly, the managerial rhetoric of "Koreanness" or the Confucian ideal did not penetrate the labor force. What prevented the demands for labor participation or higher wages was not ideological indoctrination but the intensive and extensive surveillance and discipline of the working population.

Needless to say, South Korean blue-collar workers did not all work at a fevered pitch. My contention is rather that, much more than white-collar workers, militarized management succeeded in ensuring infrastructural power over them. In this regard, the active policy of the state to disorganize workers and to quell unions robbed the workers' ability to resist managerial dictates. Hence, labor exploitation in South Korea was, in all its brutality, quite "successful." Militarized management is a major factor in accounting for the success of South Korea's export-oriented industrialization.

The Confucian managerial discourse

Very few scholars have discussed the inefficiency of white-collar work or the impact of the military upon South Korean labor management. Instead, in the 1980s, Confucianism dominated the discussion of South Korean management. Authoritarian managerial practice was widely viewed as an expression of traditional Korean or Confucian culture (Chang and Chang 1994; Sin 1984). This is puzzling because the early South Korean management literature consisted largely of rehashing American, and to a lesser extent, Japanese, verities on business management. Only in the 1980s did Confucianism become a popular topic for South Korean business scholars and managers. One could hardly read through company pamphlets or founders' writings without coming across the themes of Confucianism and the family. South Korean managers invoked Confucianism as the source and stressed the family as the quintessence of South Korean management. My inebriated superior was far from unique in equating Confucianism, diligence, and South Korean development.

Confucian ideals did in fact color South Korean managerial values. However, we should not confuse reality with ideology. The values of Confucianism and the family informed the dominant South Korean managerial ideology.

It is no secret that any ideology should draw upon existing traditions; this is no different for management ideologies (Bendix 1956). Confucianism was the ruling ideology during the Chosŏn Dynasty period. The family is in most, if not all, societies a very popular institution and ideal. Hence, it should not be surprising that corporate ideologists seized on the traditional themes of Confucianism and the family. The use of family ties in employment recruitment – even if largely for social control, as I argue – articulates well with the regnant personalistic ethic (Chang 1991). Roger Janelli (1993: 108) remarks in this regard that the company he studied "offered an embarrassment of ideological riches."

The emphasis upon the family ideal was mandated in part because South Korean corporations, as I have implied, departed so much from it. Corporate loyalty was weak, as evinced by high inter-company mobility. Hence, the family ideology sought to buttress corporate loyalty. *Chaebŏl* trained workers and attempted to instill a sense of loyalty. For example, many corporations gave employees gifts on holidays, as parents might give presents to their children. Another manifestation of the familial ideology was the Factory *Saemaŭl* (New Community) Movement, which was an offshoot of a rural development program. It sought to enhance industrial productivity by propagating the ideology of labor–capital harmony in the 1970s (Choi 1989: 181–190). A typical slogan urged: "Treat employees like family; Do factory work like your own personal work" (Choi 1989: 183). Nonetheless, the effort to transform a corporation into a family foundered on the simple fact that most corporations recklessly exploited workers.

Furthermore, social control became important in the late 1980s, a time of turbulent labor–management relations. Government officials and managers lambasted Western individualism for inciting labor militancy and appealed to the conservative Confucian ideology – with its stress on hierarchy and order as normative ideals – to achieve labor–management harmony. The ideal of the family functioned as a means of employee control. A corporate personnel manager told Robert Kearney (1991: 157) that he was looking for "the most normal people. If the office is a family, then those from ordinary families can easily adapt, but those who have had trouble giving up will be likely to encounter trouble in the office." Hence, the corporate personnel office searched employees' parental marital status as an indicator of employee adaptability. Companies recruited workers through employee networks, which ensured a web of responsibility that disciplined workers and prevented subversive activities (Bae 1987: 44). Four-fifths of the Hyundai factory workers whom Bae

(1987: 44) studied were "recommended by their relatives or friends" in order to be hired by Hyundai. Should a worker take part in union activities, for example, not only would her or his parents be informed of their child's "communist" activities, but her or his relatives in the same company would be prevented from winning internal promotion (Lee 1988: 142). The theme of social control extended well beyond the corporate managerial ideology. As Lucian Pye (1985: 227) argues: "Modernization has thus brought increasing tensions to [South] Korean society, which the government seeks to alleviate by appealing to traditional sentiment." He continues: "The government advanced the doctrine that as a Confucian society [South] Korea did not need the 'wasteful' confrontations of Western labor–management relations" (Pye 1985: 226). In the context of labor militancy in the 1980s, South Korean management theorists and practitioners invoked Confucianism as a normative ideal to attain labor–management harmony. The president of the company I worked for constantly discoursed on Confucianism whenever he deemed that his workers were not being diligent or loyal. In this context, perhaps the vice-president was doing important work for the company by rereading the Confucian classics.

Finally, the Confucian managerial ideology justified family ownership and management, and countered constant criticism not only in the media but also among employees. Family ownership and control characterized virtually all the conglomerates in the 1970s and 1980s (see Chapter 4, this volume). Family ownership and management stem from the importance of trust in corporate management. As late as 1984, only two out of the fifty largest conglomerates were headed by professional managers (Kuk 1988: 128). Family and kinship networks provided the personnel to staff *chaebŏl* expansion. Especially in the 1970s, patrimonial ties constituted the corporate hierarchy. In addition, former military officers, politicians, and bureaucrats staffed *chaebŏl* managerial hierarchies (Lim and Paek 1987: 26). Donald Christie (1972: 219) writes of the "Korean way" to promotion as not "through hard work, but through conniving and connections" (see also Hattori 1988: 116). When I worked at a *chaebŏl*, many mid-level executives complained constantly about the family "mafia" that controlled the corporate group (see also Janelli 1993:199–200). Against the meritocratic ideology they espoused, family ownership and management was not only repugnant, but was also widely believed to be inefficient. The Confucian family ideology sought to justify family ownership and management.

The prevailing and popular discourse tends to reproduce itself. I was present on many occasions when foreign scholars and policy-makers visited the corporation I worked at in order to study South Korean management and economy. The president of my company would inevitably ask me to tell the visitors about Confucianism and the family. The foreign pundits in turn readily and eagerly articulated their assent, and wrote articles and books expressing the truths they found in South Korea.

Conclusion

In this chapter, I criticized the celebratory accounts of South Korean *chaebŏl* development and managerial practice and ideology. I stressed the importance of state patronage in shaping corporate success and downplayed the role of entrepreneurship. I suggested that white-collar workplaces were far from efficient and effective, while factories were characterized by militarized management. Finally, I argued that Confucian managerial philosophy is fundamentally an ideology – a set of ideas to justify power relations.

In closing, I would like to stress that most blue-collar workers did work long and hard, goaded in large part by militarized management. Indeed, South Korean workers were the veritable and essential fuel of the economic engine. Nonetheless, their exploitation often remains beyond the purview of many scholars who purport to explain South Korean economic development. This is the supreme irony of so many accounts of the South Korean "miracle." The South Korean workers, whose blood and sweat propelled the economy, were neglected in the pages of history and social science books. Instead, their "masters" got all the credit. The world is patently unfair.

Notes

1 Just as there are significant differences between white-collar and blue-collar workers, there are also major distinctions between male and female workers or workers in the heavy and light industries. In this section I am referring primarily to male workers in the heavy industry in the 1980s. Hence, I pass over distinctions based on historical periods, sectors, gender, and so on.

2 Harbison and Myers (1959: 87) also note: "An almost self-evident proposition in our analysis, therefore, is that the capacity of a country to industrialize is dependent upon its ability to find, develop, commit, and effectively utilize the high-level human resources required by modern industrial enterprises."

References

Amsden, Alice H. 1989. *Asia's Next Giant: South Korea and Late Industrialization.* New York: Oxford University Press.

Bae, Kyuhan. 1987. *Automobile Workers in Korea.* Seoul: Seoul National University Press.

Bae, Kyuhan and William Form. 1986. "Payment Strategy in South Korea's Advanced Economic Sector." *American Sociological Review* 51: 120–131.

Bark, Dong Suh. 1984. "The American-educated Elite in Korean Society," in Youngnok Koo and Dae-Sook Suh (eds). *Korea and the United States: A Century of Cooperation.* Honolulu: University of Hawaii Press, pp. 263–280.

Bendix, Reinhard. 1956. *Work and Authority in Industry: Ideologies of Management in the Course of Industrialization.* New York: John Wiley.

Chang, Chan Sup and Nahn Joo Chang. 1994. *The Korean Management System: Cultural Political Economic Foundations.* Westport, CT: Quorum Books.

Chang, Yunshik. 1991. "The Personalist Ethic and the Market in Korea," *Comparative Studies in Society and History* 33: 106–129.

Choi, Jang Jip. 1989. *Labor and the Authoritarian State: Labor Unions in South Korean Manufacturing Industries, 1961–1988*. Seoul: Korea University Press.

Chon, Soohyun. 1992. "Political Economy of Regional Development in Korea," in Richard P. Appelbaum and Jeffrey Henderson (eds). *States and Development in the Asian Pacific Rim*. Newbury Park, CA: Sage, pp. 150–175.

Chŏng, Ku-hyŏn. 1989. "Han'guk esŏ ŭi chŏngbu wa kiŏp kan ŭi kwan'gye," in Hak-Chong Lee, Ku-hyŏn Chŏng, and Kae H. Chung (eds). *Han'guk kiŏp wa chŏllyak*. Seoul: Pŏmmunsa.

Christie, Donald Earle. 1972. "Seoul's Organization Men: The Ethnography of a Businessmen's Association in Industrializing Korea," Ph.D. dissertation, University of Illinois at Urbana-Champaign.

Clark, Mark W. 1954. *From the Danube to the Yalu*. New York: Harper & Brothers.

Clifford, Mark L. 1994. *Troubled Tiger: Businessmen, Bureaucrats, and Generals in South Korea*. Armonk, NY: M.E. Sharpe.

Gerschenkron, Alexander. 1962. *Economic Backwardness in Historical Perspective and Other Essays*. Cambridge, MA: Harvard University Press.

Harbison, Frederick and Charles A. Myers. 1959. *Management in the Industrial World: An International Analysis*. New York: McGraw-Hill.

Hattori, Tamio. 1984. "Kōdo seichōki ni okeru sangyō erīto no keisei", in Teiichi Itō (ed.). *Hatten tojōkoku no bijinesu rīdāshippu*. Tokyo: Ajia Keizai Kenkyūsho, pp. 157–186.

——. 1988. *Kankoku no keiei hatten*. Tokyo: Bunshindō.

Hong, Wontack. 1976. *Factor Supply and Factor Intensity of Trade in Korea*. Seoul: Korea Development Institute.

Janelli, Roger L. with Dawnhee Yim. 1993. *Making Capitalism: The Social and Cultural Construction of a South Korean Conglomerate*. Stanford, CA: Stanford University Press.

Jones, Leroy P. and Il SaKong. 1980. *Government, Business, and Entrepreneurship in Economic Development: The Korean Case*. Cambridge, MA: Council on East Asian Studies, Harvard University.

Kearney, Robert P. 1991. *The Warrior Worker: The Challenge of the Korean Way of Working*. New York: Henry Holt.

Kim, Seok Ki. 1987. "Business Concentration and Government Policy: A Study of the Phenomenon of Business Groups in Korea, 1945–1985," DBA dissertation, Harvard University.

Kim, Yŏng-nok. [1964] 1973. "On Korean Entrepreneurship," trans. T'ae-yông Pak, in Marshall R. Pihl (ed.). *Listening to Korea: A Korean Anthology*. New York: Prager, pp. 227–237.

Kirk, Donald. 1994. *Korean Dynasty: Hyundai and Chung Ju Yung*. Armonk, NY: M.E. Sharpe.

Koo, Hagen and Eun Mee Kim. 1992. "The Developmental State and Capital Accumulation in South Korea," in Richard P. Appelbaum and Jeffrey Henderson (eds). *States and Development in the Asian Pacific Rim*. Newbury Park, CA: Sage, pp. 121–149.

Koo, Suk Mo. 1994. "Korea's Big Business Groups and International Competitiveness," in Seung Yeung Kwack (ed.). *The Korean Economy at a Crossroad: Development Prospects, Liberalization, and South–North Economic Integration*. Westport, CT: Praeger, pp. 151–166.

Kuk, Minho. 1988. "The Governmental Role in the Making of Chaebŏl in the Industrial Development of South Korea." *Asian Perspective* 12: 107–133.

Lee, Jeong Taik. 1988. "Dynamics of Labor Control and Labor Protest in the Process of Export-oriented Industrialization in South Korea," *Asian Perspective* 12: 134–158.

Lie, John. 1988. "The Ssangyong Group: An Introductory Survey of a Korean Conglomerate," *Asian Profile* 16: 487–499.

——. 1990. "Is Korean Management Just Like Japanese Management?," *Management International Review* 30: 113–118.

——. 1998. *Han Unbound: The Political Economy of South Korea.* Stanford, CA: Stanford University Press.

Lim, Hyun-Chin and Noon-Sean Paek. 1987. "State Autonomy in Modern Korea: Institutional Possibility and Structural Limits," *Korea Journal* 27 (11): 19–32.

Mann, Michael. 1986. *The Sources of Social Power.* Vol. 1: *A History of Power from the Beginning to A.D. 1760.* Cambridge: Cambridge University Press.

Martin, James R. 1973. "Institutionalization and Professionalization of the Republic of Korea Army: The Impact of United States Military Assistance through Development of a Military School System," Ph.D. dissertation, Harvard University.

Pak, Kun-ho. 1993. *Kankoku no keizai hatten to Betonamu sensō.* Tokyo: Ochanomizu Shobo.

Pye, Lucian W. 1985. *Asian Power and Politics: The Cultural Dimensions of Authority.* Cambridge, MA: Harvard University Press.

Shim, Jae Hoon and Andrew Sherry. 1995. "Absolute Power," *Far Eastern Economic Review*, November 30.

Sin, Yu-gun. 1984. *Han'guk kiŏp ŭi t'uksŏng kwa kwaje.* Seoul: Seoul Taehakkyo Ch'ulp'anbu.

Steers, Richard, Shin Yoo Keun, and Gerardo R. Ungson. 1989. *The Chaebŏl: Korea's New Industrial Might.* New York: Harper & Row.

Stephens, Bernard. 1988. "Labor Resurgence in South Korea," *Nation*, November 19.

Suh, Suk Tai. 1975. *Import Substitution and Economic Development in Korea.* Seoul: Korea Development Institute.

Thompson, E.P. [1967] 1991. "Time, Work-discipline and Industrial Capitalism," in *Customs in Common: Studies in Traditional Popular Culture.* New York: New Press, pp. 352–403.

Woo, Jung-en. 1991. *Race to the Swift: State and Finance in Korean Industrialization.* New York: Columbia University Press.

Part III

Transformations in the state

6 Development without democracy

The political economy of US–South Korea relations, 1958–1961

Steven Hugh Lee

The late 1950s and early 1960s was a formative era in the history of South Korean politics and economic development. Between 1958 and 1961 Korean society experienced significant social and political turmoil associated with increased tensions in US–Korea relations, the violent end of Syngman Rhee's administration, the formation of a democratic government under Prime Minister Chang Myŏn in August 1960, and the overthrow of that regime by the instigators of the May 1961 military coup. During these years, policy-makers and bureaucrats in the republic also established some of the foundations for the longer term accelerated integration of the peninsula into the capitalist world system, a process that has been described as Korea's "globalization." For US officials, the late 1950s marked the start of a transition in policy away from a primary reliance on American bilateral aid to prop up the Korean state toward strategies designed to foster multilateral political and economic ties between Korea and the United States' "free world" allies.

Our knowledge of Korea's political economy in this era has grown considerably in recent years. The literature has outlined the import substitution industrialization (ISI) strategies of the Rhee government, the Liberal Party's proclivity to hand out business favors to enhance its political power, the importance of the pre-1961 period in understanding the origins of the Park Chung Hee regime's long-term economic planning bureaucracy, and the quantitative differences in growth between the Rhee and Park eras (Ahn 1992; Cumings 1981; Haggard 1990; Haggard and Moon 1993; Haggard *et al.* 1991; Lee 2002; Yi 1998). In addition, there is a general consensus that the United States played a major role in shaping Korea's five-year plan and its rapid development in the 1960s. Stephan Haggard and Chung-In Moon have written that "American influence was crucial" in determining the outcome of President Park's economic reforms, while Bruce Cumings has noted that South Korea's "export led program was decided by the US" (Haggard and Moon 1993: 864; Cumings 1981: 70).[1]

Historians and political scientists, however, have not been sensitive enough to the underlying political conflict between successive Korean and

American administrations over economic issues. Although state department policy-makers had emphasized since 1948 the importance of improving Japanese–Korean relations, and had pressured Korean bureaucrats to adopt a non-inflationary stabilization program and a more realistic exchange rate for the overvalued Korean currency, attaining these objectives became more important after 1958, as economic considerations came to play a more prominent role in United States diplomacy toward Northeast Asia. Korean officials were concerned about tensions in the bilateral partnership as they viewed healthy Korean–American relations as an important source of internal legitimacy and stability. Sustained US pressure for Korean economic reform sent signals to Korean politicians that the United States might ultimately be willing to support a different Korean government.

Protracted US–Korean disputes over economic issues thus contained significant implications for the political stability of the first and second republics. A particular source of discord was the dollar–*hwan* exchange rate. One of President Rhee's cardinal financial policies was the maintenance of an overvalued *hwan* relative to the American dollar. This was done partly to keep Korean expenditures on American aid goods as low as possible, but it was precisely this form of perceived dependence upon aid that US diplomats tried to weaken in the late 1950s. In the context of a growing crisis in Korean–American relations, they used economic reform as part of a broader strategy for restructuring the internal political dynamics of Rhee's government. The Chang regime inherited some of the monetary practices of the Rhee era, but articulated a different philosophical approach to development. Chang's high-ranking advisers drew their key ideas about economic growth from Walt Rostow's modernization theory. Their goals were to engage American bureaucrats, to attract US support, to maintain the flow of aid, and to utilize a modern development model to gain greater credibility for their regime. Despite these efforts, the momentum which emerged in the Eisenhower period to reshape Korea's political economy carried over into the diplomacy of the Kennedy administration. Washington officials remained critical of Korea's monetary policies and unsympathetic to the political dilemmas that economic reforms signified for Prime Minister Chang.

Prior to the 1961 military coup, then, Korean governments faced increased external pressures from American policy-makers who made it clear that they preferred a modernization ethos which combined conservative monetary policy with strong elements of state dirigisme. US planners rejected the Rhee regime because its internal corruption threatened to radicalize the Korean public and to initiate a period of significant social conflict in the republic from which the Left might benefit. By 1961, officials like Walt Rostow viewed Chang's government as ineffective and unable to implement economic reform. They accepted the military regime because they believed its authoritarian style of governance would be more efficient than the second republic in mobilizing the nation's resources for development. The US–Korean partnership remained close for the rest of the Kennedy and Johnson years, not only due to shared cold war ideals, but also because the two allies believed the main priority of the Korean government should be to foster economic growth. Building a democratic state remained a secondary objective of the leadership of both countries, and development in the absence of democracy became an enduring aspect of Korea's capitalist modernity during the Park era and after. This chapter examines the period leading up to the coup as a way of understanding the historical roots of this story. We begin our analysis with an overview of the political economy of American–Korean relations in the decade following 1948.

State-building: US–ROK relations, 1948–1958

In the early cold war, American and Korean officials were primarily concerned with preserving the integrity of the new South Korean state. In light of the ongoing violent clashes between Leftists and Rightists in the South, President Rhee declared in early 1950 that "national security [was] the most important problem facing the Republic" (United States National Archives [hereafter USNA] RG469E-80 1950). The Truman administration included Korea in its foreign aid programs in order to sustain Rhee's anti-communist stance. National Security Council document NSC 8/2, approved in the late winter of 1949, articulated the United States' major objectives vis-à-vis Korea. It argued that the pro-Western orientation of the ROK could be maintained if the US continued to provide military aid to the regime. The goal was to integrate South Korea into America's global security and economic nexus, and in the long term to ensure that the ROK would be capable of sustaining itself without substantial amounts of foreign aid (Lee 1996: 187–191; United States Department of State 1976: 975–978).

The Korean conflict increased South Korea's dependence on the US but it also resulted in a tremendous expansion of the Korean army – from a force of about 95,000 at the outbreak of the war to 655,000 by March 1954.[2] Partly as a result of the increased global costs of military assistance and the consequences of negotiating an armistice in Korea, the US government reorganized its relief program for the peninsula in August 1953. The new set-up reflected a desire to underwrite Korea's military power as the first priority of economic assistance. The Commander-in-Chief of the United Nations Command (CINCUNC) became responsible for overall relief, reconstruction, and rehabilitation of the ROK economy, and a civilian administrator was appointed to his staff to ensure coordination of US aid with Korean resources. The principal Washington agency for delivering assistance was the newly established Foreign Operations Administration, which became the International Cooperation Administration (ICA) in 1955 and the Agency for International Development (AID) in 1961. In addition, the United Nations Korean Reconstruction Agency planned reconstruction projects in areas such as power, mining, fisheries, education, and industry (Lee 2002; United States Information Agency 1956).

By the mid-1950s the American government was spending more than US$500 million annually in support of Korea's armed forces (United States Department of State 1993: 315–316). Korean recruits were much less expensive to maintain than US troops, and the United States designed the new proxy army to help carry America's global containment burden. Nevertheless, the weight of this military establishment had tremendous implications for the Korean economy. Although it facilitated the import substitution strategies of the government to some degree, it also drained resources which otherwise could have gone into development programs. The Rhee government, dissatisfied with the armistice, criticized the foreign assistance program for being inefficient and for spending too much in Japan on the procurement of goods for Korea. Officials also urgently insisted on an additional fifteen to twenty divisions for the army – a doubling of existing force ceilings – with the hope that they could restart the war against the north and carry out the military reunification of the peninsula. Although these demands have been seen by historians in military terms, they also reflected prevailing assumptions in the republic about the limited capacity of the South Korean economy, and a belief that unification would re-create conditions under which a strong economy could emerge. Minister of Foreign Affairs Pyŏn Yŏng-t'ae supported the President's desire to attack North Korea, saying at a meeting with US officials in January 1954 that it was his government's wish to have a "balanced" military force of thirty-five divisions. Unless this were done, South Korea might "eventually fall of [its] own weight and be incorporated in Communist Korea" (USNA RG59 1954).

Many American bureaucrats were similarly pessimistic about South Korea's economic prospects. In October 1956, Walter Dowling, the American ambassador stationed in Seoul, reviewed America's aid programs to Korea. He wrote that "Korea can become self-supporting only when the country is unified." In light of this, it was important to "develop in the economy an ability to contribute to its own support and provide a basis for a minimum rate of growth." Much of his report emphasized the importance of expanding Korea's primary agricultural and mineral export potential. He showed only a passing interest in industrial development, though his analysis did express concern about the balance of payments deficit: in the 1956 fiscal year Korea imported $95 million in goods while exporting only $17 million (USNA RG84 1956b). Policy-makers like William Warne, the UNC economic coordinator, were more experienced and knowledgable about the difficulties Korean manufacturers faced in international markets, but we should be careful not to exaggerate the ability of American officials to provide solutions to the challenges of Korean development in the 1950s and 1960s.

Korean policy-makers also took their own economic initiatives, and in the mid-1950s began to develop longer range economic plans. Although the Korean economy in the 1950s is sometimes portrayed as stagnant, recent work has demonstrated that industrial production grew significantly for a number of years in the latter part of the decade (Woo 1991: ch. 3). The period from 1955 to 1958 in particular was one of relatively low inflation, price stability, and accelerated industrial production. Even so, the country had a very high unemployment rate – as many as 1,135,000 people in a population of twenty-two million were without jobs in 1956. In the context of this critical unemployment problem, Korean officials pushed for more help from the US. In March 1956 the economic coordinator, Paek Tu-chin, told secretary Dulles and other high-ranking officials that the war had caused $5 billion in damage, and that additional assistance should accompany a long-range plan for the economy. He revealed that the Korean government was currently working on such a plan, and that bureaucrats estimated that the economy would need an injection of $2.4 billion over the next five years. Citing Korea's high unemployment and underemployment figures, he stated that "the five year plan did not take into account military requirements." Paek's request for economic support was thus also designed to raise the level of American military aid. Dulles made no commitment to the proposal, but warned that "American economic aid was not accorded on the basis of friendship but as a contribution to winning the cold war" (USNA RG84 1956a). The United States soon cut its assistance program to Korea.

By 1956, the Eisenhower administration was under significant pressure to reduce its budget and foreign aid programs. Economic conditions in the US, and American's position in the global political economy, now shaped the government's response to Korean initiatives. In June 1956, the Chair of the House Foreign Affairs Committee, Democratic congressman James P. Richards, told House representatives that the changed international situation since the end of the Korean War had required significant cuts to the administration's Foreign Assistance Bill. Although he supported the mutual security program as a means of reducing America's overall national security expenditures, he pointed out that there were several "situations in the world which make it clear that we should not continue to spend money in the same old way or in the same old places as we have in the past" (United States Congress 1956: 9668).

Congressional dissatisfaction with the high costs of aid influenced the Eisenhower administration's diplomacy toward Korea. In 1957 and 1958 the United States began to revise the framework in which its economic aid to the country operated. While renewing their emphasis on achieving an economically viable state, officials now called for decreases in the size of the ROK military. In January 1957, Secretary of the Treasury George Humphrey told the National Security Council that "[we] must clearly realize that the United States cannot go on for another ten years, as it had for the past ten years, spending our resources on military aid programs currently in effect. Such a course would be suicidal for the United States." He recommended that "the Council fit Korea into a general program which would notably reduce the size and expenditures for our military assistance programs world-wide." Secretary of State John Foster Dulles agreed with Humphrey's arguments. In August he stated that "the United States was not in a position to sustain the costs of supporting the present level of the South Korean forces to the tune of $700 million a year. Congress was going to insist on a very sharp cut in our military assistance and defense support programs world-wide" (United States Department of State 1993: 397, 483).

A new national security report on Korea, NSC 5702/2, embodied this revised thinking. Adopted in August 1957, the document reflected a strategy of "getting more for giving less." It recommended reductions in Korea's armed forces and new strategies for dealing with economic problems. These included "reducing Korean dependence on U.S. assistance and making greater progress toward the ultimate goal of a self-supporting economy." The Korean government should use aid more effectively to implement "sound economic and fiscal policies," to direct growth into investment rather than into consumption, and to stimulate private investment. In addition, the US should "encourage the ROK to take the necessary steps toward normal commercial relations with other Free World countries, particularly Japan" (United States Department of State 1993: 493–495).

Until the late 1950s, Korea's economic performance had fostered a belief that more time would be necessary before the country could be firmly integrated into the Northeast Asian political economy, but pressures to link Korea and Japan were increasing in the face of Japan's growing economic productivity. Linking the Japanese and South Korean economies into an Asian anti-communist regional nexus was a crucial part of America's global containment strategy. Although ROK–Japan relations in the period 1958 to 1960 were poor, partly due to the Japanese decision to return ethnic Koreans living in Japan to North Korea, Japan's increasing prosperity and its new presence in international forums such as the General Agreement on Tariffs and Trade contributed to the Eisenhower administration's decision to intervene more decisively in Korean economic issues. Secretary Dulles told the Chiefs of Mission Conference in 1958:

> we have the feeling that Japan has tended to resume, for the first time since its defeat in World War II, its role as a major power of the world. We also feel that U.S. policy will be furthered by accepting that role rather than by trying to maintain Japan in a somewhat secondary or subservient position. . . . Japan has already started to play a role in the balance of power in the Far East and we think it likely that they would be disposed to orient their policies further in that direction.
>
> (USNA RG84 1958a)

Such strategic and economic thinking became a significant source of conflict between the Rhee and Eisenhower administrations. President Rhee was very critical of a policy he perceived as undermining joint Korean and American interests. In the summer of 1958, for example, the President told several reporters:

> We Koreans have not forgotten. Neither have other free Asians and neither should Americans. Nor should we forget the Japanese atrocities of a historical era that is so recent.... Neither have I heard the Japanese Government nor the Japanese people publicly express regret for the great crimes committed against their friendly ally of today, the United States of America.
>
> (Republic of Korea Washington Embassy 1957)

ROK officials also publicly expressed their suspicions of Japanese diplomacy toward the communist world. They believed that the Japanese government's willingness to normalize relations with the Soviet Union, to trade with communist China, and to negotiate with North Korea demonstrated that it was not fully committed to fighting the cold war. In May 1958 Korea's ambassador in Washington, Yang You-chan, warned a group of political and social scientists in Philadelphia that Japan "is working out its own mode of 'neutralist' relations with the Communist nations.... The Communist countries offer what seems to the Japanese commercial interest an attractive alternative" (Republic of Korea Washington Embassy 1958).

By 1958 American officials had rejected South Korean arguments about the need for immediate unification, increased economic assistance, expanding the size of the ROK military, and strategy toward Japan. Furthermore, they were now inclined to take a more direct role in shaping Korea's economic policies. At the March 1958 Chiefs of Mission Conference ambassador Dowling reported that the United States government should now place more emphasis on dealing with Korea's economic problems. US assistance packages would work properly only if local governments pursued strategies consistent with development, and it was now appropriate for the US to "encourage recipient governments to adopt sound policies." American aid programs should be used "when possible, as leverage in getting them to institute necessary reforms." Dowling was "convinced that if more of our energies were devoted to these internal policy questions, the overall effectiveness of our efforts would be substantially increased" (USNA RG84 1958b).

Although there had been significant policy differences in Korean–American relations prior to 1958, this year was a turning point for the Eisenhower administration's diplomacy toward the peninsula. It now became increasingly hostile to the Rhee regime, and tensions escalated when officials decided in 1959 and 1960 to push harder to achieve a set of economic stabilization reforms associated with the dollar–*hwan* exchange rate. To understand the political dimensions of these events, we need briefly to examine how American officials viewed the question of President Rhee's succession and how the Korean Liberal Party used the aid regime in the 1950s to strengthen its internal political position.

US economic planning for Korea in the 1950s was bound up in the question of what the government should do in the event that President Rhee passed away. The issue of succession was first raised in a significant way during the 1952 political crisis when the Korean government used intimidation tactics and coercion to persuade the national assembly to pass a constitutional amendment which permitted the President to run for reelection. At the time, Army Chief-of-Staff Lee Choung Chang approached Counselor H. Allen Lightner with a plan to use UN and Korean military forces to depose Rhee and to set up an interim administration. The temporary government would stay in power until free elections were held (see Keefer 1991; Lee 1994). In Washington, a decision was taken not to depose Rhee, largely because no secure political alternative was thought to be available. Initially the events of 1952 seemed to confirm the importance of maintaining US support for Rhee. After the war, American officials believed that no other Korean leader had the ability or legitimacy to maintain the country's political stability. In the mid-1950s, however, much thought began to be given to the question of Rhee's successor. In February 1956, Secretary Dulles remarked:

> with respect to the problem of President Rhee's death, this could conceivably end up in a situation which would enable the United States to deal more rationally with the problem of Korea. . . . [If] Rhee should die and we could get through the immediate crisis which would follow, we might end up with a better situation. Until then, it was hard to see what else we can do in Korea than what we are doing.
>
> (United States Department of State 1993: 218)

At the time, American diplomats hoped and believed that the speaker of the national assembly, Yi Ki-bung, would succeed the aging president, but this scenario became complicated when Chang Myŏn, a member of the opposition Democratic Party, was elected to the vice-presidency in 1956. Yi's health also began to decline in the later 1950s. By 1958, on the eve of the extended crisis in Korea–US relations, American officials were upset by Rhee's persistent efforts to go against America's containment strategy for Northeast Asia and yet uncertain about who could replace him without seriously threatening political stability. The frustration was personified by Secretary Dulles, when, at a meeting of the National Security Council on 8 August 1958, he "expressed some frank and unflattering views of President Rhee." President Dwight D. Eisenhower and Secretary Dulles both held negative and stereotyped images of Rhee. Dulles even referred to the Korean President as an "Oriental bargainer" and a "master of evasion" (cited in Cumings 1997: 306). As late as 30 January 1959, the Director of the Office of Northeast Asian Affairs, Howard J. Parsons, argued that "With respect to Presidential succession in the ROK . . . we are uncertain that Yi Ki-bung could succeed, but do not know who would take his place" (United States Department of State 1993: 485).

In 1959 and 1960, concern about who would replace Rhee became secondary to the larger problem of finding a way to deflect the government from pursuing policies which the US feared might lead to its overthrow in a potentially violent and unpredictable revolt. Officials expressed exaggerated worries that "communists" would take advantage of popular unrest and bring a Leftist government to power. This would significantly limit the United States' influence in Korea and weaken America's global prestige.

The political economy of corruption and the emerging crisis in US–Korea relations, 1958–1959

In the 1950s, major benefactors of the Korean government's foreign aid regime and low exchange rates were Korean companies that produced goods based on imports from the US. These businesses included various sugar, flour, and textile corporations, some of which, like Samsung's Cheil Sugar, began to dominate the Korean market in this era. The overvalued *hwan* provided the Liberal Party with significant kickbacks, as licenses to import US goods could only be issued by the Korean government (Haggard *et al.* 1991: 854). Since the state also controlled reconstruction contracts, the government played a very large role in determining which companies received the benefits of US rehabilitation projects. Contracts were often a function of political dealings, and businesses frequently paid money to the ruling party after receiving government favors. After the collapse of the Rhee regime, one businessman reflected: "Just by saving what I used to give the Liberals in bribes . . . I can re-equip my plant within a year" (cited in Lie 1998: 33–34).

The financial benefits which the Liberal Party received from America's extended aid program in the mid-1950s were thus significant. In the context of declining American aid to South Korea after 1957, however, members of the party began to consider other methods of retaining power. They soon began to intimidate and persecute their political opposition and to consider using fraudulent means to fix elections.

An initial indicator of this corruption appeared in early 1958 when the Korean government arrested Cho Bong-am, chairman of the Korean Progressive [Socialist] Party and prominent opponent of the President. The state charged Cho with violating the ROK National Security Act. Cho was a strong contender for the 1960 presidential race, and the reason for his arrest was political: to weaken the Progressives in the national assembly prior to the spring elections, and to eliminate opposition to President Rhee.[3] US diplomats were concerned about the domestic and international implications of the arrest and trial of Cho, but their representations made no difference and he was hanged on 31 July 1959 for espionage.

In November 1958 the ROK government took another step toward repressing the opposition by submitting a new national security law to the national assembly. The bill included a clause stating that "anyone who has benefited the enemy by disturbing the people by reporting or spreading false facts or distorted news" could be punished (USNA RG84 1958c). The hardliners who believed a stronger national security act and state repression would sustain them in power included Home Minister Ch'oe In-gyu, a major organizer of the election fraud in 1960, National Police Director Yi Kang-hak, and Justice Minister Hong Chin-ki. One person who stood to gain from their policies was Yi Ki-bung, the vice-presidential candidate in the 1960 elections, and would-be successor to Rhee. Given his ongoing health problems and physical weakness, Yi may also have been a convenient figurehead for the machinations of the other hardliners in cabinet. In the aftermath of the violence and fraud of the 1960 elections Yi and his family committed suicide.

The increased state repression in Korea was closely monitored by the United States Embassy in Seoul. An alarmed Ambassador Dowling wrote Washington in late 1958 that if those who wanted to rig the 1960 election succeeded in dominating the Liberal Party, there would be a steady deterioration in the political situation over the coming year. If, on the other hand, the hardliners failed, the more moderate elements of the party would be able to reassert themselves. According to Dowling, the outcome of the struggle would be "decisive for [the] political future of Korea" (USNA RG84 1958d).

The ambassador's prognosis for US–Korea relations soon became more pessimistic. On 22 December he wrote the State Department that if the National Security Act amendment was passed, it would "set in motion series of actions resulting in complete discredit ROK Government on international scene, and which will require active opposition of U.S. at one stage or another. . . . I fear that we run grave risk of serious loss of influence here if ROK government persists in enactment present version of amendment, and then 'gets away with it'" (United States Department of State 1994: 519). Two days later, the government pushed through the amendment to the law by forcibly preventing opposition members from attending the national assembly meeting and by locking them in basement rooms.

In Washington, Assistant Secretary of State for Far Eastern Affairs Walter S. Robertson met with the Korean ambassador to the US, Yang You-chan, to express his displeasure with the tactics and decisions of the Korean government. Yang agreed that the methods used to pass the law were "not good" but implied that they were needed to prevent the government from being overthrown by "its enemies." To this, Robertson replied that "the type of action which was taken on 24 December is the kind that can lead to the eventual overthrow of the Republic of Korea by giving ammunition to the real foes of Korea" (United States Department of State 1994: 528).

At this point the American Embassy in Korea recommended that additional pressure be placed on the regime to alter its policies. In late January 1959 Dowling wrote to Robertson:

> When President Rhee is no longer on the scene (he is now 84 years old), the Liberal Party will probably be unable for long to maintain control even by continued use of forceful measures ... to adopt a passive role will mean that we must face a constantly deteriorating situation leading almost certainly to civil turmoil – a situation the Communists will be quick to exploit.

He recommended that American journalists be sent to Korea to report on political events; that prominent members of Congress be encouraged to moderate the position of Rhee and the dangerous elements of the Liberal Party; that further economic aid be withheld; and that the US government formally protest the failure of the ROK to enact sound economic reforms (United States Department of State 1994: 537–540). The courses of action recommended by Dowling to deal with the internal situation in Korea were approved somewhat reluctantly by Secretary Dulles on 27 January 1959 (United States Department of State 1994: 540 fn 3).[4]

Significantly, US policy-makers now associated economic progress with political stability. In 1959 they began to put pressure on the Korean government to alter its financial policy as part of an effort to weaken the position of the hardliners and to demonstrate American dissatisfaction with the regime's corrupt and authoritarian practices. In this way economic modernization was linked to efforts to sustain US political influence on the peninsula. A key US objective was the promotion and emergence of a moderate leadership group who would sustain the confidence of the Korean public and maintain a strong commitment to anticommunism. Diplomats couched their arguments in terms of the need to protect and develop Korea's democratic values, but their primary fear was that the US might not be able to preserve the political viability of their alliance partner. J. Graham Parsons, Assistant Secretary of State for Far Eastern Affairs, wrote:

> the failure of democracy in Korea at this critical juncture can only lead to the disillusionment of the Korean people, not only with democratic principles and practices, but with the United States to whom these people for over the past decade looked for leadership

> and guidance. In the ensuing vacuum, we fear that only extremist solutions can result.
>
> (United States Department of State 1994: 592)

Indeed, a political catastrophe in Korea, defined as continued authoritarian rule leading to the emergence of a Leftist government susceptible to "communist" influence, would be a disaster for US policies throughout the developing world. According to Parsons, "the failure of democracy in Korea would be considered by many nations as the total failure of the applicability of our system for the nations of Afro-Asia, with the subsequent decline of American influence and prestige within this area" (United States Department of State 1994: 590). Ultimately, American policy-makers were more concerned with stability and their global prestige than with democratic practice.

Parsons believed that the United States had the capability of dealing with Korea's "flagrant abuses of democratic institutions" provided it chose its "weapons carefully and employ[ed] them firmly but discreetly. Such actions would have the support of the majority of the Korean people and moderate leadership groups even within the Liberal Party and Government" (United States Department of State 1994: 591). But who were the moderates in Rhee's government? What interests did they represent? There never seems to have been any sophisticated analysis of the "moderate" and "hardline" factions in the Rhee government. Those people whom the United States associated with more moderate positions included the ex-Minister of Reconstruction and current Minister of Finance Sŏng Insang, Defense Minister Kim Chung-yuk, Minister of Reconstruction Shin Hyŏn-hwak, and Minister of Commerce Kim Yong-chan. Many of these officials were defined as moderates because they were sympathetic to America's plans for Korea's economic development, including reforms of the *hwan*–dollar exchange rate.

Economic reform, the exchange rate, and the 1960 political crisis

Ambassador Dowling's recommendations to stabilize the Korean political situation were implemented by the Department of State over the course of 1959 and 1960. However, some of these policies threatened America's short-term partnership with the "moderates" in the Rhee Cabinet. The problem facing US officials was that the moderate faction played a politically marginal role in Cabinet and were therefore vulnerable allies. Up to 1960 the Rhee government had needed the moderates to maintain power. Sŏng In-sang, for example, represented a symbol of limited cooperation with American objectives in Korea. As long as there had been some Koreans willing to go along with US advice, American policy-makers had been prepared to accept ROK economic inefficiencies and political authoritarianism as the price of political stability. Between 1958 and 1960 that implicit political bargain between the US and the ROK began weakening, and in 1960 it fell apart, since the US government was prepared to sacrifice moderates as part of a broader strategy of shifting the balance of power away from hardliners in the Korean Cabinet.

The major reform which US policy-makers began to consider in late 1959 dealt with the exchange rate. The ROK–US stabilization programs of the mid-1950s had not been aimed at undermining the so-called "rent-seeking sector" of the Korean economy, associated with the use of foreign aid to build up the power of the Liberal Party. The United States now decided to attack the abuses of that system to indicate its discontent with the political strategies of the regime. Throughout the next three months the Secretary of State and the Northeast Asian Affairs Bureau showed no willingness to compromise with the Rhee government. This policy reflected the decline in the Korean–American partnership and showed that the US was unconcerned with the significant political dilemmas which economic reform caused in Korea. In short, the American government was indicating that it wanted changes in the political direction of the Liberal Party, and indeed the government as a whole.

A 1955 agreement between South Korea and the United States had pegged the exchange rate at 500 *hwan* to the dollar, and in 1957 the two governments agreed that the rate would remain the same so long as the Seoul wholesale price index did not increase more than an average of 25 percent over a six-month period – January to July, or July to December – compared to the index for September 1955. In the second half of 1959 the wholesale price index averaged 30 percent above the 1955 prices, and on 18 December 1959 Washington told the embassy in Seoul to inform the Korean government that, following the arrangements made in 1957, the *hwan*–dollar rate should be changed to 650–1 before 20 January 1960. In addition, negotiations with the Korean government should begin for a 1,200–1,400 rate for all UNC expenditures. "Tourists" – that is, American civilians and officials in Korea – should also receive this rate, though the US government was prepared to settle for a 1,000 *hwan* rate for both the UNC and civilians. The ROK could have a six-month grace period to implement the 650 *hwan* adjustment if it agreed before 20 January to a minimum exchange rate of 1,000-1 for the UNC and for US personnel in Korea (USNA RG84 1959c).

In economic terms, American pressure in 1960 to alter Korea's exchange rate underlined a stronger US determination to encourage Korean exports. A lower-valued *hwan* would make Korean goods more competitive in foreign markets. At the same time, the new rate would help the executive branch deal with Congressional criticism, since it would raise the amount of counterpart funds available for aid projects decided jointly by the Korean and American governments. Every dollar of US aid would thus generate more *hwan* for Korean development. The Korean government, however, opposed the American initiative.

Since his appointment in 1955 to head the new Ministry of Reconstruction, Sŏng In-sang had worked closely with American diplomats. In early 1960 he became subjected to a major political battle between the Rhee and American governments. The Korean government viewed the exchange rate as a critical element of its economic program, and, in the context of the upcoming general elections, hardliners saw the US demands as a threat. Sŏng met with embassy officials on a number of occasions from December 1959 to February 1960 to discuss exchange rate reform. In these meetings the Minister expressed his surprise about the US position and warned that it could create a crisis in the relationship between the two countries (USNA RG84 1960a). He suggested that if the ROK, at US insistence, honored its economic commitments under the 1955 agreement, the government would then not be willing to alter the UNC and "tourist" rates. At a meeting with the new American Ambassador, Walter P. McConaughy, Sŏng said the 500-1 rate was the "cornerstone" of the President's economic policy and that the rate problem was "particularly sensitive from both political and economic viewpoints." He queried why the US had suddenly shifted its position. Change should come gradually, he opined, "not by pushing hard at the front door." An adjustment would require a major amendment to the new budget and would give "political advantage" to the opposition party in the forthcoming election. Bureaucrats in Washington anticipated this link between the elections and the exchange rate. Privately, embassy officials believed that the Minister was sympathetic to the US position but that he was in a difficult position due to his inability to convince the President and other Cabinet members of the correctness of the American recommendations (USNA RG84 1960b).

Ambassador McConaughy initially supported Washington's new negotiating position. Although he recognized that US pressure would hurt the bilateral relationship in the short term, and might even result in the resignation of Sŏng, he believed the exchange rate was "so basic to achievement of our economic objectives in Korea that it should not be avoided any longer. To do so would mean prolonging and aggravating disruptive economic effects of present rate, continuing payment excessive costs maintenance U.S. forces in Korea, and obtaining less than fully effective use [of] U.S. aid." The Ambassador also acknowledged that the increase in counterpart funds resulting from a rate change would increase America's "voice in ROK financial affairs" and that this would probably not be welcomed by the Rhee regime. The chances of maintaining price stability after the election would be enhanced if Rhee was in office, and his "effective and highly centralized control of government apparatus would be instrumental in achieving successful transition to new rate" (USNA RG84 1960c). Officials in Washington, however, were more concerned with altering the relative power balance in the Rhee government than was McConaughy, and this became more evident in late January and February.

During a series of meetings with embassy officials early in 1960 Sŏng made several compromise proposals to the United States government. On 28 January, for example, he suggested a delay in implementing the 650 *hwan* rate until after the elections in return for an agreement to set the tourist rate at 1,000-1 and to expand Korean service contracts with the UNC by several million dollars. McConaughy now recommended that Washington accept Sŏng's compromises, saying they represented important concessions that met American economic demands. An agreement now would also save the Minister's career and keep US–Korea relations on a good footing (USNA RG84 1960d). He also argued that the events surrounding Cho's execution and the passing of the National Security Law were not representative of wider trends in the relationship between the Korean executive and the legislative branches of government. Over the past several years, he noted, the Korean executive had developed a "healthy respect for legislative prerogatives." Since the proposed revision to the exchange rate also related to taxation issues which were a prerogative of the national assembly, pushing forward with the exchange reform would create angry accusations that the executive was overstepping its power and undermining legislative prerogative (USNA RG84 1960f).

Washington bureaucrats dismissed these arguments and demanded that Korea meet its full obligations under the 1957 agreement. On 24 January, Secretary Herter wrote that "If Minister Song [is] expendable on this issue he may be expendable whenever it suits ROKG purposes" (USNA RG84 1960e). The department also cited its concerns about congressional reactions. These factored very heavily in its deliberations. Accepting the ROK position would put the executive branch in the untenable position of telling Congress that it agreed to postpone action on the exchange rate "merely because of possible effect on ROK elections" (USNA RG84 1960h). On 29 January, during the ongoing negotiations with the Koreans, the American Embassy in Seoul, under directions from Washington, issued a unilateral declaration stating that commencing on 29 January the official exchange rate would be 650 to 1. President Rhee then issued a statement saying his government would uphold its international agreement but that negotiations with the Americans over exchange rate issues were still underway (USNA RG59 1960b).

The United States government's willingness to compromise had been severely eroded by the ROK government's political policies since 1958, and state department officials were no longer concerned about the political impact of a breach in US–ROK relations. For Washington planners, the exchange rate issue became a larger symbol of the ROK government's willingness to assume more responsible economic and political positions. US pressure to change the rate would demonstrate a new-found seriousness to US negotiating strategy, and would contribute to a wider policy of confronting the hardliners. Since Sŏng was forced to negotiate on the basis of hardliners' arguments, Sŏng's own position in the ROK government became temporarily expendable. He was not to be used by the existing government to escape changes in the exchange rate.

From Washington's point of view, McConaughy's arguments failed to see that lessening the pressure at this time would be a concession to the hardliners in the Liberal Party, whose plans to win the next election through fraudulent means might lead the country into chaos, and possibly revolution. Now, more than ever, it was important to make the ROK a viable economic entity, capable of operating in the long term without continued substantial amounts of US aid. On 11 February Secretary Herter wrote McConaughy that "ROKG failure to make immediate adjustment in direction of major reform would be evidence ROK did not intend to contribute to its own economic development and stability and assure maximum effectiveness of U.S. aid" (USNA RG84 1960h). His message had the support of top officials in the Departments of State, the Treasury, Defense, and the International Cooperation Administration. Herter "fully appreciated" the position of the embassy but South Korea had lost support both in the administration and Congress as a result of the "events of past year beginning with December 24, 1958 incident involving passage of national security law" (USNA RG84 1960g).

Ultimately, Rhee was not prepared to create a breach in his government's relations with the United States, and on 23 February Sŏng announced his government's decision to devalue the *hwan* to 650–1. Negotiations would be held later in the year to discuss a more realistic exchange rate. Washington's strategy had achieved its immediate economic goals, but the crisis in US–ROK had not yet reached its peak. The balance of power within the Rhee government remained the same. The defeat of the hardliners on the exchange rate issue did not prevent them from organizing fraudulent elections.

On 3 February, amidst the intense negotiations over the exchange rate, the Korean government announced that the presidential election would be held on 15 March 1960, and not in May or later as had been hoped by the opposition Democratic Party. May elections had been an established practice in the ROK, but even before the winter of 1959 President Rhee had spoken publicly about the possibility of moving the date forward to 1960. By January and February 1960, the tenor of discussions over the exchange rate could only have reinforced in party officials' minds the advantages of holding early elections.

The rise in the exchange rate adversely affected those who were dependent upon imported aid goods from the United States. This included farmers, whose fertilizer was supplied indirectly through American aid provided by the International Cooperation Administration. In announcing the revised rate on 23 February, Minister Sŏng stated that it would have a "significant effect on the rural economy" and that the government was considering measures to deal with problems which would arise in the countryside. Partly to compensate for the increased costs of purchasing fertilizer, the Korean government requested the Americans to allow counterpart funds originating from ICA fertilizer purchases to be calculated at the old 500–1 exchange rate. This request was rejected by the United States Operating Mission in Seoul in late February (USNA RG59 1960c). Several weeks later, the Rhee administration adopted a new bond program which provided long-term loans with low interest to people engaged in farming and fishing. Although the program was only announced on 4 March, the government intended that the first round of bond sales, worth 2.5 billion *hwan*, would end by 10 March, only five days before the election (USNA RG59 1960d).

By this time, the Democratic Party leaders were accusing the Liberals of planning to hold fraudulent elections and of using intimidation tactics against voters. The Democratic Party had itself been significantly penalized by the calling of the early elections. At the time the elections were announced, party leader Cho Pyŏng-ok was undertaking medical treatment in Washington for cancer, and it was unclear when he might recover. He subsequently died on 16 February, leaving the party leaderless in the election. This meant that the real contest in the upcoming vote would be for the vice-presidential position, and the candidates for that were the incumbent Chang Myŏn and Yi Ki-bung. On 1 March, the Democratic Party exposed a plan by Liberal Party members to rig the election so that it would appear that 85 percent of the vote had gone to President Rhee and Yi Ki-bung. To do this the party would stuff ballot boxes with forged votes, permit double-counting by Liberal voters, prohibit known opposition party supporters from casting a ballot, and turn various anticommunist youth groups against the opposition. American officials continued to express their deep concern about events on the peninsula. A memorandum from the acting Secretary of State, John M. Steeves, to Herter on 10 March pointed out that reports that the Liberal Party planned "to perpetrate massive election frauds" might be authentic. Steeves concluded that the elections would cause a "serious setback" to democracy in the ROK, undermine the two-party political system, weaken Korea's international prestige, undermine the US Congress's willingness to support Korea's economic aid program, and make the Rhee regime even more intransigent in its relations with the US (United States Department of State 1994: 602).

Riots which broke out in Masan city on the day of the election confirmed the administration's worst fears about the consequences of government corruption. Just two days after the election the embassy recommended economic sanctions and reported that "if we define basis US objective in Korea as the encouragement of a politically stable and militarily strong nation which is pro-US and anti-Communist in character, then these objectives fundamentally threatened by direction of current events" (United States Department of State 1994: 609). After several weeks of persistent demonstrations against the Rhee regime, McConaughy warned Washington:

> there is growing atmosphere of popular resentment which could suddenly take most dangerous turn leaving situation wide open for Communist manipulation. Severe repressive ROKG measures to control such situation would only deepen popular antagonism, blacken ROKG reputation before world, and leave this nation even more susceptible to Communist subversion.
>
> (United States Department of State 1994: 618)

On 19 April Rhee declared a state of martial law in Seoul. On that day alone, clashes between civilians on the one hand, and the military and police forces on the other, resulted in 115 deaths and 773 injuries in urban areas across the country. In the United States, President Eisenhower spoke with Secretary Herter aboard the presidential yacht *Augusta.* "We just have to get tough with Rhee," Eisenhower admonished, "and tell him that we fought for the freedom of South Korea and that unless Rhee permits free elections and the people are given the right to vote, there is just no sense in our being in Korea." Herter replied: "while we are technically interfering with the internal affairs of Korea, there are special justifications in this case" (United States Department of State 1994: 623). Washington instructed the embassy in Seoul on the same day to meet with "responsible" ROK leaders and to inform the Rhee government that it must repeal the controversial articles of the National Security Law, reopen the offices of the newspaper associated with the opposition Democratic Party, the *Kyŏnghyang Sinmun,* remove officials responsible for election fraud, and give the Korean people an opportunity for free elections (United States Department of State 1994: 624–626).

The Eisenhower administration now told Rhee to hold new elections. In the face of tremendous American and public pressure, Rhee ordered Yi Ki-bung to resign; Ambassador McConaughy effectively secured the President's resignation during a meeting with him on 26 April. This was a logical end to a policy which had been emerging in the United States since 1958. Top officials in the Department of State, including Under-Secretary of State for Political Affairs Livingston Merchant, and Assistant Secretary of State for Far Eastern Affairs J. Graham Parsons, acknowledged this in April when they approved a telegram instructing McConaughy to maintain a firm stance against Rhee "in light what Dept considers to have been effective results new policy adopted last January." Only by getting the Korean government "to pursue constructive programs both domestically and internationally" could the US avoid the risks of a "gradual deterioration" or even a "disintegration" in the longer term Korean–American relationship (United States Department of State 1994: 635). In a similar vein, Loy Henderson, Deputy Under-Secretary of State, wrote to McConaughy:

"we had concluded here that time had come for Rhee to step down if public confidence in ROKG was to be restored and even more explosive situation susceptible Communist exploitation prevented from developing." Now that Rhee had resigned, "real new vistas in entirely new era US–Korean relations open before us which will require our best imaginative efforts on priority basis" (United States Department of State 1994: 645–646).

Henderson's optimism was misplaced. The economic challenges which faced the Republic of Korea in 1959 and 1960 remained following Rhee's removal from power. Furthermore, there was a high degree of continuity in US diplomacy. While American plans for Korea were rooted in economic and strategic factors which challenged the global power of the United States in the late 1950s, the willingness of American officials to press for reform was also intimately linked to their experiences in the final year of the Syngman Rhee regime, and to a fear that unless they involved themselves deeply in the affairs of Korea, they might lose their influence over "the Republic of Korea," an erstwhile ally and cold war partner.

It is true that by early 1960 the broad framework around which the American government would try to shape Korean economic development in the next three years was in place. Renewed emphasis on exchange rate reform, improved Japanese and Korean economic relations, emphasis on an export economy, and closer linkages between economic aid programs and Korean fiscal and monetary policy – all these themes would be stressed with greater vigor after 1960. But Korean planners had their own forward-looking plans for the economy. In February 1960, for example, the Ministry of Commerce and Industry submitted proposals to improve Korean exports to the ROK Balance of Payments Committee. The recommendations included the creation of an export-import bank, tax exemptions for companies engaging in export, the creation of an export promotion corporation, and improving Korean commercial and sales knowledge (USNA RG59 1960a). Officials also developed a three-year plan which envisaged large increases in exports and high GNP growth rates. These were criticized by members of the United States operating mission for being too high, but they were a reflection of ambitions which Korean bureaucrats articulated for their economy (USNA RG59 1960e).

The second republic, Walt Rostow, and modernization theory

The Chang Myŏn regime, which came to power in the summer of 1960 after the newly formed second republic held democratic national elections, adopted many policies which American officials had sought to achieve in the late Rhee era. The platform of the Democratic Party had been articulated amidst the growing tensions in American–Korean relations in the late 1950s, and had been designed to demonstrate to the

United States the party's disillusionment with the economic and political strategies adopted by Rhee's administration.

In 1958 and 1959 Chang Myŏn and others in the Democratic Party had tried to convey to American officials that they would be better allies to work with than the existing government. In February 1959, party representatives met with William H. Draper, a former general and a key figure in designing America's global economic and containment strategies. He had been economic adviser to General Lucius Clay in occupied Germany, and, in 1948, as Under-Secretary of the Army, had played a leading role in rehabilitating the Japanese economy and launching the "reverse course." In 1959 he visited Korea as part of a broader investigation into America's Mutual Security Program in Asia. His presence in the republic reflected the changing circumstances in which American aid programs were operating, as well as a new sense of urgency in Washington to streamline aid programs and to make them more productive.

A group of Democratic National Assemblymen led by Dr. Cho Pyŏng-ok met with Draper. The representatives told the visiting senior statesperson that Korea should negotiate more realistic exchange rates, place greater emphasis on long-term planning, and develop its export industries (USNA RG84 1959a). Draper understood well the connection between exchange rates and exports, and was sympathetic to the delegation's recommendations. Indeed, one of his major findings was that more serious consideration should be given to improving Korea's ability to export. During a discussion with high-ranking officials in the Department on 28 February 1959, he argued that "it was a long haul toward viability in Korea, [but] more effort should be made and a long range plan for exports is needed" (USNA RG84 1959b).

Party officials also informed American policy-makers of their desire to normalize relations with Japan. Democrats criticized the Rhee regime's handling of Korean–Japan relations and hoped to improve ties with Korea's neighbor as a way of increasing ROK trade and generally ameliorating the country's economic prospects. A couple of months prior to becoming Prime Minister, Chang told the Korean press that the Democratic Party would overcome the problems in the bilateral relationship caused by Japanese "deportation" of Koreans to North Korea by concluding trade and fisheries agreements with Japan (USNA RG84 1960i). The interim government of Huh Chung also took concrete steps to improve relations with Japan by releasing Japanese fishermen who had been arrested by the ROK Coast Guard for fishing within the "Rhee Line" (USNA RG84 1960j).

A further indication of the regime's hopes for a close working relationship with America was its appointment of Cabinet members who embraced Walt Rostow's modernization "theory." The theory began gaining adherents in the late 1950s, and bureaucrats in Chang's government were among the first to accept a number of its key tenets. Walter

Rostow had been Professor of Economics at the Massachusetts Institute of Technology and a speech writer for Senator Kennedy prior to joining the Kennedy administration in 1961 as Deputy Special Assistant to the President for National Security Affairs. Although Rostow became famous for his 1960 book, *The Stages of Economic Growth: A Non-Communist Manifesto,* several articles he published in the 1950s, including "The Take-off into Self-sustained Growth" (1956), and "The Stages of Economic Growth" (1959), anticipated the book's conclusions. In these essays Rostow postulated his "theory" that all modern economies had gone through five stages of development. Economic growth began in "traditional society," which could then develop the preconditions for a period of rapid compressed economic growth. Once a "take-off" occurred, a further drive toward "mature" growth, and then an era of mass consumption ensued. For Rostow, the decisive period was the "take-off" stage, which could "usefully be regarded as centering on a relatively brief time interval of two or three decades when the economy and the society of which it is a part transform themselves in such ways that economic growth is, subsequently, more or less automatic." The "take-off" required a high rate of investment – around 10 percent of national income – a significant manufacturing base, and institutions which exploited the sustained growth and made it self-sustaining. Unlike later dependency theorists who argued that production of raw materials for export reflected structural and imposed inequalities in the international system, Rostow believed that the export of resources could contribute to the take-off. He also postulated that states needed to invest heavily in infrastructure and housing, what he called "social overhead capital." Thus:

> whatever its strategic role, the proportion of investment required for growth which goes into industry is relatively small compared to that required for utilities, transport and the housing of enlarged urban populations. And foreign capital can be mightily useful in helping carry the burden of these overhead items.
>
> (Rostow 1956: 25, 32, 40)

Rostow's writings influenced Korean policy-makers, and partly account for the willingness of the Chang regime to support exchange and utility rate reform, as well as its efforts to get more American aid from the United States. ROK government planners presented a summary of their economic policies to the Eisenhower administration in late August 1960. A draft *aide-mémoire* addressed to the President argued that Korea, in "a new spirit," declared its intention to negotiate in good faith to resolve "all outstanding issues" in the economic field between the two countries. These included the exchange and utility rates, and Japan–Korea relations. Chang promised to work closely with the US in implementing the aid program and in steering the country's development (USNA RG84 1960k).

The final version of the *aide-mémoire* reflected the strong influence of Rostow's modernization theory. Although many of the themes in the document were not new – the Rhee government, for example, had called for more monies to develop Korea's productive capacity – references to investment, "social overhead costs," maintaining "self-sustaining growth," and a projected "take-off" for the Korean economy all showed that Korean planners had digested Rostow's writings and were now trying to get American planners to support the "modern" economic planning that was occurring in the new republic.

The memo argued that the time had come "to shift the emphasis of the aid program away from rebuilding and maintaining consumption to accelerating investment and expanding production." Korean planners listed a dozen aid projects which were deemed essential "to achieve self-sustaining growth and a viable economy." Many of these related to infrastructure, and included railway construction, highways, telecommunications, harbors, and waterworks projects. The successful design and implementation of these projects would break Korea's "vicious circle of poverty" and provide a base for "internally generated development." The country needed a "crash" program to "elevate the Korean economy to the 'take-off stage' of development." Since it was unlikely that the southern part of the peninsula would in the near future be able to become financially strong, or even be able to provide for its resources, continued US aid was necessary (USNA RG59 1960f).

Dr. Tchah (Ch'a) Kyun-hi, the Vice-Minister of Reconstruction, was one of the key officials who helped prepare the document. On 12 October Tchah told acting Secretary of State Douglas Dillon that additional American economic aid, distributed over five years, would spark a Korean economic "take-off." Such an aid program would save the United States money over the long term and permit Korea to contribute its share of the costs of economic growth (USNA RG84 1960o). Another official who used the rhetoric of modernization in his discussions with Americans was Minister of Commerce and Industry, Chu Yo-han. In late August 1960 the director of the US operations mission to Korea, Raymond T. Moyer, pointed out that the phrase "take-off stage" appeared "to be becoming a fixed part of the policy of the present government." Minister Chu had recently "said that his party was committed to special attention to economic development with a view to reaching the 'take-off' stage within two or three years" (USNA RG84 1960m).

Korean policy-makers' embrace of modernization theory sheds light on the wider genealogy of the developmental state, and shows that Korean bureaucrats drew upon several different economic "models" to help define their own policies and agendas. Thus when planners considered the experience of Japan as an exporting nation, they could also reflect on the even more recent history of Hong Kong: "As positive measures we will concentrate our efforts to utilize the industrious and intelligent labor of Korea to produce commodities for export, as successfully demonstrated by

Japan in the early stages of industrialization and by Hong Kong more recently" (USNA RG59 1960f). Koreans drew lessons from the history of late industrializers such as Japan or Hong Kong, but they also turned to contemporary American social science for explanations of how and why states could modernize their economy. When Rostow wrote that a successful economic take-off could not happen until "a definitive political transformation occurs – which harnesses national energies, talents, and resources around the concrete tasks of economic growth," Chang and his advisers saw their own history unfolding (Rostow 1956: 6–7). Indeed, the regime said as much in its October memo to Herter:

> The burning desire of Korean people to win democratic freedom has been well manifested by the spontaneous April uprising which resulted in the downfall of the archaic and dictatorial regime of Syngman Rhee. The new government, with the support of the people, is resolved to adopt a bold new program of action directed toward accelerated growth.

In short, for a brief period in Korea's postwar history, development and democracy were pursued with enthusiasm and hope by government officials.

Unfortunately for the Chang regime, however, neither Rostow nor other officials in either the Eisenhower or the Kennedy administrations viewed the situation in Korea in 1960 and early 1961 in these terms. One paragraph from Rostow's (1959) article sums up the perspective in Washington during this period:

> While a reactive nationalism has been a powerful engine of modernization it also posed problems for economic development; for it did not immediately and directly prepare men to face and handle the homely economic tasks of the preconditions and the take-off. On the contrary, when a new national government was achieved – in the face of the colonial power, the traditional society, or both in combination – its leaders were tempted to go on with the familiar game of politics and power rather than to turn promptly to the domestic tasks of modernization. There were real or believed external wrongs and humiliations to be righted; there were still rear-guard actions from elements in the traditional society to be dealt with; and much energy and resource could be allocated to the political – and sometimes military – problem of consolidating the power of the centre over the old regional forces.
>
> (Rostow 1959: 6)

In short, the 1960 revolution had failed, and the "definitive political transformation" which would lead Koreans to turn "wholeheartedly to the technical tasks of economic growth" had not yet occurred (Rostow 1959: 6–7).

The end of modernity: toward military dictatorship

The response of the Eisenhower and Kennedy administrations to the Korean government's new economic initiatives was lukewarm, ambiguous, and equivocal. Policy-makers welcomed the long-range planning in which the republic was involved, yet believed that requests for more economic aid were not viable solutions to the problems at hand. They continued to emphasize the importance of getting the Koreans to be less dependent on American aid in developing their economy, and used the meetings in Washington in the fall of 1960 to push forward with earlier efforts to get the Korean government to alter its exchange rate and to adopt other reforms. The Director of the Office of Northeast Asian Affairs, David Bane, told Vice-Minister Tchah on 11 October that it was important to adopt as soon as possible those "exchange and related reform measures so necessary for Korean economic development and social stability." The US executive branch of government was limited in what it could do by "the overall appropriation limits set by the Congress." Since the aid program to Korea was the largest in the world, the ROK government should use the maximum amount of its own resources to deal with the economy. In addition, normalizing relations with Japan "should pave the way for Japanese economic assistance so necessary, in our view, to supplement U.S. resources available for Korean economic development over the coming years" (USNA RG84 1960n).

South Korean officials viewed American demands for immediate reforms with concern, not because of a lack of desire to develop the country, but because the proposals created significant economic and political difficulties for the government. The Prime Minister had expressed his worries about his government's ability to hold on to power in an interview with Ambassador McConaughy as early as 25 August 1960. Chang stated that the "old faction" of the party might "engage in obstructionist and harassment tactics in [an] effort [to] weaken his Administration." Such tactics were not based on "principle or conscientious objections" but were simply an "effort to block and embarrass his government." Efforts to improve Japanese–Korean relations were vulnerable to such attacks, and his adversaries were "trying to brand him as 'pro-Japanese'." These kinds of methods might work in bringing public opinion against the regime. Marshall Green, the Deputy Chief of Mission in Seoul, agreed with Chang's assessment, noting that party infighting "will undoubtedly serve to inhibit Chang Myon from getting too far out in front on question long dear to his heart of improving relations with Japan" (USNA RG84 1960l).

The US decision in 1960 to cut back its defense support aid from $180 million to $165 million also greatly worried the Koreans. In October, Tchah told State Department diplomats that if the US aid amounts were revealed to the Korean public, the government would receive a "death sentence." Chang would lose power and the country might be taken over by the communists (USNA RG84 1960o).

Enacting exchange rate reform could similarly be dangerous for the government. Although Finance Minister Kim Yong-sun agreed with the importance of altering the exchange rate, he felt that the American demand to change the effective rate to 1,300 *hwan* to the dollar was too extreme. Instead, he favored a temporary 1,000 to 1 ratio since that was the rate at which the government had prepared the 1961 government budget. Any alteration of that rate before the end of 1960 might result in a motion leading to the withdrawal of the budget bill and to the defeat of the government in the legislature (USNA RG84 1960p). On this issue the Americans were frustrated with Korean policy-making, as they had been earlier in the year in their negotiations with Sŏng and the Rhee administration. Marshall Green wrote to the State Department that the embassy could find nothing in the Korean constitution which would automatically result in a non-confidence motion in Parliament if the budget were withdrawn from the National Assembly. In short, Chang was being too cautious in his approach to Parliament and should take firmer action (USNA RG84 1960q).

In late October American and Korean officials negotiated a deal. Under-Secretary of State Douglas Dillon and Minister of Finance Kim Yong-sun agreed that if South Korea followed through on exchange, transportation, and electricity rate reforms, "rationalized" certain aid-supported industries, and negotiated a new bilateral aid agreement, the US would provide $20 million to Korea to help deal with the consequences of the change in the exchange rate, $5 million in additional defense support aid, and $10 million for imported agricultural commodities from the United States. In this way the United States used its economic aid program to get the South Korean government to make economic decisions which were seen to be beneficial both for the United States and Korea (USNA RG84 1960r). The letter to the Korean Prime Minister which outlined the details of this agreement subsequently became known as the "Dillon letter."

Between October 1960 and March 1961, Chang Myŏn showed his good faith by implementing the reforms required by the Dillon letter: the 1,300 *hwan* to $1 exchange rate was in place by the beginning of March 1961, the government negotiated a new bilateral aid agreement, and it substantially increased electricity and transportation rates. The US released the promised additional funds to the Korean government just before the military coup in 1961.

Over the course of late 1960 and early 1961, however, American policy-makers began to grow more concerned about the ability of the Prime Minister and his Cabinet to govern the country effectively and efficiently. On the issue of exchange rate reform, for example, Washington appeared to be willing to push the Chang government as far as it had the Rhee regime. In early December 1960, Chang requested a one-month extension on meeting the conditions of the October 1960 agreement, citing recent problems which his government had encountered in the legislature over power rate increases and the budget (USNA RG84 1960s). In response, Secretary Herter wrote that the Korean government "should be made understand failure fulfill conditions outlined Dillon letter will mean loss of $35 million supplemental aid with all that implies politically for existence Chang Myon Government" (USNA RG84 1960t). Although the ambassador and other American diplomats in Korea had shown more support for the Chang administration, in Washington, Chang's government was seen as potentially expendable, months before the military coup in May 1961. The telegram reflected an underlying belief that progress in economic reforms could override considerations of democratic governance. Indeed, it demonstrated an arrogance and insensitivity toward the fledgling democracy that Prime Minister Chang was trying to build.

American officials' growing frustration with the second republic was evident in a number of telegrams produced during the period. In December 1960, for example, Hugh Farley, Assistant Director for Technical Cooperation in the US operating mission, told former interim Prime Minister Huh Chung that the April revolution had "torn the veil" from the previous pattern of corruption in government and society, and that there had been "great hopes" that Korea "would move on the necessary great reforms." It was becoming increasingly clear, however, that these reforms might not be initiated. Rather, "the tie between money and politics, between public life and private profit seemed as strong as before." In spite of the high hopes for reform, "it was beginning to look as though the Chang Government was getting deeper and more inextricably involved in the old fabric of behavior, was powerless to shake free [of it]" (USNA RG84 1960u).

Official perceptions of events in Korea did not change after the Kennedy administration took office in January 1961. In mid-March, Walt Rostow, now Kennedy's deputy Special Assistant for National Security Affairs, wrote the President that "all hands agree that the situation in Korea is not good; and American policy in Korea requires a fresh look." What was required, argued Rostow, was to find a way "to get our massive aid to Korea shifted around in a way which would not merely keep Korea from going down for the third time, but would begin to get Korea moving forward." He felt that there might be some Koreans who could help out in this project, but that there was no guarantee of this, and they could also "turn against us" (United States Department of State 1996: 428).

A special national intelligence estimate produced the same month came to a similar conclusion: "little real progress has been made in the past year on the basic social and economic problems which confront the ROK Government and people ... there are mounting signs of frustration and resentment directed at the government and, increasingly, at the US, over the slow pace of reform and progress in South Korea" (United States

Department of State 1996: 431). Washington's distress over events in Korea was conveyed in a State Department telegram to Seoul approved by Avery Peterson, the deputy Assistant Secretary of State for Far Eastern Economic Affairs. The telegram referred to fears in the department that the situation in Korea might facilitate the spread of communism: "When sufficiently revolted by apathetic drifting and by illegal gains for the elite, the totalitarian aspects of communism appear less fearsome and its austerity and determined purposes may become positively attractive." The Chang regime had "too often ... plotted its course from old landmarks ... and has failed to recognize the commanding importance of youthful element in the political spectrum which accomplished the April revolution." As a result of this a "bemused ROKG" failed to see that it needed to improve the economic and social prospects of the Korean youth. "Otherwise it might be replaced by some political element equally myopic which if in turn overthrown could leave a highly volatile dangerous situation in which the appeal of unification of the country might be so great as to tempt the South Korean people to enter the Communist crab pot" (United States Department of State 1996: 436–437).

There were thus significant elements of continuity between the Eisenhower and Kennedy administrations' policies toward Korea: officials were most concerned with preventing Koreans from turning to communism as a solution to their political and economic ills. These same fears motivated those in Korea who were plotting the overthrow of the Chang regime: they worried that North Korea's economic strength relative to South Korea's "weakness" could lead over time to communist domination of the peninsula. Given the Kennedy administration's general disillusionment with Chang and the second republic, and the wider history of Korean–American relations in the late 1950s and early 1960s, it should not be surprising that the American government did so little to find ways to back Chang in the aftermath of the *coup d'état* in May 1961. Part of the difficulty lay with the Prime Minister himself, who made no contact with the American authorities in the immediate aftermath of the coup. But Washington officials were willing quite early on to accept the new military regime, even though they recognized that the military government would likely not be as willing to work with them as the Chang Myŏn regime had been. Washington was mainly concerned with economic development, and issues of democratic governance were of secondary importance. A more sympathetic view of the second republic by the United States government would have helped to shore up the Chang regime's position domestically. On the other hand, the early decision to work with Park Chung Hee helped to ensure that Korea's future would emphasize modernization and development over democracy.

Given Korean policy-makers' decision to adopt the broad tenets of modernization theory, it is ironic that Rostow criticized the Chang regime and supported Park's military government, since, indeed, within the

Kennedy administration, Rostow was one of the key supporters of the new military junta in the immediate weeks following the coup. At a meeting of the National Security Council in mid-June 1961, President Kennedy "expressed the view that the economic and political situation in and about Korea were such as to present a hopeless situation." Walter McConaughy, now promoted to the position of Assistant Secretary of State for Far Eastern Affairs, shared the President's pessimism, but Rostow disagreed with these opinions, arguing that there were three factors in Korea which allowed for "a certain degree of optimism." These were the establishment of "new effective economic and social planning," the emergence of "young, aggressive, capable people in government," and "better relations with Japan" (United States Department of State 1996: 481). This position was consistent with Rostow's interpretation of economic and political development in Asia. As early as 1955 Rostow had written, in collaboration with Richard Hatch, that the presence of mass illiteracy and "traditional cultures" in Asia meant that "initiative must come from the top down." In Asia, "private capitalism" was "much less automatically an adjunct to democracy. . . . Generally speaking, we must expect a more powerful and especially more direct state control of economic activities in Asia than in the United States" (Rostow, in collaboration with Hatch 1955: 10–11). In mid-1961, then, it appeared to Rostow that the new Korean leaders could now meet a number of his requirements for achieving an "economic takeoff." But his support for the military regime also reflected the contradictions and limitations in his own theory. For many decades after 1961, Korean economic development came at the price of political freedom. This seems a logical yet also tragic conclusion to the modernization theory postulated by Rostow in the 1950s, as the Korean state took on a developmental ethos, but one without a democratic base.

Notes

1 Cumings argues that Taiwan's export program was also heavily shaped by United States government policies. See also Satterwhite 1994.

2 In November 1954 Korean and American representatives negotiated an "Agreed Minute of Understanding" which authorized the size of the Korean armed forces at 730,000 men.

3 In the 1956 presidential election Cho had received 2.1 million votes while Rhee had received 5 million. The presidential candidate for the Democratic Party, Shin Ikhi, died just before the election.

4 On 20 March 1959 President Eisenhower directed that all ambassadors be held responsible for coordinating the distribution and implementation of US aid. For Korea, this meant a weakening of the power of the CINCUNC, though the Commander retained the authority to control the distribution of military aid. It also meant that the ambassador had more control over the decision-making process regarding US economic aid. In August, several months after John Foster Dulles' death, and in anticipation of Ambassador Dowling's impending departure and replacement, Howard J. Parsons requested a reassessment of the Korean political situation. Dowling's subsequent recommendations to the State Department

reiterated those he had made in January, and they were forwarded to the new Secretary of State, Christian Herter, in late October 1959. There is no indication that Herter formally approved them, but US policy toward Korea between the fall of 1959 and the spring of 1960 indicates that they were accepted and implemented by the administration.

References

Ahn, Yeonmi. 1992. "The Political Economy of Foreign Aid: The Nature of American Aid and its Impact on the State–Business Relationship in South Korea." Ph.D. thesis, Yale University.

Cumings, Bruce. 1981. "The Origins and the Development of the Northeast Asian Political Economy," *International Organization* 38: 1–40.

——. 1997. *Korea's Place in the Sun: A Modern History*. New York: Norton.

Haggard, Stephan. 1990. *Pathways From the Periphery: The Politics of Growth in the Newly Industrializing Countries*. Ithaca, NY: Cornell University Press.

Haggard, Stephan and Chung-In Moon. 1993. "The State, Politics, and Economic Development in Postwar South Korea," in Hagen Koo (ed.). *State and Society in Contemporary Korea*. Ithaca, NY: Cornell University Press, pp. 51–93.

Haggard, Stephan, Byung-kuk Kim, and Chung-In Moon. 1991. "The Transition to Export-led Growth in South Korea: 1954–1966," *Journal of Asian Studies* 50: 850–873.

Keefer, Edward. 1991. "The Truman Administration and the South Korean Political Crisis of 1952: Democracy's Failure?" *Pacific Historical Review* 145–168.

Lee, Steven Hugh. 1994. "US–Korean Relations, 1950–1954: Historiography and Documentary Record." Paper presented to the 2nd Pacific Basin Conference on Korean Studies, Tokyo, July.

——. 1996. *Outposts of Empire: Korea, Vietnam, and the Origins of the Cold War in Asia, 1949–1954*. Montreal: McGill Queen's Press.

——. 2002. "The United Nations Korean Reconstruction Agency in War and Peace: An Economic and Social History of Korea in the 1950s," in Chae-Jin Lee and Young Ick Lew (eds). *Hangukkwa 6.25 Chŏnchaeng* (Korea and the Korean War). Seoul: Yonsei University Press, pp. 357–397.

Lie, John. 1998. *Han Unbound: The Political Economy of South Korea*. Stanford, CA: Stanford University Press.

Republic of Korea Washington Embassy. 1957. "The Korean Information Bulletin," August–September.

Republic of Korea Washington Embassy. 1958. "The Korean Information Bulletin," May.

Rostow, W.W. 1956."The Take-off Into Self-sustained Growth," *The Economic Journal* 66: 25–48.

——. 1959. "The Stages of Economic Growth," *The Economic History Review* (New Series) 12: 1–16.

——. 1960. *The Stages of Economic Growth: A Non-Communist Manifesto*. Cambridge: Cambridge University Press.

Rostow, W.W. in collaboration with Richard W. Hatch. 1955. *An American Policy in Asia*. New York: The Technology Press of Massachusetts Institute of Technology and John Wiley & Sons.

Satterwhite, David. 1994. "The Politics of Economic Development: Coup, State,

and the Republic of Korea's First Five-year Economic Development Plan (1962–1966)." Ph.D. thesis, University of Washington.
United States Congress. *Congressional Record*, 6 June, 1956, p. 9668.
United States Department of State. 1976. *Foreign Relations of the United States* 1949. VI part 2. Washington: Government Printing Office.
United States Department of State. 1993. *Foreign Relations of the United States* 1955–1957. XXIII part 2. Washington: Government Printing Office.
United States Department of State. 1994. *Foreign Relations of the United States* 1958–1960. XVIII. Washington: Government Printing Office.
United States Department of State. 1996. *Foreign Relations of the United States* 1961–1963. XIX. Washington: Government Printing Office.
United States Information Agency. 1956. *Korea: In the Common Interest.* Washington: US Information Agency.
United States National Archives (hereafter USNA) RG59. 1954. 795B.5 MSP/1-2354, Seoul to Secretary of State No. 704, 24 January.
USNA RG59. 1960a. 895B.00/1-1560, Seoul to Secretary of State, January 15.
USNA RG59. 1960b. 895B.00/2-560, Seoul to Secretary of State no. 387, 5 February.
USNA RG59. 1960c. 895B.00/2-2660, Seoul to Department of State no. 447, 26 February.
USNA RG59. 1960d. 895B.00/3-1160, Seoul to Department of State no. 487, 11 March.
USNA RG59. 1960e. 895B.00/3-1860, Seoul to Department of State no. 494, 18 March.
USNA RG59 1960f. 895B.00/10-460, *Aide-memoire* addressed to Secretary of State Christian Herter, 4 October.
USNA RG84. 1956a. Box 2 file 320.1, "Memorandum of Conversation," 17 March.
USNA RG84. 1956b. Box 2 file 320.1, "Current Review of U.S. Programs in Korea," 10 October.
USNA RG84. 1958a. Box 2 file 310, Chiefs of Mission Conference, "Far East Chiefs of Mission Conference," 27 March.
USNA RG84. 1958b. Box 2 file 310, Chiefs of Mission Conference, "Confidential" memo, March.
USNA RG84. 1958c. Box 7 file 363.3, "Memo of Conversation, Proposed Amendment ROK National Security Law," 5 December.
USNA RG84. 1958d. Box 7 file 363.3, Seoul to Secretary of State no. 255, 16 December.
USNA RG84. 1959a. Box 11 file 400 MAP, Seoul to Department of State no. 452, 24 February.
USNA RG84. 1959b. Box 11 file 400 MAP, "Memorandum of Conversation," 24 February.
USNA RG84. 1959c. Box 13 file 501.51, Secretary of State to Seoul no. 423, 19 December.
USNA RG84. 1960a. Box 22 file 501.51, Seoul to Secretary of State no. 477, 2 January.
USNA RG84. 1960b. Box 22 file 501.51, Seoul to State Department No. 489, 7 January.
USNA RG84. 1960c. Box 22 file 501.51, Seoul to Secretary of State, G-57, 8 January.
USNA RG84. 1960d. Box 22 file 501.51, Seoul to Secretary of State no. 532, 21 January.

USNA RG84. 1960e. Box 22 file 501.51, Secretary of State to Seoul no. 511, 23 January.

USNA RG84. 1960f. Box 22 file 501.51, Seoul to Secretary of State no. 572, 1 February.

USNA RG84. 1960g. Box 22 file 501.51, Christian Herter to Walter McConaughy no. 566, 12 February.

USNA RG84. 1960h. Box 22 file 501.51, Vettel to Green, 20 March.

USNA RG84. 1960i. Box 15 file 320.1, ROK–Japan, Seoul to Washington no. 1212, 25 May.

USNA RG84. 1960j. Box 16 file 320.1, ROK–Japan Repatriation, Seoul to Washington, no. 112, 28 July.

USNA RG84. 1960k. Box 21 File 500, Chang Myon to Dwight Eisenhower, "Draft Aide Memoire," 23 August.

USNA RG84. 1960l. Box 15 file 320.1, ROK–Japan Seoul to Secretary of State no. 255, 27 August.

USNA RG84 1960m. Box 21 file 500, Moyer to Walter McConaughy, with enclosures, 1 September.

USNA RG84 1960n. Box 21 file 500, "Memorandum of Conversation," 11 October.

USNA RG84 1960o. Box 21 file 501.51, Draft "Record of Discussion," 12 October.

USNA RG84. 1960p. Box 22 file 501.51, Seoul to Washington no. 468, 17 October.

USNA RG84. 1960q. Box 22 file 501.51, Seoul to Washington no. 478, 18 October.

USNA RG84. 1960r. Box 22 file 500, Economic Aid Program, Washington to Seoul, no. 382, 26 October.

USNA RG84. 1960s. Box 21 file 500, Seoul to Secretary of State, no. 676, 5 December.

USNA RG84. 1960t. Box 21 file 500, Washington to Seoul, no. 548, 8 December.

USNA RG 84. 1960u. Box 21 file 350, Korea Seoul to Washington TOICA A-2149, 14 December.

USNA RG469E-80. 1950. Box 19, Korea – Economic Conditions Minutes February–May 1950. Fifth Conference of the Economic Stabilization Committee with President Rhee, 4 March.

Woo, Jung-En. 1991. *Race to the Swift: State and Finance in Korean Industrialization.* New York: Columbia University Press.

Yi, Wŏn-bŏm. 1998. "1950 Nyŏndae Huban'gi ŭi Chŏngch'w ŭiki wa Miguk ŭi Taeŭng: 1958 nyŏn ŭi Kukkaboanpŏp kaejŏng P'atongul Chungsimuro" (The Political Crisis of Second Half of the 1950s and the US Response in the Aftermath of the Revision of the National Security Act), in Han Hŭng-su, Kim Kyŏng-il, Han To-hyŏn, Sim Chi-yŏn, Yi Wŏn-bŏm, Kim Dae-hwan, and Chŏng Yong-uk, (eds), *Han'guk Hyŏndaesa ŭi Chaeinsik 4: 1950 Nyŏndae Huban'gi ŭi Han'guksa Haewa Yi Sŭng-man Chŏngbu ŭi pungkui* (Rethinking Modern History 4: Korean Society in the Second Half of the 1950s and the Collapse of Syngman Rhee's Government). Seoul: Oruem Publishing, pp. 137–191.

7 Cut from the same cloth

Bureaucracies and rulers in South Korea, 1948–1979

David Kang

Introduction

Chapter 6 demonstrated that the South Korean bureaucracy worked closely with the state in formulating economic policy and in shaping Korea's capitalist modernity. This chapter will re-examine the role of the bureaucracy in light of another prominent field of inquiry in this volume: the workings of Korea's developmental state (see Amsden 1989; Evans 1995; Haggard 1991; Johnson 1982, 1987; Önis 1991; Wade 1990). The existing literature on this subject postulates two major arguments. The first is that the state was largely, although not completely, autonomous from society.[1] The second central tenet follows from the first: shielded from politics, a technocratic Weberian bureaucracy designed efficient policies and pursued a national agenda of development.[2] In the classic explication of the developmental state, Chalmers Johnson argued that in Japan politicians reigned while rulers ruled: "the elite bureaucracy of Japan makes most major decisions . . . and is the source of all major policy innovations in the system" (Johnson 1982: 20–21; see also Najita and Koschmann 1982). Along with Japan and Taiwan, during the period of high growth, Korea is often portrayed as a relatively depoliticized state which was run by austere technocrats and stern military leaders who focused on national economic development as a priority.

Is this picture accurate? What role did politics play in influencing the direction of state policy? Given the centrality of the bureaucracy in discussions of the developmental state, detailed studies are surprisingly rare. New, primary information about the bureaucracy in Korea challenges the consensus about the developmental state and shows that political and technocratic considerations were closely intertwined. I argue that technocratic views of public administration ignore the political milieu within which bureaucrats operated and that political calculations were a central feature of Korea's developmental state. The organization of the bureaucracy was much less significant in explaining Korean policy-making than the nature of the political leadership that sat atop that bureaucracy, and the social forces it sought to organize or disorganize in order to maintain power. In short, the state was not very autonomous, meritocratic appointment was not common, and the bureaucracy had relatively little protection from societal interests. These were thus key features of Korea's capitalist modernity even in the period of high economic growth in the 1960s and 1970s.

The significance of this chapter lies in its explication of the political bases of the developmental state and the evolution of Korean capitalism. The developmental states of Asia were not divorced from society, floating above politics and making disinterested decisions. To understand further both how the process worked, and why these states were successful, we must first realize that the bureaucracy was politicized, and not a neutral site of technocratic mediation and compromise.

This chapter addresses two key issues that relate to the organization of the Korean state and the character of the policy-making process. First, identifying organizational attributes does not allow us to make *ex-ante* predictions about the developmental efficiency of a particular state. I take the central aspect of the institutionalist argument – the role of the bureaucracy – and subject it to empirical scrutiny. Korean rulers have reigned *and* ruled, and the bureaucracy has not been autonomous from political regime interests. We witnessed aspects of this relationship between the state and bureaucracy in Larry Burmeister's discussion of the integration of the National Agricultural Cooperative Federation into the state's development project (Chapter 2). My argument, which complements Burmeister's conclusions, is that policy decisions reflected regime interests designed to reward good coalitional partners and to punish potential opponents. The developmental statist wisdom about growth is built on the premise that the Korean state under Park was structurally different. But clientelism and corruption existed to an astonishing degree even in the 1960s. Reviewing the *ex-ante* measures of independent variables associated with Weberian bureaucracies, I thus provide a revisionist account for Syngman Rhee, South Korea's first leader (1948–1960). Indeed, most work on the Rhee period has characterized the bureaucracy as weak and laid blame for slow development and incoherent economic policies squarely on the shoulders of Rhee.[3] Lee (Chapter 6) showed that after difficult bargaining, the Rhee regime was willing to make compromises with the Americans on the exchange rate issue. I examine the institutional constraints that Rhee faced, and show that in most ways his ruling style and relations with the bureaucracy were similar to those of Park Chung Hee. Many of the supposed reforms under Park were less fundamental than the literature has recognized.

Second, policy choices reflected political, and to an extent, developmental priorities. We need a better understanding of the political incentive structure within which actors make economic decisions. In this context, I discuss Park's use of policy and patronage for the purposes of building political coalitions. The real action of Korean development supposedly occurred in the government's guidance of business, and in that arena the conventional wisdom is that politics was scrupulously avoided. This, unfortunately, was not the case. The use of exports as an indicator of success, the willingness of Park to let poorly managed firms fail on economic grounds, and the objectivity of the entire process was far less prevalent than is currently believed. Political leaders used pork and public goods strategically: neither pork nor policy is preordained, and both have political benefits and costs.

The natural question that follows from my study is how growth and politics are related. Elsewhere I directly address this question, arguing that under certain, specifiable conditions, corruption may be growth-enhancing.[4] Here my goal is more modest: to focus on the institutions of the state. Indeed, any explanation about why Korea developed has given the bureaucracy pride of place, and it thus makes sense to begin by closely examining the state itself.

This chapter is organized in three sections. I begin with a discussion of the theoretical literature, and show how a more explicit consideration of politics will refine our understanding of the developmental state. The second section compares Korea's first two rulers, Syngman Rhee and Park Chung Hee, and argues that many of the supposed reforms under Park were less obvious than might be expected. The final section examines the policy-making process. It demonstrates that political considerations mattered as much as efficiency in determining developmental policy.

Towards a micro-foundation of the state

In this section I introduce politics to the propositions found in the developmental state. While the statists emphasize efficiency in policy choices and autonomy in the organization of the state, a political explanation focuses on the politician's incentive to control the bureaucracy and the use of policy to create coalitional support. Woven into more general discussions of the developmental state lies the argument that the organization of bureaucracies has a direct influence on development strategies and success. Scholars argue that autonomous and insulated bureaucracies are more effective, initiate major policy innovations, and implement their development policies in an objective and rational manner. This "Weberian" bureaucracy is insulated from social demands, internally coherent, relatively uncorrupt, staffed with far-sighted technocrats who put the national welfare above their individual needs, and yet it retains ties to the business community with which it must interact. In many instances this bureaucracy has a single "pilot" agency that takes the overall lead in guiding and leading development.

From this viewpoint, many scholars have focused on the period of rule by Park Chung Hee (1961–1979) and its strong state – its relatively uncorrupt, autonomous, and insulated bureaucracy, its rational economic planning, and its unselfish leadership – as central to South Korea's economic development. Among many who hold this view, Peter Evans has argued that "the internal organization of developmental states comes much closer to approximating a Weberian bureaucracy. Highly selective meritocratic recruitment and long-term career rewards create commitment and a sense of corporate coherence" (Evans 1995: 2). Alice Amsden has also written that "economic success in Korea challenges the assumption . . . that government intervention degenerates into 'rent-seeking'."[5] Some authors, including Chalmers Johnson and Jung-en Woo, have emphasized the centrality of external threats in some successful developers (see Johnson 1982; Kang 2002; Woo 1991: chs 3 and 4). This does help explain the differences in *preferences* across states; but preferences are only part of the story: we need to look at how preferences are translated into policy, and that means we need to look at institutions.

In the literature, the actual organizational attributes of the developmental state remain relatively understudied. This is surprising, given its centrality to the literature. While the Korean state is often cast as an important actor in explaining both economic policy and the politics behind policy choices, few systematic studies of the internal workings of the state are available. To the extent that the literature examines the state, it tends to imply that bureaucracies and policy choices in South Korea have been shielded from political influences.

However, the role of the bureaucracy within the state is unclear in the statist literature. Do politicians allow technocrats to work alone, without guidance or sanction? If so, why is this possible? Why would technocrats care about the national interest? If bureaucrats have better information and are insulated from politics, why do they not use informational asymmetries to maximize budgets at the expense of larger developmental goals? Alternatively, how do rulers control and sanction bureaus? Do rulers force the bureaucracy to comply with their wishes? In the abstract it is possible to pose two mutually exclusive hypotheses. The first explains why rulers might rationally delegate critical control over policy-making to bureaucrats, while the second explains why rulers might wish to retain control in their own hands.

The first hypothesis involves a scenario in which industrialists and other social coalitions may be skeptical that the ruler has a genuine commitment to implementing efficient economic policies and reform. Thus the ruler's predicament is to convince these groups to support the ruler's development strategies. One way the ruler can communicate a sincere desire to reform is institutional. This strategy involves the voluntary delegation of political authority to disinterested technocrats: a "tying of hands" by political elites that will restrain their ability to interfere for political reasons in the formulation of economic policy.[6] In a political restatement of the developmental state, Robert Bates and Anne Krueger have argued that delegating authority to a disinterested and technocratic elite can have positive feedback. They argue that sophisticated politicians may possess a response to this dilemma: the creation of new agencies to which politicians delegate the responsibility for a particular policy domain. These public institutions' mission is to defend the collective welfare rather than the private political interests of particular politicians (Bates and Krueger 1993: 464; see also Bawn 1995; McCubbins and Schwartz 1984: 165–179; Moe 1991: 102–129). Policies can be chosen on the basis of efficiency, rather than on the basis of political calculations. In this manner rent-seeking behavior is minimized.

There is, however, a competing hypothesis. In this scenario, no matter what their motives, be they venal or altruistic, rulers need to retain power. The ruler presumably also has some idea of the direction in which he wishes to lead the country. In this case, the ruler has preferences over the use of political resources and the pursuit of substantive goals, and the bureaucracy and policies are powerful political resources. The more closely he can control bureaucrats, the more likely the ruler is able to implement his desired preferences and also retain power by providing benefits to important social coalitions.

This alternative hypothesis calls into question the meaning of bureaucratic autonomy. Prima facie, it seems hard to imagine what, exactly, an "autonomous" bureaucracy is, since bureaucracies are hierarchically ordered organizations that are nominally controlled by political superiors. At issue is whether, how, and from whom bureaucracies gain autonomy and independence. Thus the problem is not merely one of "freedom" from political interference. The problem of shirking by bureaucrats also exists, and both issues need combined as well as separate treatment (see Ramseyer and Rosenbluth 1994). Given no direction or oversight, agencies may well develop their own internal agendas aimed at maximizing budgets, lifetime tenure, or other unproductive (from society's viewpoint) activities, while excessive political interference can limit the agency's initiative and goal orientation.[7]

In addition, government policy is a powerful tool that enables rulers to reward supporters and punish competitors. Policies used wisely can enhance coalitional support, disrupt the opposition, or lure a fence-sitter to one's side. Rodden and Rose-Ackerman argue that "In order to stay in office, leaders must respond to the institutional incentive structures set up by party organizations, electoral rules, campaign finance laws, and a host of other structures. Even authoritarian leaders must protect their positions by pleasing party, bureaucratic, and military constituencies, by building coalitions, and by staving off costly riots and unrest."[8] Politics is active and constant: rulers struggle to cobble together supporters and coalitions and to fend off enemies. Politics and policy become deeply intertwined in such an environment.

These competing hypotheses point to opposite results, and it is thus possible to test them empirically against one another. The following sections focus on two key variables about a developmental state. Did these states have an autonomous and meritocratic bureaucracy? Did political influences operate in economic decisions, or did an autonomous bureaucracy initiate policy? In looking for evidence of internal cohesion and strength, I focus on personnel policies and institutional reform. In examining policy, I focus on who received preferential treatment and why.

Personnel policy and the organization of the Civil Service in South Korea

Authors of all stripes have labeled the Rhee period (1948–1960) as "weak" and the Park Chung Hee period (1961–1979) as "strong." In general, this perception has arisen due to economic performance; South Korea under Park experienced rapid economic development; therefore Park *must have* presided over a strong state. By contrast, due to poor economic outcomes, Syngman Rhee has been criticized in the literature for using the bureaucracy as a place for his patronage appointments, and for subordinating bureaucratic consistency to political expediency (see, e.g., Bark 1982; Kim 1991; Lee 1982). For example, Peter Evans writes that "Rhee's dependence on private-sector donations to finance his political dominance made him dependent on clientelistic ties with individual businesspeople" (Evans 1995: 52).

Ironically, while Western scholars have focused on the meritocratic and competent Korean bureaucracy, Korean scholars have emphasized the theme of corruption during the twenty years Park was in power (see, e.g., Bark 1961; Cho 1968; Chŏng 1987; Jung 1989; Yi 1966; Yoon 1994). However, when we compare the political institutions under Park and Rhee, the supposed *ad hoc* cronyism of the latter appears less great than is generally believed. Many of the indicators that seemingly indicate comprehensive reform of the bureaucracy under Park Chung Hee are ambiguous at best. Rhee was creating a nation, and filling an entire bureaucratic apparatus from scratch, and the few bureaucrats who had worked under the previous Japanese administration tended to be low-level functionaries, unsuited to running bureaucracies.[9] Rhee needed to fill the rest of the bureaucracy with appointments, as the exam system could not provide sufficient numbers of civil servants to fill the entire apparatus. Let us first examine the issue of continuity of Cabinet appointments under Rhee and Park.

Cabinet composition

As evidence of incoherence in Rhee's policy-making, scholars have often criticized the "revolving-door" character of Rhee's political appointments. Too much turnover in policy-makers leads to an absence of stability and short time-horizons. Table 7.1 shows the average tenure of Cabinet

Table 7.1 Cabinet turnover under Rhee and Park (average tenure in months in parentheses)

	Syngman Rhee	*Park Chung Hee*
Foreign affairs	6 (23.5)	11 (20.0)
Finance	9 (15.6)	16 (13.8)
Health	6 (23.5)	10 (22.1)
Education	6 (23.5)	14 (15.7)
Communication	8 (17.6)	14 (15.7)
National defense	7 (20.1)	10 (22.1)
Transportation	8 (17.6)	12 (18.4)
Justice	9 (15.6)	13 (17.0)
Prime Minister	8 (17.6)	8 (27.6)
Commerce and industry	10 (14.1)	10 (22.1)
Agriculture and forestry	16 (8.8)	14 (15.7)
Home affairs	20 (7.0)	14 (15.7)
Construction	–	15 (14.7)

Source: Compiled from Ministry of Governmental Affairs.

ministers under both Rhee and Park. What is most striking is the absence of a clear trend. While Rhee's Ministers of Foreign Affairs, Finance, Health, Education, and Communication served *longer* average terms than their counterparts under Park, the Ministers of Home Affairs, Commerce and Industry, and Agriculture and Forestry had markedly shorter average tenures under Rhee than under Park.

Examination procedures

Another aspect of the developmental state that has received attention is the use of the Civil Service examinations for entry into the higher Civil Service. Again, the differences between Rhee and Park are not as clear as might be expected. Table 7.2 provides the data for the exams from 1949 to 1979, the most important to us being the Public Administration exam, or *haengsi.* During the period of Rhee's rule (1949–1960), an average of twenty-two aspirants passed each exam. The competition ranged from a low of nine attempts per each successful exam-taker in 1951 (probably due to the disruption of the war); to a high of 315 aspirants per each successful exam-taker in 1957. Under Park we also see a clear trend: in the first decade of his rule, from 1961 to 1970, the numbers are only slightly higher than Rhee's. From 1961 to 1970, an average of 36.9 aspirants passed each exam, while the difficulty ranged from a low of twenty-two attempts per each exam-taker in 1966 to a high of seventy-three aspirants per each successful exam-taker in 1967.

However, in 1971 there is a clear jump in the number of successful exam-takers. In 1971 alone, 188 aspirants passed the *haengsi,* or more than half of the entire number of aspirants who had passed the exam in the

Table 7.2 Higher Civil Service exam, 1949 to 1979

Year	*Absolute no. accepted*	*Attempts per success*
1949	5	100
1951	38	9
1952	16	14
1953	24	22
	9	75
1954	13	74
1955	58	29
1956	11	214
1957	7	315
1958	27	65
1959	36	47
1960	20	154
1961	72	21
1962	38	42
1963	40	37
1964	24	62
1965	28	25
1966	50	22
1967	24	73
1968	45	32
1969	55	36
1970	38	43
	27	70
1971	188	18
1972	41	94
	47	71
1973	96	43
	116	36
1974	47	92
	68	59
1975	100	44
	101	44
1976	73	93
1977	55	92
	131	38
1978	250	31
1979	248	41

Source: Ministry of Governmental Affairs.

preceding decade. From 1971 to 1979, an average of 111.5 aspirants passed each exam, while the difficulty remained similar; a low of 18:1 in 1971 and a high of 93:1 in 1976. What might explain these outcomes? The small number of initially successful applicants is not surprising; as I have argued elsewhere, in the late 1940s there was a complete lack of educated and qualified Korean aspirants for the Civil Service; this is reflected not only in the smaller numbers of successful examinees, but also in the higher number of *teukche*, or special appointments (see Haggard *et al.*

1997: 873). This is also shown in the lower educational achievement of the Rhee bureaucracy, and the inevitably higher numbers of external promotions: by 1960 even the first of those bureaucrats recruited at the *samugwan*, or Grade III level, had had only twelve years within which to rise through the various ministries. Park Chung Hee's regime benefited from the growing number of educated Koreans, as well as the chance to promote more bureaucrats through internal means.

Internal promotion

Tables 7.3 and 7.4 include interesting data regarding the promotion patterns within the Rhee bureaucracy. The data are mixed. Table 7.3 compares Rhee and Park in their recruitment and promotion of higher civil servants. For the highest levels, the numbers are almost reversed: under Rhee, about 64 percent of Grade I civil servants were special appointments, while under Park, about 65 percent of Grade I appointments were internal promotions. At the entry level (Grade III-B) under Rhee only 4 percent of appointments were through the *haengsi* exam, while over 20 percent of Park's entry-level appointments were through the exam. Again, however, it needs to be remembered that the typical bureaucratic career path in Korea takes about ten years to go from Grade III-B to Grade III-A. Another decade winnows out membership at Grade II, and leaves a few who rise to Grade I. Thus under Rhee it was impossible that by 1960 internal promotions could have filled much of the bureaucracy, whereas Park benefited from the thirteen years preceding him. This is not to say that the only differences between Rhee and Park were structural. Such differences did, however, exist, and they clearly created constraints for Rhee that did not exist for Park.

Table 7.4 shows the pattern of recruitment under Rhee. Grades III-B through II are the "heart" of the bureaucracy – Grade III-B is a subsection chief, Grade II bureau director. It is interesting that by 1960 fully 78 percent of the Grade II (bureau directors) had been promoted from

Table 7.3 Pattern of recruitment and promotion of higher civil servants under Rhee and Park (by grades, in percentages)

	1948–1961				*1977–1980*		
	Hengsi	*Special*	*Internal*		*Hengsi*	*Special*	*Internal*
1	–	63.9	36.1	1	–	34.5	65.5
2	–	52.9	47.1	2A	–	6.8	93.2
	–	–	–	2B	–	6.5	93.5
3A	–	39.8	60.2	3A	–	8.1	91.9
3B	4.1	30.6	65.3	3B	20.6	10.8	68.5

Source: Ministry of Government Affairs. Quoted in Byung-kook (1988: 101).

Table 7.4 Pattern of recruitment and promotion of higher civil servants (by grades, in percentages)

Process of recruitment and promotion	*Incumbents as of January 1960, occupying positions of:*		
	Grade III-B	*Grade III-A*	*Grade II*
Grade II			
Originally recruited at Grade II	–	–	21.1
Promoted from below	–	–	78.9
Grade III-A			
Originally recruited at Grade III-A	–	20.4	43.7
Promoted from below	–	79.6	35.0
Grade III-B			
Originally recruited at Grade III-B	19.4	28.8	26.2
Promoted from below	80.6	50.7	8.8

Source: Bark (1961: 206).

within the bureaucracy, and almost 9 percent of those bureau directors had risen from below the rank of Grade II-B. In addition, almost 80 percent of Grade III-A civil servants were promoted from below, and 80 percent of Grade III-B civil servants were promoted from below.

Graduates of four-year colleges accounted for 29.9 percent of all bureau directors in the Korean bureaucracy in 1960; all bureau directors at the Ministry of Reconstruction, by contrast, had completed college. The Ministry of Reconstruction, the Ministry of Finance, and the banks were also the major beneficiaries of the US program in public administration that exposed government officials to overseas training. Of 225 people trained in the program through 1961, thirty-nine came from the Ministry of Reconstruction, fifty-nine from the Ministry of Finance, and forty-one from the banking community (a total of 139).[10] The training of these people in the United States may help account for the American influences in Korean planning which were discussed in Chapter 6.

Other evidence of differences between the two systems is also unclear. In the Korean bureaucracy, internal promotion was always based more on seniority than on any type of merit; for example, it is simply impossible to find a forty-year-old Grade II civil servant. Ministers do not rotate through various ministries and gain varied expertise; rather, they rise through a single ministry in their entire career. As their class rises through the bureaucratic ranks, they begin slowly to fall off for various reasons. After ten years or so they can expect to rise to Grade III-A level, and after another decade to Grade II. By the time one of their members of their class is eligible for a political post at vice-minister level, their ranks have thinned. When one of them is successful in rising to the political appointment, the rest then exit the bureaucracy and retire to other posts. They will not remain after one of their cohort has risen too high.

Thus to conclude that Syngman Rhee's personnel policies were consciously clientelistic in nature is unfair; he faced a number of constraints on reforming the bureaucracy that Park did not face. At the same time, the evidence does not reveal that Park Chung Hee was interested in reform.

Monitoring and enforcing bureaucratic compliance with Rhee and Park

One difference between Rhee and Park concerns the method by which these rulers monitored and enforced bureaucratic compliance with top political leadership's goals. There is a large literature on how political principals control bureaucratic agents. Matthew McCubbins and Thomas Schwartz have identified two generic strategies: police patrols or fire alarms (1984). "Police patrols" is a regular, routine, information-gathering exercise whereby the principal learns from the agent about various activities that have taken place, while "fire-alarms" involves the principal waiting until someone pulls the cord and says out loud that there is a problem. For Rhee, oversight involved the use of fire-alarms, and his leadership style was hands-off until certain actions had been taken. Park, on the other hand, made extensive use of "police patrol" systems, whereby he regularly met with bureaucrats and made instant decisions about what to do.

Did Rhee interfere? My research corroborates Lee's work on this period. Sŏng In-sang told me that "Rhee gave me three rules, and then he left me alone (as Reconstruction Minister): first, keep trade with Japan as small as possible. Second, defend the Exchange rate. Finally, never, *ever* sign anything in English until Rhee had read it first. My English was not very good at that time!"(Author's interview, 17 October 1996).

Far from Park Chung Hee creating an independent and neutral bureaucracy, the evidence suggests that Park conducted regular police patrols of the various bureaus. This included the monthly trade promotion meetings, "on-the-spot" guidance, and episodic purges. Under the military junta, the "Extraordinary Measures for National Reconstruction Law" allowed the suspension of all civil rights. Under this law, 2,000 military officers, including fifty-five generals, were dismissed on charges of factionalism and corruption (Henderson 1968: 183). After the coup, 4,000 civil servants were dismissed or arrested on various charges (Huer 1989: 97). The Revolutionary Tribunal was enacted in July 1961 and within ten months had prosecuted 901 trials, involving 1,474 persons. The Political Purification Law of 1962 barred 4,369 persons from political activity. The junta ended up dismissing 35,684 civil servants on various charges (Yi 1966: 310). Even when Park's rule was relatively consolidated, under the *Yusin* (Revitalizing Reform) constitution, Park dismissed 331 officials in

April 1974 for corruption, including fifty-two holding posts higher than section chief (Jun 1985: 63). In March 1977, 420 employees were purged. In 1976, 15,000 officials were reprimanded and sanctioned for corruption.

Virtually no one believed, however, that Park was engaged in purges in order to clean up society. Declaring politicians and other leaders to be corrupt, promulgating lists of men deemed unfit to hold office, and punishing alleged wrongdoers was a legitimizing tactic used by Korean military dictators to justify *coups d'état*: Park did it in 1961 and again in 1971 when he declared martial law preparatory to promulgating the *Yusin* constitution. Chun imitated his predecessor in 1980. Although this allowed both leaders to present themselves as simple and pure soldiers intervening to punish the corrupt and rescue the nation, the main thrust was legitimization of the new regimes and neutralization of their political opponents. Most Koreans believed that the purges were motivated by an attempt to divert public attention away from larger political problems, and that even so, the purges targeted small fry and rarely prosecuted the major infractions.[11]

Such monitoring and enforcement created a bureaucracy that responded quite clearly to regime interests. Both major and minor policy decisions were reached at the highest levels, and then justified by the various ministries. Even though Park supported and protected the economic technocrats in his government from other branches of government and from certain social pressures, it is a mistake to see the technocrats as independent from the executive. The decision to launch the Heavy and Chemical Industry Plan and the *Saemaŭl Undong* (New Village Movement) in the early 1970s provides examples of how the short-run political objectives of the executive could prevail over and ultimately circumvent the bureaucracy. In both instances, existing bureaucratic structures were bypassed and new ones directly responsible to the President were created.[12]

Thus the bureaucracy's role was to justify and implement economic choices made by politicians. In an interview, Hahn-been Lee told me that "Of course the political leadership made all the major decisions about projects. We were there to provide a rationale for the decisions the regime had already made, and then to implement them. The approval guidelines were there to help, but were not strictly enforced" (author's interview, 22 October 1996).

This evidence suggests that Park was more interventionist than Rhee, and his bureaucracy clearly paid close attention to the wishes of political superiors. An autonomous or insulated bureaucracy is not one where the agent keeps close tabs on what the principal wants. By most measures, Rhee and Park look similar. Far from delegating responsibility and autonomy to a technocratic elite, the evidence shows that Park kept a very firm grip over the entire state.

A full discussion of Park's political choices is beyond the scope of this chapter. Clientelism and patronage are far more subtle than either/or propositions, as are the issues of embeddedness, delegation, rent-seeking, and policy choice. It should be clear from this discussion that the full story of how elites managed political coalitions and bureaucrats and policy choices is extremely complex, and requires a level of empirical detail that is still generally lacking in the extant literature. If this is true, the question naturally arises as to how political control affected the second major statist claim, that policy-making was relatively divorced from politics. It is to this issue that we now turn.

Korean balancing and mutual hostages

Can we now begin to flesh out a political story which might explain the choices that actors made? Economic policy choice is only one of many issues about which political elites must concern themselves. A political-economy explanation must focus closely on how preferences emerge and the institutions that direct the implementation of those preferences. Such an explanation must be sensitive to the nature of the political coalition that supported the elites, to the nature of intra-elite rivalries, and to the resource constraints and vulnerability that elites faced. Given that elites must constantly be concerned about retaining power, corruption and policy access can be powerful political tools.

Political considerations had always been important in Korean policy-making, and Park Chung Hee was no exception. Our task is to describe the policy-making process and to explain "why who got what." After showing that economic and political elites balanced each other in a process that limited their ability to the advantage of the other, I then show why the large *chaebŏl* valued size over efficiency, and why the decision-making process in the Korean state also emphasized size over efficiency.

In the Park regime, government intervention was subject to political influence in a number of ways that reduced both rent-seeking on the part of the entrepreneurs, and transaction costs for the politicians and bureaucrats involved in monitoring the policy process. While the "strong state" has been the focus of much of the literature, the surprising strength of the business sector has received less attention. State control over the financial sector had enormous consequences for the organization and conduct of business in Korea (Chang 1994; Cole and Park 1983: 173; Jones and SaKong 1990; Woo 1991). Suh and Kwon have discussed the important role the state played in shaping the fortunes of the Hyundai corporation. The state could, in fact, control business through its control over the flow of finance. Since Korean companies were highly leveraged, these were vulnerable to state control. Paradoxically, this weakness became a source of strength relative to the state. The Park regime – intentionally or unintentionally – actively encouraged the centralization and enhancement of economic power in the *chaebŏl*. From Park's initial decision in 1961 to pardon the "Illicit Wealth Accumulators" to the bail-out of highly leveraged firms in August 1972 to the 1976 decision to promote General Trading Companies,[13] there have been continuous policy moves by the state to encourage the rise of the *chaebŏl*.

If the state has control over various policy instruments, can control or manipulate the judiciary and the legislature, and can redesign the terms of any agreement it makes at will, the problem will be that no action it takes will be credible. The far-sighted ruler who realizes that his state is at risk will take action to infuse greater confidence. One way the state can make a believable commitment to various policy initiatives is by fostering domestic sources of power in specific areas – power centers that would be tremendously costly to overcome. A "mutual hostage" situation exists whenever two actors have significant vulnerability relative to each other. This can arise from either an explicit or an implicit exchange of hostages. In so doing, each side thus has an incentive both to continue the relationship, and also to limit taking advantage of the other party. Exchanging hostages as a generic strategy involves exposure to the potentially affected party.

By encouraging the formation of conglomerates that accounted for large percentages of the Korean economy, the state and *chaebŏl* in effect became "mutual hostages" with each other (See Tables 7.5 and 7.6). Each needing the other, neither able to gain fully the upper hand, state and *chaebŏl* were forced to work together. This view emphasizes the continuing collaboration between big business and the state, the state's reliance on the *chaebŏl* for political funds, and the inability of the state to push too strongly in directions that the *chaebŏl* did not wish to pursue (Lew 1992; Park: 1982).

Table 7.5 Mutual hostages, Part I: *Chaebŏl* value-added, 1973 to 1975 (% of non-agricultural GDP)

Chaebŏl *(ranking)*	*1973*	*1974*	*1975*
Top 5	5.1	5.6	7.1
Top 10	7.9	8.5	10.7
Top 20	10.9	11.8	14.7

Source: Jones and SaKong (1980: 268).

Table 7.6 Mutual hostages, Part II: Debt/equity ratio of manufacturing firms in selected countries, 1972 to 1984 (%)

Year	*Korea*	*U.S.*	*Taiwan*
1972	313.4	–	–
1975	339.5	60.6	99.3
1980	487.9	177.0	82.5
1984	342.7	134.5	110.1

Source: Adapted from Leipziger (1988: 128).

Thus, mutual hostages constrained collusion between political and economic elites. Firms rushed headlong to become larger as a way of both justifying continued cheap money and also of making themselves so large that the government would have no choice but to bail them out. A flow of political payoffs to politicians cemented this pipeline of easy money. For politicians, the need for political funds to run elections and other political activities, as well as a natural proclivity towards greed, gave them no incentive to sanction companies unless the business managers were utterly incompetent.

Why bigger was better

In the context of an authoritarian regime that is selectively handing out favors, size is always an advantage. Given the Korean state's total control over the financial sector in the 1960s and 1970s, there was naturally intense interest on the part of business in gaining access to the enormous rents that accrued to a *chaebŏl* if it received a low interest rate loan.

Historically, the *chaebŏl* have *always* been heavily indebted. Rents accrued merely from the interest differential between state-sponsored loans and the real interest rate. Capital was so scarce in developing Korea that the curb (or informal) market interest rate in 1964 was 61.4 percent per annum. The opposition party in the National Assembly concluded that of the ten largest creditors, eight were "disguised curb market loans" (Yi 1985: 273–274). In 1970, estimates of the size of the curb market exceeded 345 billion won, which was 80 percent of the money supply (M2 basis) and 34 percent of the outstanding domestic credit held by the banking sector (see Ministry of Finance 1978: 155). Thus having access to low-interest government loans was a license to print money.

In fact, the Economic Planning Board had advocated a "more is better" approach to foreign borrowing during the 1960s. It was common for firms to borrow foreign funds in order to "gain construction materials to build a factory, run the factory, and repay the debts" (Economic Planning Board 1983: 88), in a circular pattern of borrowing.

In addition, debt provided a number of economic benefits that raising capital by other means did not (see, e.g., Williamson 1988). Debt is cheaper than equity, because there are generally tax write-offs for interest payments. With high inflation, as existed in the 1960s in Korea, the real interest rate actually could become negative, making debt a superior form of financing. In addition, taking on debt is more secure than equity: the businessman retains control of the company, and loans create fewer transaction costs than equity. Debt also allows more political pressure on banks, and with good political connections debt was relatively easy to acquire from the government. Finally, larger political needs had an influence: the Koreans were generally quite worried about the Japanese coming in and buying up their entire country, but with debt there is no foreign control.

So as a practice of restricting foreign influence, debt is far superior to equity financing or FDI. Creating equity markets is also much harder than taking on debt: capital markets require a legal and institutional infrastructure that is far more nuanced and sophisticated than merely borrowing money on the international market. With personal guarantees made by close political connections, debt also lowered transaction costs of monitoring and enforcing agreements. Debt also gives the politicians a measure of control over the *chaebŏl*: raising capital through issuing equity would have severed that connection. Debt financing has thus acquired a very critical place in the story of Korea's capitalist modernity.

There were also political reasons why government intervention favored the largest *chaebŏl* in a number of other ways. A capitalist who had already acquired a license to invest in a project was at a great advantage in acquiring further credit allocation from the government. Since there were only a small number of capitalists who had shown their ability to produce in the past, they stood out.

Given the bureaucrat's innate disposition to avoid risky decisions and to rely on past performance as an indicator of future success, "the rich got richer." The few large firms were considered better risks, regardless of the quality of the actual business plan submitted to the government. In addition, most decisions were made at the highest levels. Thus, having "smoky, back-door" access through personal connections as to precisely what officials at the top of the regime desired meant that some *chaebŏls* were able to submit applications designed specifically to fit the regime's political and economic goals. This became a reinforcing cycle, where bigger was better, the rich got richer, and political connections were thus a very important factor in getting decisions. Park Byung-yoon noted that:

> If a high-ranking bureaucrat made a decision to support a less-well known small applicant, rather than an established *chaebŏl*, there followed invariably public suspicion: "Even large *chaebŏls* couldn't get it. How could a small unknown man get such support? There must have been a hidden reason or bribery."
>
> (Interview, quoted in Kim 1987: 110)

In addition, bureaucrats attempting to advance along their own career paths had their progress closely monitored by Park Chung Hee and the political leadership. The best way to advance was to be successful, and spreading scarce government-allocated capital around many small firms was less likely to be impressive than picking proven winners. Monitoring and enforcement were much easier with smaller numbers than with larger numbers. In addition, the larger *chaebŏls* were more likely to give the bureaucrat a job upon retirement. In Korea, though perhaps not as extensively as in Japan, *amakudari*, or "descent from heaven" also occurs. Table 7.7 shows that of 231 Chairmen or Vice-chairmen of Federation of Korean

Table 7.7 Previous careers of officers of FKI member companies, 1989

Previous career	*Chairman and Vice-Chairman*	*President and Vice-President*	*Managing Director*
Executive administration	46 (20.0)	84 (12.6)	47 (8.6)
Military	3 (1.3)	44 (6.6)	15 (2.7)
Banking	28 (12.1)	102 (15.3)	60 (11.0)
Business associations	55 (23.8)	55 (8.2)	5 (0.9)
Academia	27 (11.7)	41 (6.1)	20 (3.7)
Other	72 (31.1)	342 (51.2)	399 (73.1)
Total	231 (100)	668 (100)	546 (100)

Source: Kang *et al.* (1991: 77).

Industry member companies in 1989, fully 20 percent had had a previous career in the executive branch of government.

All these factors combined to make it politically more wise for bureaucrats to reward size. Thus bureaucrats were more likely to approve projects based on track record, personal connections, and historical background rather than on the pure merit of the proposed project.

Finally, social and political strength came from size: profitability was not nearly as important as survival and growth. Most Korean firms have had lax accounting procedures, and siphoning off funds was very easy to do. In addition, much of the conspicuous consumption was for social purposes. Having a limousine, driver, and money for entertaining was the way to political and social success. As long as the firm did not go bankrupt, there was always a way to get discretionary cash. Thus a number of factors, both economic and political, led to the enormous indebtedness of the *chaebŏl* in Korea and a focus on expansion as rapidly as possible.

Political connections: inmaek and honmaek[14]

It is almost a cliché to point out that personal connections are important in Asia. Our task is to show that these connections mattered to the point of overriding efficiency concerns. Not surprisingly, size correlated with close personal relations. Park Byung-yoon points out that in 1964, 40 percent of total bank loans – 44 percent of M1 money supply – were given to only nine *chaebŏl* (1982: 198–199). The largest borrowers of foreign capital were Ssangyong, Lucky, Korea Explosive, Shinjin, Samho, Kolon, Panbon, Hanil, and Samchuk Samup, all of which had family members in powerful positions in the ruling party or in the bureaucracy (1982: 210). The *quid pro quo*? During the 1960s, the expected "donation" in order to receive loans became an informal norm of between 10 and 20 percent of the value of the loan (for more information, see Kang (2002); Kim (1985)). Figure 7.1 shows a very selective map of relationships among the political and economic elites in Korea. Most of the major businessmen

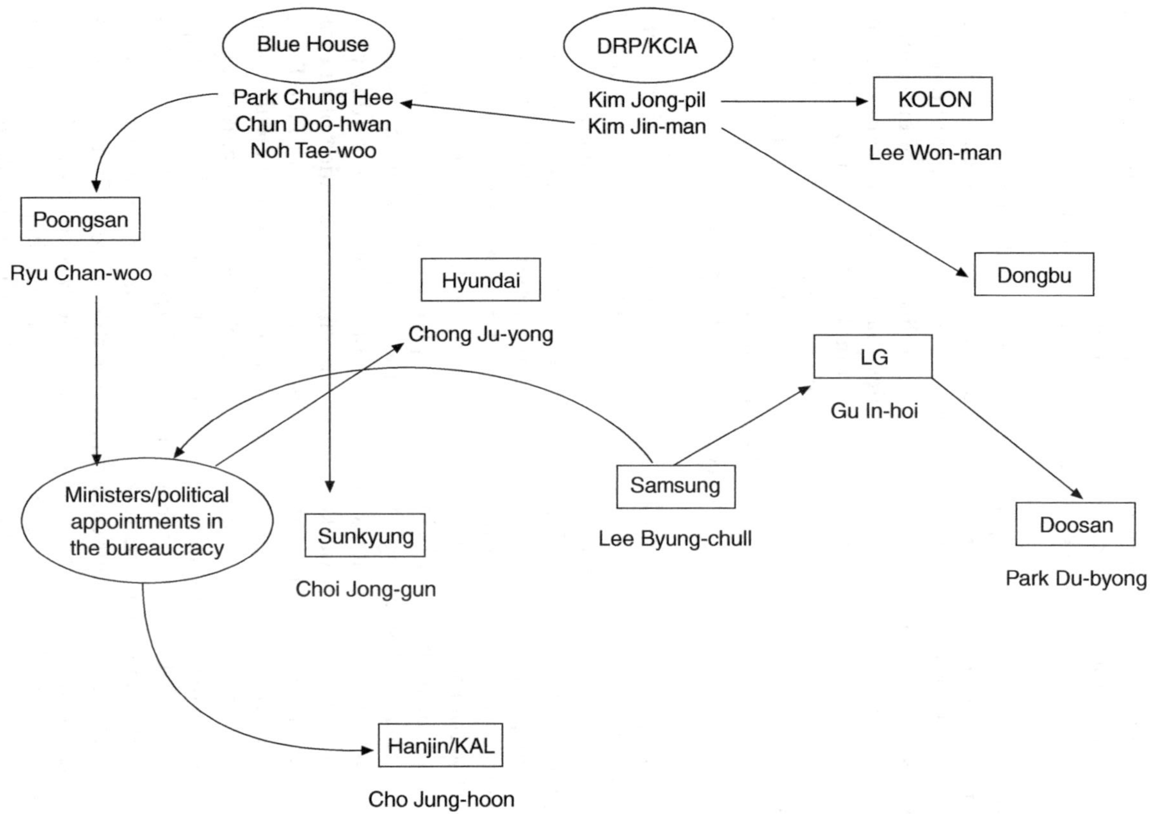

Figure 7.1 A highly selected sample of family relations in Korea (source: adapted from Sung-ryol 1988: 49–60; Kang *et al.* 80–81.

have marriage relations with major political figures, and all assiduously cultivate personal relationships.

However, there existed a downside to close relations with Park, as well as a positive side. Those who fell foul of Park were in exposed positions, and Park was not afraid to use his power to destroy those who had angered him. Before the US Congress, Kim Hyung-wook testified that:

> Mr. Park imposed severe pressures and sanctions on businessmen who did not give him their undivided loyalty. In many cases, charges were fabricated and these individuals were sent to jail. In addition to imprisonment, the businesses of these individuals were often confiscated. Some of the business companies that were destroyed or taken over were Yonhap Steel Co., Sinjin Automobile Co., Chungang Industries and Builders, Tongkwang Business, Koryo Shipbuilding Co., Kwang Myong Printing Co., Koryo Food Co., Kyungnam Business Co., Tachan Transportation Co., and the Cheju Bank.
>
> (US House of Representatives 1977: 11)

Since bigger was better and led more easily to rewards, and since personal connections and size were a mutual reinforcing virtuous cycle, many firms either massaged or fabricated their export data during the period of high growth. While it is true that firms in Korea did export a large percentage of their production, those numbers were frequently inflated. In addition, most applications for government support did not require the type of financial accounting and transparency that are well known in the West, and past performance and being a past recipient of government aid was used as a means of selecting those companies that might succeed in the future. Thus numbers about the Korean economy should be regarded with care. A businessman who worked out of the chairman's office of one of Korea's largest *chaebŏl* told me that the numbers they reported to the Bank of Korea, the World Bank, and to major publications such as *Fortune* were all highly inflated. "Of course we made them [the trade figures] up. I would wait for the Chairman to let me know what the numbers were supposed to be and then find a way to make it so" (personal interview with a member of the Chairman's secretariat of a major *chaebŏl*, 14 March 1993).

There is also independent confirmation of this process. Table 7.8 shows the over-invoicing of Korean exports. This table was compiled by taking Korean export statistics and comparing them to US import statistics, on the assumption that the US both had more legal rules in place to force accurate reporting, and no inherent incentive to inflate the numbers. The discrepancy shows that throughout the 1970s and 1980s, South Korean companies overestimated their exports by hundreds of millions of dollars, a result that squares both with the anecdotal evidence told to me by actual managers who inflated the numbers to please their superiors, and the sense that the Korean state was not as successful as it claimed it was.

Table 7.8 Overestimation of Korean exports, 1970 to 1985 (million US$)

	Over-invoicing of exports
1970	87
1971	145
1972	174
1973	396
1974	93
1975	206
1976	123
1977	403
1978	921
1979	1,172
1980	1,128
1981	2,073
1982	2,764
1983	3,650
1984	4,354
1985	2,597

Source: Gulati (1987: 72).

Overcapacity

The state's inability to control firms and their growth led to endemic overcapacity. Firms rushed willy-nilly to expand at all costs, whether or not it was economically feasible. The result was that in most major sectors of the economy there was excess capacity, and overlapping and duplication of efforts as each *chaebŏl* tried to be the biggest.

The car industry serves as a good example. Despite numerous attempts to rationalize the automobile industry and force domestic firms to concentrate on core competencies, throughout the 1970s Korea had more capacity and more players than was considered economically feasible (see Table 7.9). To return to Hyundai for a moment, in 1969 Hyundai motors operated at 49 percent of capacity, and in 1972 at only 25.8 percent of capacity. The rest of the industry was no better. Even by 1979, after the rationalization efforts had begun, total Korean passenger car production was operating at 48.6 percent of capacity.

On the other hand, observers of the automobile industry have noted that continuous attempts by the government to impose a unitary automobile producer in Korea (beginning with the 1963 "unitarization plan") have been singularly unsuccessful, due to the ability of local capitalists to resist government intervention. An effort by Kim Jong-pil, then head of the Korean CIA, to assemble Nissan vehicles, collapsed in 1963 in part due to protests from Korean parts manufacturers that imports of Nissan parts would eradicate the home market. When Park Chung Hee attempted to consolidate industry around Shinjin as an assembler of Toyotas, he failed as well. Park Byung-yoon argues that industry has seen the government as

Table 7.9(a) Production and capacity of Hyundai Motor Company, 1969 to 1972 (%)

	1969	*1970*	*1971*	*1972*
Passenger cars	52.0	19.6	20.0	21.8
Trucks	62.0	33.1	3.9	7.5
Buses	17.5	67.2	53.5	68.3
Total	49.0	27.3	22.2	25.8

Source: HMC (1987: 138).

Table 7.9(b) Passenger car production and capacity, 1979 (%)

	Production/capacity
Hyundai	61.8
Saehan/Daewoo	24.6
Kia	55.4
Total	48.6

Source: KDB (1980: 114–115).

ineffective and "a weak organization that lacks the will and resources to implement its own policy. If the government had tried to enforce policies against the interests of industry, the government could not have done anything to make the business community comply with its program" (1979: 76, quoted in Lew 1992).

Finally, between August and October 1980, the Korean government ordered the automobile industry to "merge by decree." The objective was to create more financially sound companies which were more willing and able both to compete in export markets and to assemble foreign-designed cars in Korea. The plan was to merge Hyundai Motors with Daewoo's *Saehan* subsidiary and to produce passenger cars, while forcing *Kia* industries out of the passenger car market. The government did not succeed (Lew 1992; see also Choi 1989: 129–130).

In fact, the influence of the automobile *chaebŏl* on Korean developmental plans has been so pervasive that one scholar has termed the policies "inconsistent and incoherent." Lew (199: 145) writes:

> the lack of insulation in the policy-making process, from the business circle or the political circle, contributed to the oscillation and the incoherent character of automobile industrial policies.... Career bureaucrats did not exercise any decisive influence on the development of the South Korean automobile industry in the 1960s.

Why did these plans fail? The mutual-hostage situation, while allowing collusion between business and political elites, also eliminated coercion as an option. As Choi Byung-sun (1989: 132) writes:

> Paradoxically, the fact that the government controlled credit allocation weakened, rather than strengthened, the force of the government's commitment to discontinue financing, because private investors knew that terminating financial assistance would be disastrous not only for themselves but probably more for the political regime. In sum, Korean government's extraordinary measures to restructure excessive heavy industrial investment projects failed.

Essentially, a non-incredible threat is the same as a credible commitment. Controllers of domestic capital knew that the state could not credibly expropriate their wealth and thus did not need to worry.

Other industries were also able successfully to resist merger decrees (Choi 189: 126–127; Kim 1987: 238). *Hyundai Yanghaeng* (Hyundai Power) was in deep trouble in the late 1970s. The business fell far below the capital–asset ratios agreed on by the World Bank and the EPB.[15] And yet, because the process of creating a power plant had had such significant sunk costs, Hyundai was reluctant to abandon the project. Daewoo and Samsung also made power, and the government attempted to rationalize them in the late 1970s into one main group; but the Park Chung Hee government was not able to rationalize the power industry.

> The government's proposal was not accepted by the rival business groups, although the former group had made some progress toward a merger. The Hyundai group pleaded for various kinds of government support and privileges, almost all of which the government grudgingly granted. Nonetheless the merger attempt was unsuccessful in the end.
> (Choi 1989: 128)

Thus the mutual-hostage situation limited the state's ability to control the *chaebŏl*. Korean government control over capital gave it a non-credible threat to cut off credit to the *chaebŏl*, because all actors knew that it would hurt the regime as much as the conglomerate. Indeed, whether or not there existed a market rationale for expansion of the firms' activities, there certainly existed a profit rationale when combined with the proper political connections. Far from limiting and controlling *chaebŏl* expansion, the Park era saw the opposite result. Table 7.10 shows the year of incorporation or establishment of subsidiary companies for the ten largest *chaebŏls* in 1984.

Sixty percent of the expansion of the *chaebŏl* occurred during the 1970s, resulting in tremendous overcapacity. The entire heavy and chemical industries project was one of massive expansion and very little oversight. The argument that the Korean state was performing an effective role in organizing and restraining *chaebŏl* growth does not appear to be supported by the data.

Table 7.10 Year of incorporation or establishment of the subsidiary companies of the ten largest *chaebŏl* in 1984

	Total	*1949*	*1950–1959*	*1960–1969*	*1970–1979*	*1980–1984*	*Missing*
Samsung	30	1	3	6	11	8	1
Hyundai	32	1	2	4	20	1	4
Lucky Goldstar	24	1	2	5	10	3	3
Daewoo	24	0	0	0	21	3	0
Sunkyung	14	0	1	1	7	3	2
Ssangyong	14	2	1	3	6	2	0
Korea Explosives	18	0	1	5	8	3	1
Kukje	18	1	0	5	7	0	0
Hanjin	12	1	0	5	7	0	0
Hyosung	20	1	2	5	12	0	0
Total	206	8	12	34	114	23	15
%	–	4	6	18	60	12	–

Source: Kuk (1995: 116).

Bail-outs

The incentive to become heavily indebted and to focus on expansion instead of efficiency had predictable results: firms borrowed whether they needed to or not. Many firms expanded far too quickly and without adequate management expertise or planning, but because there were so few *chaebŏl*, it was politically dangerous to allow them to fail. As a result, the Korean state *did* bail out weak companies, and rewarded political relations, not necessarily economic success. Far from imposing performance standards, the Korean government was continually forced to bail out inefficient firms that had overextended themselves. Table 7.11 shows the changing debt–equity ratios of major Korean *chaebŏls*.

Indeed, as far back as 1971 the United States government alerted South Korea to the problems it faced due to the personalistic manner in which foreign aid and loans were disbursed. At a meeting on 30 March 1971 between EPB officials and US Treasury and State Department officials, the Americans stressed that

> insolvent industries, caused by political favoritism in earlier years, represented a major problem. They stressed that foreign banks looked closely at the prevalence of favoritism towards basically unsound companies. [EPB vice-minister] Lee acknowledged the problem and indicated that President Park had directed that these companies be "rationalized" in the near future through a process of changing principal investors and mergers where appropriate.
>
> (US House of Representatives 1978: 189 and fn. 120)

Table 7.11 Debt/equity of the ten largest *chaebŏl*, 1970 to 1983

Rank[a]	Chaebŏl	*1970*	*1975*	*1980*	*1983*
1	Hyundai	2.9	6.1	3.7	3.0
2	Samsung	3.2	2.5	7.4	8.0
3	Daewoo	7.0	4.9	3.7	6.1
4	Lucky Goldstar	1.6	3.9	5.5	4.7
5	Ssangyong	2.4	2.8	7.2	5.5
6	Sunkyong	n.a.	6.1	11.5	5.4
7	Korea Explosives	3.2	7.1	7.7	3.2
8	Hanjin	3.8	17.5	10.5	5.1
9	Kukje	4.7	3.7	5.5	9.5
10	Daelim	1.8	1.6	2.2	3.2

Source: Kim (1987: 106).

Note
a Ranking based on total assets, sales, and capital in 1983.

However, the firms were rarely rationalized in the manner promised by Park.

Perhaps the best example of inefficient but large and politically connected firms receiving government aid is the 3 August 1972 "Presidential Emergency Decree on Economic Stabilization and Development" (informally known as the *pal-sam* decree or the 8-3 decree) when Park Chung Hee decided to freeze high-interest informal ("curb") market loans and replace them with long-term bank loans. By early 1972, many highly indebted firms were facing economic difficulties, and the FKI was meeting daily in order to deal with the problem of excessive indebtedness to the curb market.

The Chairman of the FKI finally decided to ask the President directly for help with the problem. After two personal meetings in June with the President, Park Chung Hee told his Chief-of-Staff, Kim Chung-nyum, along with Presidential Secretary Kim Yong-hwan, to prepare an emergency decree.[16] Designed by Park Chung Hee to alleviate the curb market, the 8-3 decree had the effect of saving the bigger *chaebŏl*, because they were more valuable to the state and had thus received more support. The decree essentially placed a moratorium on new loans, and old loans were rescheduled to be paid back over five years, after a three-year grace period. Special Finance Bonds up to two billion *wŏn* were be issued in order to alleviate the debt burden of major corporations, and the government established a loan interest and long-term Industry Rationalization Fund.[17]

This case is instructive for two reasons. First, the FKI was in fact able to appeal directly to the President and to exert some influence, because this was a situation in which the FKI was able to speak for all the *chaebŏl* (Eckert 1993: 108). Second, those companies that had been most poorly managed and hence heavily indebted were those that gained the most from the 8-3 decree.

The picture of policy-making I have presented here complements and in some ways supersedes the pattern described by the statists. The bureaucracy was marginal, political connections were central, and little oversight was undertaken. Corruption was rampant, allowing political leaders to finance their parties and retain power. Large firms benefited at the expense of small firms, and the resulting overcapacity and high indebtedness has been an endemic feature of Korea's political economy well into the 1990s.

Maintaining rule while still reigning effectively

In this final section I discuss how Park Chung Hee managed his clientelistic relations with his military cronies. In Korea, the "state" under Park Chung Hee was an amorphous entity that comprised the ruling party (DRP), the military, the KCIA, the bureaucracy, the national assembly, and the executive and judicial branches. A conventional wisdom exists that the military officers who descended upon the South Korean bureaucracy after the *coup d'état* in 1961 provided a more principled focus on economic development, a rationalistic and goal-oriented perspective, in contrast to the corrupt and inefficient civil servants. This vision of Korea, for example, informed Walt Rostow's perceptions in 1961. In addition, the military allegedly possessed organizational skills honed during the war (see, e.g., Huer 1989: 80–81). These beliefs are so accepted an article of faith that the assumptions underlying them are rarely questioned: Why would military officers, trained in the arts of war, have any better idea about how to manage an entire national economy than the civilian bureaucracy? It is also not clear why officers who had retired from the military would be less inclined than bureaucrats to use their position to line their pockets. Indeed, Park compensated for a lack of economic expertise by keeping military cronies out of important fiscal bureaus. This strategy was evident to domestic capitalists, and allowed Park a measure of freedom in his dealings with both the military and the capitalists.

Park carefully orchestrated bureaucratic appointments in order to allow for both patronage *and* reform. Initially, Park Chung Hee needed military support in all sectors of the bureaucracy as a means of consolidating and keeping control; yet he gradually phased out the military's influence in some areas, thereby creating more efficient bureaucracies. This allowed Park to achieve domestic control by buying off supporters, and also to create pockets of efficiency that were oriented towards promoting defense and development.[18]

Table 7.12 shows a ministry-by-ministry breakdown of the origins of ministers and vice-ministers. The "fiscal" ministries (EPB, Finance, MTI) had relatively little military infiltration. By contrast, ministries not directly related to development were staffed heavily with ex-military officials. For example, the Ministry of Construction, widely regarded as one of the most

Table 7.12 Career backgrounds of vice-ministers and higher (1963–1983)

Bureau	*Total number*	*Prior career*
		Military
Prime Minister	11	3
EPB		
M	13	1
VM	13	0
Presidential Secretary		
Chief Secretary	8	2
Economic Secretary	9	0
Finance		
M	14	0
VM	18	0
Trade and Industry		
M	11	2
VM	9	0
Agriculture and Forestry		
M	15	0
VM	11	0
Energy and Resources		
M	7	1
VM	3	0
Construction		
M	15	6
VM	10	2
Transportation		
M	16	11
VM	13	2
Defense		
M	9	9
VM	9	6
Home Affairs		
M	13	9
VM	13	3
KCIA		
Director	9	7

Source: Kim (1988: 119); Ministry of Governmental Affairs.

Notes
M: Minister; VM: Vice-minister.

corrupt ministries in Korea, saw a large number of military appointments, eight out of a possible twenty-five. In South Korea, public works contracts and construction in general are poorly controlled.

In addition, Park Chung Hee was assiduous in creating what one ex-bureaucrat called a "three-levels-deep" political network in all the ministries. "Don't forget that Park was also using a criterion of skill; if you didn't perform, he always had an assistant Vice-Minister and a Planning Coordination Officer in the wings, waiting for their chance. So it wasn't just patronage, it was effective competition for Park's favor that induced such responsiveness" (author's interview with a bureaucrat who wishes to remain unidentified). Cronies who had become dangerous or lost their favor were sent to ambassadorial posts in second- or third-rate countries, far away from the action.

In fact, Park's networks comprised a set of concentric circles around him. For political purposes, the most important posts were the Seoul Defense Command (*Sudokyŏngbi-sa*) and the heads of the CIA and the National Defense Security Command (*boansa*, which Chun Doo Hwan would later command). The headquarters of the Seoul Defense Command is located next to *Kyŏngbokgung*, and the commander was one of the few generals who had instant and direct access to Park. This was a military regime, existing under the shadow of war with the north. Thus, for Park, managing the Civil Service was only one aspect to the larger political problem of maintaining rule while leading the country in the direction he wished.

The point of this section has been to show that the military and patronage appointments under Park Chung Hee, while prevalent and necessary for means of political control, were also selectively implemented. Park was able to create a bifurcated bureaucracy, directing patronage appointments to domestic "service" ministries, while maintaining the professionalism of the "fiscal" ministries.

Conclusion

Understanding the political bases of the developmental state not only furthers our empirical knowledge, it also provides us with a better explanation for how and why these states developed. If the criterion is "growth of the *chaebŏl*" then Park Chung Hee was more influential in the rise of the few major conglomerates than was Rhee. Whether or not intentionally, under Park the largest firms benefited enormously, often at the expense of the smaller firms. If the criterion is "consistency of political appointments," again, Park and Rhee look remarkably similar. Under Park, neither patronage appointments nor the consistency of Cabinet-level appointments shows any clear difference from Rhee in terms of either length in office or of type of personnel. If the criterion is "insulating the bureaucracy and allowing it to develop initiatives," again Park and Rhee, although with different styles, look very similar. Neither Park nor Rhee allowed the bureaucracy to operate independently of political control.

This chapter has argued that new questions need to be asked about the development of the Asian economies and the evolution of Asian capitalist modernity. Substantively, I have focused on an empirical argument that revises some of our stylized facts about Korea. However, my work builds upon – rather than negates – the spate of new theoretical work in the field.

New developments in micro-economics, sociology, and anthropology have underlined the role of institutions in East Asia's economic performance (see, e.g., Chang 1993). Rather than seeing markets as the frictionless intersection of supply and demand curves, markets are being reinterpreted as complexes of principal–agent relationships in which problems of imperfect and asymmetric information, contracting and credibility are ubiquitous. The smooth functioning of markets is not simply a matter of getting policies, incentives, or prices right, but of public and private institutions that facilitate market exchange from the legal system and a clear delineation of property rights; to the public provision of information; and to social networks that build trust. This theoretical work is absolutely essential; yet it is not by itself sufficient for the field to move forward. It is important that we remember to combine theoretical work with careful and intensive empirical detail. The controversy in the discipline over the role of area studies and theory is largely misguided – both are critical to the intellectual process. In this chapter I begin the process of creating a theory that looks inside the state, and provides micro-foundations for individual behavior. The approach offered here suggests that we shift our attention away from broad notions of the state, and also away from the role of individual personalities, and look for empirical and theoretical micro-foundations of how leaders, bureaucrats, social coalitions, and institutions interact with each other.

Notes

1 For example, Peter Evans writes that "the internal organization of developmental states comes much closer to approximating a Weberian bureaucracy. Highly selective meritocratic recruitment and long-term career rewards create commitment and a sense of corporate coherence" (Evans 1995: 12; see also Geddes 1990: 217–234; Muramatsu and Krauss 1984: 126–146; Schneider 1993: 331–350).

2 Alice Amsden's celebrated work has emphasized the economic rationale for state discipline over big business by examining "two interrelated dimensions: (a) penalizing poor performers; and (b) rewarding only good ones" (Amsden 1989: 15).

3 Jung-en Woo's *Race to the Swift* finds a "method to Rhee's madness" (see also Moon and Rhyu 1997).

4 For work that directly addresses the question of growth, see Kang (2002).

5 Amsden (1989: 327). For other specific instances, see Evans (1995: 51–53),

Fields (1997: 126–128), Johnson (1987: 152–155), Önis (1991: 114), Rhee *et al.* (1984), and Schneider and Maxfield (1997: 17).

6 Chalmers Johnson's discussion of the Japanese developmental state implicitly uses voluntary delegation of power to the bureaucracy as the basis of the Japanese success (see Johnson 1982: 21).

7 See Bendor (1988: 365). In an intriguing study of machine politics in Chicago, Steve Erie notes that the Irish "machine" reformed certain sectors of the bureaucracy with an eye toward efficiency. Such reform allowed the machine to capture the resulting efficiency gains for itself. See Erie (1988).

8 Rodden and Rose-Ackerman (1997: 1535). Much of the literature in American politics uses only the assumption that politicians want to be re-elected. The classic work is by Mayhew (1974).

9 For more detail on the Japanese period, see Haggard *et al.* (1997: 867–881). For those who see the Japanese influence as positive or even formative, see Kohli (1994).

10 Under Park, the reverse brain drain truly began. The first wave of Koreans to study in the US in the 1950s began to return to Korea in the 1960s, many going on to play key roles in the bureaucracy under Park. See Ahn (1990) and Kim (1991).

11 Personal communication with John Duncan, 12 October 1997. For similar skepticism, see Rahman (1986: 122). For a detailed account which argues that Park's moves in 1961 were a cynical propaganda attempt to justify a coup, see Satterwhite (1994).

12 For a more detailed discussion of how political interests overrode the technocrat's suggestions in South Korea, see Kang (2002) and Yong (1985).

13 On *Chonghap sangsa* (GTCs), see Cho (1987), and Jo (1991).

14 "Personal connections" and "marriage relations."

15 By 1978, Hyundai Yanghaeng had invested $200 million in a huge integrated machinery plant, and needed $200 million more to finish the project. Capital asset ratios were 8 percent by December 1978, far short of the target levels: 30 percent by 1979 (EPB 1981: 1149–1173).

16 Lee (1985). See also *Kyŏnghyang Ilbo*, 31 August 1991. This account, too, has contradictions. Lew (1992: 162) notes that Kim Yong-hwan argues that the preparations for the 8-3 Decree began in February 1971, long before the FKI became involved.

17 For these details, see the *Seoul Kyŏngje Sinmun*, 3 August 1972.

18 For a good overview from American politics that examines the electoral connection in policy-making, see Shepsle and Weingast (1994), and the subsequent articles in vol. 19. See also Frieden (1991); Przeworski and Limongi (1993).

References

Ahn, Byung-yung. 1990. "Chonhwaki hankuk kwallyoche ŭi kaltŭng kwa palchŏn panghyang (Development and Discord in Bureaucratic Transitions)." *Gyegan Sasang*: 63–104.

Amsden, Alice. 1989. *Asia's Next Giant?* Oxford: Oxford University Press.

Bark, Dong-suh. 1961. *Han'guk kwallyo ch'edo ŭi yŏkssajŏk kaebal* (The Historical Development of the Korean Bureaucratic System). Seoul: Hanguk Yŏn'guso.

——. 1982. "Haengchong kwallyo ŭi hyŏngsŏng (The Formation of Bureaucrats)." *Sindonga*: 5–16.

Bates, Robert H. and Anne O. Krueger. 1993. "Generalizations from the Country

Studies," in Robert Bates and Anne Krueger (eds). *Political and Economic Interactions in Economic Policy Reform.* Oxford: Blackwell.

Bawn, Kathleen. 1995. "Political Control versus Expertise: Congressional Choices about Administrative Procedures." *American Political Science Review* 89: 62–74.

Bendor, Jonathan. 1998. "Formal Models of Bureaucracy." *British Journal of Political Science* 18: 353–395.

Byung-kook, Kim, 1988. "Bringing and Managing Socioeconomic Change." Ph.D. dissertation, Harvard University.

Chang, Ha-joon. 1993. *The Political Economy of Industrial Policy.* New York: St. Martin's Press.

Chang, Ha-joon. 1994. "Organising Development: Comparing the National Systems of Entrepreneurship in Sweden and South Korea." *The Journal of Development Studies* 30: 859–891.

Cho, Dong-sung. 1987. *The General Trading Company: Concept and Strategy.* Lexington, MA: Lexington Books.

Cho, Suk-chun. 1968. "Han'guk kunsa chŏngbuha ŭi issŏsŏ ŭi tugaji e kwanhan pigyo yŏn'gu (A Comparative Study of Two Administrative Reforms Under the Korean Military Government)." *Han'guk Haengjong Nonch'ong* (Korean Journal of Public Administration) 6: 98–121.

Choi, Byung-sun. 1989. "Institutionalizing a Liberal Economic Order in Korea." Ph.D. dissertation, Harvard University.

Chong Ilgwon. 1987. "Nawa Pak Daetongnyŏng: 'Kun gwa chŏngch'i chagumŭn kwallyŏ hajimasio' (President Park and I: Do Not Meddle in Military Affairs and Political Funds)." *Sindong'a*: 251–267.

Cole, David and Yung Chul Park. 1983. *Financial Development in the Republic of Korea 1945–1978.* Cambridge, MA: Harvard University, Council on East Asian Studies.

Eckert, Carter. 1993. "The South Korean Bourgeoisie: A Class in Search of Hegemony," in Hagen Koo (ed.). *State and Society in Contemporary Korea.* Ithaca, NY: Cornell University Press.

Economic Planning Board (EPB). 1981. "Hyundai Yanghaeng Changwon Kongjanmit Okpo Chosensoe Kwanhan Taech'aek (Measures Regarding Hyundai International's Changwon Plant and Okpo Shipyard)," in *Kyongjeanjonghwa Sich'aek Charyojip* (Collected Documents of Economic Stabilization Measures), Korean Development Institute. Seoul: Korean Development Institute, pp. 1149–1173.

Economic Planning Board (EPB). 1983. *Kyonje kihoekwon isipnyonsa* (Twenty Year History of the EPB). Seoul: EPB.

Erie, Steve. 1988. *Rainbow's End: Irish-Americans and the Dilemmas of Urban Machine Politics, 1840–1985.* Berkeley: University of California Press.

Evans, Peter. 1995. *Embedded Autonomy.* Princeton, NJ: Princeton University Press.

Fields, Karl. 1997. "Strong States and Business Organization in Korea and Taiwan," in Sylvia Maxfield and Ben Ross Schneider (eds). *Business and the State in Developing Countries.* Ithaca, NY: Cornell University Press.

Frieden, Jeffrey. 1991. *Debt, Development, and Democracy.* Princeton, NJ: Princeton University Press.

Galati, Sunil K. 1987. "A Note on Trade Misinvoicing," in Donald Lessard and John Williamson (eds). *Capital Flight and Third World Debt.* Washington, DC: Institute for International Economics.

Geddes, Barbara. 1990. "Building 'State' Autonomy in Brazil, 1930–1964." *Comparative Politics* 22: 217–234.

Haggard, Stephan. 1991. *Pathways from the Periphery.* Ithaca, NY: Cornell University Press.

Haggard, Stephan, David Kang, and Chung-in Moon. 1997. "Japanese Colonialism and Korean Development: A Critique." *World Development* 27: 867–881.

Henderson, Gregory. 1968. *Korea, the Politics of the Vortex.* Cambridge, MA: Harvard University Press.

Huer, John. 1989. *Marching Orders: The Role of the Military in South Korea's Economic Miracle.* New York: Greenwood Press.

Hyundai Motor Company (HMC). 1987. *Hyundai Chadongch'a Isipyŏnsa* (A Twenty-year History of the Hyundai Motor Company). Seoul: HMC.

Jo, Sung-Hwan. 1991. "Promotion Measures for General Trading Companies," in Lee-Jay Cho and Yoon Hyung Kim (eds). *Economic Development in Korea: A Policy Perspective.* Honolulu: East–West Center.

Johnson, Chalmers. 1982. *MITI and the Japanese Miracle.* Stanford, CA: Stanford University Press.

Johnson, Chalmers. 1987. "Institutions and Economic Performance in South Korea and Taiwan," in Frederic Deyo (ed.). *The Political Economy of the Newly Industrializing Countries in Asia.* Ithaca, NY: Cornell University Press.

Jones, Leroy and Sakong Il. 1980. *Government, Business, and Entrepreneurship in Economic Development.* Cambridge, MA: Harvard University Press.

Jun Jong-sup. 1985. "The Paradoxes of Development: Problems of Korea's Transformation," in Bun Woong Kim, David S. Bell, Jr., and Chong Bum Lee (eds). *Administrative Dynamics and Development: The Korean Experience.* Seoul: Kyobo Publishers.

Jung Jung-gil. 1989. "Daetongyŏng ŭi kwallyo wa ŭi kwan'gye (Presidential Decision-Making and Bureaucratic Expertise)." *Han'guk Haenjong Hakbo* 23: 73–90.

Kang, Chol-gyu, Jong-pyo Choi, and Jisang Jang. 1991. *Chaebŏl: sŏngjang ŭi chuyŏk in'ga tamyŏk ŭi hwasin inga* (*Chaebŏl*: Pivotal Role in Growth or Paragon of Greed?). Seoul: Kyŏngje Chŏngŭi Chŏnsiminyŏnhap.

Kang, David. 2002. *Crony Capitalism: Corruption and Development in South Korea and the Philippines.* Cambridge: Cambridge University Press.

Kim, Alexander Joungwon. 1985. *Divided Korea: The Politics of Development, 1945–1972.* Cambridge, MA: Harvard University Press.

Kim Eun-mee. 1987. "From Dominance to Symbiosis: *Chaebŏl* and Development in Korea." Ph.D. dissertation, Brown University.

Kim Kwang-woong. 1991. *Han'guk ŭi kwallyo chedo yŏn'gu* (Research on the Korean Bureaucracy). Seoul: Taeyong Munhwasa.

Kim, Seok-ki. 1987. "Business Concentration and Government Policy: A Study of the Phenomenon of Business Groups in Korea, 1945–1985." Ph.D. dissertation, Harvard University.

Kohli, Atul. 1994. "Where do High-growth Political Economies Come From? The Japanese Legacy in South Korean Development." *World Development* 22: 1269–1293.

Korea Development Bank (KDB). 1980. *Trends in Automotive Sector.* Seoul: KDB.

Korea Development Institute. 1981. "Hyundai Yanghaeng Changwŏn kongjan mit Okpo Chosŏnso e kwanhan taech'aek (Measures Regarding Hyundai International's Changwon Plant and Okpo Shipyard)," in *Kyŏngje anchonghwa sich'aek charyojip* (Collected Documents of Economic Stabilization Measures). Seoul: KDI.

Kuk, Mino. 1995. "The Governmental Role in the Making of *Chaebŏl* in the Industrial Development of South Korea." *Asian Perspective*: 107–133.

Lee, Hahn Been. 1968. *Time, Change, and Administration*. Honolulu, HI: East–West Center.

——. 1982. *Future, Innovation and Development*. Seoul: Panmun Book Co.

Lee, Young-hwan. 1985. "Hanguk ui Gyongje Danche-was Jongchekgyolchung Gujo (Corporatist Development and the Structure of Policy-making in Korea)," in Lee Young-hwan (ed.). *Han'guk kiŏp ŭi segyehwa chollyak* (Strategies for Globalizing Korean Business). Seoul: Chulparsa.

Leipziger, Danny M. 1988. "Industrial Restructuring in Korea." *World Development* 16: 121–135.

Lew, Seok-jin. 1992. "Bringing Capital Back In: A Case Study of South Korean Automobile Industrialization." Ph.D. dissertation, Yale University.

McCubbins, Matt and Thomas Schwartz. 1984. "Congressional Oversight Overlooked: Police Patrols versus Fire Alarms," *American Journal of Political Science* 28:165–179.

Mayhew, David. 1974. *Congress: The Electoral Connection*. New Haven, CT: Yale University Press.

Ministry of Finance. 1978. *Chaejŏng kŭmyung samsipnyŏnsa* (Thirty-year History of Fiscal and Monetary Policy). Seoul: Ministry of Finance.

Moe, Terry. 1991. "Politics and the Theory of Organization." *Journal of Law, Economics, and Organizations* 7: 106–129.

Moon, Chung-in and Sang-young Rhyu. 1997. "Overdeveloped State and the Political Economy of Development in the 1950s: A Reinterpretation." Seoul: Yonsei University, ms.

Muramatsu, Michio and Ellis Krauss. 1984. "Bureaucrats and Politicians in Policymaking: The Case of Japan." *American Political Science Review* 78: 126–146.

Najita, Tetsuo and J. Victor Koschmann (eds). 1982. *Conflict in Modern Japanese History: The Neglected Tradition*. Princeton, NJ: Princeton University Press.

Önis, Ziya. 1991. "The Logic of the Developmental State." *Comparative Politics* 24: 109–126.

Park, Byung-yoon. 1982. *Chaebŏl kwa chŏngch'i*. Seoul: Hankuk Yŏn'guso.

——. 1992. "The Inside Story of the Automobile Industry." *Shindonga*: 176.

Przeworski, Adam and Fernando Limongi. 1993. "Political Regimes and Economic Growth." *Journal of Economic Perspectives* 7: 51–69.

Rahman, T. Rafique. 1986. "Legal and Administrative Measures Against Bureaucratic Corruption in Asia," in Ledivina V. Carino (ed.). *Bureaucratic Corruption in Asia: Causes, Consequences, and Controls*. Quezon City: JMC Press.

Ramseyer, Mark and Frances Rosenbluth. 1994. *Japan's Political Marketplace*. Cambridge, MA: Harvard University Press.

Rhee, Yung-whan, Bruce Ross-Larson, and Gary Pursell. 1984. *Korea's Competitive Edge: Managing the Entry into World Markets*. Baltimore, MD: Johns Hopkins University Press.

Rodden, Jonathan and Susan Rose-Ackerman. 1997. "Does Federalism Preserve Markets?" *Virginia Law Review* 83: 1521–1572.

Satterwhite, David. 1994. "The Politics of Economic Development: Coup, State, and the Republic of Korea's First Five-year Economic Development Plan (1962–1966)." Ph.D. dissertation, University of Washington.

Schneider, Ben Ross. 1993. "The Career Connection: A Comparative Analysis of Bureaucratic Preferences and Insulation." *Comparative Politics* 25: 331–350.

Schneider, Ben Ross and Sylvia Maxfield. 1997. "Business, the State, and Economic Performance in Developing Countries," in Sylvia Maxfield and Ben Ross Schneider (eds). *Business and the State in Developing Countries.* Ithaca, NY: Cornell University Press.

Shepsle, Kenneth and Barry Weingast. 1994. "Positive Theories of Congressional Institutions." *Legislative Studies Quarterly* 19: 149–179.

Silberman, Bernard. 1982. "The Bureaucratic State in Japan: The Problem of Authority and Legitimacy," in Tetsuo Najita and J. Victor Koschman (eds). *Conflict in Modern Japanese History: The Neglected Tradition.* Princeton, NJ: Princeton University Press.

Sung-ryol, Baek. 1988. *Chaebŏlga ŭi saramdul: 22 dae Chaebŏl Group-ŭi ch'angup, sŏnjang, hyonhwang, inmaek, honmaek story* (The Men of the *Chaebŏl*: The Story of the Founding, Growth, Present Condition, Personal Relations and Marriage Relations of the 22 Largest *Chaebŏl* Groups). Seoul: Dosuh Chulpansa.

US House of Representatives. 1977. *Investigation of Korean–American Relations* (Hearing Before the Subcommittee on International Organizations of the Committee on International Relations, House of Representatives, Ninety-Fifth Congress), Part I, June 22.

Wade, Robert. 1990. *Governing the Market.* Princeton, NJ: Princeton University Press.

Williamson, Oliver. 1988. "Corporate Finance and Corporate Governance." *Journal of Finance* 43: 567–591.

Woo, Jung-en. 1991. *Race to the Swift: State and Finance in Korean Industrialization.* New York: Columbia University Press.

Yi, Mun-yong. 1966. "Kongmuwŏn pup'ae isipnyŏnsa (Twenty Years of Civil Service Corruption)." *Sasang'gye*: 107–123.

Yi Sung-hyong. 1985. "Kukka kyekŭp mit chabon ch'ukchŏk: 8, 3 chochi'rul chungsimuro (State, class, and capital accumulation: The president's decree of 8-3-72)," in Choi Jang-jip (ed.). *Han'guk chabonjuŭi wa kukka* (Korean Capitalism and the State). Seoul: Hanwul.

Yi, Young-hwan. 1995. "Han'guk ŭi kyŏngje tanch'e wa chŏngch'aek kyŏlchŏng kujo (Corporatist Development and the Structure of Policymaking in Korea)," in Lee Young-hwan (ed.). *Hankuk kiŏpŭi segyehwa chollyak* (Strategies to Globalize Korean Industry). Seoul: Ch'ulpansa.

Yong, Gwan. 1985. "Kwallyo chŏk kwŏlli chuŭi ŭi t'aedo wa chunghwahak kongŏp chŏngch'aek (The Emergence of the Bureaucratic Authoritarianism and Policies of the Heavy Chemical Industries)," in Han Sang-jin (ed.). *Han'guk sahoe pyŏndong kwa kukka yŏkhwal e kwanhan yŏn'gu* (Studies on the Changes in Korean Society and the Role of the State). Seoul: Hyundai Sahoe Yŏn'guso.

Yoon, Tae-bom. 1994. "Han'guk kwallyo ŭi pup'ae (Bureaucratic Corruption in Korea)." *Hankuk Haengchong Hakbo* 28: 169–186.

Part IV

Transforming culture and ideology

8 Confucianism, democracy, and the individual in Korean modernization

Uchang Kim

1

In his *Age of Extremes,* Eric Hobsbawm calls the recent transformation of South Korean society "as spectacular an industrial success story as any in history" (Hobsbawm 1994: 362). There have been attempts to understand the circumstances of this emergence of Korea and other societies, in its initial phase grouped together as the newly industrializing economies (NIES), and understood as industrial economies, if not democratic polities. Studies have been made of the processes of industrial development; explanations have been offered to identify the forces that have driven and characterized this development, for example, workable political organization, shrewd industrial policies, and fortunate conjunctions of various factors in the world economy as well as cultural causes.

Understanding the case of Korea and other new industrial societies in terms of Confucianism has also been tried. This is useful for societies situated in East Asia – the area formed, broadly speaking, under the Sinitic influence, whose chief cultural orientation was shaped by Confucianism. Confucianism is certainly relevant in the case of Korea. It had indeed been the hegemonic ideology in Korean society more than in any other Asian society, and must have been an important factor in Korea's modern transformation. It was adopted as the state ideology for 500 years from the founding of the last dynastic regime in 1392, and was systematically imposed upon Korean society through to the end of the nineteenth century. Dynastic Korea was perhaps a unique case in pre-modern times of a state created and destroyed, somewhat similar to the Soviet state, by a systematic and secular ideology. In Korea's case that ideology was Confucianism. It is therefore natural to look to Confucianism to explain Korea, from its past supremacy to its present influence. But in trying to relate Confucianism to the modern situation, academics have mainly considered Korea's industrial development. Does Confucianism also apply to Korea's development as a nascent democracy?

To answer this question, empirical studies in the political arena need to analyze the Confucian legacy operating in contemporary culture, society, and the economy. What I propose to do here is to approach this question from a philosophical angle, trying mainly to compare essential aspects of the development of the Western ideal of democracy with democratic development in Korea. Do ideas, especially philosophical ones, have anything to do with democracy or political regimes? The question suggests itself in view of an assumption, naïve and yet widely held by politicians, that importing good ideas could develop a democratic regime in traditional societies. Of course it would be equally naïve to hold that ideas do not count, even the ideas of an abstruse philosophical kind. But if they do count, it is crucial to understand how ideas insinuate themselves into political reality; what is important is to locate the conjunction of the logic of ideas and that of political processes. Nevertheless, ideas also serve heuristic purposes in understanding more complex phenomena resistant to their influence.

There are some obvious words that express certain political ideas important in the conception of democracy: liberty, equality, rule of law, and so on. Then there are ideas of a more philosophical kind; ideas that could constitute a philosophical anthropology concerning the nature of human beings as individual and social beings and, inevitably, the place of humans in the larger scheme of things. Even if we do not subscribe to the idea that there could be found in the buzzing, blooming confusion of the lived world a more or less logical order susceptible to rigorous philosophical analysis, in the world of political practice some ideas appear to be at work, grounded philosophically. The idea of Cartesian subjectivity seems to be, for instance, such a constitutive idea in Western democracy, since it concerns the process by which the individual and the world are simultaneously institutionalized. In Cartesian reflection, the individual, retreating to his or her interior, becomes the subject of thought, but also the master of the world, for the subjectivity of the thinking self also founds the world as an objective order which can be commanded. But the condition attached to this process is that the individual finds his or her essence in being the purified carrier of reason. The formula can be simplistically applied to the democratic political order, and it seems possible that the Western democratic order is the working out of this co-foundation of the individual and the world in political institutions. There cannot be a democracy without the recognition of the individual as a being, by principle, irreducible to the collectivity to which he or she belongs. It is this recognition that marks a democratic order, while primacy of collectivity over the individual characterizes more traditional non-democratic societies. In addition, of course, there cannot be an orderly polity without ways and means by which these individuals would come together in a collectivity. This is done mainly through public and rational debate, which is then institutionalized by law into a system of government.

The important point here concerns the co-foundation of the two poles of a democratic polity, the individual and the collectivity, through the mediation of rationality. This is what was foreshadowed in Descartes' philosophical procedures. If we assume that this institution of Cartesian subjectivity is necessary as the basic constitutive principle of Western democracy, do we need a new institution of Cartesian subjectivity for Asian democracies? Is it possible to have democracy without this? It is also possible to ask: In the Asian tradition was there something equivalent to Cartesian subjectivity even before the advent of Western discovery and influence?

These are questions we would like to consider here. However, a preliminary survey of more familiar problems of democracy in Korea will be necessary to provide some context: a rough review of the modernization, and the democratization of Korea. This survey would involve cataloging the political economy of development, which would apply not only to Korea but also to many other similar societies in today's world. But at the same time it will be seen that Korea's cultural heritage, especially in the form of Confucianism, played a unique role in bringing Korea to its current capitalist and democratic state. Confucianism has lent a dynamic force to its modern development, no doubt. However, the main question we will be asking is: What role has it played in the construction of a new polity, and in history? This point concerns whether some kind of subjectivity was posited in Confucianism and, if so, how it was constituted and how it was distinct from Cartesian subjectivity.

2

If Confucianism has played a causal or at least an accessory role in industrial development, similar to Weber's Protestantism in the rise of Western capitalism, its role in the political development of Korea must have been a very complex one, and not simply because of its oblique or negative character in relation to what it takes to become a modern nation. What is often overlooked in studying the recent Korean resurgence in relation to its cultural heritage is the fact that one of the most turbulent centuries of Korean history had preceded it. This possibly cleared the historical slate so that there could be a new beginning. One of the major events that happened during this interregnum was the destruction of Confucianism. If Confucianism played a role in recent Korean development, it was as much through the effects of its destruction as its continuation. There is, for example, a general agreement that government initiative – in other words, the strong state, as a political scientist put it – is chiefly responsible for this recent development (Choi 1993). The strong state could come into existence simultaneously with the weakening of civil society, which might have opposed it. Here, civil society means, especially in the earlier phase, the social formation under the Confucian regime. This process occurred through several catastrophic events in modern Korean history. Japanese colonialism, while dealing a death blow to the prestige and legitimacy of the old regime and devastating Korean society as a whole, replaced it with the rationality of colonial mobilization. Land reform in the post-liberation era deprived the landowning class (the bearers of Confucian ideology) of its economic and political base; the Korean War and the post-war continuation of the tension between the two Koreas helped destroy social classes. These historical events posed the threat of equal pauperization for all classes. Another effect of this tragic history, though mainly of the post-Korean War tension, was the pretext given to the state to make security its prime objective and to concentrate power in its hands. These events and circumstances, along with the erosion of traditional ways (pried from their institutional moorings) laid the groundwork for a strong state with the functional rationality necessary for modern industrial development. They prepared for a military regime which took over the reins of power in 1961 and began with military orderliness to implement its plan for economic development.

However, by this time Confucianism had long lost its prestige as ideology. From the beginning of the modern era in the twentieth century, it had begun, as in other East Asian countries, to decline as it became the target of vigorous attack by political critics. If this attack was not as vigorous as in other Asian countries such as China, it was because Japanese imperialism soon became Korea's primary enemy. From the beginning of the modern era, it became almost the axiom of independence fighters, patriots, and nation-builders in Korea that what the nation needed was not the restoration of the Confucian regime but its destruction. Confucianism was an obstacle; modernity could establish itself only in the place vacated by Confucianism. The violent history of the twentieth century only completed the practical work of destruction of an ideology that had lost its hold on the cultural world. It is true, however, that a worldview providing 500 years of a comprehensive action program for society would not disappear overnight, even under the heavy onslaught of a violent history. It would at least survive as a tribal memory subliminally retained in mind and practice. There have also been attempts to revive it by various groups who have found in it a convenient resource for their own purposes. This is especially so with authoritarian or conservative groups in power. Certain Confucian precepts were important to Japanese militarism. The military regimes in Korea from the 1960s through the 1980s also intermittently dragged out the Confucian concepts of loyalty and filial piety, working them into an attitude of deferential obedience to authoritarian rule. Even today, filial piety, now divorced from loyalty due to the bad odor it acquired in its association with authoritarianism, is incessantly put forward by some conservative groups as the core of traditional morality which constitutes, as it is asserted by them, the essence of Korean culture, and especially as the cure for dysfunctional social consequences of recent capitalist development.

To consider the case of filial piety, advocated as a virtue to be protected in modern society, even as a private virtue uncoupled from its social implications, it was important in the Korean understanding of Confucian ethics, since it was a nodal point where natural affection, property relations, and authority are knotted together. Those who would like to see this virtue as a fundamental cornerstone of the ethical life of human existence are not exactly opposed to capitalism; indeed, they are in most cases its enthusiastic supporters. They think that by reviving filial piety and concomitant Confucian virtues they can pressure capitalist development into a form, possibly authoritarian and moralistic, free from its ill-effects. In addition, as they conceive of it, filial piety would be adequate for the fulfillment of the aspirations of Korean nationalism, and in the process, they would like to think, Confucian virtues were chiefly responsible for Korea's industrialization. In this respect, their thinking is more in the nature of broader ideological apologetics as found in some American observers of East Asian development such as Herman Kahn, Peter Berger, Roderick MacFarquhar and others. They were, according to a recent critique mounted by Arif Dirlik, basically looking for an alternative to Western capitalism in crisis. In their view, East Asia's Confucian culture made it possible to develop a stronger kind of capitalism without the liberal values usually associated with Western capitalism. Instead, the virtues derived from Confucian legacy which support East Asian capitalism are, according to Dirlik's summary of the views of Kahn and Berger, "(1) a high evaluation of education and dedication to hard work, (2) the priority given group over individual interests, beginning with the family but extended to social life in general, and (3) emphasis on 'harmonious human relations' in organization" (Dirlik 1995: 246). Dirlik's critical view is that these Confucian virtues, as the enabling cultural values for East Asian capitalism, have more to do with the circumstances of global capitalism in search of remedial visions than with the real dynamics of East Asian society or, for that matter, the reality of historic Confucianism.

However, the case is a little more ambiguous and complicated. The emphasis on collectivity or mutuality was real in Confucian ideology and may have helped East Asian development. The collectivism, as Kahn says, was characterized by "a sense of hierarchy" or "a sense of complementarity of relations" (Kahn 1979, quoted in Dirlik 1995: 246). This hierarchical or complementary collectivism goes well, in the Korean case, with the requirement of the polity becoming the "strong state." Besides this, there are elements in Confucianism which may have contributed to the emergence of East Asian modernity: its secularism which had given it, long before the West, a disenchanted world and a kind of rationalism (Weberian requisites for capitalist development); a strong sense of social justice, albeit paternalistic, that helped the somewhat equitable distribution of the fruits of economic development and thereby stimulated acquisitive and productive motivation widely across the classes; and a concept of the popular basis of political authority, though mixed with other ideas such as the idea of the mandate of heaven, which placed the origin of the political authority of the ruler in the transcendental realm. These could all have contributed to the strengthening of collectivity in its enterprise of modernization.

To say that these and other past cultural forces must have helped Korean or East Asian modernization may be correct, but this is not necessarily to say that they are the agents of the transformation. They are only some of the resources that could be mobilized, and the real question concerns assessing responsibility for this mobilization by looking at the internal and external social and political forces that fostered a directed subjectivity of the process.

3

If Confucianism contributed to Korea's capitalist development, whether by its withdrawal from history or by its availability as a resource, its contribution seems to consist in its enhancement of the authoritarian character of development. If so, where does democracy fit into this scheme? The easiest explanation for the emergence of democracy in Korea in recent years is that liberal democracy is an inevitable consequence of a maturing industrial capitalism. If this is the case, we may say that even if it is set in motion by a developmental authoritarian government, as Korean political scientists often characterize the military regime of Park Chung Hee, it has a mechanism of reversing itself, authoritarianism completing itself in its own dissolution, on account of historical forces generated by itself in the form of democratic opposition.

This emerging democracy is not quite the same kind of democracy as one would see in the West, either due to its political immaturity or different historical circumstances. In East Asia, one would suppose that democracy retains a strong native coloration of Confucian culture, which in the earlier phase provided support for authoritarian politics. Could this then result in a peculiarly collectivist kind of democracy? There has been some speculation about the possible emergence of egalitarian or communitarian capitalism which some of the observers of East Asian capitalism entertained. In most cases it was based on the post-1945 Japanese example, already a mature capitalist economy and a kind of liberal democracy, whose corporate ethos once seemed to produce a peculiarly Japanese style of management, enviously efficient and successful while also cooperative and caring. Taiwan, Korea, or Singapore would present different examples. It is not unreasonable, in any case, to expect that East Asia would produce a subspecies of democracy different from the West. This becomes possible only on the basis of successful capitalist development, which could then draw upon the cultural capital unique to Japanese or other Asian traditions. In this respect history is reinscribing the past in the present, on the basis of the strength of this present.

It would not be entirely correct to say, however, that democracy is only an accompaniment to capitalist development; it is even possible that it is not a Western import if we take into account historical democratic yearnings found in many societies and possibly divergent forms of government that could accommodate them, though one can speak of the priming effect of the Western model on non-Western developments. The historical experience of the Korean people has its own story to tell. Apart from the question of the putative pre-modern origins of democratic impulses, in the modern period democracy has formed from the beginning part of the national program in the struggle of the Korean people for modernity and independence. In the late nineteenth century, when Koreans began to realize the need to join the modern world and throw off its East Asian particularity, they first viewed democracy in its monarchical form. Soon after the annexation of Korea by Japan in 1910, however, patriots working for the cause of national independence began thinking of the future polity of the nation only in terms of a popular government without the monarchical compromise. The ideal of popular sovereignty was already captivating the Korean mind. Since then monarchical restoration has never been an issue. A Japanese reporter writing as late as the 1970s expressed his puzzlement over the total absence of royalists or royalist sympathy in Korean politics. Korea had been, after all, ruled by royalty for several millennia – in fact, all throughout its history except in this century (Kuroda 1993: 103–115). Needless to say, monarchy is not contradictory to democracy, but the Korean negation of its monarchical past is an indication of the strength of the idea of popular sovereignty in the public mind. At the time of liberation in 1945, it was taken for granted that the form of government could only be a democratic one. In North Korea a socialist state was established, but it was still called a people's democracy, and was understood as a purer and more radical form of government by the people. Of course, neither the idea of popular sovereignty nor popular aspiration for democracy is sufficient to make democracy a reality. If South Korea is now considered a democracy, it has become one, not with the formal inauguration of a republican form of government in 1948, but through unceasing popular struggle, which has involved occasional violence and enormous sacrifice on the part of its people. Landmarks in recent Korean history all denote the stages of the struggle for democracy. This brief recall of Korea's modern history highlights the aspiration and struggle for democracy of the Korean people, despite its enormous costs. It also makes us note the fact that democracy could become a reality, and replace the Confucian politics of the last dynasty based on hierarchy, class injustice, and traditionalism, though it could be considered to have formed powerful counter-currents.

At the same time, the Confucian past provides usable resources for a new political order, including not only industrial capitalism but also democratic politics. Enduring arrangements of collective living, developed over centuries or millennia, are likely to contain provisions for doing justice to the contradictory claims of individual and collective living. Their ideological supports also last only if they supply resources for these provisions. Past history contains motifs that can take on different meaning, depending upon overall configurations of historical forces incorporating them. I have already enumerated some representative Confucian values which have putatively contributed to capitalist development: the ideal of social harmony; the sense of justice; and the ambivalent belief in the need for popular justification of political power. These are also obvious values useful for democracy. There are less obvious ideas and habits that comprise the fund of ideas for democracy. Of these ideas, the collectivism of Confucianism is significant in the development of democracy, since those I have enumerated could all be subsumed into Confucian collectivism. This would be a central issue not only in capitalist but also democratic development. We cannot dismiss it even in our consideration of the possibility of democracy from Confucian traditions. In spite of the suspicion likely to attach to any idea of collectivism, it is hard to deny that a collective sense is the basis of any society (including a liberal-democratic one) as a condition of state formation. We can begin by noting the formal significance of collectivism: that it enables one to conceive of society as an ordered totality, and this conceivability itself emerges only in long historical practice. This is not a trivial observation, as can be confirmed in the evident difficulty many new nations experience in becoming clearly defined national entities. A total conception of society and state could, to be sure, easily lead to an authoritarian type of political organization, which is what happened in Korea in the past and in its military regime. Nevertheless, the first requisite of a democratic society is the possibility of a social order, which is often forgotten in favor of freedom, too often taken to be the sole distinguishing mark of a democratic society. In the case of Western societies, what often strikes an Asian visitor at first is not freedom but the orderliness of society. There could be in this orderliness a set of strong social and political constraints delimiting human freedom, but one's sense of freedom in a society is often a function of the degree of acculturation into the social norms of that culture which makes the acculturated forget, but the unacculturated feel their coercive character. The question of social constraint versus individual freedom is a relative one, and more importantly, it exists only in a delicate balance with the possibility of an ordered collectivity.

The collectivist heritage has other implications for the emergence of democracy. Capitalist society conceived of in the Confucian spirit is, in its apologists' mind, a model of society which flourishes in collective harmony without the aggravations of individualism. What is referred to is in reality the authoritarian capitalist state, but the virtue extolled is not the form of the state itself but of social virtues found within it. Although these social virtues usually play a part in the political maneuver and rhetoric of the ruling class, it is also true that corporatist pretension sets some limits to the open pursuit of individualist gains, even by the ruling class. During the period of modernization under the military in Korea, there had been a constant collective emphasis as the government tried to mobilize the nation for its modernization efforts. The military regime was by definition authoritarian. It was convenient for it to employ collectivist rhetoric, in the absence of the abdicated ideology of personal loyalty to the monarch or to the charismatic leader. The most convenient excuse was collective security against the communist regime to the north. There were other sources of collectivism, in a more substantive way. For instance, there was nationalism as the legacy of the patriotic struggle under Japanese colonialism, but the Confucian idea of a just society, too – just for the people as a whole – might have prepared the soil for all these collective pretexts. These are all elements of collectivism, which can remain abstract, with a strong emphasis on a totalistic conception of the nation as a whole, but they had to be filled from time to time with concrete substance under the pressure of the masses clamoring for a greater share of the fruits of modernization. As the collective pretension was challenged, the abstract rhetoric had to be turned into an idea of communitarian solidarity and a standard against which the ruling power was asked to measure itself. There were results, too. Evidence of this is, as has often been noted, a smaller income gap among the classes or, more graphically, between the salaries of the top executives and the lowest paid in the business firms when compared with the developed West or other developing countries. This is to say that the collective ethos of Confucianism could eventually be modulated into the ideal of equality, an important component in the democratic ideals as conceived of in the West.

Ideas formed in the past may be used for new politics: creating a sense of the state as a political unity, recognizing equality in a community, or making people into the ultimate source of legitimization or the ideal of social justice. Yet these ideas can be mobilized for very different forms of government. What is important is the overall configuration in the political structure in which they are put, and also the way they are modified according to the structure that envelops them. For example, we can take the idea of equality, certainly an important component in the ideology of democracy. Whatever equality was achieved in the authoritarian regimes tended to be only in the macro view, but not in the micro. Equality comes into its own in the modern sense only when combined with the affirmation of the individual, another important component in the concept of democracy. If collectivism is to lead to egalitarian achievement in the modern sense, it has to step out of an abstract corporatism and get in touch with the concrete content of the collectivity; articulated by individuals. Thus we come face to face with an idea that is central to the democratic organization of society: the individual. This is what requires democracy to play a legitimate part in the political life of people.

By contrast, the idea of the individual as an end in itself seems to be one of the most difficult things to recognize, either ideologically or institutionally, in the Confucian tradition. What is involved is the historical process giving birth to a distinctively modern form of the individual, but one may examine the problem of discursive articulation, which differentiates constitutive units of society before they can be put into its inclusive order. This must then be included in the institutional make-up of society. As we will see, the emergence of a certain possibility in the formal ordering of social relations occurs simultaneously with the development of the individual.

To say that what is really lacking in Korean society today or in its Confucian past is the clear idea of the individual is to note a crude abstract category and to miss important distinctions in reality. In present-day Korea there are people motivated by ideas of individual gain in spite of the predominance of nationalist rhetoric which, in the last resort, is the ultimate coercive rhetoric of Korean politics, whether of the Left or Right. In today's Korea more individuals ruthlessly pursue individual aims than ever before in Korea's history. We cannot say that in traditional Korea no individuals acted and lived on motives coming from their own mind, not out of deference to socially prescribed conformist norms, though their motives would often be not material gains but inner compulsions. It is even possible that there were more authentic individuals then than in modern times, though cast entirely in a different mold than the individual we think of in relation to modern democracy.

If this is the case, we must define more carefully the democratic individual, who may be regarded as unlike the individual we see in past or present Korea. We can only look to the Western model. This search, however, does not necessarily assume that this is a desirable model in all respects, since a critical examination will reveal its achievements as well as its failures. When we speak of the individual in Western democracy, we should note that the individual does not simply refer to a biological being, but to a formal or normative status recognized by the formal institutions and cultural habits of society. This status ensures a clear public space or a space of public restraint free from religious, moral, or external social compulsion. Yet this space existing within the larger space of society also subjects the individual to the normative regulation of society. The individual is free only as part of the formal institution of society, assertively recognized but also definitely within the constraint of the formal arrangement of society as a whole.

The formal nature of this status is best recognized in the legal system. In this respect, the Western individual is foremost a juridical being, the bearer of rights recognized by law. Charles Taylor, while discussing the question of human rights, asserts that the West alone has had provisions for giving strong protection to the individual as the bearer of rights: "personal rights" (*droits subjectifs*). This has to do with a particular tradition and concept of human being which the West has developed, as will be discussed below. The important point is that the rights of a person here do not refer merely to an ethical requirement or an appeal on the ground of moral sentiment, but to legal recognition, with the possibility of the individual contesting interference from the public sphere by resorting to the public institution itself. Taylor says that a fundamental law of a society may have provisions for a civilized life, protecting a person from arbitrary killing, imprisonment, or imposition of silence, but that society can be without rights in the modern sense. It is fundamentally the system of personal rights that makes an individual an individual in modern democracy, as "(a) it places limits on the actions of governments and on collective decisions by offering a measure of protection to individuals and specific groups; [and] (b) it offers individuals and specific groups the right to seek redress and gives them a margin of liberty in the imposition of these limits" (Taylor 1986: 48).

Whatever status the individual may have had in the Confucian scheme, the rights of the individual were not yet established in Korea even by the late 1980s; not exactly in the sense of (a) above, but, more emphatically, not in the sense of (b). There are laws granting the individual rights modeled after the West, but there is not yet a culture in society that would support whatever laws exist concerning these rights, though the struggle for democracy has gained for these laws some experiential reality (which I hope would be further expanded in the course of time). The lack of a solid legal base for the rights of the individual is not simply due to the authoritarian regimes in Korea that have suppressed these rights. The collective ethos is too strong to make room for them, especially when the collectivity is seen as justified. We can see here that the strongest influence of Confucianism is still very much alive. Usually the claim of morality it puts forward suppresses the assertion of individual rights, and the Confucian political ideology, relying on this aspect, makes no provision for the freedom of the individual (that could be formally defined) separate from the morality of any concrete case in question. The morality, in turn, derives its authority from the claim of collectivity on the individual.

4

The individual, understood as having formal status in a polity, makes us realize that he or she is a product of a complex historical process, and the question concerns the cultural and social dynamic in the modernization of Korea (and by analogy other East Asian societies) that may or may not have produced the individual. The idea of the individual in the West is a product of historical processes that have precipitated the whole system of social and political institutions and cultural practices warranting legitimate recognition to the individual. As Taylor points out, the Western concept of personal rights has many historical roots. The idea of the priority of the individual over society was clearly articulated in seventeenth-century political thought; this idea was further enriched by the Kantian ideal of the individual as an end, or the Romantic notion of full personal development. Going further back in history, the system of rights may be said to have its roots in feudal society. To recall this historical background is to be reminded of the fact that Korea or any other society cannot import a whole cultural history, even if it could borrow some fragmentary ideas or external trappings that stem from it. If Korea has difficulty in establishing institutions providing for the rights of the individual or the rule of law on the whole in its social practices, it is not simply due to the inertia of the past tradition, which would have to be overcome or removed, or lack of a persuasive advocacy of the benefits of individualism, which will move Korea closer to the Western model of democracy. The difficulty is that of transplanting an institution from one tradition to another, and that institution being inextricably embedded in the network of other institutions.

To assume, perhaps for our convenience, that there could be a unitary creative genius orchestrating various resources behind the evolution of culture, real difficulty lies in transplanting creative resources of social construction that have generated these institutions, especially a peculiar mechanism by which the individual becomes an agent that masters these resources for social construction, and at the same time becomes a functioning part of a society now having validity in an objective world. For the individual must emerge as a site in which the activity of cultural and political constitution is performed, and from which the individual, polity, and the world are born as historical realities. In this complex constructive process, we may assume, if there is a genius of the cultural dynamic involving the individual, that epistemological reflection plays a central role as graft-stock for this constitution in which the individual is conscious of itself as the subject, and eventually becomes this subject of history. In Western intellectual history, the Cartesian meditation on the *cogito* carries an immense historical importance. It develops subjectivity as the epistemic theater where this historical dynamic is protogenetically or symbolically represented and enacted in a mysterious distillation of history, although its full institutional realization will have to wait for a long historical unfolding through the Enlightenment and various civil and revolutionary movements down to the early twentieth century.

We should note that the individual emerges not simply as an active agent – a subject – but also as a passive entity in the dynamic matrix of a system. This double aspect emerges from a single process. A person is a subject, his or her own agent, but if the individual is also an entity definable in reference to a system of positive laws, then he or she is negated as an active agent; the analogy is a physical object in the Newtonian universe. However, the system itself is the individual's achievement, which eventually restores his or her status as agency, though through a complex mediation. It is precisely in epistemology that the status of the subject is worked into this kind of necessary ambiguity. The subject is, in its epistemological exploration, an active agent, but at the same time it is in the service of truth – truth adequate to the object of cognition. This epistemological operation finds its homolog in the social construction of the individual as well. It is clear that though this relation must be more rigorously worked out, philosophical projects of epistemological nature reveal the central societal dynamics of reality construction, both cognitive and social. The relation of the individual in modern Western civilization is thus worked out in the philosophy of subjectivity, epitomizing in its essential outline the gigantomachia in the larger arena of history.

This double process of articulating the individual in society as an active and passive element is more clearly recognized from a critical perspective that tries to prove that the freedom of modern Western human beings is not really as complete as is claimed. In an interesting essay, Etienne Balibar points out that the Western attempt at institutionalizing a human being as the subject of his or her own life also subjected the individual to the society that was being created by this institution. He conveniently sums up this fateful vicissitude in terms of the changing meaning of the subject (Balibar 1991). From Roman times to the early modern era, man[1] was the subject, defined as a juridical being, by authority or a system of laws, subjected to the prince and the imperial order or spiritual authority. However, with the rupture effected by the French Revolution he becomes the subject in the sense that he is master of his own fate, better expressed, in Balibar's opinion, by the term "citizen," a free political agent. Balibar clearly sees this rupture enacted in Kant's philosophy of transcendental subjectivity. As he puts it, the moment at which Kant produces "the transcendental subject" is precisely that moment at which politics destroys the "subject" of the prince in order to replace him with the republican citizen (Cadava *et al.* 1991: 39). For Kant, the subject is the bearer of the synthetic unity of the conditions of objectivity, but the subject has no substantive or phenomenal anchoring in the empirical world. As Balibar's critique would emphasize, it is simply reflexivity and self-consciousness accompanying representations. In this Kantian formulation, Balibar finds an ambiguous legacy which helped establish the individual as an active agent; that is, only epistemologically, while emasculating him as a citizen, since he is subject to the laws and institutions of the bourgeois state, reduced to the legal subject. This, in a way, reinstates the story of the king's subject, alleging absolute obedience to the laws of the state. This is inevitable, for Kant's philosophy reflects the predicament of the Western individual defined as a free subject and at the same time as an object caught in the collectivity constituted by the activity of free subjectivity. Balibar's analysis is a critique and exposé of the idea of individual freedom claimed as a unique Western achievement. Yet it tells an essential truth about the way the individual constructs society and then becomes subject to its rules.

What is important here for our purpose is not the kind of freedom the individual enjoys in the West, but the fact that the individual and society proceed from a single epistemological and historical matrix. Although it is not the point he wants to make, this comes out clearly in Balibar's analysis of the enchainment of the individual to the bourgeois state.

Now we return to East Asia. How can we understand the dynamic involved in defining the status of the individual in East Asian society? In asking this question, we must acknowledge that we are assuming that the individual is, contrary to some common prejudice, an inerasable actuality of human life, not only in the Western tradition, but also in other traditions as well, and is also constituted as subject in a different guise and different network of relations. Both the individual and the subject are the product of a different process by which the world and society are organized, and the particular way they are articulated in the original philosophical project is different, with huge differential results in the status of the individual in society and politics. If a non-Western society like Korea is to move towards democracy based on the Western model, the move would involve reconstitution of the human being as the individual and the subject of social construction in its original unitary process, which remains problematic even if it succeeds.

As a kind of preliminary exercise, we may also ask if this reconstitution is desirable or necessary. If we accept the axiom that Western subjectivity is not the only way of existing as a human individual, there could be other ways of becoming the subject. It would even be possible, in view of postmodern critiques of the Western conception of human subjectivity, to abandon the narrowly conceived entity called subjectivity in favor of something more open and fluid. Even if we do not question the problematic nature of the subject as conceived in the West and accept the necessity of its installation in an alien society, it would pose a problem. It means, from the assumption that there is always an individual and a subject in any civilization, that we supplant the native subject with an alien subject, thereby destroying its own subjectivity as the source of coherence in various creative processes of human practice. The fragmentation and disorder one observes in many developing societies is probably due as much to the destruction of the subjective competence in a society to create its own world as to the lack of development according to the Western model. Even the ugliest form of individualism or the relentless pursuit of material advantages one may find in developing societies today is also caused by the loss of the subjectivity that would take upon itself as part of the price of its constitution as subjectivity some necessary restraint coming from the discipline of mutually coherent institutions. Native subjectivity can be supplanted only with grave consequences.

In spite of these radical possibilities, it is realistic to accept that a reconstitution of the traditional idea of the individual is in order. It is occurring already and would bring a new focus to the emerging reality of an industrial and democratic order in Korea. To recall what might have been in the past and compare it with the Western model, we rely upon the shorthand of epistemology. Confucianism was a system of thought acutely aware of the dialectic of the individual and society, and directed its main effort to understanding this. What is not often recognized is that there was an epistemological self-reflection underlying its understanding of this dynamic. It too had an interest in the process by which the individual was constituted as subject; only it could not be said to have displayed the same sophistication and acuteness in analyzing the process as in the Kantian or Cartesian epistemology of subjectivity. But, in a way, Confucian understanding of the constitution of subjectivity did more justice to complex human possibilities that could be put to use in various constructive projects, mostly ethical, of the social existence of humans, though at the cost of theoretical thoroughness.

For the sake of comparison, we may recall briefly the basic operation of subjectivity in Descartes' philosophy. For him, the *cogito*, discovered through the procedure of radical doubt, is the ground of certainty. In the rigorous test of doubt, nothing can be ascertained as truth, except on the strength of clarity and evidence as it appears to the *cogito*, and by rules of reason that connect what is clear and evident in a lawful order. The world is justified and constructed according to this procedure, and the ego acquires self-certainty as the thinking subject, and could become the master and possessor of the world. But the operation of the reduction applied to the sensory manifold of the world in search of certainty at the same time reduces the human person to the function of cogitation, that is, reason – especially reason as a means for instrumental mastery of the self and the world, including now the excluded passions of the soul. This reading is what is often applied to Descartes and the evolution of his thought in history. It would be erroneous to trace all the achievements and failures of modern society to Cartesian origins, but the assertion is often repeated, especially as a critique of its failures, that the instrumentalization of reason or a conspiracy for domination concealed in the Western projection of reason can be traced to the philosophy of subjectivity, of which Descartes may certainly be held as a powerful progenitor. But what should not be overlooked are multiple possibilities in the Cartesian projection. The achievements in the legal institution of personal rights and other social, political, and above all, scientific and technological development, are traceable to these origins; critiques of the philosophy of subjectivity themselves owe their impetus to them. Beginning with epistemology always opens up the possibility of beginning anew, though the critique thus begun usually has limits, since it cannot go behind the fundamental principle that moves it: Cartesian reason.

Confucian philosophy lacks the theoretical purity of Western rationalistic epistemology but, as we have observed, it too has an epistemological foundation. As is well known, the primary concern of Confucian philosophy is ethics or proper regulation of social relations. Central in its ethical thought are the four cardinal principles of human conduct: humanity, righteousness, propriety, and knowledge as the irreducible originary points of departure for understanding human beings and their social relations. These principles, repeated endlessly in all Confucian writings and passed into mindless clichés, appear arbitrary, lacking proper philosophical rigor. But they have derived from a reflective exploration into human nature. The locus classicus of the question of human nature in Confucianism is the book of Mencius, wherein Mencius tries to ascertain the baseline of the psychic endowment of humanity, from which all thought of ethical rules must start. What is to be noted is a reflective rigor by which Mencius tries, through a procedure of negation, to arrive at an indubitable point of departure, defining the mind that cannot bear *(burinjisim* in Korean, *burenzhixin* in Chinese), the point in the working of mind beyond which it cannot proceed without ceasing to be itself.

> All men have the mind which cannot bear [to see the suffering of] others. . . . When I say that all men have the mind which cannot bear to see the suffering of others, my meaning may be illustrated thus: Now, when men suddenly see a child about to fall into a well, they all have a feeling of alarm and distress, not to gain friendship with the child's parents, nor to seek the praise of their neighbors and friends, nor because they dislike the reputation [of lack of humanity if they did not rescue the child]. From such a case, we see that a man without the feeling of commiseration is not a man; a man without the feeling of shame and dislike is not a man; a man without the feeling of deference and compliance is not a man; and a man without the feeling of right and wrong is not a man. The feeling of commiseration is the beginning of humanity; the feeling of shame and dislike is the beginning of righteousness; the feeling of deference and compliance is the beginning of propriety; and the feeling of right and wrong is the beginning of wisdom. Men have these Four Beginnings, as they have their four limbs. Having these Four Beginnings, but saying that they cannot develop them, is to destroy themselves.
>
> (Mencius in Chan 1963: 65)

Although Mencius and Descartes are truly worlds apart from each other in time, place, and in the direction of their inquiry, there is something similar in their resolution to arrive at a point that cannot be doubted. We may compare, for example, the above passage with a passage where Descartes describes his discovery of *cogito ergo sum*:

> I resolved to pretend that all the things that had ever entered my mind were no more true than the illusions of my dreams. But immediately I noticed that while I was trying thus to think everything false, it

> was necessary that I, who was thinking this, was something. And observing that his truth *"I am thinking, therefore I exist"* was so firm and sure that all the most extravagant suppositions of the skeptics were incapable of shaking it, I decided that I could accept it without scruple as the first principle of the philosophy I was seeking.
>
> (Descartes 1985: 127)

The thinking subject ascertained by Descartes is the carrier of reason. In fact, what he needed to ascertain was also reason as the principle of the world. In the passage quoted earlier, Mencius ascertains the goodness of human nature as a basis for proper rules of society and the state. The goodness of human nature pronounced thus by Mencius formed an indubitable foundation of all Confucian ethics and political philosophy. Thus it formed the cornerstone of philosophical thinking on personal and social ethic in Korean Neo-Confucianism. Its central philosophical concern was directed more towards the elements that constituted the originary nature of goodness: the four beginnings of the ethical mind. Nurturing these incipient tendencies of the mind into maturity, especially in relation to other properties of the mind-heart (i.e., desire, hate, love, fear, grief, anger and joy) formed the core of inquiry into moral cultivation. Self-cultivation was, however, not only for the good of individual man; it also helped to maintain social and political order on the correct foundation. The state was to embody these ethical principles in its workings. At its apex was of course the king. His responsibility was also defined in these terms: it was to perfect his moral mind, so that he could be a guarantor of the moral order of society by his example and administration, and take up the task, delegated by heaven, of looking after his people through commiseration and wisdom. Toegye, for instance, lays it out as the plan of an ethical state in his advice to the king (Yi 1972). Thus there could be an integrative order for the self and the world.

The ideal was that of a theocracy or ethicocracy. This ideal has often ended up in a regime of repression and hypocrisy. This was the case even in Korea. However, it is not without elements that can be carried over to the modern age with its more liberal mind free from prescriptive moral imperatives. What should be noted is that Korean ethical politics did not necessarily consist in the implementation of a set of fundamentalist articles of faith, at least in its philosophical rendition. The advantage of beginning with self-reflexive epistemology is that it does not require the positing of precepts and maxims in advance, but subscribes to a mind open to critical investigation, though its openness tends to turn to closure too soon. The first condition of moral cultivation is the nurturing of a vigilant mind. The emphasis on it has the intention of making the moral person constantly watch for Confucian principles. This vigilance is, instead of an itemized examination of rules of conduct, performed more simply by keeping the mind clear as a whole. Keeping the mind free of subservience to details brings on its liberation to the original state of fluidity.

What is important is this vigilance in itself, not necessarily its moral and practical consequences. The vigilant mind is the ground of all, for it is not only the guarantor of moral conduct, but also the condition of discernment in Confucian self-cultivation and moral conduct, and the investigation of things, as the morality must have an underpinning of the cosmological truths. The mind whose clarity is so important in moral conduct is a more inclusive principle than an adjudicator of moral precepts. Clarity of the mind is not simply the same as moral purity, but an epistemological condition. *Kyŏng* is, in Neo-Confucianism, a word designating the vigilant state of mind underlying all moral conduct. As may be seen in its frequent translation into English as "mindfulness," it often designates simply attentiveness, or it can mean more appropriately apprehensive awareness. *Kyŏng* is also "reverence"; therefore it has associations with deferential morality, but deeply serious attentiveness often goes along with reverence or respect for what is being attended to. It is undeniable that, even if it is usually coupled with a moral attitude, an unfettered mind, moving in response to the fluidity of things, was an important object of Confucian self-cultivation. To do so, one has to clear the mind of dogmatic positivities and revert to the state of negativity. As Toegye puts it, "Things, good or evil, large or small should not be kept in the mind as positivity. Positivity means to be attached to things in an imbalanced way, and it gives rise to the evils of a fixed mind, unfair hasty striving, profit-seeking. Avoiding attachment [means to be] . . . in the state of apprehensive awareness of things" (Yi 1982: 119). Here he is affirming Chu Hsi's idea that "the mind must remain centered and unitary, tranquilly unmoving in the absence of things to attend to, and moving responsively when there are things to attend to and yet stopping before overflowing into other things, thereby ensuring the undwelling singleness of the mind moving with ten thousand things" (Yi 1982: 117). The primary object that emerges in the fluid attentiveness of the mind is its responsiveness to other human beings from which the ethical principles arise, but the object could also be other things, even performance of daily chores. Eventually the mind must be open to minute nuances and the entirety of nature and the world. What is assumed is the congruence between the correct perception of human needs and the nuanced perception of the things of the world, all achieved by the act of looking inward, coinciding with outward-looking responsiveness.

The aim of Confucian self-reflection is this congruent inwardness, the undwelling singleness of the mind open to the world, and this was to be the sole point of support for all constructive endeavors of Confucian society, including the pursuit of authentic individuation, which could be as individualist as in any other cultural scheme, though mostly within the Confucian possibilities of human society.

In this constant concern to define the self and the world in the double-headed single process, there is a parallel between the working of the mind as conceived in Confucian philosophy and the process of the Cartesian *cogito*. If the Cartesian *cogito* is the foyer of analytical-referential deployment of the self and the world, Confucianism, too, has its epistemological foyer in the undwelling singleness of the mind where the positivities of the world are dissolved and redeployed in a single unitary process. Both cases speak of a constitutive principle of the world abstracted from empirical reality: the subject as the substratum of the synthetic unity of the world arrived at through a process of philosophical reduction (of varying degrees of purity and complexity). However, whether Confucian or Cartesian, this subjectivity is presuppositionless by principle, but in reality contains the vectors of pragmatic interest originating in the empirical world. It is not only that both subjectivities are in reality located in the empirical ego. In the Cartesian reduction, the process of doubt and certainty already moves in favor of *mattiesis universalis* and reason, and, as has been pointed out in critiques of Cartesianism, the will to domination. In the Confucian *ascesis* or the mind, the undwelling singleness of the mind is already motivated by moral certainty and social relations ordered by indubitable ethical laws, which are really a reflection of the existing order of things in an archaic society. There is in both cases a kind of reason as the central principle of operation, and in this reason, mathematical or ethical, as *parti pri*, in turn prefigures the future fate of both Eastern and Western societies; the instrumentalization of reason for one and the ever-rigidifying institutionalization of ethical reason for the other. In Asia, or more specifically in Korea, the fluidity of the mind is easily forgotten and ideological rigor mortis sets in, as the mind deteriorates into ritual and institutional details, ever refined in a scholastic exercise in futility.

5

The parallel between Cartesian subjectivity and Confucian subjectivity brings us to the earlier observation about the difficulty of transplanting Western subjectivity to an East Asia society. If the individual (in the Western sense) does not yet have a normative standing in Korean society, it is because he does not yet have legitimacy as the subject of social processes; and this is not simply, as I have observed above, the question of vigorous advocacy or even legislation. It is not even that we have not had the concept of the individual, but this individual is already caught in the dialectic of subjectivity that made it the nodal point of ethical relations, and of cosmic relations as well, with the deepening of these relations taken as the fulfillment of selfhood in cosmic harmony.

This, however, is not the individual or the world called for in an industrial democracy. A modern individual cannot be invented overnight and simply added on to what has existed. The terms of the whole social process must be reset so that it can be remade along with its world on a new basis in a syntactically binding reconstitution. The modernization of the past several decades has gone far in destroying the ancient regime of Confucian subjectivity, but the new regime has not yet been established, except in externalities.

Besides the inherent difficulty of a new instauration, another question is whether this new dispensation would promise a better world. True, there were many reasons why the old subjectivity had to be destroyed. One simple fact was that it was out of phase with the movement of world history, which was being shaped by the West. The old regime failed to produce viable instrumentalities for survival in the modern world. There are also old repressions, still at work, transformed as they are by the force of a newly acquired modernity. Abuse of rights is still here, though there has been in recent decades a great deal of progress in reducing it. The moral paternalism of a society has a more ambiguous significance, with its communitarian suggestions. This communitarian moralism, however, does not change the repressiveness of institutionalized moralism (as morality becomes here a claim on an individual by others in the political arena, and could easily turn into a rhetorical cover for coercion). What is called for is a new rational articulation of the relation between the individual and the collectivity.

Nevertheless, there could be regret for excluding the principle of moral concern at the heart of the institution of politics. Further, the processes of Confucian subjectivity seem to reveal more insight into the possibility of authentic individuation. If Confucianism is repressive, it is not only because of coercion imposed from outside. It is also part of a moral program, regrettable as its repressive implication is, demanding a more rigorous introspection which would put a person in closer touch with the authentic needs of the individual, and would help the person succeed in attuning himself or herself with the needs of society. In the best instance, perhaps it may lead to a joyous asceticism, a glad acceptance of the pleasure as well as the responsibility of attending to things in the world. It would call for acknowledging one's authentic needs and also for willing restraint of inauthentic desires, which will be needed in the work of a more harmonious social order. This joyous asceticism cannot help but stand opposed to the philosophy of self-aggrandizement that rules today's world. The pressure and lure to join this modern world cannot be greater. It does not come simply from its material success, but this promise of liberation, as conceived in the Western Enlightenment, from all regimes of repression, political and moral, is more beguiling. Deeply involved in this modern development is Cartesian rationalism, its preoccupation with the instrumental mastery of the world. More disturbing is oblivion, in Cartesianism, of the origin of rationality in the deeper recesses of the human interior, wherein multiple other ways of conceiving the human selfhood and its relation to the world are located. The Cartesian subjectivity is not the only way of being a subject in the world. To some viewpoints, Confucianism, along with all the past records of repressiveness, seems to present a different way of being in the world, for individuals and for society, requiring ethical restraint but promising harmony and equilibrium.

Some see in Confucianism the possibility of a new social and political order. Tu Weiming, a philosopher of Confucian self-cultivation, believes that Confucian communitarianism, broadly conceived to include Taoist wisdom as well, can be an alternative social ideal with operative efficacy even in today's world. He writes:

> The ideal state is, first of all, extremely small. (Take the Daoist vision: the ideal state was thought to be a neighborhood community.) It is not authoritarian. Instead, it is participatory and communal. Mencius' ideal state is very much an agricultural community, resembling what Marx called a primitive commune. Given the complexity of modern or post-modern political development, that is not necessarily an outdated notion.
>
> (Tu 1984, quoted in Dirlik 1995: 64)

The above quotation from Tu Weiming is from Arif Dirlik's critique of the modern vision of Confucian society. Dirlik's suggestion is that the ideal Confucian state is spurious, not per se, but in the modern context in which in it is placed, put forward as an apology for Asian industrial authoritarianism and for global capitalism of which it is a part. Apart from its apologetic nature, we ought to say that Tu Weiming's picture of an ideal Confucian state as a small agricultural community is totally unrealistic. But this spurious and unrealistic picture should not obscure the primary importance conceded in Confucian thought to ethical concern and its origins in the ontological needs of humans, whether looking for individual fulfillment or a harmonious social order. Yun Sa-sun, a representative interpreter of traditional Korean philosophy, looks back on the Confucian heritage, paying attention only to the ethical aspect of Confucianism. He writes:

> [T]he trouble with Western modernity is to conceive of human nature in terms of individualist desire, which resulted in utilitarian philosophy and the absolutizing of selfishness, destroying the foundation of collective life, the solidary relationship with human beings.
>
> (Yun 1996: 132)

This is to be remedied by Confucian moral philosophy. One important element to be rescued from Confucianism is affectivity as a fundamental mediatory agent in the relation of the human being to the world and other humans. Especially significant is the social affectivity of reciprocity, expressed in Confucian terms as: "Do not do to others what you do not want them to do to you" (Analects 12: 2); and "A man of humanity wishing to establish his own character, also establishes the character of others, and wishing to be prominent himself, also helps others to be prominent" (Analects 6: 28).[2]

One can sympathize with this kind of restorative work from the past by such a philosopher as Yun; but one wonders whether odd pieces from here and there could really affect a larger social change that is progressing according to its own logic. Even as an interpretation of the past, ideas belonging to a larger structure of a *Weltanschauung* must be seen as part of this structure, not as locally detachable pieces. They have their significance as part of the original matrix from which the individual, society, and the world were born in a single constitutive dynamic. The original insight into Confucianism on the responsibility of reciprocity in the relation of humans to fellow humans and to the world lies in the possibility that authentic needs and fulfillment of individual life require the responsibility of reciprocity. Even in the past regime of Confucian politics and morality, forgetting the original matrix for the generation of the individual and the world was the beginning of its repressive turn. Morality and ethics often come from this imposition from outside, not the fulfillment of inner needs. Even in the case of modern Confucians, if moral remedy is prescribed simply as re-importation of a collective ethic from the past, it would end up re-enacting the repressive regime of ethicocracy of the past.

Even if it is possible for Confucianism to offer remedial measures to modern society, these are likely to return as so many problems. The major problem with visions of a Confucian utopia is not with the visions themselves but their fit with historical and modern reality. Dirlik's critique reminds us that what is really at issue is not the question of choice at the level of ideas, but the dynamic of the reality of the national and global situation today. The question is how we determine a more just and peaceful society, a more harmonious and more fulfilling world. If that is the case, the choice is not simply, to use again that reductive shorthand, between Cartesian or Confucian subjectivity. Remaining on a purely philosophical level, we may say it is not without relevance to think about the two forms of subjectivity briefly noted above as somehow involved in the practical task of the world, even as a mere shadow play of larger historical processes. Koreans are presented with a philosophical choice and asked to choose Cartesian or Confucian subjectivity, however flawed they are. Koreans are for the first time in their history beginning to experience the ravages of the instrumental rationality in capitalism traceable, in a shorthand fashion, to the Cartesian philosophy of subjectivity, with its objective counterpart in this value-free *Zweck-rationalitaet* defined most narrowly as economic aggrandizement. But they also feel that the progress of rationality in society and politics would perhaps contribute to the containment of these ravages; there are clearly areas of social life which could benefit from increased rationality in society, in firmer establishment of procedural democracy and the rule of law. But the pull from Confucianism still remains strong, not only for the authoritarian ideologs, but also for those who are looking for alternative ways of making history and constructing human existence.

In view of the strong legacy of repressive and regressive politics from Confucianism, there must be some way of overcoming this repressive legacy. It may be found not in getting away from it but in going back to the origins of Confucian self-reflection – not the moral principles, but to the condition of apprehensive awareness as the beginning of reflective reconstruction of humans and society – without presuppositions, with no *parti pri*, and above all, avoiding the traps of premature closure. This condition of openness seems to coincide with the original epoch in Cartesian *cogito*, suspension of positivities, soon closed off as mathematical reason. This coincidence seems to point to a new possibility. As noted above, Cartesian subjectivity has been the object of an intense critique from various quarters in recent years, either for harboring a will to dominate or for its illusory search for foundation. The same critique could be applied to Confucian subjectivity. It is not easy to find a way between the two subjectivities and beyond. Yet from comparison of the two subjectivities the important thing seems to be to maintain this condition of reflective vigilance, not veering off from it to deconstructive nihilism or to a premature leap into positivities; to remain attentive to the scientific and practical needs on the one hand, and to the inner and moral needs of humanity on the other. On this foundation, also important is not abandoning the generative dynamic of subjectivity, and to consider new possibilities of a world to come.

What is called for is indeed the fusion of Cartesian and Confucian subjectivities. In this fusion, however, I would say, at least for this period of Korean history, that Cartesian subjectivity would have a methodological priority in that it offers a principle of a more radical and lawful construction. Only within the radical and lawful reflexivity that goes along with constructive effort will it be possible to preserve the authority of reason as well as the other non-rational elements of human nature that Confucian philosophy found innate to humans, though the danger of Cartesian simplification is real enough, as has been pointed out in many postmodern philosophies. Part of the political problem with Confucian philosophy is its insufficiency in the power of differential articulation in its communitarian holism. Even if we would like to preserve a more broad-minded conception of human subjectivity than in Cartesianism, we need to see this subjectivity as based on the moment of self-reflection and self-evidence. This moment is best guaranteed its independence and freedom within the social institutions made possible by Cartesian rationalism.[3]

Notes

1 Here the male pronoun is unavoidable due to its historical accuracy.
2 All quotations from Confucius are from Chan (1963: 39, 31).

3 The power of formal articulation seems to be little noticed as a significant factor in the historical development of institutions, as I have hinted above. If communality of man is important, it is so not only for men as an aggregate but also for men as differentiated individuals. An unmediated emphasis on the communality of man seems to lead to a state where individuals cease to be, and then there is no need to emphasize the communality. Professor Misoguchi Yuzo of Tokyo University presented an interesting argument in his paper "Japanese Economic Development and Traditional Elements" given at the Symposium on Eastern Thought and Social Development, Seoul, 1996. He noted that while the Chinese tradition always emphasized the ethics of communal solidarity with no clear articulation of individuals, the Japanese feudal system sharply separated the two realms of the lord, the public realm, and the subject. He contends that this separation was an element that helped the early modernization of Japan. It appears that modern society must be constituted as an articulated whole, not as an undifferentiated aggregate.

References

Balibar, Etienne. 1991. "Citizen Subject," in Eduardo Cadava, Peter Connor and Jean-Luc Nancy (eds). *Who Comes After the Subject?* London: Routledge.

Cadava, Eduardo, Peter Connor and Jean-Luc Nancy (eds). 1991. *Who Comes After the Subject?* London: Routledge.

Chan, Wing-tsit. 1963. *A Source Book in Chinese Philosophy.* Princeton, NJ: Princeton University Press.

Choi, Jang-jip. 1993. "Building a Strong State in South Korea: The State and Cultural Transformation: Perspectives from East Asia," in Kenichi Hirano (ed.). *The State and Cultural Transformation: Perspectives from East Asia.* Tokyo: United Nations University Press.

Descartes, Rene. 1985. *The Philosophical Writings of Descartes,* trans. John Cottingham, Robert Stoothoff, and Dugald Murdoch. Cambridge: Cambridge University Press.

Dirlik, Arif. 1995. "Confucius in the Borderlands: Global Capitalism and the Reinvention of Confucianism." *Boundary* 2 (22/3): 229–273.

Hobsbawn, Eric. 1994. *Age of Extremes: The Short Twentieth Century, 1913–1997.* London: Michael Joseph.

Kahn, Herman. 1979. *World Economic Development: 1979 and Beyond.* New York: Morrow Quill Paperbacks.

Kuroda, Katsuhiro. 1993. *Han'gukin dangsineun nuguin'ga* [The Korean, Who Are You]. Seoul: Moeumsa.

Taylor, Charles. 1986. *Human Rights: The Legal Culture. Philosophical Foundations of Human Rights,* ed. Aiwin Diemer *et al.* Paris: UNESCO.

Yi Toegye. 1972. "Mujinyukchosŏ" [Memorial to the King in the Year of Mujin; Six Articles], in Yi Hwang, *Han'guk ŭi sasang chŏnjip X* [Korean Thought X]. Seoul: Tonghwachulpansa.

Yi Toegye. 1982. *Toegye sŏnjip* [Selected Works of Toegye], trans. Yun Sasun. Seoul: Hyŏnamsa.

Yun, Sa-sun. 1996. *Sinsilhak sasangron* [A Treatise on New Practical Learning]. Seoul: Yemunsŏwŏn.

9 Monumental histories

Manliness, the military, and the War Memorial

Sheila Miyoshi Jager

> Our ancestors were manly men until the middle ages, but this masculine character disappeared by the time of the establishment of the Chosŏn dynasty.... Sorrow is the only reward we can get from surveying our past history.
>
> President Park Chung Hee, 1962, quoted in Park 1970: 167

How does one commemorate a war that technically is still not over? While the Korean War, at least for the Americans, "ended" in 1953, the discourses of commemoration about the war have not been brought to a closure in Korean society.[1] How does one bring closure to a war for which the central narrative is one of division and dissent, a war whose history is still in the process of being made?

In South Korea, the official commemoration of the Korean War has always taken on an anti-North Korean stance. However, this official view was suddenly questioned in the wake of Kim Dae Jung's historic meeting in Pyŏngyang with North Korean leader Kim Jong-il in June 2000. Indeed, to the surprise (and dismay) of the hundreds of veterans who had gathered in Seoul to commemorate the fiftieth anniversary of the Korean War in June 2000, it was announced that most of the planned commemorative events, including a large city parade and an historical re-enactment of the 1950 Inchŏn landing, were to be canceled.

Of course, the singular and official historical narrative of the Korean War, including the anti-North Korean rhetoric that was embedded within it, has always been open to question in South Korea, although it was not until very recently that these new views, and especially new perceptions of North Korea, have been able to be freely aired. While any commemorative act, particularly about wars, is a form of history-making that aims to promote and secure a particular interpretation of events while at the same time blocking or erasing potentially contestatory readings, in South Korea, official memory about the war has always been constituted within a discourse of national self-definition aimed to promote the legitimacy of the state. In the Korean official culture of commemoration, the Korean War has played a fundamental role in defining the masculinist language of national self-definition and state legitimacy in South Korea. Not only has this official commemorative culture perpetuated and generated a view of the past in terms of a particular masculine ideal; memories of the war have also affirmed the identification of the national subject with the authority of these masculine images aimed to perpetuate the state's vision of a future reunified Korea.

The purpose of this chapter is to explore the masculinist logic of this official commemorative culture through a detailed examination of the War Memorial, a huge architectural complex located in Yongsan-gu, Seoul. Conceived under the Roh Tae Woo regime in 1988, the Memorial was opened to the public in 1994, soon after the election of Korea's first civilian president, Kim Young Sam, in over thirty years of military rule (Figure 9.1). While the War Memorial glorifies the ancient or eternal character of the nation which it links to the lost "manly" past of a forgotten martial tradition, it seeks simultaneously to emphasize the unprecedented novelty of the modern nation which it links to the "recovery" of ancient military values. The connection made between the military, manliness, and nationalism throughout the War Memorial thus presents us with a window to view not only how history was written by those who saw themselves as the privileged "subjects" of the nation, but also, and more importantly, how the gender ideals implicit in that history – in this case, martial masculinity – were appropriated by the state for political ends to *affirm* its legitimacy *vis-à-vis* North Korea. The War Memorial not only tells the story of the manly and strong nation against the plight of its war-torn past; it

Figure 9.1 The War Memorial, Yongsan-gu, Seoul.

also advocated manliness and brotherly strength as patriotic *values* against the plight of its divided future.

The cult of virile (military) manhood that was expounded in Sin's nationalist histories and later reinforced during the Park regime is thus essential to understanding how the legacy of Korea's military past continues to influence civilian politics in South Korea today. During the economic crises of 1998, for example, the recuperation of Korea's "warrior culture" was suggested by the Kim government as a way to get South Koreans out of their economic slump. Moreover, the robust efforts made by President Kim Dae Jung to honor the legacy of Park Chung Hee reveal that the narrative about manly "redemption" that was cultivated during the Park era is *still* being used as a solution to all kinds of problems.[2]

Sincere efforts to reproduce, memorialize, and concretize this warrior past were made, strikingly, during a period that was witness to the historic culmination of nearly thirty years of military rule in South Korea. Far from being merely a poignant reminder of state military power, however, the War Memorial is heir to the particular historical legacy of social Darwinism, militarism, and nationalism that sought to link national "progress" with martial prowess, economic "survival" with the cult of martial masculinity. Moreover, as the central locus for commemorating the Korean War, the War Memorial has played a significant role in the historization and rehistorization of the military in South Korean society by forging a consensus version of the events aimed to bring together military leaders and the "people" of North Korea and South Korea. The cultural memory of the Korean War is evoked in the context of memories about other wars, so that the "healing" process associated with the division of the peninsula appears to be metaphorically related to other moments of healing in Korean history brought about by heroic soldiers and martial leaders.

The War Memorial

When the War Memorial opened its doors to the public in 1994, it created a minor, although vocal, public outcry from certain sectors of society. To dissident intellectuals and students, the opening of the War Memorial signaled the continuation of state authoritarian power through the forced celebration of a patriotic history imposed upon the public from above. Spectacular and triumphant, the Memorial was deemed nothing more than a calculated tribute to bolster state authority and established interests. Evoking feelings of insecurity and anxiety, the War Memorial, its critics claimed, makes the visitor "feel vulnerable" in the presence of state power (Kim 1994: 171; Chong 1994). Alternatively, compared to Stalin's Soviet Palace, Hitler's Berlin Square, Mussolini's Rome, and Mao's Mausoleum, the War Memorial's severest critics unanimously deemed it "a wicked plot," "a bastard that should never have been born," "an illegitimate child that should never have seen the light of day" (Yi 1997a).

What is, of course, interesting about these criticisms, above and beyond their attacks on the Memorial as a vehicle of state power, is the very language in which they chose to condemn it: the Memorial as an illegitimate child. By attacking its legitimacy in familial terms, these critics unwittingly attacked the very basis upon which the War Memorial was founded: to establish a link between family and nation, ancestral lineage and state pedigree, "blood inheritance" and state legitimacy.

The idea that Korea's war heroes, from the establishment of the ROK Army during the Korean War era, to its deployment overseas during the Vietnam and Gulf Wars, could be traced back to a single "patriotic" (male) warrior lineage, beginning with the Three Kingdom period, lies at the very core of the Memorial's significance as a state monument and a national museum. In this sense, the Memorial's monumentality derives from its latent insecurity; its aim is not only to "prove" its legitimacy in the eyes of the public, but also to challenge other family/national histories that may lay claim to the heroic (martial) history which the state deemed to be its very own. The timeless past of Korea's heroic history was thus presented as an unbroken warrior tradition; the intent of the Memorial is not to periodize history, but to link separated historical phases into a continuum.

The first clue of the Memorial's self-preoccupation with its own "bloodline" legitimacy may be seen at the Central Plaza. A vast open area embraced on either side by the right and left Galleries, the Central Plaza (also called the War Memorial Plaza) is an empty space except for two reliefs carved at each end facing the main stairway. They both reveal a familiar scene: in Figure 9.2a, we see the belligerent poses of the common citizens on their way to battle their Japanese colonial oppressors. In Figure 9.2b, we see the Righteous Army itself, armed in full battle gear, accompanied with this telling inscription:

> Ah, our proud Army!
> Inherit the anti-Japanese Righteous Soldier's sacrificial spirit,
> Devote yourselves to restoring our national pride,
> Hear the battle cry of the Independence Army and the Restoration Army,
> You are the honor restored by their souls!

Implied within the obvious link made between the Righteous Army (*ŭibyŏng*), the Independence Army (*tongnip kun*), and the Restoration Army (*kwangbok kun*) is a familiar familial code:[3] the "inheritance" of the spirit of resistance passed down through the generations. But the inscription has other key codes that link these historical phases into a family continuum: father and son form the vanguard of the people's army on the left wall, a generational continuum which is reinforced by the "embracing" presence of the left and the right Galleries which house the names of

(a)

(b)

Figure 9.2 Relief of the Righteous Army.

South Korea's Korean War "martyrs." Thus visually represented is the symbolic familial link between the anti-Japanese war heroes of the Righteous Army and the Independence Army which are in turn surrounded by the anti-communist war heroes of the modern ROK Army. Still, the reliefs in the Central Plaza contain a third code in its narrative structure: the link between the military and the people. To those who oversaw the planning and construction of the War Memorial, this link was central to the legitimizing presence of the structure itself: military heroes as the people's heroes. In fact, this link is presented as soon as the visitor first steps onto the Memorial complex. On the right-hand side of the pathway that leads towards the Central Plaza is the following inscription, carved in granite, which reads:

> Suffused with the everlasting breaths of our noble and majestic countrymen,
> This is the living domain of the sacred spirit of national defense,
> This is where one's love of country magnificently bursts forth.
>
> The brilliant services of the heroes,
> Who protected our inherited self-respect and our land,
> It is they who are responsible for the peaceful rays
> of the sun and the moon over this land.
>
> By pursuing the spirit of our martyrs who defeated invasions,
> By spreading the gospel of love of country.
> Here forever will be preserved the proud history of our people.

The dual purpose of the War Memorial thus becomes clear: as a museum, its function was to educate and reform; as a memorial, its purpose was to bless that newly acquired education with a spirit of reverence. Through it, the inevitable outcome was a correct and unanimous understanding of Korea's patriotic history as both intimate yet eternal, fleeting yet immortal.

The ritual honoring of "one hero every month" in the Central Hall merely reinforced this idea of familiarity within the vast continuum of "inherited" patriotic history. Chosen on a rotating basis from among the fifty or so statues represented in the Hall of Heroes, the purpose of paying homage to a new hero every month was "to laud their ethos and achievements thereby making them a shining example to the new generation" (CCKNK 1990: 12). Thus honored, the hero stands between an immortalized past and glorious future ("a shining example to the new generation"). The temporal logic of this presentation of patriotic history was to forge a homogeneous and continuous national subject who is both unique and yet the same, distinct yet indifferentiable. It is the spirit of patriotism, not the hero's particular patriotic act(s), that is being commemorated.

From this individual encounter with a single hero, the visitor walks down through the Hall of Heroes towards the darker recesses of the Memorial Hall (see Figure 9.3). The Hall of Heroes is structured in such a way that the deeper one travels down the Hall, the further back in time one finds oneself (from the Korean War period to the Three Kingdoms period). National history is told in flashback: it is a retrospective reconstruction of the past from a current vantage point of repetition. Here, Koguryŏ's struggles against the Sui in AD 598 become the "ancestral" predecessors of South Korea's struggles against North Korean communists in 1950. By conceiving of the past in this way, history becomes a process of the continual development of the same (Duara 1995). The visitor thus finds himself caught between two temporalities: an ageless and glorious past which in turn becomes the foundation for an equally ageless and glorious future.

Here, time and space appear separated but unambiguously linked: history and nation meet as one entity born and reborn over and over again in one long genealogical sequence of fathers, sons, and grandsons. It is the "spirit" of patriotism passed down through the generations, not the individual (lost) battles themselves, that are being commemorated. And it is precisely this historical continuum, expressed visually by the repetition of column-like forms, which leads the visitor from the contemplative space of the Central Hall (present), to the long walk down the Hall of Heroes (past), and into the dark recesses of the Memorial Hall (ancient past). While the walk back in Korea's past is supposed to evoke the glorious past of Korea's triumphant history, the very monumentality of the Memorial structure itself stands for the present and future of that patriotic history.

Figure 9.3 The Hall of Heroes.

The exhibitions

So what exactly *is* the nation's past, and how was it supposed to be exhibited? For the overseers of the Memorial, this question had everything to do with the mythologized history of the nation's struggle against foreign domination and the pivotal role the military had played in Korea's history of national self-defense: "The primary reason why our people have been able to turn back so many foreign invasions and maintain an unbroken 5,000 year history has been due to the patriotic (*aeguk*) and selfless (*salsin sŏngin*) service of our national heroes" (CCKNK 1990: 11–12). Through the sacred contemplation of past heroic deeds, the future reunification of the nation could be realized. As the exhibition manual explains:

> The object of the War Memorial is to act as a place that *pledges realization of the national dream of unification by learning from the heroes through the presentation of their pride and love of country.* In order to achieve the objective presented above, the following basic principles are established . . .:
>
> (a) Make people *aware that only the solidarity of the people, the government and the army can help a nation withstand national suffering* . . .
>
> (b) Remind visitors that to *reach our present state of national prosperity, the armed forces had to suffer all kinds of sacrifices and tribulations.* Through this presentation, create not only a proud image of our army but also make people realize that the army and the people are one.
>
> (c) *Foster not only trust in the military, but also firm trust in the nation by clearly showing how nations, regardless of who they are, will stand at the crossroads of fate if they allow their military to become weak.*
>
> (CCKNK 1990: 11–12; emphasis added)

The recurrence of such words as "solidarity," "unity," "strength," and "trust" which either appear or are alluded to in this passage are used throughout the entire "master plan" for the War Memorial. This repetition itself points to a predominant theme running through Korea's modern history: the triumph of strength over weakness, solidarity over division, faith over distrust. The celebration of the nation's "strength," which could only be guaranteed by the people's recognition of the military as a legitimate force in society, would also guarantee the eventual strengthening and reunification of the nation. Just as the solidarity of the military and the people resulted in the prosperous South Korean state, so the happy unity of South and North Korea would eventually be realized by the same strength evinced by those fruitful bonds.

The Chosŏn *Dynasty exhibit and Admiral Yi Sun-sin*

The history that was celebrated by the War Memorial everywhere portrayed the force of the fundamental alliance and unity between the people and the military as *the* primary condition for a prosperous (unified) future. The nation's victories were represented not merely as the triumph of the military in battle, but the triumph of the Korean people over both internal and external adversity. The message is clear: a divided people leads to national ruin; a unified people leads to prosperity and peace ("divided we fall; united we stand"). From this perspective, the extensive exhibition space devoted to Yi Sun-sin's (1545–1598) triumphant role during the Hideyoshi invasions (1592, 1597), when Koreans were able to overcome impending national disaster by relying on the magnetism of his "unifying" force, becomes a clear metaphor for the present state of national division. In each case, the historical analogy symbolically presented by the prominent display of Yi Sun-sin's Turtle Ship becomes a testament to a past and a present of the Korean nation and the military's vital role in both (see Figure 9.4). According to the exhibition manual, the

Figure 9.4 Admiral Yi Sun-sin's Turtle Ship.

Japanese invasions of the peninsula occurred because "the nation had fallen into distress" as a result of "a divided national opinion" (CCKNK 1990: 82–83). The aim of the display was to "lead the visitors to believe in the necessity of the unity of the people" as demonstrated "during times of imminent national danger by Admiral Yi Sun-sin's leadership" (CCKNK 1990: 82–83). The exhibition manual further relates:

> Make it a well known fact that the source of our 5000 years of long history and brilliant culture, as well as the force that effectively handled countless numbers of national crisis, arose from the manifestations of the Korean's unique love of country and of people as demonstrated during times of imminent national danger by Yi Sun-sin's leadership, and the uprising of Righteous soldiers. . . . In particular, by emphasizing the uprising of the Righteous soldiers and the many incidents of resistance, put forth the proposition *that the Korean War period soldier's self-sacrificial ethos during that tragic internecine war began with the martyrdom ethos of the Righteous soldiers who were willing to sacrifice their lives for their country during a national crisis, an ethos that was passed on to the (colonial period) Righteous soldiers and the Independence Army in their struggle against Japanese Imperialism.*
>
> (CCKNK 1990: 82–83)

Two points are of particular interest in this passage. The first concerns the issue of legitimacy. In tracing the "blood-line" heritage of the ROK Army to the Righteous soldiers and the Independence Army, Japan's formative role in the establishment of the South Korean military is strikingly absent.[4] Clearly, if such a lineage had to be drawn, it was the DPRK Army, and not the ROK Army, that had accumulated the vast majority of anti-Japanese Independence fighters within its ranks (Cumings 1981). The obfuscation of this fact once again indicates the present-minded vantage point of the Memorial: the possibility of laying claim to Korea's (anti-Japanese) "patriotic" past could be made only by illuminating the victorious state's *ultimate* triumph over its enemies (Japanese imperialism and North Korea communism) through the grandiose display of power and prosperity embodied by the very structure of the Memorial itself. It was precisely this assertion of *ultimate* victory that allowed the South Korean State to lay claim to Korea's patriotic tradition because North Korea (and the DPRK military) had *ultimately* failed.

Furthermore, the possibility of summarizing the past as victory clearly manifested some historical problems. In particular, the Memorial's portrayal of the Chosŏn Dynasty (1392–1910) is singularly problematic. (Not coincidentally, it was also this period of history that was given significantly more exhibition space compared to any other period of Korea's ancient history.) Inventing a newer, stronger, and militarily more powerful image of Chosŏn Korea, the War Memorial sought to rewrite the history of the

Chosŏn Dynasty from the vantage point of military strength and not of bureaucratic weakness. Because this period in Korean history was widely considered to be the most "shameful" chapter in Korean history due to its "dependence" on China, the aim of the Memorial was to lay claim currently for a stronger, more "manly," military tradition that had been, in reality, non-existent. This forging of a new history of the Chosŏn period on behalf of a "victorious" present is explicitly demonstrated in the exhibition manual:

> (a) Show how generals and warriors [during the Chosŏn Dynasty] possessed intellect, virtue and physical strength by explaining the Chosŏn period military system.... *Show how the national defense posture improved during the Chosŏn Dynasty* as a result of the soldier's going to battle with a strong military spirit and a firm belief in the nation....
>
> (b) *Organize the exhibit to wipe out the stereotype that the Chosŏn period had a weakened national defense as a result of bureaucracy (munch'ichuŭi)* by displaying various actual and replicated weapons.
>
> (c) Make it possible to directly experience our ancestor's "providing is preventing" philosophy of national defense, *and their progressive and active will to expand our territory* by exhibiting how the Chosŏn Dynasty conquered Tsushima island, a Japanese den, and how it drew the northern barbarian Juchens out and established outposts along the Yalu river and garrison forts along the Tumen River.
>
> (CCKNK 1990: 82)

Portrayed not merely as a military power able to defend the nation from external threats, but one also bent on territorial expansion, the aim of the display was to rewrite the history of the Chosŏn Dynasty in terms that marginalized the prominent role played by the Confucian high literati culture during that period. Furthermore, the portrayal of the "Great Taehan Empire" (1897–1910) which marks the end of the dynasty was accomplished in such a way as to draw a comparative link between Korea and other contemporary "great" imperial military powers. This connection was made by the strikingly visual connection posed between Korea's military uniforms with those of Britain, Germany, Japan, the United States, and China.

Ironically, the display of "The Military Uniforms of the Great Taehan Empire" starkly contrasts with the actual events which took place during that period of Korean history: it was during this "Great Empire," after all, which lasted a mere thirteen years, that the Korean people witnessed the collapse of their nation as a sovereign state and the colonization of the peninsula by Japan (1910–1945). Indeed, Japan's colonization of the peninsula is hardly discussed at all, becoming instead a mere blank period in the genealogical line of commemorated battles and celebrated military "victories." (Significantly, it is the battle of Ch'ŏngsal-ri in October 1920 –

entitled "The Great Battle at Chŏngsari" – which represented the Independence Army's first major military victory over the Japanese in Manchuria that is highlighted.)

If Korea's colonization by Japan was given only passing mention in the history of Chosŏn Korea, its triumph over Japan 400 years earlier was celebrated as one of Korea's greatest achievements. Not only is Yi Sun-sin's victory over Japan allotted extensive exhibition space; the strategic position of Yi Sun-sin's Turtle Ship within the museum, situated in the center Left Hall, was constructed in such a way that the visitor cannot help but come across it several times during the course of a visit. As one "travels" through the course of Korea's ancient history, the triumphant figure of Yi Sun-sin's Turtle Ship, which one encounters again and again, becomes testament to a past that is both heroic and triumphant. The strategic placement of Yi's Turtle Ship was thus meant to create a past that could give meaning to the present and the future: Yi's triumph over foreign adversity and domestic strife would become an analogy for South Korea's (eventual) triumph over North Korean communism and national division. By holding up this period in the history of the nation as an example for future generations, the War Memorial sought to legitimize the state as Yi Sun-sin's "filial" successor.

The Korean War exhibit

The second main exhibition area after the Chosŏn Period rooms is the Korean War exhibition which is located on the second and third floors. Although the exhibition downplays anti-North Korean propaganda ("Quickly get over the fact that the Korean War was an act of provocation by North Korea" (CCKNK 1990: 342)), the visitor is nevertheless presented with clear evidence that the War was instigated by the North ("Present clearly with actual evidence that the Korean War was an illegal attack by North Korean communists who received support from the Soviet Union" (CCKNK 1990: 342)). Divided into four main rooms, the exhibition is presented in the following chronological order: (1) the background to the Korean War; (2) the North Korean invasion; (3) Defense Operations at Nakdong River; (4) the Inch'ŏn Landing; (5) Northward Advancement of the Armed Forces; (6) Intervention by Chinese Communists; (7) Stalemate Battle Phases; (8) and the Armistice. The last room, created almost as an afterthought, is devoted to the UN participation in the Korean War (which merely displays uniforms worn by UN soldiers), wartime life and weapons. Indeed, one of the more striking features of the Korean War exhibition is the attempt to highlight the South Korean army as the *principle* (heroic) subject of the war, so that the conflict is portrayed as being fought chiefly between the South Korean Army and North Korean *and* Chinese communist forces (with little reference given to the vital role that the US played in the conflict). Moreover, unlike the strategic role played by UN forces during the War, Chinese aid to North Korea is emphasized. The exhibition manual explains:

> Although the early period of the invasion was disadvantageous for our army, *present the fact that even in such a situation, our brave soldiers displayed a self-sacrificial patriotic spirit that arose from their love of country and the people....*
>
> By vividly showing the Battle of the Hills during the Armistice talks, where both sides struggled to take a little more of the land, *convey our brave soldier's spirit of national defense and make the visitors feel grateful towards our heroes.*
>
> (CCKNK 1990: 342; emphasis added)

Two points are significant here. The first concerns the idea of history as a righteous struggle to overcome adversity. The narrative is a familiar one: Yi Sun-sin's struggle against the Japanese in 1592 and 1597; the Independence Army's struggle against Japanese colonialists; South Korea's struggle against North Korean communists. As with similar wars witnessed in the preceding exhibition spaces, the Memorial treats the Korean War like a *continuum* of righteous struggle. The second point, concerning the idea of "gratitude" ("Make our visitors feel grateful towards our heroes") which is linked with similar ideas associated with "reverence" (*kŏngŭi*), "homage" (*kyŏngae*), and "piety" (*kyŏnggŏn*), is also significant. Not only were the visitors to the Memorial urged to honor their war dead; the very idea of honor was written into the history of the post-1945 liberation period itself. The Expeditionary Forces Room, which follows the Korean War exhibition, and displays artifacts dealing with South Korea's involvement in Vietnam, the Gulf War, and peace-keeping operations in Somalia, West Sahara, and Angola shows "how we South Koreans helped our friends in the cause of freedom" (Chang Chŏng-dŏk 1997).

Rising from the ashes of the Korean War, South Korea thus emerges as an internationally recognized power, a loyal friend, a trusted world partner fighting side by side with other world powers for the cause of freedom. A nation which has fought for freedom within its borders, South Korea also fights for freedom in the world. As an honored member of the international community which shares its "righteous" cause, the military once again becomes the subject of honor by the people.

The Armed Forces Room and the outdoor exhibition area

So how exactly did the planners of the War Memorial attempt to reinforce the inherent link between the military and the people, and between military power and national prosperity? The first step was to re-emphasize the historical link between the modern ROK Army and its "original" predecessors. Once again, the visitor is confronted with the same "historical" chart, which is accompanied by this explanation of sorts:

> When the military forces of the Chosŏn dynasty were forcibly dissolved by the Japanese in August 1907, Righteous Armies arose in defiance all across the nation. Upon the Japanese annexation of Korea in 1910, the Righteous Armies were organized in the Independence Army to continue their anti-Japanese struggle.
>
> Righteous Army (*ŭi byŏng*)
> Korean Independence Army (*tongnip kunhwaldong*)
> Revival Army (*kwangbok kun*)
> National Constabulary (*kukbang gyŏngpidae*)
> ROK Army (*yukkun*)

The idea of the ROK Army as *the* subject of the linear (patriotic) history of the Korean nation exposes one of the most persistent splits in nationalist histories: that between the atavism of the nation and its telos of modernity (Duara 1995). Here, the ROK Army is conceived of as the end-product of the "natural" evolutionary process of the Korean nation, so that what is considered to be the "authentic" warrior spirit of the nation is now "atavistically recovered" as something new and entirely modern. Hence, Duara's point that "as the subject of History, the nation must daily reproduce the project of recovering its national essence – to secure its transparency as the already-always of the nation-space – especially to external challenges to this claim" (Duara 1995: 29). In the case of Korea, this "essence" became affiliated with a largely mythical military culture which now served as the "master subject" of the nation, and with this assumption of national continuity came other claims, to history, tradition, and culture for all of "its" nation's past and future. Hence, the War Memorial's attempt to privilege the military as *the* principal agent defining the national community and "the people." The modern period is thus conceived of as a period of renewal – the "recovery" of a lost past even as one forges into the future. By positing the military-people (the "people's army") as the new subject of national history, the planners of the War Memorial sought to "recover" the continuity of culture and the people even as they fashioned the people's "future":

> The Army has performed its duties as the army of the people during those times when the nation faced difficulties and its people suffered misfortunes.... *The army became the foundation of today's nation and society because, not only did it provide direct support to various (civil) construction projects, but because military training became closely connected to normal day-to-day social education.*... The Army is the object of terror and threat to the enemy, *the symbol of trust and devotion to the people, and*

> *the buttress of the nation's prosperity and its (goal of) reunification.* The army builds its image as a fresh and progressive institution that is *fulfilling these roles as the army of the people.*
>
> (CCKNK 1990: 202; emphasis added)

If the "people's army" emerged in the name of the "people," the implication is that the people-nation had always been present historically. But who exactly were the people? As the basis of the nation's sovereignty, the people were supposed to be very old. And yet, in order for the people to partake of the "fresh and progressive" future – and particularly the future of national reunification – they also had to be remade to fit their newly acquired "modern" status. In order to serve as a source of legitimization of the new nation of the "people's army," the "people" themselves had to be remade. In this way, the planners of the War Memorial undertook the pedagogy of the people in which the military now assumed a new and vital role in the lives of the people. Serving both as a repository of traditional authentic Korean "values" *and* as the vehicle of the "people's" modernization, the people's army now becomes synonymous with the people-nation itself. The "awakening" of the spirit of national self-defense was thus conceived as a "reawakening" of the original people-army-nation.

We can now understand the importance the Memorial's organizers attached to the physical bonding between the people and the military of the "new" people-army-nation. The Large Equipment room, but mostly the outdoor exhibition area, invite the visitor to actually touch the machines of war, to roam freely among them, to interact with them (Figure 9.5). The merging on a geographically symbolic plain between the army and the people, the people and the patriotic history of self-defense, would also give credence to the legitimacy of the military as "the army of the people." The goal was to bring together state power and the public in a familiarly intimate way. This familiar (and familial) demonstration of military strength was calculated to illustrate the continuity of an "authentic" core culture rejuvenated within modern South Korean society.

Reverence and embrace

As much as the visitor's freedom is encouraged in the outdoor exhibition area, however, it is severely restricted in the Central Plaza area. This vast open space leading up to the entrance of the War Memorial was designed to promote a "feeling of reverence" (Yi 1997b). It was within this space that the "petty" concerns of everyday life "were supposed to be brushed aside so that the visitor can confront the extraordinary meaning of war, sacrifice and patriotism" (Yi 1997b). Enveloping the Plaza with its "arms," the visual effect of the Galleries on this space was "to imbue it with a sense of inclusiveness, warmth, and even love" (Yi 1997b). It was within this inclusive space that the heroic past and the glorious present, the people

Figure 9.5 The outdoor exhibition area.

and the nation, the individual and history, were supposed to come together in the staged dramaturgy of national unity, reverence, and shared memory.

The repetitive placement of columns and tablets (inscribed with the names of over 100,000 Korean dead since 1945) within the space of the Galleries themselves merely accentuated this temporal preoccupation with national history and memory. The historical continuum expresses itself in the repetition of forms. This space was supposed to evoke "a quality of reverence and remembrance" which was "enhanced by the calm shadows which lengthen with the changing position of the sun, thus evoking the passage of time" (Yi 1997b). This movement of shadows, "formed by the columns and the tablets inscribed with the names of the dead interspersed with sunlight which shines through the empty spaces in between them," was supposed to produce "a revelatory and repetitive sequence of death and life, anger and repose, past and present" (Yi 1997b) (see Figure 9.6).

However, the idea of "embrace," associated here with the meeting of the people and their history, offers still another interpretation: the embrace of *all* Koreans (including North Korea) by the nation's southern Korean War martyrs. The brotherly magnanimity of that visual embrace – accentuated here by the building's triumphant celebration of "manly" strength – was supposed to underlie the War Memorial's significance as a "monument devoted to the peaceful reunification of the land" (Yi 1997b). The out-

Figure 9.6 The Central Plaza area.

stretched and open "arms" of the Galleries, which are visually reinforced by the statue of embracing brothers to the Memorial's left, denote both "forgiveness" as well as triumph, love as well as victory. The story of national reunification is written as a narrative of brotherly reunion. Significantly, the meeting between brothers – one strong and one weak, one elder and the other younger – is portrayed in such a way that the genealogy of the ancestral blood "line" was never questioned: South Korea is the elder son, the legitimate "heir" of Korea's patriotic warrior tradition whose forgiveness of his weaker, wayward brother becomes the condition upon which North Korea is finally allowed to return to the "arms" of the family/nation fold.

Fraternal embrace

The Statue of Brothers was conceived after the plans for the War Memorial had already been approved; nevertheless, its message of reunion through "manly" strength merely reinforces the masculine celebration of national triumph evinced by the War Memorial structure itself. Located on the left-hand side of the Memorial complex, the first thing which strikes the viewer about The Statue of Brothers is the enormous discrepancy in the size between the two figures (see Figure 9.7). Clasping his smaller brother to his heart, the South Korean soldier's emotion-laden face stares intently at his younger North Korean brother while the latter looks up at him with admiring, grateful, and (one imagines) tearful eyes. The contrast between these poses is further enhanced by the fact that only the elder brother wears a weapon; the younger one is as defenseless as he appears weak. According to Choi Young-jeep, the statue's sculptor, the "forgiving" embrace of the South Korean soldier is "enhanced by the weapon which points outwards in a non-threatening manner" (Choi 1997). Yet the very fact that he wears a rifle at all signifies that the "South is prepared for war should the nation be ever provoked again. It is only when nations are weak that wars become inevitable." Furthermore, the portrayal of the younger brother as weak and defenseless was supposed

Figure 9.7 The Statue of Brothers.

to show "the defeat of communism and the victory of South Korean democracy."

The legitimacy of the state, which became inextricably linked with this narrative of triumphant (or failed) manhood, was therefore couched in very familiar terms: one brother was heroic and virtuous, the legitimate "heir" of Korea's victorious "manly" past. The other brother was weak, effeminate and, by extension, illegitimate. The rhetoric of fraternity was therefore not incompatible with an extremely strict sense of familial hierarchy. This is because the unity of the nation could be secured only by acknowledging the true "blood-line" descendants of the original ancestors: South Korea as the eldest brother and, hence, the *only* legitimate heir.

Reunion and rebirth

Given this reading of the Statue of Brothers, what are we to make of the circular dome which forms its pedestal? According to Choi, the pedestal is modeled after a Silla Kingdom tomb mound. Given the Silla's role in the unification of the Three Kingdoms in AD 668, the historical analogy between the ancient past and the divided present becomes strikingly apparent. Rising up out of the "tomb," a reunified peninsula is reborn as a nation of brothers. The cracks at the bottom of the pedestal become smaller as the two figures, standing on two sides of a divided dome, embrace each other to form one single entity (Figure 9.7). As Choi Youngjeep remarked:

> My idea of using a (Silla) tomb as a pedestal was not intended to evoke the idea of death. On the contrary, it was intended to evoke ideas of hope and rebirth, the cycles of history, so to speak. The two brothers are reborn out of the womb of the past to be one again in the future.
>
> (Choi 1997)

The notion of national rebirth was also enhanced by the strategic placement of the Statue of Brothers in relation to the other objects within the War Memorial complex. Standing to the right of the Memorial at the opposite end of the Statue of Brothers is a reproduction of the large Memorial stele to King Kwanggaet'o the Great (the original stands in Jian City, Jilin Prefecture, China), perhaps the most celebrated king of the Kingdom of Koguryŏ. Engraved on all four sides are the mythical story of the founding of Koguryŏ, the meritorious deeds of Kwanggaet'o the Great, and the rules for the care of the tomb (see Figure 9.8). Erected by King Kwanggaet'o's son King Changsu in AD 414 in order to commemorate his father's great national achievements, the placement of the stele in the War Memorial grounds is significant. While standing for Korea's

Figure 9.8 Reproduction of Memorial to King Kwanggaet'o the Great.

heroic national past, the monument also announces the nation's glorious "rebirth." Likewise, in its celebration of a "victorious" present, the War Memorial creates both a past and a future of a mythologized Koguryŏ history that becomes as much a tribute to the heroic dead as it is to the living and the unborn. The triangular placement of these objects within the Memorial complex thus, each in their own way, stood for both the past and present, past and future, history and national "rebirth." Figure 9.9 shows the symbolic structure of the War Memorial complex.

The triangular scheme of this monumental complex demonstrates the state's vision of history and the nation on a geographic plane. Just as the future of a unified Korea finds its legacy in the Silla (left), so the future of

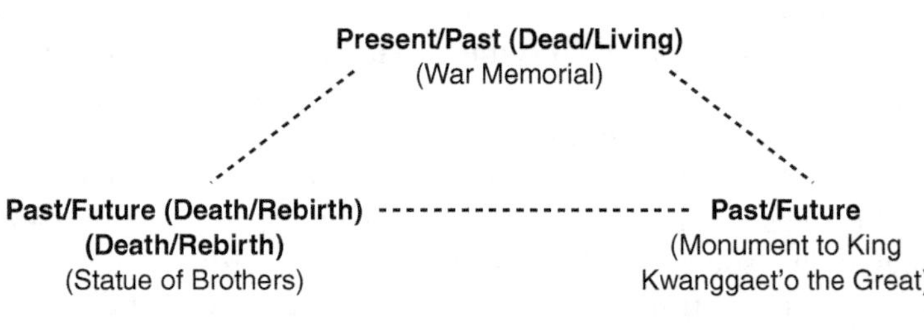

Figure 9.9 The symbolic structure of the War Memorial complex.

the vigorous ("manly") nation-state is modeled after the Koguryŏ (right). Past meets future in the moment of a victorious present.

The trope of brotherhood thus served the state well to fuse its two primary concerns: the need to construct a racial community of (warrior) men who are the "authentic" (legitimate) descendants of the original ancestors, and the need to establish a modern society. In order to recover the "lost" past of a glorious (primordial) military tradition, and hence forge a homogeneous and continuous national subject, the War Memorial had to search for alternative traditions to Confucianism within Korean history. In the process, North Korea was symbolically subsumed by the Memorial's appropriation of Koguyrŏ's history as its own. As we have seen, this history was the story of a Korean military heritage that had, for the most part, ceased to play a vibrant role in the past 500 years of Korean history (1392–1910). The problem of "recovery" thus also becomes the problem of shedding certain accretions of an "effete" middle-age. What began as a project of commemorating the past thus turns into the familiar project of reconstructing the nation's (reunified) future.

War and peace

If the painful memories of the Korean War have been temporarily overshadowed by the startling images of Kim Dae Jung and Kim Jong-il in brotherly embrace, what role will the War Memorial play in this drama, I wonder, in the minds of future generations? Will its monumental tribute to the dead and future soldiers of the nation still be read as an official testimonial to peace or as an ominous prelude to yet another war? Will the Statue of Brothers – the submissive gaze, the manly posture, the forgiving embrace, the ready rifle – signify hoped-for reunion or future conflict? Will the monument to the military be read as a reminder of the violent excesses of past military regimes or will it be viewed as a symbol of inclusion and peaceful transition to democracy? The ambiguity of these conflicting possibilities offered by the War Memorial has, of course, everything to do with the ambiguity of the Korean War experience itself, a war which has not yet ended, and for which no closure has yet been reached. Couched within the powerful monumentality of its masculine gaze is an equally powerful offering of reconciliation and peace, although it is a peace that can only be represented by a memorial to war.

Notes

1 In July 1953, North Korea, China and the United States signed an armistice agreement (South Korea refused to be a signatory). There was no peace treaty signed among the participants.

2 A good case in point is the inauguration of the Second *Saemaŭl Undong* (New Village Movement) and the Second Nation-building Movement (*Chae 2ŭi kŏnkuk*) in 1998, both of which were modeled after successful national campaign

movements initiated by former president Park Chung Hee in the 1970s. In addition, Kim's ebullient praise of Park Chung Hee, which came just two days before the thirty-seventh anniversary of Park's May 16, 1961 *coup d'etat*, was viewed as a historical revaluation of Park's place in Korean history. Further efforts to "make peace" with past military leaders were displayed in the dispatch of President Kim Dae Jung's junior coalition partner, Prime Minister Kim Jong-pil, to Kwangju for a ceremony commemoration of the nineteenth anniversary of the Kwanjgu Uprising on May 18, 1999.

3 The Righteous Army *(ŭibyŏng)* refers here to the guerrilla forces that sprang up against the Japanese led by Hideyoshi in 1592; the Independence Army (*tongnip ŭikun*) refers to the guerrilla army (also known as *ŭibyŏng*) raised against the Japanese shortly after the assassination of Queen Min in 1895, and the Restoration Army (*kwangbok kun*) refers to the Korean Provincial Government (KPG) and Kuomintang Allied Army, whose officers later came to dominate the top levels of the Republic of Korea Army (ROKA).

4 According to the actual record of Korean graduates from the Japanese Army Officer Military Academy, none went to North Korea. Instead, all of those who went on to pursue a military profession went into the South Korean military, many of them occupying key positions in the ROK military in the 1940s through the 1960s. See Yi Ki-dong (1982).

References

Chang, Chŏng-dŏk. 1997. Interview by author. Seoul, April 21.

Choi, Young-jeep. 1997. Interview by author. Seoul, March 25.

Chŏnjaeng Kinyŏmkwan chŏnsi yŏnch'ul kyehoek. 1990. [Exhibition display plans for the War Memorial]. CCKNK: 12.

Chong, Ki-hong. 1994. Kwŏllyŏk kwa mulsinchuŭi [Power and Fetishism]. *Plus* 7: 166–169.

Cumings, Bruce. 1981. *The Origins of the Korean War. Vol. I. Liberation and the Emergence of Separate Regimes, 1945–1947.* Princeton, NJ: Princeton University Press.

Duara, Prasenjit. 1995. *Rescuing History from the Nation: Questioning Narratives of Modern China.* Chicago: University of Chicago Press.

Kim, Ran-gi. 1994. "Kinyŏmkwaninga pangmulkwaninga?" [Is it a Memorial or a Museum?]. *Plus* 7: 170–173.

Park Chung Hee. 1970. *Our Nation's Path: Ideology and Social Reconstruction* (2nd edn). Seoul: Hollym Corporation Publishers.

Yi, Ki-dong. 1982. *Pigŭk ŭi kunindŭl: Ilbon kunin ŭi yŏksa* [Tragic Soldiers: History of the Graduates of the Japanese Army Officers Academy]. Seoul: Ilchogak.

Yi, Sung-kwan. 1997a. *Chŏnjaeng kinyŏmgwan ihu* [Beyond the War Memorial].

——. 1997b. Interview by author. Seoul, April 2.

10 Modernization theory, ideology, and economic success

Putting Korea's development in comparative perspective

Daniel Chirot

Social theory and ideology in the twentieth century

Now that the twentieth century is over, it is time to take stock and see what we have learned from it. It has been a century whose last quarter has produced so many unexpected outcomes that both social theory and more broadly based social and political ideologies have not caught up and absorbed all the changes that have occurred.

It is a platitude to say that when it comes to macro-social theory, whether it is concerned with social, political, or economic structures, social scientists cannot carry out the kinds of controlled experiments that micro-theorists are able to perform. We can, at best, use a comparative approach to produce quasi-experimental situations. The more data, be it quantitative or qualitative, from the more cases we have, the better-off we are, but we are unable to set up anything close to conclusive laboratory experiments. Therefore, theoretical and ideological debates continue long after common sense might suggest that answers to some major controversies are available.

There have been many large scale attempts to create new kinds of societies in the twentieth century. None of these have met the criteria of purely objective, controlled laboratory experiments, and many have included elements from several ideological and theoretical traditions. Still, they offer us an unprecedented kind of practical testing ground. By now we have seen enough successes and failures to allow some strong conclusions. However, the close connection between ideology and theory, each of which is difficult enough to judge objectively, makes the task of drawing useful lessons from the experiences of our century difficult.

By far the two most original ideological movements in the twentieth century were revolutionary fascist corporatism and revolutionary Marxism. Each had an accompanying set of social theories that preceded their coming to power. In fact, both political movements came originally from social theories produced by intellectuals, and they were later disseminated and popularized by activists. As social and political systems, both have failed catastrophically. Many, though not all, of their faithful followers who have survived have partly abandoned their original premises, though often not their core beliefs.

The other major ideological movements of the twentieth century have somewhat older origins than fascism and communism. One came from the European Enlightenment of the eighteenth century, and emerged in the nineteenth century as what is broadly called *liberalism.* This called for respect for individual over collective rights, a firm faith in human rationality, a conviction that on the whole individual choice expressed in open markets (that is, political democracy and economic capitalism) should determine most of the direction of both political and economic activity, and finally, a belief that it is impossible to devise perfect answers to social problems. It appeared, first, as a set of rather abstract philosophical principles, but eventually became the basis for some powerful political movements. In the first three-quarters of the twentieth century the theoretical view of society that is linked to political liberalism seemed to be in decline, but, in the final quarter, the success of the liberal, democratic capitalist systems reversed this trend.[1]

Then there has been nationalism, but nationalism may be consistent with fascism, communism, or liberalism, and with sentiments of ethnic and religious communal solidarity that are far older than any of the modern ideologies. It has to be worked into any discussion about the major ideological trends in the twentieth century, but case by case rather than as a complete ideology by itself. This is theoretically awkward, but there is no way to avoid it. One thing that may be said about nationalism, however, is that in one important way it resembles the other major ideological movements that have so upset our century. Modern nationalism originated as a set of ideas among intellectuals, and has spread from there to the general population.[2]

The major social theories constructed in the nineteenth and twentieth centuries have been tied intimately to important political ideologies. That is certainly obvious with Marxist social theory which was the intellectual base of communism, or with social Darwinism combined with eugenics theory and corporatism that became the foundation of Nazism and some other fascist movements. To take a liberal example, the same close connection may be found between the evolution of neoclassical economic theory and the legitimating ideologies that buttress free market economies. This makes the dispassionate examination of these theories all the more difficult, as they are firmly associated with particular political ideologies that appeal as much to emotion and faith as they do to objective social theorizing. Yet, logically, we should make some attempt to unbundle social theory from ideology. The failure of communism or of Nazism may cast strong doubt on some of the social theories that supported them, but Marxist, social Darwinian, and corporatist theories (which are actually not incompatible with each other) may still have something useful to tell us.[3]

What does all this have to do with Korea? In a sense, at least from an academic's viewpoint, it has a lot to do with both the recent Korean past and its future. The major social, political, and economic issue of the twentieth century has been, and continues to be, how well various societies will adapt to the immense, rapid set of changes forced on the entire globe by the Industrial Revolution that began in Europe in the eighteenth century. These changes have now encompassed every corner of the globe, but now, as was the case 100 ago, the most important question to ask about any society is: How well has it modernized and coped with all of its associated upheavals?[4]

There is a contemporary literary fashion that has spread into all humanistic studies and into many of the social sciences that calls the late twentieth century "postmodern." Applied to serious issues of social change, the attempt to import notions of postmodernism is completely misleading.[5] Modernization – that is, urbanization, the rapid increase in productivity, the increasing mechanization of every aspect of our lives, dramatic improvements in standards of living and life spans, our ability to transmit information ever more rapidly, and the spread of education – these are changes that are far from being finished. Even in the most advanced industrial countries such as those of Western Europe and the United States, rapid change continues as a result of modernization. In France as recently as two generations ago, peasants were the largest class of inhabitants, and women obtained the vote less than sixty years ago, in 1946. In the United States, prior to World War II, the south, its largest region, was still a largely agrarian, caste-based, quasi-feudal, poorly educated, traditional society. Japan, for all its bristling militarism in the 1930s, was also a society dominated by an agrarian-feudal ethos and deep traditionalism. Postmodern? We have hardly begun the modern age, and we barely understand its social ramifications. Only those with no sense of history or technology think that somehow we have come to the end of the modern age.

Korea, as we all know, has had one of the most rapid and dramatic experiences with modernization in the second half of the twentieth century, and, as in every other part of the world, it has had to struggle to find a way of adapting. Its great success, which hardly anyone expected fifty years ago, has not freed it from anxiety about what path to take in the future. The debates about the best way of coping with continuing rapid change, the ideological camps which have existed in the recent past, and will exist in this new century, and the theories on which these various proposed solutions are based are all matters of contention. Nothing is firmly settled. This has been, after all, the condition of modernity for 200 years. For that reason, theoretical conclusions we may draw from observations about the twentieth century are directly relevant to any interpretation of Korea's recent success, and to the debates about its future. Korea is in no sense unique in this respect. Weighing the validity of various competing social theories of modernization, and of the political ideologies and strategies that derive from them, is a vital task everywhere.

What works?

In a fascinating, very widely read book by the world's most eminent Marxist historian, Eric Hobsbawm revealed his feelings in a way few of his readers have seen before. In a chapter entitled "The Crisis Decades" in *The Age of Extremes* (Hobsbawm 1994), he suggests that the moral and economic decline of Western liberal societies marks the failure of free market liberalism just as surely as the fall of communism in Eastern Europe and the USSR marks the failure of socialism. In his concluding chapter, Hobsbawm remarks that the failure of liberalism when it was actually practiced in its extreme form with post-communist economic shock therapy in Eastern Europe, or Mrs. Thatcher's attempt to impose it upon Great Britain, show that it is theoretically bankrupt as well as practically impossible.

It takes a socialist like Hobsbawm, or in a somewhat different context, a communitarian like Robert Bellah, to come up with a strange conclusion such as this (Bellah *et al.* 1992). In the 1990s Eastern Europe successfully underwent a painful transition from suffering inefficient communist economies with depressed standards of living to having much more competitive and better-off ones. From 1993 to 2003 the Czech Republic's Gross Domestic Product (GDP) grew at an average of 2.2 percent a year, Hungary's at 3.5 percent, Slovakia's at 4.3 percent, and Poland's at 4.4 percent at a time when the Euro area, on average, grew at 2.3 percent a year (OECD 2004: 14–15). The Baltic countries of Estonia, Latvia, and Lithuania have seen GDP growth rates averaging over 6.5 percent a year in the 2000s. The poorer countries of Bulgaria and Romania, after going through very difficult times during the period of adjustment in the 1990s, have been growing, respectively, at 5.1 percent and 4.5 percent per year in the 2000s (World Bank 2004: 14–16, 182–184). Hobsbawm is right, of course, that absolute free market conditions were not tried, and never could be because they are only a theoretical construct. The point, however, is that these societies did experience a serious shock as they moved toward a capitalist system; it was painful, but ultimately they have benefited and shown that market-oriented reforms do work. Holding on to the stagnant economic systems that had prevailed before 1989 would have led to continuing decline and suffering.

The former Soviet countries (outside the three Baltic ones) have also experienced significant growth in the early 2000s, largely due to high energy prices that have benefited Russia's and Central Asia's oil- and gas-dependent economies, even though they have not reformed nearly as much as have Eastern Europe and the Baltic. But an interesting aspect of this is that these former Soviet countries are following a path unlikely to lead to significant long-term development. A good indicator of this is that those former Soviet countries that have remained least reformed have had noticeable increases in poverty and hunger, whereas those that have become capitalist democracies, namely the small Baltic countries of Estonia, Latvia, and Lithuania, have had sharp drops in hunger from 1993 to 2003. For former Soviet countries (excluding the Baltic), the proportion of the population that is malnourished has risen from 7 percent to 9 percent during this time, whereas for the Baltic countries it has fallen from 5 percent to 2 percent. Even more dramatically, a look at the two largest Central Asian countries of the former Soviet Union, Kazakhstan and Uzbekistan (the two contain about 72 percent of Central Asia's population), shows that in the former the proportion of the population that is malnourished has risen from 1 percent to 13 percent, and in the latter from 8 percent to 26 percent (FAO 2004: 6, 38). Clearly, to end socialism while replacing it with an autocratic, corrupt state-run economy that remains unreformed does produce negative effects, but the critics of capitalism are wrong to blame this on liberalization of the economy.

As for the United Kingdom and the United States, so despised by their critics, there is very little evidence that either have been ruined by the revival, and recent dominance of what are now called "neoliberal" economic policies. On the contrary, all the evidence points to the robustness of their economies which continue to grow faster and have considerably less unemployment than the less "neoliberal" continental economies, most notably France and Germany. From 1993 to 2003 America's average annual GDP growth rate was 3.2 percent, Britain's 2.9 percent, and the Euro zone's was 2.3 percent. In 2004 America's growth rate was 4.0 percent, and Britain's 3.1 percent, while the Euro area's growth rate was limited to 1.8 percent (OECD 2004: 14–15; *The Economist*, December 18, 2004: 162).

The point is not to make too much of relatively minor differences in the economic growth rates of very rich OECD countries, all of whom are substantially capitalist and democratic, but to emphasize the point that liberalism is very from being a failure. The same holds when the statistics for former communist countries are compared. The situation is complex, and it is not the formal abandonment of communism that is at issue, but the degree to which liberal market reforms have been implemented. China, of course, growing at about 7 percent to 8 percent a year for well over two decades, is a case in point. It is far from being a democracy, and many of its economic sectors are not free of state control, but it has prospered by opening itself up to the world market, by allowing entrepreneurial activity, and by allowing its people ever increasing amounts of personal freedom (Lardy 2002; OECD 2003).

What offends the critics of liberalism such as Hobsbawm and Bellah is the amorality and impersonality of markets, be they economic, cultural, or political. Measures of economic performance could hardly convince them to change their minds. As long as there exist any signs of economic difficulty (which are always easy to find in any system) the critics of liberal capitalism will use these to support their criticism, and largely neglect the bigger picture which shows that on the whole the more liberalized an economy the more able it is to adapt to change, to grow, and to provide more of its people with a comfortable life.

In judging which political ideologies and modernization strategies are more or less successful we can turn to old-fashioned functionalist-evolutionary criteria and ask simply: What has worked and what reproduces itself successfully? Specifically, in our times, the question is: What has allowed some societies to modernize successfully, while so many have succeeded less well or failed dramatically?

It is not possible to solve definitively the acrimonious debates about what kinds of policies lead to rapid economic development. Is it necessary to "get the price right" or, as Alice Amsden suggested for South Korea, to "get it wrong," but in the right way (Amsden 1989: 139–155)? Is a developmental state necessary, or can *laissez-faire* handle development? Perhaps it is best to remark, as Stephan Haggard and Tun-jen Cheng once did, that each case history is somewhat different, and even within East Asia, much less the entire world, it is difficult to draw clear policy conclusions from past experience (Haggard and Cheng 1987: 128–129).

Nevertheless, a few very broad lessons may be drawn. Markets work. Centrally planned economies, especially insofar as they are able to also resist competitive pressures from the outside, work poorly. The more advanced the global economy, the less adaptive socialist, closed economies become. We could argue about the details, but this fact is so obvious that its central validity is no longer subject to argument. An economy such as South Korea's may have had a high level of government involvement and planning in its successful development, and it may continue to be substantially protected from certain forms of outside competition. But if it had sealed itself off from the global market and not become so dependent on exporting to the rest of the world, it would have been in as ruinous a condition as North Korea's economy. Further, with continuing technological progress in the world economy, the South Korean economy will continue to prosper by becoming less dependent on government favors and regulation, more open, and even more competitive. To go back to a more controlled, less open economy would only erode some of the astounding progress of the past fifty years.[6]

There is not even any strong evidence that the kind of corporatist, protectionist policy followed by the government of South Korea, and the fostering of the huge corporations that dominated the Korean economy during its period of most rapid growth, have been an important reason for Korea's success. Judging from the performance of some other East and Southeast Asian economies, it is conceivable that greater decentralization and less government control from the start might have done the job even better. Certainly that has been the case in two of the new "little dragon" economies of East Asia, Hong Kong, and Taiwan. Without large amounts of American aid following the Korean War, heavy American involvement in training personnel in the 1950s and 1960s, and eventually an American ultimatum in the early 1960s to force Korea to develop faster in order to reduce the burden on American foreign aid, the South Korean model might not have worked all that well.[7]

The record in East Asia is quite clear. Between 1980 and 1990 South Korea's economy grew at an average rate of 8.4 percent a year. From 1990 to 2002, despite the "Asian economic crisis" of the late 1990s, it grew at an average of 5.6 percent a year. China's comparable growth rates during this time were 8 percent a year from 1980 to 1990, and 7.3 percent a year from 1990 to 2002 (World Bank 2004: 182–184). North Korean economic statistics are not available, but there is an estimate of malnutrition in that country. In China, the proportion of the population that was malnourished in 1990 to 1992 was 16 percent, and by 2000 to 2002 had fallen to 11 percent. South Korea's proportion fell from just above to just below 2 percent in that time. Meanwhile, North Korea's malnourished increased from 18 percent of the population to 36 percent, by far the highest in East Asia and at a level above that of even most impoverished countries in Africa (FAO 2004: 36). China is far from being an ultra-liberal country, and even South Korea does not adhere to an extreme form of neoliberalism, but the trend in both has been toward ever greater liberalization, and, even in areas highly regulated by their government, firms have been increasingly forced to compete in the open world market. This is what has enabled them to adapt and grow.

If arguments persist about how much state intervention was necessary for Korea to succeed, or for any modern economy to progress, it is easier to conclude that the prescriptions of what is called "dependency theory" or sometimes "world system theory" turn out to be completely wrong. Ultimately, they called for some form of closure to the capitalist global economy, because development from that point of view has to be a zero-sum game. Any one economy's gain is another's loss, and the strong ruthlessly exploit the weak. Bruce Cumings put it nicely some years ago in a well-known article which predicted that there was room only for one "semiperipheral" success in East Asia, and South Korea was destined to not be the one (Cumings 1987: 78–81).

These kinds of theoretical prescriptions, demanding closure, import substitution, and generally eschewing the world market have actually been turned into functioning policies in many places in the second half of the twentieth century: all the communist countries before China began to reform itself under Deng Xiaoping, Italy under Mussolini (his failures in foreign policy have obscured his regime's dismal record in promoting economic growth), Argentina from the 1930s to the 1980s, Peru in the 1970s and 1980s, Burma, India from independence until the 1980s, and others. All have been long-term failures.[8]

India is particularly interesting in this respect. Its average GDP growth between 1965 and 1980 was 3.7 percent a year, but due to its high birth rates, per capita GDP in those years grew at only about 1.8 percent a year. As India started to open up its economy to the outside world in the 1980s, its growth rate increased to 5.7 percent per year in that decade, and to an average of 5.8 percent per year from 1990 to 2002. As its population growth has slowed, another by-product of modernization, its per capita product has been increasing at about 4 percent a year, more than double the old rate (World Bank 1989: 164–166; World Bank 2004: 39, 183). In 2004 India's GDP grew at the rate of 7.4 percent a year, surpassed in the world only by China and Singapore's growth rates for that year (not counting economies whose entire GDP fluctuates wildly according to the price of oil because they are so dependent on petroleum exports) (*The Economist*, December 18, 2004: 162).

It is important to remember that dependency theory originated as a German nationalist economic theory in the nineteenth century. It was adopted by both Marxists and corporatists in the early twentieth century. In the period between World Wars I and II fascists applied the theory at almost the same time as did Stalin's Soviet Union. Later it turned out to be compatible with the mild socialism espoused by independent India's first generation of leaders, and by a variety of other regimes. This shows how carefully we must tread when discussing global ideological and theoretical schools of thought, especially when it may be that ultimately nationalism has been the most enduring and potent ideological force in the twentieth century, as well as the most threatening to liberalism.[9]

It has not just been the communist and some fascist-corporatist attempts to modernize that have resulted in catastrophe. Looking across Africa since the establishment of independent states some three to four decades ago (but only two decades ago for the former Portuguese colonies), one sees an almost unbroken pattern of failure. Harsh communist regimes such as those in Guinea or Ethiopia, milder socialist ones that prevailed throughout most of the continent as in, until the late 1980s, Ghana, Tanzania, or Zambia, or even relatively non-socialist governments such as in Nigeria, Zaire, and the Ivory Coast (once black Africa's most promising experiment with capitalism) have little to boast about. Immense, almost unbelievable corruption in places where there were valuable natural resources to be looted, as in Nigeria and Congo (Zaire), very weak loyalty to existing state institutions and boundaries, a virtual absence of strong bureaucratic traditions to guide civil servants, low levels of modern education, and autocratic but inept political elites have made most of the continent inhospitable to outside as well as to domestic investors. Despite a very low standard of living, African economies have been unable to take advantage of their low wage rates, unlike some of the Southeast Asian economies such as Indonesia and Thailand.[10]

There are many cases around the world of weak, corrupt states that have caused economic havoc. Pakistan comes to mind, and there are many candidates for this kind of failure among the post-Soviet states, particularly in Central Asia. An inability to maintain a stable currency, enforce contracts or even basic law and order, and systematic corruption made many Latin American economies perform anemically for a long time, and we cannot be sure that even substantial economies such as Mexico can avoid falling back into this kind of calamitous spiral in the future. The Philippines under Marcos may have turned in such a weak performance for precisely these reasons rather than due to any obvious policy error or more fundamental economic flaws. Even within otherwise prosperous and successful modern economies we can find the same phenomenon at work at the regional level. Southern Italy, for all of the billions of dollars' worth of subsidies poured into it by the Italian government, remains far poorer than it should be due to corruption and a local social system unable to enforce basic norms of honesty. Corruption and the fact that government subsidies have been used inefficiently keep southern Italy relatively backward to this day.[11]

What this suggests is that it takes more than lack of government control to produce economic success and make societies capable of adapting to the modern world. There also need to be states strong enough to insure domestic tranquility, protect property rights and enforce contracts, and bureaucracies able to maintain decent infrastructures and communications. Economic growth requires, as Douglass North has been arguing for several decades, institutions that lower transaction costs, secure property rights, and make information widely available (North and Thomas 1973; North 1981, 1990). States unable to carry out these functions, or ones that deliberately block them, either for ideological, anti-market reasons or for corruption's sake, to be better able to steal, will slow down economic progress. One can add a large list of desirable governmental actions, though most of them would fall under the categories stressed by North. The point is that no reasonable observer would deny the important tasks that governments have to be able to carry out, but in the absence of market mechanisms, even governments that build infrastructures, educate their populations, and maintain law and order will fail. This is what happened in European communist states. They did everything more or less right except that they were socialist and disregarded both internal and world markets, or at least they tried to ignore markets until it was too late.[12]

Legitimizing capitalism

This brings up another key function that modern states have to carry out. They have to legitimize markets. Markets, like all uncontrolled evolutionary processes in which the successful survive and others perish or fail to reproduce, have nothing inherently fair about them unless one considers utilitarianism to be the basis of an ethical doctrine. This is the principal reason for which almost all civilized societies in the past looked down on commercial activity as unclean money-grubbing. Honor, noble blood lines, gracious comportment, learning, or at least skill in some obvious physical endeavor rather than the mere ability to manipulate goods and financial instruments always struck the upper classes in agrarian societies as more appropriate ways of assigning rank and prestige. Among agrarian societies, for most of their existence there persisted among the mass of peasants a strong inclination to demand equality and to disapprove of those who tried to forge ahead too quickly. All of this may have been quite functional in the agrarian age that lasted until the Industrial Revolution. It was obviously useful much earlier than that when humans lived in small bands that had to stick together in a friendly way in order to survive, but market societies are in flagrant violation of all the old virtues, whether of nobles, learned officials, or egalitarian peasants. This is why, as Ezra Vogel has pointed out, it was necessary for the old Confucian order to be thoroughly discredited in East Asia before economic growth could take off (Vogel 1991: 83–84).[13] Albert Hirschman reaches a similar conclusion in a different way in his examination of why Enlightenment philosophers had to legitimize capitalism before it existed in order to make a capitalist order possible in Western Europe (Hirschman 1977).

The problems of legitimization of markets, of inequality, and of open competition are not trivial, and many difficulties in modernizing societies can be ascribed to the unwillingness of most classes to change their minds on these issues. Yet, it must be done, and here state sponsored educational institutions can play a major role. The absolute unwillingness to do this in communist schools and communist regimes' officially disseminated culture turned out to be one of the greatest barriers to further modernization and economic success, and now, in some of these post-communist societies, it will take decades of work to change prevailing sentiments which are as traditional and deeply rooted as in pre-modern agrarian societies.

It is in this domain that intellectuals can play a particularly important role, either in blocking or accelerating successful modernization. Many of the theories of change popular among intellectuals, whether of the fascist-corporatist or of the socialist variety, have contributed mightily to slowing down modernization insofar as they have been taught in school systems. The successes of leftist and rightist revolutionary parties in mobilizing students and intellectuals all over the world throughout most of the twentieth century are a testament to this. As has now been shown, particularly by the pioneering work of political scientists such as Zeev Sternhell, the common element of most of the major revolutionary doctrines of the twentieth century was hostility to liberal individualism and to capitalist markets (Sternhell 1995).

In short, despite the successes of a liberal approach to development, its future acceptance is no more guaranteed now than it was at the start of the twentieth century, when all these lessons were already available. The resistance to change among theorists, ideologs, and among large proportions of populations everywhere has not been eliminated, though some of the most egregiously harmful alternatives to liberal capitalist modernization have been disgraced. If it were only a matter of Marxism, or fascist corporatism, it would be possible to say that these have been shown to be failures, so they will not be repeated. But anti-liberal nationalism, especially in the form of resentment against the rich and powerful nations of the West, has in no sense disappeared. It will find new theories, neo-Marxist, fascist, religious, or who knows what to serve as the basis of movements and parties determined to resist the Western form of modernization.

Theoretical implications

If we look at Walt Rostow's venerable and often mocked book, *The Stages of Economic Growth: A Non-Communist Manifesto,* we find that his typology still holds up. Economic modernization begins with the establishment of essential preconditions for an economic take-off (Rostow 1960). In the case of Korea, this happened under Japanese colonial rule when the necessary infrastructure was built, agriculture was marketized, and a modern Civil Service was instituted. The somewhat strained efforts by Korean nationalist historians to find sprouts of capitalism in pre-colonial Korea do not prove a contrary position. At best, they suggest that Korea might have been able to do this on its own, and that may be the case, but for better or for worse, it was under Japanese rule that it happened.[14]

The same preconditions are always necessary. Rostow's list includes non-economic factors taken from the writings of the functionalist theorists of the mid-twentieth century, and they remain valid today. At the heart of all necessary changes is the spread of new aspirations and broadened horizons that can tolerate, even welcome, change. Everywhere, colonialism increased migration, monetized the economy, and promoted new forms of social mobility, but the Japanese, in that sense, were the most thoroughly modernizing colonizers.

Then there was the take-off. This may have begun in the very late colonial period in Korea, but what was built then was destroyed during the Korean War, so that the real take-off dates only to the early 1960s. Here we know that American aid contributed at a time when an unfavorable balance of trade may otherwise have damaged South Korea's take-off. As such, it was a substitute for the kinds of foreign investment brought in by the presence of exportable natural resources.[15] In the 1970s and early 1980s Korea became what Rostow calls a "mature" economy, that is, a diversified, technologically modern economy. In the late 1980s and 1990s, it has become a high mass consumption economy.

It was not the typology itself that was so important for Rostow, nor what made his book so hated among his critics. What was crucial was his functionalist-evolutionary theoretical base. Rostow suggested, first, that the way in which some Western societies, primarily Great Britain and the United States, have developed corresponded to a general pattern that had to be followed more or less by everyone. This did not mean that France, Germany, Great Britain, and the United States all had identical economic histories or that they developed the same institutions, but that they had to fulfill certain functional requirements for development.

Communist societies could create all the preconditions for take-off and provide the investment and discipline for such a take-off, but they were unable to run diversified, mature industrial economies because the absence of markets blocked the signals needed to improve efficiency and continue the pace of technological progress. This blockage made even the wealthiest communist economies unable to reach successfully the stage of high mass consumption.

The underlying theme of all functionalist theory is not inherently ideological; it demands only that we look at what succeeded, and draw appropriate lessons. It was precisely because the British, Americans, and some other Western Europeans thrived as their societies and economies became more liberal and capitalist that anti-Western nationalists throughout the twentieth century have grasped for one theory or another which would permit them to modernize their societies without becoming too Western; that is, too liberal and capitalist. And the fact that, inescapably, functionalist theorists in the 1950s concluded that there must be something working in the United States, or else it would not have become so powerful and rich, antagonized younger social scientists (both within and outside America) who bitterly resented American power and the unfairness of American society.

In a sense, in Korea we see something resembling this with respect to the Japanese model. South Korea has, in fact, followed the Japanese model quite closely, but this raises problems for its nationalists who would prefer to find alternative models of development. And the fact that the Japanese model of development has come to fruition only after it was opened up under American hegemony has made American liberalism suspect, too. Dependency theory, Marxism, or, for quite a time, Kim Il Sungism seemed more appropriate for nationalist intellectuals than liberalism or its seeming theoretical corollaries, functionalism, and neoclassical economic theory.

In that respect, Bruce Cumings' analysis of Korea is perfectly correct. North Korea, independent of American hegemony and the world capitalist system, has been able to follow a far purer nationalism than South Korea. Cumings has also been right to say that the natural inclination of many of South Korea's elites has been similarly corporatist (because that is what North Korea has – national socialism in its purest corporatist form).[16] The very fact that South Korea was too dependent on American hegemony has kept it in the world market, has opened it up to the outside, and has ultimately allowed its democratic forces to triumph. In forcing South Korea into this path, America's hegemony has created the conditions that insured its success.

It is worth noting that it was precisely because South Korea had been transformed by American pressure into a more open, more liberal, and more democratic society that it pulled out of the serious Asian economic crisis that hit it so hard in 1997 to 1998. This is the lesson Meredith Woo-Cumings draws from the astounding Korean recovery (Woo-Cumings 1999: 134).

This might suggest that dependency theory and world-system theory have it all exactly backward. The more tightly connected a periphery (originally, a society and economy that has not yet begun to modernize) to a more advanced core, the more likely it is that it will be modernized and obtain the conditions necessary for development.

We have had many cases of economic take-offs that have been aborted or have gone off in unsustainable directions due to policies designed to limit the power of markets and to keep out the influence of the world system. To some extent, almost all governments have tried to do this at one time or another during the process of modernization. But in this respect the most successful, the most closed, the most determined to be self-reliant, such as North Korea, have been the greatest failures.

The biggest theoretical question is: Why is this so? What is it about open societies with open markets that makes them so adaptable?

Quite simply, any social, political, or economic system that allows experiments to occur, and which permits signals about the failure and success of these experiments to circulate and influence future decisions, will be more successful. It is the messiness of open politics and market economies that provides their strength, just as it was the hard-fought establishment of key corners of intellectual freedom that allowed the scientific and technological revolution in Western Europe to flourish in the early modern age. Immanuel Wallerstein, no matter how wrong he has been about many other aspects of the modern world system, was right about this: the very disunity of capitalist world economies was the key to their success (Wallerstein 1974). Competition and the inability to impose monopolies, despite the many attempts to do so, have remained the ultimate strength of liberal societies. In the long run, the centrally planned, ideologically dictated, politically unfree societies that competed with the liberal democracies in the twentieth century proved unable to maintain the flexibility required to adapt to changing circumstances. Messages about failed policies did not circulate well enough; free thought, and therefore innovation, were partially or entirely stifled; popular discontent did not surface until it had become explosive; failure in the international arena, be it economic or political, was not permitted to affect central institutions or policies until it was too late and the failure had become catastrophic.

All this has been known for a very long time, but enemies of liberal, market societies continue to insist that there must be a better, fairer way than open competition, that there must be an absolute truth in some ideology or religion, and that open societies are too corrupt, dissolute, and disorganized to survive much longer. The same sentiment that makes so many opponents of modern capitalism say that there must be something more than a bottom line do not recognize that bottom lines are not simply matters of profits, at least not when it comes to whole societies, but of how well a society functions. The advantage which capitalist businesses have is that they can sometimes see something measurable going wrong with their bottom lines before the company has collapsed. If they fail to adapt, they fail, and are replaced by those who are better adapted, but the system never fails entirely because it consists of so many different kinds of firms. Closed monopolies, whether they are businesses or political systems, lack this adaptive capacity, and if an entire economy is centrally controlled, catastrophic failure may occur because smaller signals of impending failure are blocked.

The dangers of utopianism, corruption, and their use by nationalists

We have seen that it is almost impossible to disentangle social theory from ideology; but some effort must be made.

Marxism as a theory of society brought out the importance of class relations, explained how new modes of production created different class structures, and emphasized the fact that until utopia was reached contradictions in any mode of production would slowly work toward creating the seeds of new modes of production. But class conflict is by no means the only or even always the primary cause of long-run social change, and in making human thought and culture epiphenomenal, Marxism excluded one of the other main aspects of social structure. Still, it was only when Marxism became a prescription for policy, and its texts supposedly infallible, that it became truly dangerous. Separated from its Enlightenment roots and turned into dogma, Marxism served as a justification for some of the most closed, tyrannical regimes in human history. Only if it is returned to its proper place, as a set of interesting and useful, but tentative and often quite wrong theoretical assumptions, can Marxism be rehabilitated.

Surely the same must be said about social Darwinism, a doctrine that was grossly misused from the late nineteenth to the mid-twentieth century. The original Darwinian assumption, that differential reproductive success within an ecosystem explains evolutionary patterns, is not vitiated by the distortions to which it was subjected by later ideologs. What works for biology works for human societies too, in the sense that social institutions best adapted to specific environments will survive, and over time, those that contribute nothing to survival, or are inimical to it, will tend to disappear. As in the case of the natural world this is a brutal process, because it means that societies with many dysfunctional aspects will suffer and ultimately fail. In the past, that could easily mean famine, conquest, or at the very least, massively disruptive events that led to suffering. It may still mean just that, as we can witness in many parts of the world, not least of all in North Korea.

That said, it must be emphasized that there is nothing in Darwinian theory to justify the notion that there are superior human "races," or that competition between these supposed races is the mainspring of human history. It is ironic, but important for understanding the tragic twentieth century, that the Marxist conception of inevitable class conflict to the bitter end, and social Darwinian ideas from the late nineteenth century about the inevitability of racial conflicts to the death, were highly compatible with each other. (Marx and Engels were great admirers of Darwin.) These notions of inevitable conflict dominated social thought and political ideology for much of the century, and their prevalence accounts for more of the terrible warfare and mass persecution throughout the century than any other phenomenon (Chirot 1995).

Evolutionary thinking does presume that there are differences between societies in their degree of adaptability. Unlike evolution in the biological world, however, societies can learn and change their institutions of their own will. This is why notions of hereditarily carried cultures, or of struggles between supposed human races for survival, make so little sense.

If evolutionary-functionalist thinking has important theoretical insights to offer us, the question posed in 1990 by Douglass North in *Institutions, Institutional Change and Economic Performance* still has to be answered. Why have economically inefficient institutions survived in so many places for so long? And why, if we live in a single, interconnected world, do such large differences remain in social and economic institutions when it should be that those which work best are adopted as the others fail? (North 1990: 7, 101).

The answer is at least partly Marxist. Those in power need not and usually do not care about maximizing general social well-being. Economic efficiency is less important to them than staying in power, and open political and economic systems present them with a continual threat to their dominance. It is not normal for those in power to want to allow competition against their own interests. Furthermore, as we have seen, even within the lower ranks of most societies, and certainly all agrarian societies, resistance to change and a stubborn egalitarianism prevented more efficient institutional arrangements from emerging.

In the twentieth century, however, the progress of a few Western societies may have served as a dramatic example that reform along Western lines was necessary for successful adaptation. Indeed, that is exactly what did happen, as modernizers took power in one place after another. Unfortunately, many of them thought it would be possible to carry out economic and technological modernization without adopting liberal political systems or tolerant intellectual atmospheres. In particular, the utopian visions of the Marxists and fascist-corporatists combined with strong anti-Western nationalist elements to offer alternative paths to modernization. Once in power, the most successful of these visionaries were able to create alternative, though ultimately unsuccessful modernizing systems. Stalin, Hitler, Mussolini, the Japanese military, Mao, Ceausescu, Pol Pot, Ne Win (at least in his earlier years as ruler of Burma), and, yes, Kim Il Sung, were not just, or even mostly, corrupt tyrants. They were men of vision who genuinely believed that they knew better than anyone else what their societies needed to become strong, independent, and modern. Secure in their ideological and theoretical errors, they refused to countenance competition or modification of their societies, and they destroyed what they had wanted to build rather than surpassing or even catching up with the hated West.[17] Exactly the same thing will happen to the Islamic extremists who want to revive a puritanical, absolutist form of early Islam. If they seize power and push their absolutist utopian dreams too far, they will also ruin their societies.

It is worth noting that despite its radical Islamic government, Iran has moved away from the abyss by being much more flexible than outsiders expected, by continuing to allow some dissent, albeit limited, and especially by avoiding the over-centralization of the economy which spelled disaster for more closed systems such as that of North Korea. Iran never abolished private property, it never established the kind of totalitarian regime that characterized the right-wing and left-wing regimes in the twentieth century, and it never invaded the privacy of the family because the Ayatollah Khomeini thought that this was a violation of Islamic law. Iran under religious rule is unlikely to adapt as successfully to modern social change as if it were more secular and open, but it is entirely conceivable that it could evolve peacefully toward a more open and adaptable system, the way China has (McDaniel 2000: 225–227).[18]

In the agrarian past, many of the institutions that made some agrarian civilizations strong were functional in the sense of maintaining order and mobilizing resources for war. Economic efficiency in a capitalist-market sense was not critically important and, in the absence of advanced technology, would not have made that much difference in determining the relative power of one society over another, at least in the short run.

With the emergence of an interdependent, highly advanced capitalist world system the situation has changed. The evolutionary process has brought forth a set of institutional arrangements which make those societies that adopt them far more efficient, powerful, and prosperous than others. Now we can compare standards of living or different levels of popular satisfaction, not just levels of military power across societies. In short, we now have ways of evaluating "bottom lines" that did not exist in the past. Only wars or catastrophes could bring out such comparisons in the past, but now it is easier. This means that the evolutionary process which has made liberal market societies so successful can function more smoothly, and North's paradox might be resolved. The world may not be moving toward a single, united political system, but economic institutions are becoming more alike as they become more efficient.

This hardly means that "history has ended" or that we can all rest assured that the future will be bright. We have much evidence that it remains possible to block liberal modernization. Intellectuals hostile to liberal capitalism all over the world, including ones in the most advanced countries, are busy cooking up new theories that will, in this new century, promise alternatives to liberal modernization, and will undoubtedly inspire new generations of eager visionary tyrants. Many of these, it now seems, will be based on religious, anti-Western utopias that claim to be able to better the modernized West at its own game by being purer and godlier (Chirot 2001).

Being aware of the dangers of ideological tyrannies, and their capacity to block progress, does not negate the fact that there is another way in which elites can retard modernization as effectively. Corrupt political elites in such disparate places as Burma, Haiti, Zimbabwe, or Nigeria can keep their populations economically and politically backward, impoverished, and brutalized. For the time being ideologically motivated elites are rare, and outside the Islamic world they have no coherent revolutionary model to inspire them. But even the most corrupt thugs in power can appeal to nationalism, and frequently do, to keep their societies from becoming free. In this respect they join hands with the most damaging ideological forms of anti-liberalism by claiming that national pride and honor demand alternative, non-Western forms of modernization.

Nor should we be overly optimistic about other forms of ideologically inspired tyranny. Dislike of modernization, of globalization, and of markets is still a powerful force, both among intellectuals throughout the world and among those who feel that they are the losers in the process of continuing modernization. New utopian dreams will undoubtedly recycle corporatist and Marxist dreams of the past, and new religious extremist utopias will emerge. These can and will block modernization in some societies, and turn them into dangerous, angry failures.

Looking at the future of South Korea, or at any other emerging modern economy and democracy, it is possible to see what kinds of danger lurk around the corner. These dangers are not economic globalization, capitalist hegemony, Western culture, or any of the other aspects of change that have come with increasing liberalization of the world. The dangers are just the opposite: economic and cultural closure, the seizure of power by corrupt, undemocratic elites, the exploitation of nationalism to block liberal reforms, and the rise of anti-liberal utopian ideologies.

We know that it is possible for economies to develop quickly if they allow entrepreneurial freedom, remain open to competition, and insure both adequate property rights and a good infrastructure. Democracy is not required at first. We also know, however, that over time the temptation to corruption by elites is such that without democratic controls progress will eventually slow down and be stifled. This is why countries such as South Korea or China could prosper without much democracy for some time, but not indefinitely. Over time, not only does greater prosperity create more of a middle class that demands more democracy, but the need for that evolution increases.

Corrupt elites in Russia or Mexico, for example, could well bring democratization and economic progress to a halt in order to maintain their power. Even China's astounding economic success could be destroyed because it is still run by a corrupt network of Party and military elites who use nationalism to legitimize their continuing hold on power. No economy can prosper indefinitely simply on cheap labor, and no rapidly growing economy in today's world can remain immune from the forces of liberal individualism, democracy, and free thought. China's rulers will have to choose: either they will have to reform and become more like South Korea in some ways, or they can hold on to power and crush future opposition by trying to close China again.

Only a country that falls into the hands of a fundamentally illiberal elite and cannot extricate itself is in long-run danger of failing in the modern world. Alas, there are many such places. Fortunately, it does not seem that South Korea is one of them. Unfortunately, North Korea is perhaps the worst example in the world.

Acknowledgment

This chapter was previously published as an article in the *Sungkyun Journal of East Asian Studies* (sponsored by The Academy of East Asian Studies of Sungkyunkwan University in Seoul) in April 2004, and is being reprinted with the Journal's permission.

Notes

1 For a good discussion of the history of liberalism, see Manent (1995). For a history of its critics, see Holmes (1993); and for a popular celebration of its recent success, Fukuyma (1992).
2 For some recent analyses of nationalism see Hobsbawm (1990); Gellner (1983); and the more controversial analysis of Greenfeld (1992).
3 A discussion of the effects of Marxism and social Darwinism on the production of tyranny in the twentieth century, and their compatibility with each other, may be found in Chirot (1996: 50–70).
4 An old, but still relevant, book about the strains of modernization is Eisenstadt's (1966) book. On the debate about competing theories of modernization and their relationship to the supposed "clash of civilizations" see Chirot (2001).

5 I agree with Gellner (1992).
6 Although her perspective on modernization is very different from mine, this was also Jung-en Woo's conclusion (Woo 1991: 202–203). Her book was written when South Korea was still much more protectionist, and its economy more state controlled than today, but the general conclusions remain valid.
7 How important the interventionist role of the state actually was in South Korea is a contentious subject. I accept Paul Kuznets's assertion on these matters (Kuznets 1994). He stresses the fact that however one interprets Korean government policy, the total percentage of public sector spending as a proportion of GDP was much lower in Korea than in other comparable countries, largely due to low spending on health, housing, and social security. On the comparison with other East Asian NICs, see Vogel (1991), particularly his remarks on Korean–American relations (pp. 52–53).
8 In Chirot (1996) I discuss the cases of Argentina and Burma in detail in chapters 8 and 9, emphasizing the disastrous results of policies that were meant to keep these countries free from "foreign" interference and markets. The case of India is more complicated, but there is little question that a recent opening which is starting to produce significant economic growth is under intense attack by nationalists incapable of understanding the harm they would inflict on their own population, particularly the poor, if they succeeded in reimposing closure of the Indian economy. On Mussolini's Italy, see Clough 1964. On India's recent rapid growth and the political dangers posed by its anti-liberal nationalists, see *The Economist* 2003: 43.
9 See the definitive new book on this subject by Joseph Love (1996).
10 In recent years Africanists have analyzed the continent's problems by pointing first to its political failures – inefficient and kleptocratic states, lack of fair judicial systems, and state breakdowns into numerous ethnic, tribal, clan, and regional wars (see Herbst 2000). See also the articles on Africa in Beissinger and Young (2002).
11 For some of the background and delusions about how to fix southern Italy's problems, see Mountjoy (1973). Southern Italy has been the only region in the European Community (prior to the addition of former communist countries) that has fallen further behind the developed parts of Europe in recent years (see Apicella 1996). The public authorities in the south are so corrupt and ineffective that, as Jobert (1995) found, money spent on education and training has no positive effect on development. Yet the rest of Italy has undergone an economic miracle since the late 1940s that is almost as impressive as what has happened in East Asia since the 1950s. Inept and corrupt government has been, in a sense, overcome by Italy's participation in the Common Market, and by a lot of semi-undercover business activity that simply bypasses the government. On the difficulties of carrying out reform in Mexico, see Centeno (1994).
12 This topic has now been explored by hundreds of studies. My position on the reasons for the collapse of communism is found in Chirot (1991).
13 This is not to deny the virtues of having a meritocratic bureaucratic ideal, a sense that the family must be nurtured and preserved, or that every individual owes his or her duty to a larger community, all stressed by many of the admirers of "neo-Confucianism," including Vogel (1991: 92–103). On the other hand, the high bureaucratic elite's ethos despised commerce and industry, and, as long as it ruled, economic progress was retarded.
14 I understand that here again there is a heated debate among specialists. But among the younger, leading scholars working in the West, there seems to be substantial agreement that the preconditions for take-off did occur in colonial times (see Eckert 1991; Woo 1991; Shin 1997).

15 Whether or not one thinks the Park Chung Hee regime that took power in a coup in 1961 deserves the credit for South Korea's subsequent economic development, as many scholars do, there is a consensus of opinion among specialists that a take-off did occur in the early 1960s. Jung-en Woo, who clearly dislikes Rostow and his theories, and is not fond of Park, nevertheless agrees that this happened (Woo 1991: 73–74).

16 This is expressed most clearly in Cumings (1982–1983). It has also been a theme in his work on the Korean War, particularly Cumings (1990: 313, 314, 332). It is a theme that also runs through his pamphlet on the possible future unification of Korea (Cumings 1995).

17 There are chapters on all these cases in Chirot (1996).

18 This is also the main message in Abrahamian's "Empire Strikes Back: Iran in U.S. Sights," in Cumings *et al.* (2004: 129–136). This highly polemical book written against George Bush's foreign policy nevertheless has some useful facts about the reality in these countries singled out as America's enemies. It is particularly interesting to contrast the Abrahamian and Cumings chapters. Abrahamian argues by looking inside Iran to show that it is not as radical or as dangerous as the Americans claim, while Cumings argues by looking primarily at past American policies on the Korean peninsula and the dangers inherent in pushing North Korea too far rather than by making any claims that internal life in North Korea is any better than its critics claim. This is because there is very little to defend about North Korea.

References

Amsden, Alice H. 1989. *Asia's Next Giant.* New York: Oxford University Press.

Apicella, V. 1996. "Southern Italy and the Underdeveloped Regions of Europe." *Review of Economic Conditions in Italy* 1 (January–June 1996): 119–127.

Beissinger, Mark and Crawford Young (eds). 2002. *Beyond State Crisis?* Washington, DC: Woodrow Wilson Center Press.

Bellah, Robert N., Richard Madsen, William M. Sullivan, Ann Swidler, and Steven M. Tipton. 1992. *The Good Society.* New York: Vintage.

Centeno, Miguel. 1994. *Democracy Within Reason.* University Park: Pennsylvania State University Press.

Chirot, Daniel. 1991. "What Happened in Eastern Europe in 1989?" In Daniel Chirot (ed.). *The Crisis of Leninism and the Decline of the Left.* Seattle: University of Washington Press, pp. 3–32.

——. 1995. "Modernism Without Liberalism: The Ideological Roots of Modern Tyranny." *Contention* 5 (1): 141–166.

——. 1996. *Modern Tyrants.* Princeton, NJ: Princeton University Press.

——. 2001. "A Clash of Civilizations or of Paradigms? Theorizing Progress and Social Change." *International Sociology* 16 (3): 341–360.

Clough, Shepard. 1964. The *Economic History of Modern Italy.* New York: Columbia University Press.

Cumings, Bruce. 1982–1983. "Corporatism in North Korea." *Journal of Korean Studies* 4: 269–294.

——. 1987. "The Origins and Development of the Northeast Asian Political Economy: Industrial Sectors, Product Cycles, and Political Consequences." In Frederic C. Deyo (ed.). *The Political Economy of the New Asian Industrialism.* Ithaca, NY: Cornell University Press, pp. 44–83.

——. 1990. *The Origins of the Korean War*, Vol. II. Princeton, NJ: Princeton University Press.

——. 1995. *Divided Korea: United Future?* New York: Foreign Policy Association, *Headline Series # 306*.

Cumings, Bruce, Evrand Abrahamian, and Moshe Ma'oz. 2004. *Inventing the Axis of Evil: The Truth About North Korea, Iran, and Syria*. New York: The New Press.

Eckert, Carter J. 1991. *Offsprings of Empire: The Koch'ang Kims and the Colonial Origins of Korean Capitalism*. Seattle: University of Washington Press.

The Economist. 2003. *The World in 2003*. London.

——. 2004. "Economic and Financial Indicators." London, December 18: 162.

Eisenstadt, Shmuel N. 1966. *Modernization: Protest and Change*. Englewood Cliffs, NJ: Prentice Hall.

Food and Agricultural Organization (FAO). 2004. *L'état de l'insécurité alimentaire dans le monde 2004*. Rome: United Nations Food and Agricultural Organization. (This report, "The state of food insecurity in the world 2004," is also available in English.)

Fukuyma, Francis. 1992. *The End of History and the Last Man*. New York: The Free Press.

Gellner, Ernest. 1983. *Nations and Nationalism*. Ithaca, NY: Cornell University Press.

——. 1992. *Postmodernism, Reason and Religion*. London: Routledge.

Greenfeld, Liah. 1992. *Nationalism: Five Roads to Modernity*. Cambridge, MA: Harvard University Press.

Haggard, Stephan and Tun-jen Cheng. 1987. "State and Foreign Capital in the East Asian NICs." In Frederic C. Deyo (ed.). *The Political Economy of the New Asian Industrialism*. Ithaca, NJ: Cornell University Press, pp. 84–135.

Hirschman, Albert O. 1977. *The Passions and the Interests*. Princeton, NJ: Princeton University Press.

Hobsbawm, Eric J. 1994. *The Age of Extremes: A History of the World, 1914–1991*. New York: Vintage Books.

Holmes, Stephen. 1993. *The Anatomy of Antiliberalism*. Cambridge, MA: Harvard University Press.

Jobert, A. 1995. "An Italian Paradox: Unemployment Among Young Graduates." *Sociologie du Travail* 37: 4.

Kuznets, Paul. 1994. *Korean Economic Development: An Interpretive Model*. Westport, CT: Praeger.

Lardy, Nicholas R. 2002. *Integrating China into the Global Economy*. Washington, DC: Brookings Institution.

Love, Joseph L. 1996. *Crafting the Third World: Theorizing Underdevelopment in Rumania and Brazil*. Stanford, CA: Stanford University Press.

McDaniel, Tim. 2000. "The Strange Career of Radical Islam." In Jeffrey Wasserstrom, Lynn Hunt, and Marilyn Young (eds). *Human Rights and Revolutions*. Lanham: Rowan and Littlefield, pp. 211–229.

Manent, Pierre. 1995. *An Intellectual History of Liberalism*. Princeton, NJ: Princeton University Press.

Mountjoy, Alan B. 1973. *The Mezzogiorno*. London: Oxford University Press.

North, Douglass C. 1981. *Structure and Change in Economic History*. Cambridge: Cambridge University Press.

——. 1990. *Institutions, Institutional Change and Economic Performance*. Cambridge: Cambridge University Press.

North, Douglass C. and Robert Paul Thomas. 1973. *The Rise of the Western World: A New Economic History*. Cambridge: Cambridge University Press.

Organization for Economic Co-operation and Development (OECD). 2003. *China: Progress and Reform Challenges*. Paris: OECD.

——. 2004. *OECD in Figures 2004*. Paris: OECD, from the web at www.oecd.org.

Rostow, Walt W. 1960. *The Stages of Economic Growth: a Non-Communist Manifesto*. Cambridge: Cambridge University Press.

Shin, Gi-Wook. 1997. *Peasant Protest and Social Change in Colonial Korea*. Seattle: University of Washington Press.

Sternhell, Zeev. 1995. *Neither Right Nor Left: Fascist Ideology in France*. Princeton, NJ: Princeton University Press, 1995.

Vogel, Ezra. 1991. *The Four Little Dragons*. Cambridge, MA: Harvard University Press.

Wallerstein, Immanuel. 1974. *The Modern World System*, Vol. I. New York: Academic Press.

Woo, Jung-en. 1991. *Race to the Swift: State and Finance in Korean Industrialization*. New York: Columbia University Press.

Woo-Cumings, Meredith (formerly Jung-en Woo). 1999. "The State, Democracy, and the Reform of the Corporate Sector in Korea." In T.J. Pempel (ed.). *The Politics of the Asian Economic Crisis*. Ithaca, NY: Cornell University Press, pp. 116–142.

World Bank. 1989. *World Development Report*. New York: Oxford University Press.

——. 2004. *World Development Indicators 2004*. Washington, DC: World Bank, from the web at www.worldbank.org/data/wdi2004/.

Part V

Social transformations

Labor, women, and the family

11 Modernization, gender roles, and marriage behavior in South Korea

Minja Kim Choe

In recent decades, profound and powerful changes in the forms and functions of family have taken place in the highly industrialized countries of Europe and North America. Young adults nowadays remain unmarried long after they achieve physical adulthood, and marriage is no longer considered to be a lifelong commitment. Sexual relationships, cohabiting, and childbearing and rearing are not limited to married couples (Bumpass 1990; Lesthaeghe 1983; Lesthaeghe and Wilson 1986). At the same time, the proportion of married women who are in paid employment has increased rapidly (Oppenheimer 1994). Rising educational standards and declining levels of fertility and mortality have given women more opportunities for employment. In addition, married women's employment has become less affected by family characteristics such as the number of babies a couple has or the age of their children (DaVanzo and Rahman 1993). These changes in lifestyle are closely related to the emergence of modern institutions that have provided modern society with social security, educational, and welfare services. Increased affluence has contributed to the growing independence of individuals because many who want to establish their own households can afford to do so. In general, higher levels of education, more contact with the outside world through mass media, and increased employment opportunities have tended to undermine values and norms supporting the "traditional" family system and gender roles (Lesthage 1983; Mason *et al.* 1998).

As the chapters in this collection have demonstrated, South Korean society has also experienced dramatic economic and social change over the second half of the twentieth century. Korea's economic development and social modernization began relatively late but it occurred at an extremely rapid pace. The republic has been transformed from a mostly rural, agriculturally based economy into a predominantly urban society where nearly 90 percent of workers are employed in non-agricultural sectors (National Statistical Office 2001: 179). Over the past two decades in particular, the country has become significantly more affluent and integrated into global economic and communication networks. Educational levels of the population have also increased significantly. Comparing educational attainment levels for men and women born from 1936 through 1970 (ages twenty-five to fifty-nine in 1995), we see that in the time span of about one generation, the high school education that was enjoyed by less than 40 percent of men and by 10 percent of women has become nearly universal. Forty-five percent of men and 36 percent of women born in 1970 have more than high school education. This shows a remarkable increase from the 16 percent figure for men and the 2 percent figure for women who were included among the 1936 birth cohort (Figure 11.1).

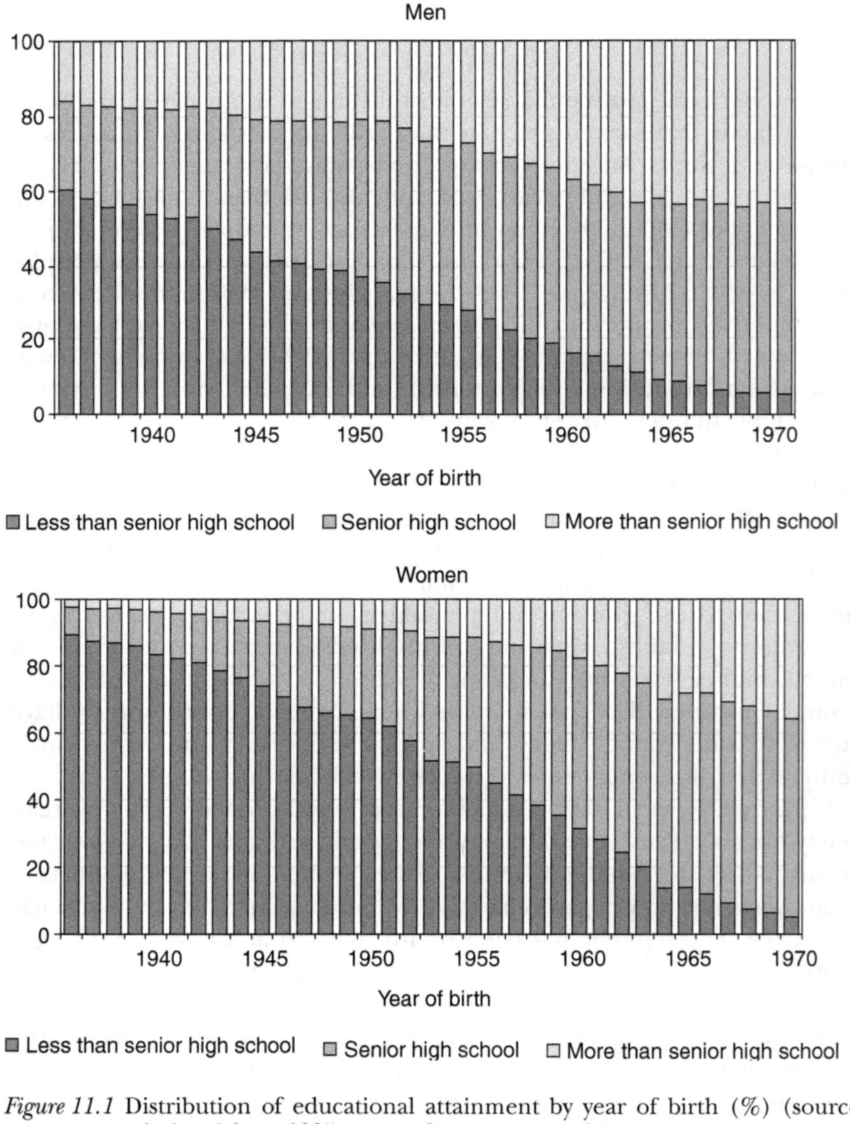

Figure 11.1 Distribution of educational attainment by year of birth (%) (source: tabulated from 1995 census, 2 percent sample).

As economic development and other aspects of modernization in South Korea approach levels reached in the advanced industrial world, the question arises about how Korean families have responded to the challenges and opportunities presented by capitalistic forms of production and consumption. This chapter examines two aspects of family change that have taken place in South Korea in recent years: shifts in gender roles and in marriage behavior. We employ data from recent national surveys, vital statistics, and census results, to examine recent attitudes and behavior regarding marriage and divorce. Shifts in attitudes about gender roles and women's employment will be discussed within the broader context of traditional norms and the economic and social modernization process.

Women, the family, and modernization in Korea

The traditional Korean family was strongly patrilineal and patriarchal. This gave sons enormous importance as preservers of the family line (Choi 1970; Kim 1968; Lee 1972). Even among East Asian countries that share a Confucian tradition, Korea stood out as a country holding on to one of the strictest forms of Confucianism (Deuchler 1992). Korea is different from other countries with Confucian traditions such as China and Japan, especially with regard to the issue of who can assume the role of a son, and whether all sons are subject to the same relationship with the father (Choi 1970; Lee 1972; Wolf and Hanley 1985). Under this family system, marriage was mandatory, early marriage was common, and men and women assumed strictly separate gender roles. These features of "traditional" norms resulted in family changes that were different from those experienced in the West. The strong patrilineal and patriarchal traditions, for example, have kept out-of-wedlock childbearing and divorce at low levels, and shifts toward more egalitarian gender relations may progress at a slower pace than alterations in other aspects of family life.

Women have been active participants in economic activities throughout twentieth-century Korean history, with a large proportion of them working in farms, factories, and family-owned businesses. The primary role of married women, however, has been taking care of the family and household. In the 1960s, large numbers of women worked in non-farming occupations but they often quit working around the time of marriage or first childbirth. Some married women worked, but they did so mainly to earn complementary income necessary for household expenditures, and they tended to be employed in the sales and service sectors. Industrial developments in the 1970s and 1980s accompanied rising levels of education, and these factors have changed the nature of economic activities among women in South Korea. There are now signs that women working in career-oriented jobs are increasing. Among women employed at establishments of ten or more workers, the proportion who have worked continuously for five years or longer has more than doubled from 14 percent in

1985 to 30 percent in 1998 (Figure 11.2). The proportion of men in this category increased only moderately, from 37 to 48 percent. It is notable, therefore, that in recent decades women have experienced greater changes in their educational and employment levels than have men. On the other hand, social norms and institutional habits such as hiring practices and employment conditions are dominated by attitudes of older members of the society, and are likely to change at a slower pace.

Attitudes on marriage and divorce: normative obligation to marry

Data from the 1994 "Survey of Quality of Life in Korea," conducted by the Korea Institute for Health and Social Affairs, collected information on attitudes of adult men and women for a range of items concerning marriage, family life, and gender roles (Chang *et al.* 1994). This study examined selected aspects of this body of information pertaining to attitudes on marriage and divorce as reported by men and women aged twenty-five to fifty-nine. In particular, it aims to understand how respondents' attitudes differed by their sex, age, and level of education. The following tables show the estimated percentages of men and women who do not hold "traditional"[1] views on marriage and divorce. The percentages have been estimated through the

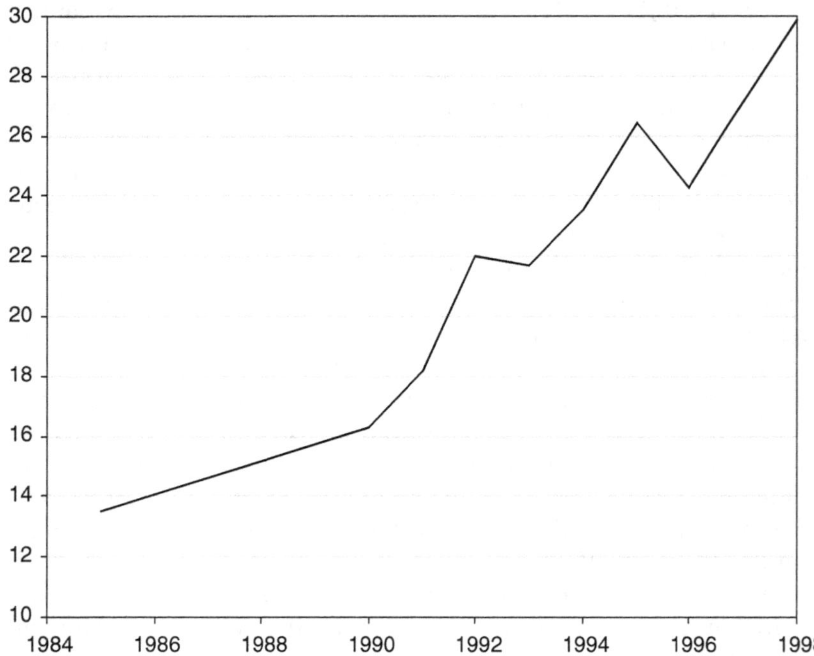

Figure 11.2 Proportions of women employees in continuous service for five years or longer (source: National Statistical Office 1998, 175; 1999: 185).

application of a series of logistic regression models, using age, sex, and years of education as the explanatory variables. To see the "net effect" of age, I estimated the proportions of males and females who did not adopt traditional attitudes toward marriage and divorce at the ages of thirty, forty, and fifty, holding their education constant at "senior high school" level. To see the "net effect" of education, I held the age constant at thirty and estimated the proportions for three levels of education: less than senior high school, senior high school, and more than senior high school.

Our first item concerns the attitude on the oughtness of marriage for women. Table 11.1 shows, for men and women of different ages and educational attainments, the estimated percentages of respondents who held non-traditional views on the oughtness of marriage for women. Respondents who disagreed with the statement "A woman can have a full and satisfying life without marrying" have been classified as having traditional views. Those who agreed with or expressed neutral opinions about the statement have been classified as having non-traditional views. We see that the majority of men and more than two-thirds of women hold non-traditional views on the oughtness of marriage. Women are much more likely than men to hold non-traditional views. Younger age and higher education are also associated with an increased likelihood of holding non-traditional views. It is interesting to note that age has a large impact on whether or not women hold non-traditional views (see first panel of Table 11.1). The impact of education on these attitudes, however, is small (see second panel of Table 11.1).

Table 11.2 shows the estimated percentages of men and women who hold non-traditional views on the oughtness of marriage for men. Younger age, having more education, and being female are all associated with adopting less traditional attitudes. Note, however, that the variations in these characteristics, especially regarding gender differences, are smaller than the variations in views on the oughtness of marriage for women. In addition, we see that views on oughtness of marriage for men remain more traditional than the views on the oughtness of marriage for women.

Table 11.1 Estimated percentages of men and women who agree with or are neutral about the statement "A woman can have a full and satisfying life without marrying" by selected characteristics, 1994, South Korea

Characteristics	*Men*	*Women*
Age 50, high school education	52	71
Age 40, high school education	62	79
Age 30, high school education	71	85
Age 30, less than high school education	69	84
Age 30, high school education	71	85
Age 30, more than high school education	75	87

Source: Adapted from Survey of Quality of Life in Korea (1994).

Table 11.2 Estimated percentages of men and women who agree with or are neutral about the statement "A man can have a full and satisfying life without marrying" by selected characteristics 1994, South Korea

Characteristics	*Men*	*Women*
Age 50, high school education	48	51
Age 40, high school education	55	58
Age 30, high school education	62	65
Age 30, less than high school education	59	62
Age 30, high school education	62	65
Age 30, more than high school education	65	68

Source: Adapted from Survey of Quality of Life in Korea (1994).

In summary, our statistics reveal that marriage is viewed as necessary for a full and satisfying life more frequently by men than by women, by older persons more than by younger persons, and by the less well educated more than by the more highly educated. Korean women tend to see marriage as less necessary for happy lifestyles than do Korean men. Finally, men and women agree more on the oughtness of marriage for men than on the oughtness of marriage for women.

Divorce and parental obligations

Studies on divorce in the United States have found that a rapid increase in the divorce rate occurred together with a rapid decline in the proportion of men and women who agreed that parents should stay together for the sake of their children, even when the marriage was in trouble (Bumpass 1990; Thornton and Freedman 1983). As a result, divorce rates rose in the United States as increasing proportions of men and women considered individual happiness to be a more important factor than their parental obligations to children.

Similar shifts in attitudes on divorce have been taking place in South Korea. Table 11.3 shows that a majority of men and women do not agree with the position that "A couple should not divorce for the sake of children even when the marriage is bad." The proportion of those not agreeing is much higher among women than among men, and among younger persons than among older persons. It is interesting to note that the percentages do not vary much by the level of education. Thus, although there seems to be a secular trend of emphasizing adult individuals' happiness over their parental obligations, there is uniformity in the view, within gender, and among persons of similar ages. The traditional view that marriage is for a lifetime is also changing. Men and women are increasingly more willing to end a difficult marriage by getting divorced. Let us now turn to examining recent changes in marriage and divorce behavior using census and vital statistics data.

Table 11.3 Estimated percentages of men and women who do not agree with or are neutral about the statement "A couple should not divorce for the sake of children even when the marriage is bad" by selected characteristics 1994, South Korea

Characteristics	*Men*	*Women*
Age 50, high school education	41	53
Age 40, high school education	50	61
Age 30, high school education	59	69
Age 30, less than high school education	58	69
Age 30, high school education	59	69
Age 30, more than high school education	59	70

Source: Adapted from Survey of Quality of Life in Korea (1994).

Marriage and divorce behavior

From each census data, we can estimate the mean age at first marriage based on the proportions of single persons tabulated by age. The estimated mean age at marriage (singulate mean age at marriage (SMAM)) increased from 21.5 for women and 25.3 for men in 1960 to 27.1 for women and 30.3 for men in 2000 (Table 11.4). By 2003, the mean average for women rose to 27.3, but the age for men declined somewhat, to 30.1 years. The differences in mean age at marriage have narrowed somewhat over the past several decades, from 3.8 years in 1960 to 2.8 years in 2003.

Vital statistics show that the divorce rate has also increased steadily. The number of divorces per 1,000 persons (crude divorce rate) increased from 0.5 in 1976 to 2.0 in 1997 (National Statistical Office 1998: 121). The crude divorce rate has increased rapidly in recent years, reaching 3.5 in 2003. Not all persons are at risk of getting a divorce and therefore the crude divorce rate does not reflect how many marriages actually end in divorce. A more refined measure of the divorce rate, based on the number of married

Table 11.4 Trends in singulate mean age of marriage (SMAM) in South Korea, 1960 to 1995

Year	*Female SMAM*	*Male SMAM*	*Difference*
1960	21.5	25.3	3.8
1965	22.8	26.7	3.9
1970	23.3	27.2	3.9
1975	23.7	27.4	3.7
1980	24.1	27.3	3.2
1985	24.7	27.8	3.1
1990	25.4	28.5	3.1
1995	26.5	29.8	3.3
2000	27.1	30.3	3.3

Source: Reports of Population and Housing Census (various years).

women classified by their age, gives an estimate of the proportions of marriages that would end up in divorce (total divorce rate). Figure 11.3 shows that the total divorce rate computed for married women between the ages thirty and forty-nine doubled in seven years between 1989 and 1996. Looking at these figures another way, in 1993 there were 59,300 cases of divorce, representing 158,600 people. In 1998 there were 116,700 cases, and in 2003 there were 167,100 cases, or 234,200 people getting divorces (National Statistical Office 2004: http://www.nso.go.kr/eng/releases/e_svpo2003.shtml).

In our analysis, we have seen that attitudes toward marriage have varied by people's age, sex, and education. We now ask how delayed marriage and increasing divorce rates relate to education levels among men and women. Figure 11.4, which shows the distribution of marital status of men and women by educational level and age, provides some clues. The top panel shows clearly that when men with high school education are compared with those with post-secondary educations, higher educational levels are associated with later marriage. At the same time, the proportions of men who eventually marry do not depend on whether or not they have more than high school education. On the other hand, men with less than high school education are more likely to stay single into their late thirties and in their forties, and probably end up never marrying.

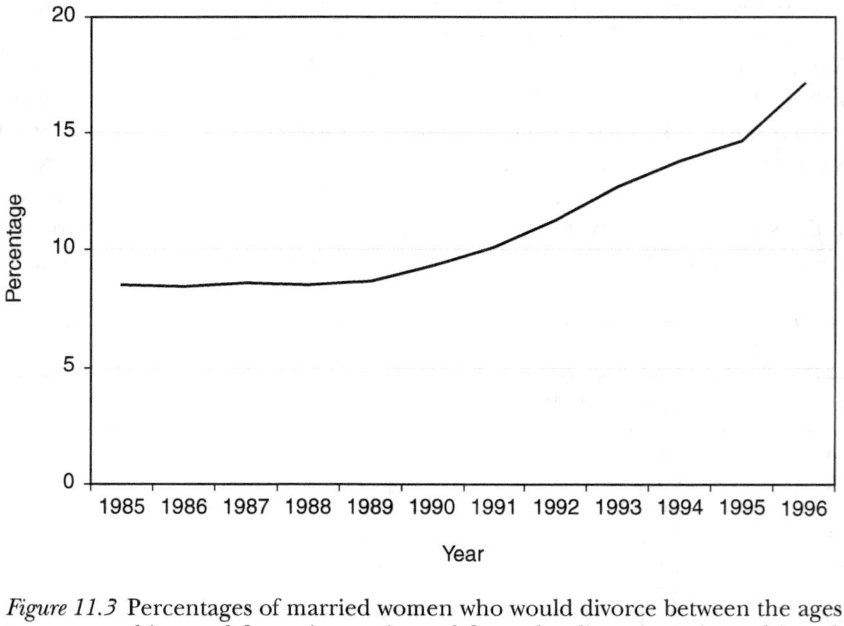

Figure 11.3 Percentages of married women who would divorce between the ages of thirty and forty-nine, estimated from the divorces registered in calendar years 1985–96 (source: Han *et al.* 2000).

Note
The percentages are estimated based on the divorces registered in each calendar year.

The bottom panel of Figure 11.4 shows quite a different pattern for females. Among Korean women, a higher level of education is associated with both later marriage and a higher likelihood of remaining single up to the age of sixty. We can contrast this recent data with information we have from 1970 which showed a different pattern: although more educated men and women were marrying at later ages, most men and women ended up marrying regardless of their level of education (Choe 1998).

Overall, our data show that a new pattern of marriage behavior has emerged over the past several decades. Increasingly larger proportions of men and women are spending a significant proportion of their adult lives

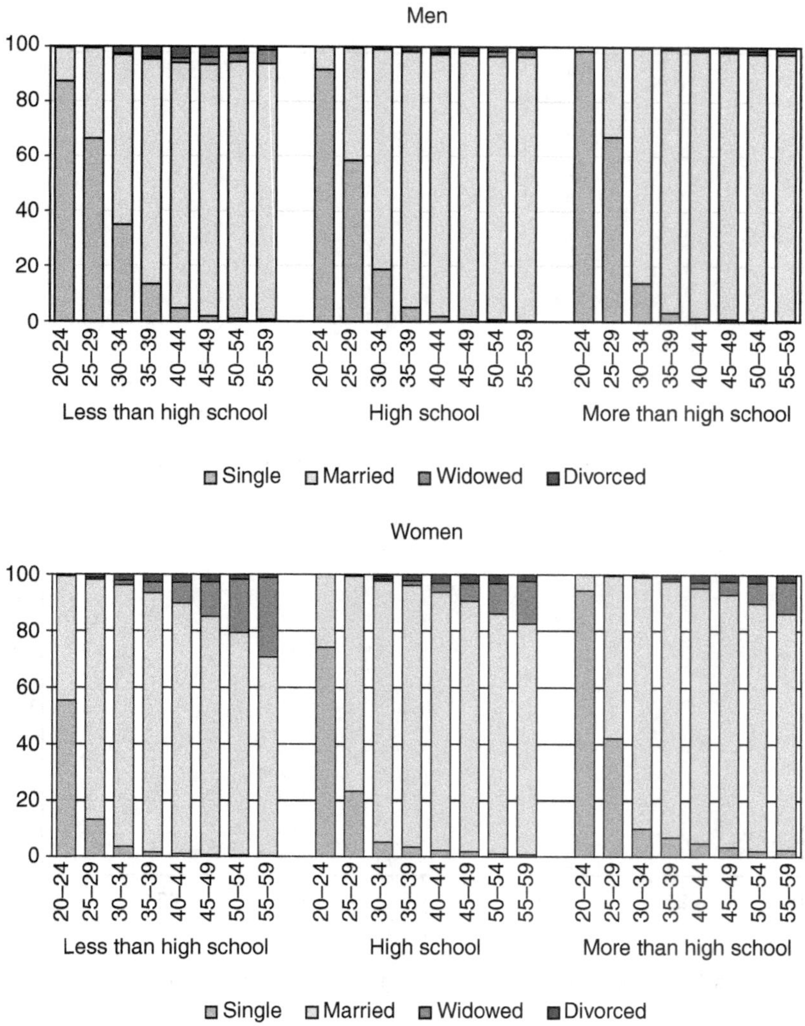

Figure 11.4 Distribution of marital status by sex, education, and age, 1995 (%) (source: tabulated from 1995 census, 2 percent sample).

single. More notably, higher proportions of women with relatively advanced levels of education are not marrying at all. They are either avoiding marriage or are having a difficult time finding marriage partners, and at increasingly higher rates.

The increasing proportions of men and women who are divorced indicate another measure of the changing significance of marriage in modern Korean society. Because divorce can take place only among married persons, we have also calculated the proportions of divorced among ever-married. Figure 11.5 shows that among men, the proportion of those who are divorced is clearly associated with their level of education, with the

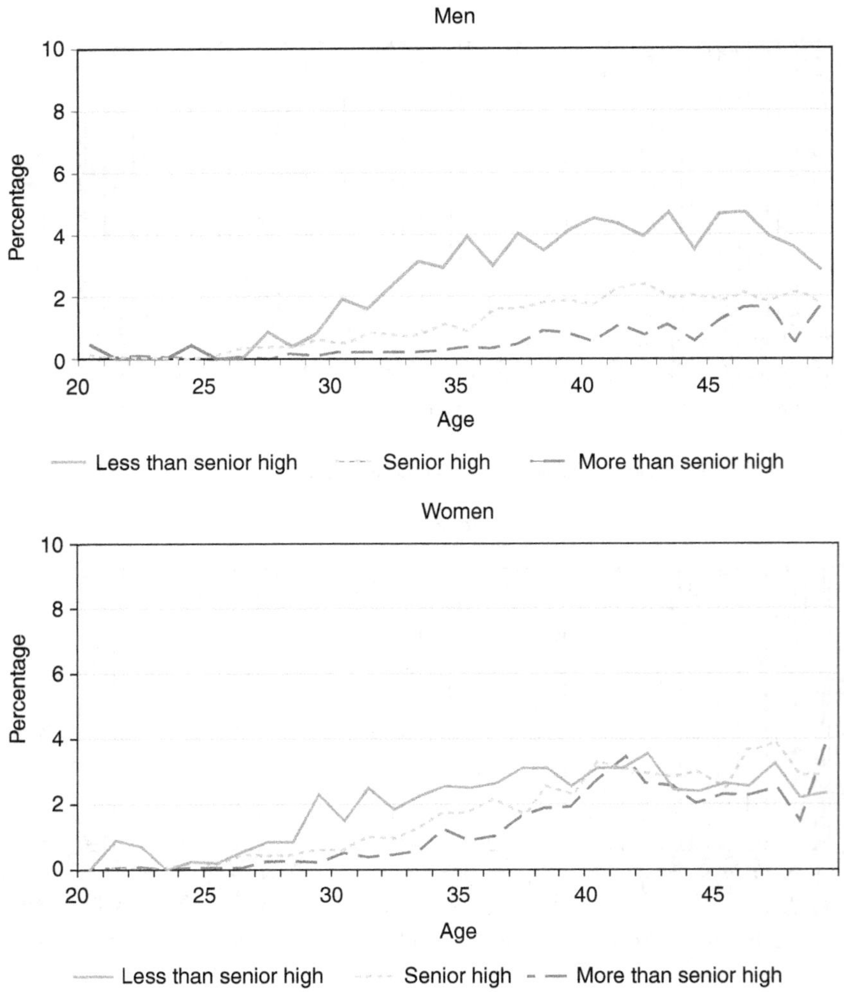

Figure 11.5 Proportion divorced among ever-married men and women by age and education, 1995 (%) (source: tabulated from 1995 census, 2 percent sample).

more highly educated being less likely to become divorced. Among women, on the other hand, we see no clear relationship between the level of education and the proportion who are divorced.

We make one final observation about Figure 11.4. The proportion of the population who are widowed is much higher among women with less than high school education than among any other group of women and men. It is possible that these women are more likely to have had husbands exposed to higher rates of mortality but the mortality differential alone is not likely to explain the large difference. It is also possible that women with low levels of education report that they are widowed when in fact they are either divorced or are separated from husbands, and that the figures on divorce hide what are in reality higher rates of failed marriage in modern Korean society.

Among men and women with the same level of education, with the exception of those with the lowest levels of education, the proportions of males and females who are divorced are higher among women than they are among men. Considering that the educational levels of husbands and wives tend to be similar, the gender differences in the proportions of those who are married indicate that men are more likely to remarry after divorce than are women. Thus, we have another indication that the significance of marriage remains stronger for men than for women.

We can now proceed to examine attitudes on gender roles and the most important aspect of changing gender roles: women's employment.

Attitudes on gender roles: the husband–wife division of labor

Using the 1994 survey data mentioned above, I examine two attitude items concerning gender roles. The first relates to attitudes about the traditional gendered division of labor and the second to views about the impact of women's employment on family life. Table 11.5 shows the estimated percentages of respondents who did not agree with the

Table 11.5 Estimated percentages of men and women who do not agree or are neutral about the statement "It is best for everyone if the husband makes the living and the wife takes care of home and family" by selected characteristics 1994, South Korea

Characteristics	*Men*	*Women*
Age 50, high school education	16	26
Age 40, high school education	18	29
Age 30, high school education	20	31
Age 30, less than high school education	18	29
Age 30, high school education	20	31
Age 30, more than high school education	23	35

Source: Adapted from Survey of Quality of Life in Korea (1994).

statement "It is best for everyone if the husband makes the living and the wife takes care of the home and family." On this item, much smaller percentages of men and women hold non-traditional views (do not agree with the statement) than on the items related to marriage and divorce discussed earlier in the chapter. A recent comparative study of attitudes on marriage and family life reports that the responses to this item varied greatly among those living in the United States, Japan, and South Korea. Among women aged thirty to thirty-nine, about 50 percent in Japan and more than 70 percent in the U.S. did not agree with the traditional view (Bumpass and Choe 2004). Relatively large differences among countries and small variations within each country suggest that this item strongly reflects existing social norms.

How do South Korean men and women evaluate married women's employment in terms of its impact upon family life and relationships among family members? Table 11.6 shows the estimated percentages of men and women who do not agree with the statement "If the wife works, family members and family life will suffer."

The majority of Korean men and women did not agree with the statement, and whether or not they agreed did not depend greatly on either their age or educational levels. There was only a 10 percent differential between men and women in these categories. In other words, South Korean men and women continue to hold quite traditional views on gender roles, and tend to endorse the traditional division of labor. At the same time, they hold less traditional attitudes about the harmfulness of married women's employment. This latter perception may partly result from the fact that many women who are employed receive help in family care and housework from parents, relatives, or private household employees (Choe *et al.* 2004). Indeed, it is likely that most women seek employment only when such arrangements can be made.

Table 11.6 Estimated percentages of men and women who do not agree or are neutral about the statement "If the wife works, family members and family life suffer" by selected characteristics 1994, South Korea

Characteristics	*Men*	*Women*
Age 50, high school education	49	60
Age 40, high school education	53	63
Age 30, high school education	56	66
Age 30, less than high school education	56	66
Age 30, high school education	56	66
Age 30, more than high school education	56	66

Source: Adapted from Survey of Quality of Life in Korea (1994).

Women's employment

Mary Brinton and Moonkyung Choi discuss women's incorporation into South Korea's urban economy in Chapter 12. However, we may note here several important trends in Korea in recent decades. One is that the overall rate of women's employment has changed little during the latter stages of the industrialization process in South Korea, increasing from slightly over 40 percent in 1976 to nearly 50 percent in 2003 (National Statistical Office 2004 website). In recent years, furthermore, there has been no appreciable change in these figures. However, the type of employment women have held, and whether or not their employment has been interrupted by marriage and childbearing, has changed in recent years. In particular, single females' work experience has increased substantially over the past several decades. According to a survey of ever-married women conducted in 1997, 91 percent of women born between 1968 and 1972 had work experience before marriage compared to 61 percent of women born between 1948 and 1952 (Cho *et al.* 1997: 232).

Recently, the employment rate among married women has been low immediately after marriage. The 1997 survey reported that 22 percent of married women aged fifteen to forty-nine were employed. The figures are especially low for women in the twenty-five to twenty-nine age bracket (8.6 percent) and the thirty to thirty-four age group (13.2 percent), periods in Korean women's life cycle when statistics show that they are more likely to have small children (Cho *et al.* 1997: 232). However, employment rates of married women relative to their education levels show an interesting pattern which suggests that other changes have occurred in women's employment. The proportion of women employed is highest among the least educated and lowest among high school graduates. Married women with more than high school education, however, are more likely to be employed than those with high school education (Cho *et al.* 1997: 232; Choe *et al.* 2004). This pattern contrasts with patterns observed in the United States, where the female employment rate is positively associated with levels of education, and with patterns observed in Japan where the female employment rate is negatively associated with levels of education (Figure 11.6). In short, at least compared to the two nations which have had a significant influence in shaping Korea's twentieth-century modernity, Korean women display unique employment patterns.

In the United States, married women's employment is determined more by individual women's characteristics and less by family situation or husband's income. In Japan, on the other hand, women's employment is determined more by husband's income and family situation (Choe *et al.* 2004). We should note, however, that the pattern of married women's employment by education in South Korea has changed since the mid-1980s. A national survey of married women conducted in 1986, for example, reported that the employment rate of women was inversely

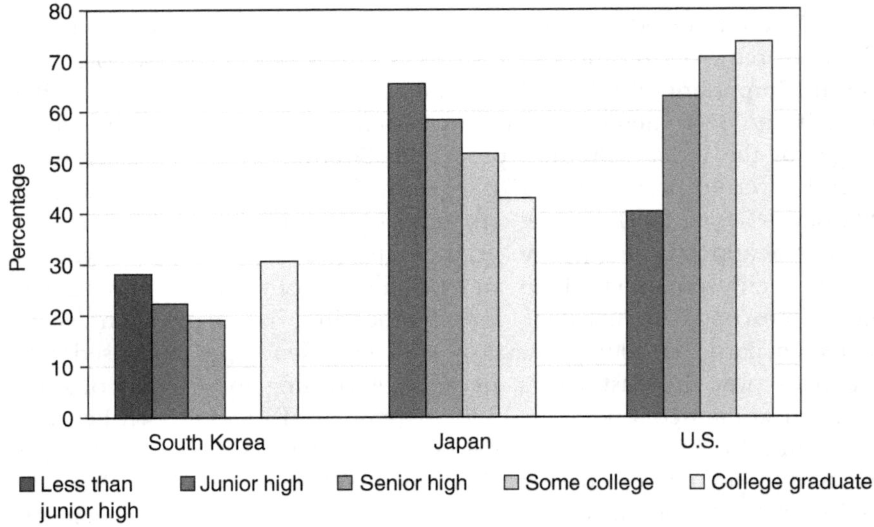

Figure 11.6 Percentages employed among married women aged twenty-five to fifty-nine by education, South Korea 1994, Japan 1994, and the United States 1992 (source: Choe *et al.* 2004).

related to their education: 4.3 percent among women with more than high school education; 15.7 percent among women with junior or senior high school education; and 53.6 percent among women with less education (Kong *et al.* 1987: 193).

We can see clues which explain why the female employment rate following marriage is lower among high school graduates by comparing the distribution of occupation of single and married women by education level around the age of marriage. Figure 11.7 shows the distribution of occupation of women aged twenty-five to thirty-four by level of education and marital status. The occupational categories are administrative/managerial/professional; technical/semi-professional; clerical; sales; "others," which include farming, production, skilled labor, and unskilled labor jobs; and women who do not work.

Figure 11.7 illustrates that marriage has a large impact on women who hold clerical and technical/semi-professional occupations. These occupations are quite common among single women, especially those with high school education, but are rare among married women. Occupations in the administrative/managerial/professional, sales, and "others" categories are affected less by marriage. Single women with high school education are most likely to have clerical or technical/semi-professional occupations, and their employment is most likely to be interrupted by marriage.

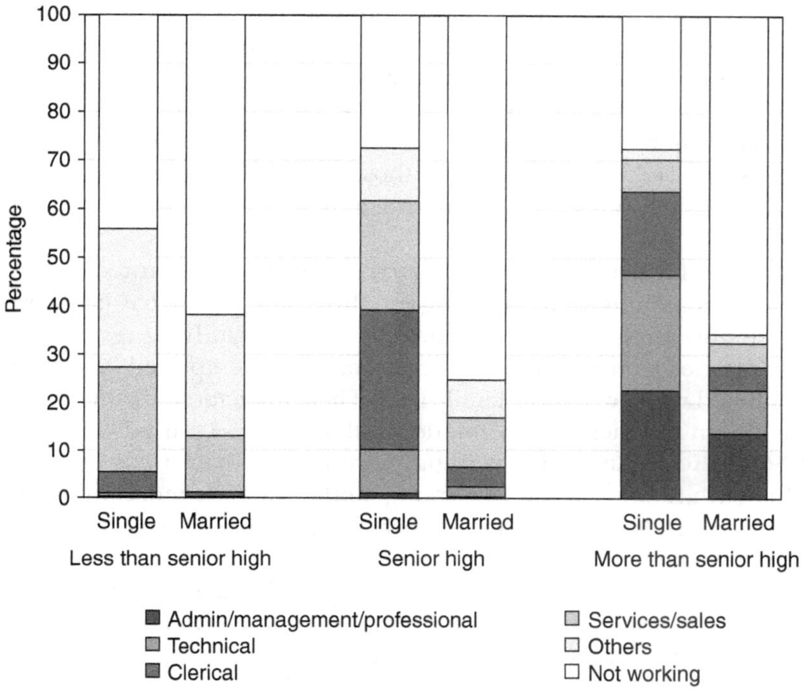

Figure 11.7 Distribution of occupation by marital status and education of women aged twenty-five to thirty-four, 1995 (%) (source: tabulated from 1995 census, 2 percent sample).

Discussion

Attitudes among Koreans on marriage and gender roles have undergone significant shifts over the past several decades. The younger a person is, and, to a lesser extent, the more highly educated a person is, the greater chance there will be that that person will maintain "non-traditional" attitudes on a range of issues relating to marriage, divorce, and gender roles. Furthermore, our study indicates that women are more likely to hold non-traditional views than men.

Marriage and divorce behavior in Korea reflects a society in transition. With some exceptions, the behavior of most men and women with high school education or less follow more traditional patterns. Most of them marry, although higher education is associated with delayed marriage. Women with more than high school education, on the other hand, show more drastic changes in behavior from previous decades, since a substantial proportion of these women now remain single into their late thirties and forties.

Gender roles in women's employment patterns reflect a complex society where old traditions and new ideas seem to coexist with each other. Today, employment of women before marriage has become nearly universal. Women with high school education who are employed in clerical or technical/semi-professional occupations tend to stop working after marriage, at least for a while. When they return to work, they are likely to work in occupations in the sales and service sectors. Women with more than high school education, especially those in professional occupations, are less likely to stop working after marriage than those with lower educational levels.

Curiously, as far as employment of married women is concerned, South Korean women seem to have already gone through a phase that Japanese women are now in, and have established a new pattern. In Korea, highly educated married women are now finding ways to be employed, and thus have combined work with their family lives. The explanation for this trend probably lies in the fact that the modernization process started relatively late in South Korea and is progressing more rapidly than it has done in Japan. In South Korea, parents of working mothers may be more willing to help out with childcare and housework than in Japan, and privately arranged personal help for housework and childcare may be found more easily and at more affordable prices than in Japan. These factors may have provided those South Korean women with a high level of education with more flexibility in re-entering the work force.

As modernization progresses, families will probably find it more difficult to rely on other family members to help out with housework and childcare. Given prevailing attitudes about women's work, it is possible that women who want to continue working after marriage will find it more difficult to combine work and family life successfully unless they are able to find satisfactory arrangements for childcare.

Studies on Japan and Taiwan indicate that highly educated women respond to potential conflicts between work and family life by postponing marriage until a very late age or by not marrying at all. In Japan 11 percent of women aged thirty-five to thirty-nine with college-level or higher education were not married in 1994. In Taiwan, 14 percent of women with more than high school education were not married in 1990. Within marriage, fertility has declined to levels that are far below the replacement level. Women in these countries seem to avoid marriage and childbearing. In Japan and Taiwan, these trends have resulted in low levels of fertility and a rapidly aging population. There are prospects of declining population sizes in the near future as well.

Perceived conflicts between work and family life have affected the quality of life of married women. A recent study points out that working married women in South Korea and Japan continue to do most of the housework, whereas in the United States, husbands help with housework substantially. This is especially true among men who are highly educated (Tsuya and Bumpass 1998). A recent survey of married women in South

Korea reports that most non-working married women (94 percent) would like to work (Cho *et al.* 1997: 236). The main reasons for them not working are the childcare problem (51 percent), followed by lack of appropriate jobs (16 percent), and the perceived need to do housework (11 percent). Married women who want to work but are not working may not be happy, and women who work are often exhausted and stressed (Choe *et al.* 2004; Liao 1998).

South Korea's modernization has thus changed many aspects of family life. In many of the issues discussed in this chapter, Korean women have experienced more changes than have their male counterparts. How future changes will take shape will depend partly upon attitudes of men and social adjustments to shifting attitudes and behavior. For example, future marriage patterns are likely to depend heavily upon how women expect their lives to change with marriage. Whether or not most women can combine work and family life successfully and satisfactorily will also depend on how men will modify their roles within the family, and if society will provide better working conditions for women and options for childcare.

Note

1 For my definition of "traditional," see below.

References

Bumpass, Larry L. 1990. "What's Happening to the Family? Interactions between Demographic and Institutional Change." *Demography* 27(4): 483–498.

Bumpass, Larry L. and Minja Kim Choe. 2004. "Attitudes Relating to Marriage and Family Life," in Noriko O. Tsuya and Larry L. Bumpass (eds). Marriage, *Work, and Family Life in Comparative Perspective: Japan, South Korea, & the United States.* Honolulu: University of Hawaii Press, pp. 19–28.

Chang, Hyŏn-Sŏp, H.-O. Kim, and H. O. Pae. 1994. *Kajok ŭi Salm ŭi Chil kwa Chŏngchaek Yŏnku* (The Quality of Family Life and Policy Implications). Seoul: Korea Institute for Health and Social Welfare.

Cho, Nam-Hun, Sŭng-Kwŭn Kim, Ae-Jŏ Cho, Yŏng-Sik Chang, and Yŏng-Hi O. 1997. *Chŏnkuk Ch'ulsanyŏk mit Kajok Pogŏn Siltae Chosa* (National Survey of Fertility and Family Health). Seoul: Korea Institute for Health and Social Affairs.

Choe, Minja Kim. 1998. "Changing Marriage Patterns in South Korea," in K. O. Mason, N. O. Tsuya, and M. K. Choe (eds). *The Changing Family in Comparative Perspective: Asia and the United States.* Honolulu: East-West Center, and Tokyo: Nihon University, pp. 43–62.

Choe, Minja Kim, Larry L. Bumpass, and Noriko O. Tsuya. 2004. "Employment," in Noriko O. Tsuya and Larry L. Bumpass (eds). *Marriage, Work, and Family Life in Comparative Perspective: Japan, South Korea, and the United States.* Honolulu: University of Hawaii Press, pp. 95–113.

Choi, Jai-Seuk. 1970. "Comparative Study on the Traditional Families in Korea,

Japan, and China," in R. Hill and R. Konig (eds). *Families in East and West: Socialization Process and Kinship Ties.* Paris: Mouton, pp. 202–210.

DaVanzo, Julie and M. Omar Rahman. 1993. *American Families: Trends and Policy Issues.* Santa Monica: RAND.

Deuchler, Martina. 1992. *The Confucian Transformation of Korea: A Study of Social Ideology.* Cambridge, MA: Council of East-Asian Studies, Harvard University.

Goode, William J. 1963. *World Revolution and Family Patterns.* New York: The Free Press.

Han, Sung-Hyan, Minja Kim Choe, and Jin-Suk Lee. 2000. "The Trend in Divorce Rate in South Korea During 1985–1996 Based on Vital Statistics Data." *Journal of the Korean Society of Health Statistics* 25(1): 1–10.

Kim, Duhŏn. 1968. *Han'guk Kajok Chedo Yŏn'gu* (Study on Korean Family System). Seoul: Seoul National University Press.

Kong, Se-Kwŏn, In-Hwa Pak, Ae-Jŏ Cho, Chin-Sŏk Kim, and Hyŏn-Sŏp Chang. 1987. *Han'guk Kajok Kujo ŭi Pyŏnhwa* (Changing Korean Family). Seoul: Korea Institute for Population and Health.

Lee, Kwang-Kyu. 1972. "The Korean Family in Changing Society." *East–West Cultural Studies* 11(1–4): 28–43.

Lesthaeghe, Ron. 1983. "A Century of Demographic and Cultural Change in Western Europe: An Exploration of Underlying Dimensions." *Population and Development Review* 9: 411–435.

Lesthaeghe, Ron and Chris Wilson. 1986. "Modes of Production, Secularization, and the Pace of the Fertility Decline in Europe, 1870–1930," in Ansley J. Coale and Susan C. Watkins (eds). *The Decline of Fertility in Europe.* Princeton, NJ: Princeton University Press, pp. 261–292.

Liao, Tim Futing. 1998. "Dealing with a Double Day: Role Strain among Married Working Women in Japan and South Korea," in K. O. Mason, N. O. Tsuya, and M. K. Choe (eds). *The Changing Family in Comparative Perspective: Asia and the United States.* Honolulu: East–West Center, and Tokyo: Nihon University, pp. 137–154.

Mason, Karen O., Noriko O. Tsuya, and Minja K. Choe. 1998. "Introduction," in K. O. Mason, N. O. Tsuya, and M. K. Choe (eds). *The Changing Family in Comparative Perspective: Asia and the United States.* Honolulu: East–West Center, and Tokyo: Nihon University, pp. 1–16.

National Statistical Office. 1998. *Social Indicators in Korea.* Taejon: National Statistical Office.

——. 1999. *Social Indicators in Korea.* Taejon: National Statistical Office.

——. 2001. *Social Indicators in Korea.* Taejon: National Statistical Office.

Oppenheimer, Valerie Kincade. 1994. "Women's Rising Employment and the Future of the Family in Industrialized Societies." *Population and Development Review* 20: 293–342.

Rindfuss, Ronald R., Karin L. Brewster, and Andrew L. Kavee. 1996. "Women, Work, and Children: Behavioral and Attitudinal Change in the United States." *Population and Development Review* 22(3): 457–482.

Thornton, Arland and Deborah Freedman. 1983. "The Changing American Family." *Population Bulletin* 38: 1–44. New York: United Nations.

Tsuya, Noriko O. and Larry L. Bumpass. 1998. "Time Allocation between Employment and Housework in Japan, South Korea, and the United States," in K. O. Mason, N. O. Tsuya, and M. K. Choe (eds). *The Changing Family in Comparative*

Perspective: Asia and the United States. Honolulu: East–West Center, and Tokyo: Nihon University, pp. 83–104.

Wolf, Arthur P. and Susan B. Hanley. 1985. "Introduction," in S. B. Hanley and A. P. Wolf (eds). *Family and Population in East Asian History*. Stanford, CA: Stanford University Press, pp. 1–12.

12 Women's incorporation into the urban economy of South Korea

Mary C. Brinton and Moonkyung Choi

Introduction

South Korea is one of several countries in East Asia to show increases in women's labor force participation during a period of extremely rapid industrialization. Annual Gross Domestic Product growth rates in South Korea were close to 9 percent for many of the years between 1960 and 1990, and the female labor force participation rate rose from 31 to 45 percent (Lim 1993). East Asian economic growth was fueled by the rapid expansion of export-oriented industry and the creation of large export-processing zones in South Korea, Singapore, Hong Kong, and Taiwan. These developments accelerated employment opportunities for women, especially in the manufacturing sector (Bai and Cho 1995; Koo 1985; Lim 1993; Wood 1991). In the wake of the 1997 Asian financial crisis and the ensuing economic difficulties of the late 1990s, the Korean economy made a speedy if painful recovery, and by 2000, Korean women's labor force participation rate had risen to 56 percent (OECD 2002).

Despite the continuing rise in Korean women's rates of participation in the economy over the period of industrialization and beyond, the employment rate for women in Korea is currently one of the lowest among all OECD countries. The average female labor force participation rate among OECD member countries in 2000 was 69 percent. In only four countries – Greece, Ireland, Italy, and Spain – did women participate in the economy at a lower rate than in Korea. Even more striking is Korea's distinctiveness when we consider the gap between the employment rates of men and women at various levels of education. Comparing the employment of men and women with upper secondary education or less, Korea shows a gender gap of twenty percentage points (that is, 20 percent fewer female than male graduates are employed), which roughly matches the OECD average. However, among the university-educated population, the gender gap in employment reaches 35 percent in Korea, over three times the OECD average.[1] Thus it is not inappropriate to say that highly educated Korean women in particular are underemployed, especially relative to their highly educated male counterparts.

The distinctiveness of highly educated Korean women's low rates of labor force participation relative to international standards is coupled with several other striking characteristics of women's economic participation in Korea, even if we restrict the international comparison only to other East Asian countries such as Japan and Taiwan. Notably, among these three countries, Korea shows: the highest rate of non-wage employment (self-employment or employment in small family enterprises) for women; the greatest gender gap in wages among paid employees; the greatest monopolization of managerial and administrative jobs by men; and the lowest rate of labor force participation for women of childbearing age among the three societies (Brinton 2001). These patterns underline the broader theme of this volume regarding the unique character of Korea's capitalist modernity.

The dominant paradigms in the literature on women and economic development seem to fit uneasily with the experience of East Asia, especially when we consider what these paradigms have to say about the experience of married women. The integration perspective, rooted in modernization theory, posits the optimistic view that economic development leads to lessened gender inequality in the labor market due to phenomena such as women's increased access to education and employers' use of universalistic rather than ascriptive evaluation criteria (Goode 1970; Inkeles and Smith 1974; Moore 1970; also see Jackson 1998). In this view, women enter wage employment in increasing numbers and patriarchy is gradually replaced by egalitarian sex roles (Davis 1984).[2] On the other hand, developmentalist or marginalization theory, with roots in Ester Boserup's classic work on women and economic development, is pessimistic; it predicts stagnation or decline in women's economic status relative to men's, at least during the early stages of industrialization (Boserup 1970). This occurs through a variety of mechanisms that block women from the "good jobs" in the expanding capitalist economy and relegate them to low-wage positions (Elliott 1977; Jacquette 1982; Papanek 1976).[3] While the integration perspective surely seems to offer predictions too rosy for the experience of women in Korea, it is nevertheless without dispute that women's employment opportunities did increase dramatically with industrialization and urbanization. The important question is how the process of industrialization and the development of Korean urban labor markets produced the distinctive female employment patterns we now observe.

In this chapter we approach this question by examining the types of work opportunities that developed for women during the course of rapid industrialization in Korea. We do this by using a dataset that provides detailed information on the work patterns of several cohorts of Korean women through 1985 and allows us to trace the types of work done by women with differing levels of education when they were single, recently married, raising their children, and moving into middle age. For reasons we explain below, we are particularly interested in how women were incorporated into the expanding formal sector (paid employment) or marginalized from it during the stage of rapid industrial development, and what role the "informal" sector – composed of self-employment, employment in small family-run enterprises, and home-based employment for large firms – played in women's array of options. Given Korea's experience of very rapid educational expansion, it is also important to consider how women with different levels of education experienced the rapid development of Korean urban labor markets.

We begin with a very brief overview of South Korean industrialization and women's standing in the economy. We then turn to the predictions that modernization and marginalization theory would generate about the incorporation of women into Korea's urban economy, and examine how our data speak to those predictions.

South Korean industrialization and women's work in comparative perspective

By the 1980s South Korea came to be known in the West as one of the "four tigers" of East Asia that experienced rapid economic growth since the 1960s. A number of chapters in this volume have examined various aspects of Korea's economic modernization since the advent of the Park regime in 1961. South Korea's industrial "takeoff" began with the implementation of the First Five-year Economic Plan in 1962 (Amsden 1989). Over the following three decades, the economy recorded an average per capita gross national product annual growth rate of 7 percent.[4] This was accompanied by massive rural–urban migration flows. In the early 1960s over half of both male and female workers lived in rural areas, but by the 1990s this was the case for only about 20 percent of all workers (Bai and Cho 1996). By the mid-1980s about half of all manufacturing workers were concentrated in the Seoul metropolitan area alone (Cheng and Gereffi 1994). As in other East Asian countries, rapid economic growth was made possible by an export-oriented industrialization strategy (Deyo 1989; Papanek 1988).[5] South Korean economic growth was characterized by its dual nature, with export-oriented industries showing more rapid growth than others. As has been documented in this volume and elsewhere, these industries were led by several business groups (*chaebŏl*) with considerable access to government subsidies, preferential loans, tax incentives, and scarce investment capital (see also Cheng and Gereffi 1994; Cumings 1984; Hamilton *et al.* 1988, 1990). By contrast, small and medium industrial enterprises had much more limited access to capital and had difficulties surviving (Jacobs 1985). The consequence was a pattern of parallel development over the course of industrialization between very large family-owned enterprises and quite small, individual- and family-run businesses. The number of enterprises in the manufacturing, sales, and service sectors with just one or two employees remained steady, the number with three to nine employees decreased, and the number with more than ten employees grew over the 1970s and 1980s (Yoon 1987).

Although Kwon and Suh wrote in Chapter 4 about the character of large corporate management in Korean *chaebŏl*, given the dual nature of South Korean economic growth, there continue to be a substantial number of self-employed and family enterprise workers in addition to workers in large enterprises (Jacobs 1985).[6] The proportion of employees (that is, wage and salary workers) in the total labor force increased dramatically during industrialization, but it was nevertheless the case that well over 30 percent of the total labor force at the beginning of the twenty-first century was in the informal sector – as self-employed workers, small-scale employers, or family enterprise workers (OECD 2000). This is the highest figure for any OECD country, including the other East Asian member country in the OECD, Japan.[7] Moreover, this holds for both men and women. Even in Taiwan, where a large proportion of the labor force works in very small enterprises, the rate of self-employment among women is lower than in Korea. The rate of people working in the informal sector varies considerably by educational level in Korea, with the least-educated men and women being the most likely to be in this sector. But the rate of informal sector work among the most educated among the populace is hardly trivial: over 20 percent of college- and university-educated men and women. This is an indicator of the presence either of strong "pull" factors for a certain segment of the highly educated into self-employment, or of "push" factors out of the formal sector.

In addition to the continued numerical significance of the informal sector in Korea, there are important characteristics of the formal sector that are not necessarily easily predicted on the basis of the economies of other East Asian countries such as Japan and Taiwan. These too bear mentioning, as they create the context within which we need to consider the work opportunities and conditions in the formal sector for single and married Korean women of varied educational backgrounds. When we consider the nature of employment conditions in the formal urban sector in Korea, one of the striking things is that it is marked by a certain degree of rigidity. This is evidenced in several ways.

First, as noted elsewhere, the concentration of the urban population in Seoul and a few other large cities and the rather weak public transportation infrastructure to date has translated into very long commuting times for many workers (Brinton 2001; Brinton *et al.* 1995). This adds to the total daily hours that full-time workers must allocate to work and related activities; this is a particularly important consideration for mothers of young children. Second, Korea has an extraordinarily low percentage of part-time jobs (defined as less than thirty hours per week) when compared with almost all other OECD countries. Fewer than 10 percent of women (and less than 5 percent of men) work part-time, whereas figures for women in a number of other OECD countries including Japan are three to four times that (OECD 2002). This is not to imply that part-time work is necessarily better, as both the hourly wage and the provision of benefits is generally worse than in full-time jobs. But the near-absence of the option to work part-time may be a significant factor in lowering the labor force participation of Korean married women with children, especially in the formal sector of the economy. Third, the number of average work hours for Koreans is higher than those for workers in other OECD countries, with half of all employees working over fifty-four hours per week (OECD 2000). This, too, constitutes a severe constraint on either fathers or mothers – but overwhelmingly on the latter – who must accommodate their work schedules to some degree to the rhythm of their children's daily lives.

These constraints are hardly uniquely Korean, but the comparison with other OECD countries is useful in illustrating that Korea is on one end of a continuum of work conditions that ranges from the flexible to the rigid. Both the availability of part-time work options and the shorter duration of the work week render the labor market in Japan slightly more hospitable to women. This is ironic, given that the structure of the Japanese employment system itself can be considered more inhospitable to working women than the analogous structure in Korea. In Japan, firm-internal labor markets in large enterprises have continued to fuel employers' reluctance to hire women into career-track jobs, as the perception is that training investments in female workers will not pay off because women may leave employment when they marry or have children (Brinton 1993). This has created a vicious cycle between employers' discriminatory behaviors and the quit behaviors of women in the labor force. By contrast, many fewer Korean enterprises adhere to the strong firm-internal training and promotion practices practiced by prototypical large Japanese firms (Genda and Yee 1998; Ito and Kang 1989). Job tenure, even for Korean men, is considerably shorter than it is for Japanese men, and some mid-career hiring does occur (Genda and Yee 1998; OECD 2000). There is also a phenomenon in Korea where men quit large enterprises in order to pursue their dream of being self-employed.

While the level of Korean women's wages in the formal sector is quite a bit lower relative to men's wages than is the case for women in either Japan or Taiwan, here again Korea is an interesting case. Those Korean women who do enter professional occupations or administrative occupations – although the latter percentage remains extremely low – experience a wage gap with men that is only slightly greater than their counterparts in Taiwan and is comparable to their counterparts in Japan (Brinton 2001). In other words, the earnings of Korean women employed in the professions – approximately 15 percent of women – compare quite favorably to those of men, whereas the earnings gap between women and men in other occupations such as clerical, manufacturing, and sales or service is much worse.

Given the rapid educational expansion experienced by Korea and the unusually high rate of university attendance for women as well as men in recent cohorts, Lee and Brinton conducted a study in the 1990s that investigated the work patterns of Korean women during the first ten years following their graduation from universities in the Seoul metropolitan area (Lee 1997, 2001; Lee and Brinton 1996). Among women graduating from universities of different prestige levels, those from top-ranked universities were the most likely to demonstrate continuous work histories, including work after marriage. A very high percentage (47 percent) of all university-educated women worked in an education-related field in their first job, compared to just 17 percent of university-educated men. There was no variation in this percentage across women according to the prestige of the university from which they had graduated. The overwhelming percentage of men (nearly 80 percent), on the other hand, entered the labor force in other white-collar occupations.

In this study, women in education-related occupations were the least likely to leave the labor force in the first ten years after starting work, followed by women in pharmaceutical jobs and nursing. By contrast, women in secretarial jobs were the most likely to exit the labor force. This indicates that professional occupations, particularly those that are traditionally female, are where highly educated Korean women are concentrated in the formal sector, and women who enter these fields demonstrate a high degree of labor force attachment.

In sum, Korean women's lower rates of overall labor force participation and lower rates of participation in the formal sector in particular seem to derive from a combination of factors that are not necessarily common to other OECD countries or to Korea's closest counterparts (Japan and Taiwan) in East Asia. The size of the informal sector has remained surprisingly stable over the past thirty-five years, and the sector comprises male and female workers of varied educational backgrounds, including the highly educated. Rigidities in working conditions in the formal sector seem particularly pronounced in Korea, even though large firms do not necessarily maintain the "permanent employment system" associated with large Japanese firms and which disadvantages women. Korean women who work as employees in the formal sector earn less on average relative to men than do their counterparts in Japan or Taiwan, but among that subset of women who enter professional occupations, the country differences are minor. Furthermore, the professions – especially education-related jobs – are the most common destination for Korean female university graduates, and women who enter these jobs are the most likely to work continuously as they marry and start a family.

We turn now to consider general perspectives on women and economic development, and the predictions that can be generated about women's participation in the Korean economy; we then pursue these predictions with our data. Our detailed data on different cohorts of women and their participation in the formal and informal sectors of the economy cover the period up until 1985. We do not claim in this chapter that we can read the present back into the recent past or, on the other hand, that we can carry the recent past up to the present and beyond in some linear, mechanistic fashion. But the advantages of the work-history data we employ are many, and we argue that in providing a recent historical backdrop they can illuminate some of the reasons behind the current patterns of Korean women's economic participation.

Theoretical predictions about women's economic incorporation

Theoretical perspectives on women and economic development should be able to generate predictions on the pace of women's incorporation into the expanding formal sector and on the characteristics of women who are likely to enter the formal or informal sector. Following what we briefly laid out in the introduction, we suggest three sets of predictions that the modernization and marginalization theses make.

Women's participation in formal sector employment

The integration or modernization perspective would predict that as the formal sector expands with industrialization, successive cohorts of women as well as men should have higher probabilities of working there. This should be enhanced by individuals' increasing access to the education necessary for work in the formal sector. On the other hand, the marginalization thesis incorporates gender more strongly into predictions about who participates in the expanding formal sector, and assumes that existing patriarchal norms privilege male workers (Anker and Hein 1985; Papanek 1976; Ward 1988). If male and female workers are preferred by different industries or occupations, women's employment in the formal sector may depend on several factors such as the size of the male labor force, the rate of increase in formal sector employment, and the particular industries or occupations that expand over time, either "naturally" or through government assistance (Pyle 1990). Consequently, the marginalization thesis would predict that greater access to the formal sector of the economy by successive cohorts of women may or may not occur; it is fundamentally contingent upon a number of contextual factors related to male labor supply and the nature of employer preferences.

Women's life-cycle patterns of labor force participation

Neither the integration nor the marginalization perspective explicitly emphasizes how women's life-cycle labor force participation patterns will change in the process of industrialization. Given the modernization perspective's emphasis on the emergence of "modern" sex role norms concomitant with economic development, it is theoretically consistent with this perspective to predict that as fertility declines and women's educational attainment increases, more and more women will remain in the labor force across their life cycle. Moreover, women's participation in the formal sector may not necessarily be compromised by family obligations, particularly if they are highly educated. These women bring significant human capital resources to the labor market and, according to modernization theory, should be the most likely to be in households where "modern" sex-role attitudes prevail (Jackson 1998).

However, observers have noted that life-cycle variation does exist in the degree of women's involvement in the formal sector in developing countries (Arizpe 1977; Tiano 1984). The typical work pattern of women in many developing countries involves participation in the formal sector in their late teens or early twenties, withdrawal from the labor force with marriage, and a return to the labor force – typically in the informal sector – in later life cycle stages (Tiano 1984).[8] The marginalization perspective predicts that the degree of women's access to the formal sector prior to marriage (albeit mainly in low-paying manufacturing jobs) increases with each new cohort, but that the degree of married women's mobility into formal sector employment does not necessarily show any relationship to cohort.

Formal sector workers and wages

Finally, it is clear that modernization theorists expect to find that formal sector employment is "better" than informal sector employment in terms of paying higher wages and providing better working conditions. It also predicts that women with greater resources (education and work experience) will be more likely than others to participate in the labor force per se, particularly in the formal sector.

This is consistent with early arguments by scholars of industrial development, who viewed the informal sector as a transitory phenomenon in peripheral economies. As a consequence of the imperfect penetration of capital markets, these scholars believed the informal sector would gradually shrink as development proceeded. However, more recent empirical studies have shown that the informal sector is not simply an abnormality of underdevelopment. Rather, it is a direct outcome of the very process of capitalist development (Castells and Portes 1989; Portes 1985; Portes and Benton 1984; Portes and Sassen-Koob 1987; Portes and Walton 1981). Although earnings of workers in the informal sector are generally lower than those of workers in the formal sector (Aronson 1991), this is not the case in all countries (e.g., see Blau (1985) on Malaysia; House (1984) on Kenya; Marcouiller *et al.* (1997) on Mexico; Smart (1990) on Hong Kong; Teilhet-Waldorf and Waldorf (1983) on Thailand; Yamada (1996) on

Peru). Some studies suggest that informal sector employment is a strategic choice of individuals. For example, Blau (1985) finds that self-employment in Malaysia is positively associated with managerial ability. Similarly, in Hong Kong, street vending is sometimes perceived to be a better choice than low-paying wage employment in terms of earnings and long-term chances for upward mobility (Smart 1990).

Much of the theoretical and empirical work on the informal sector does not take gender into account (Ward 1990), but women tend to be over-represented in the informal sector in most countries and to hold lower-status jobs in that sector than do men.[9] Some studies have found that the earnings differential between workers in the formal and informal sectors is greater for women than for men (Aronson 1991; ICRW 1980a). Furthermore, some empirical work has shown that informal sector employment is often a transitional state for male workers as they shift from agriculture to the modern sector, thus representing upward mobility. By contrast, mobility out of the informal sector is much less likely for women workers (Arizpe 1977; ICRW 1980b; Schmink 1986; Truelove 1987). Married women's work in the informal sector may also be viewed by their husbands as an extension of housework rather than as "work." It is thus unclear whether informal sector work provides women with increased power vis-à-vis men.[10]

Marginalization theorists typically assert that women's work in the informal sector is not highly valued in modern capitalist economies and is poorly rewarded. They argue that women's concentration in the informal sector is therefore an indicator of the degree of women's marginalization in the economy (Arizpe 1977; Ward 1984, 1988, 1990). That is, women enter the informal sector because their only choice is "creating their own demand out of desperation" (Arizpe 1977: 37), since employers' preferences for male workers limit the demand for female employment in the formal sector (Anker and Hein 1985). Conversely, the degree of women's involvement in the formal sector indicates women's integration into the economy. Therefore, marginalization theorists generally consider formal sector employment to be the main indicator of women's integration into the urban economy.

Marginalization theory also predicts that women with fewer, not more, human capital resources are more likely to be in the labor force, because their households require their earnings. On this point it diverges from modernization theory, which places emphasis on how economic development draws educated women into the labor force. However, given that women do engage in remunerative work, marginalization theory would predict that those with greater human capital are more likely to work in the formal sector where, as modernization theory would predict, jobs generate higher earnings than in the informal sector. On this point alone, the two theories converge.

Table 12.1 summarizes the expectations of modernization and margin-

Table 12.1 Predictions of two theoretical frameworks on women's incorporation into the South Korean urban economy

	Modernization (integration) theory	*Marginalization (developmentalist) theory*
Women's life-cycle labor force participation patterns	Become more continuous with increased industrialization	Remain discontinuous
Historical change in women's participation in formal sector employment	Married women as well as single women gain access to formal sector employment	Participation in formal sector is strongly limited to women's premarital life-cycle stage
Characteristics of women in the labor force vs. women out of the labor force	High human capital	Low human capital
Characteristics of women in the formal vs. informal sector	High human capital	High human capital
Income of women in the formal vs. informal sector	High	High

alization theories and provides a reference for our examination of the South Korean development experience.

Data and methods

We use data from the *Survey on Women's Labor Force Participation: Focus on Married Women,* collected by the Korean Women's Development Institute in 1985. This is a national random sample of ever-married women between the ages of fourteen and sixty-five years old. Each of the 4,316 respondents was asked in detail about their current work. In addition, questions were asked regarding work experience and the "major job" (job held for the longest period) in each of four life-cycle stages – from fourteen years old to marriage, from marriage to the birth of the first child, from the birth of the first to the birth of the last child, and after the birth of the last child. Since women were asked only about the major job they held in each life-cycle stage, we do not have a complete history of all of their jobs. Nonetheless, the cumulative duration of the major jobs comprises an average of 92 percent of these women's complete work histories. Therefore, we consider the information on major jobs to be representative of past work experiences.

We analyzed a subset of the sample. First, since we are interested in women's work opportunities in urban settings, we selected women who have lived in urban areas since they were fourteen years old. Second, we chose women between the ages of 30 and 54. Younger women were excluded because of potential selectivity problems related to their age at marriage, and older women were excluded because the impact of industrialization would be limited only to their later life-cycle stages. The final sample consisted of 1,065 women.

We carried out a number of descriptive and causal analyses in order to test the hypotheses derived from the two theoretical perspectives on women and development. Our first task was to look at the life-cycle patterns of economic participation for successive cohorts of women to see what has and has not changed over time in terms of "retirement" from the labor force due to marriage or childbearing. We then examined cohort patterns of entering the labor force and specifically the formal sector before marriage and after marriage, and considered what characteristics of women predict these patterns. Third, we assessed whether more highly educated women tend to participate in the formal rather than the informal sector, as the optimistic modernization theory would predict. Fourth, we considered whether our results indicated that the formal sector was "better" for South Korean women in terms of earnings than the informal sector.

Life-cycle labor force participation patterns

Table 12.2 shows the most common life-cycle patterns of economic participation for women in different cohorts.[11] The oldest cohort (aged fifty to fifty-four in 1985) consists of women born between 1931 and 1935, who would have begun work at a time well before the high economic growth period. By the time the second-youngest cohort, born between 1946 and 1950, reached their mid-teens, economic growth was on the upswing. As Table 12.2 shows, the proportion of women in each cohort who have never worked in the economy *declined* slightly throughout the twenty-five-year period represented by the five cohorts, from close to 20 percent in the oldest cohort to 15 percent in the youngest. But the proportion who worked continuously from before marriage through their childrearing years and beyond also declines across these cohorts from about 15 percent of women to 9 percent. This shows that continuous participation in the work force, whether in the formal or informal sector or both, is not at all the typical pattern for South Korean women and in fact became slightly less common during the high economic growth years. Together the two "extreme" work patterns – never worked and continuously worked – are typical of between a quarter to one-third of each cohort.

The most common pattern of work shifted across the five cohorts from being a pattern of working only after the last child was born – over 20 percent of women in the oldest cohort – to being a pattern of working until marriage and not returning to the labor force after that. This latter pattern reached a high of 27 percent in the youngest cohort; it was

Table 12.2 Life-cycle labor force participation patterns: five cohorts of South Korean women

	Birth cohort				
	1931–1935	*1936–1940*	*1941–1945*	*1946–1950*	*1951–1955*
	Age in 1985				
	50–54	*45–49*	*40–44*	*35–39*	*30–34*
Percentage who:					
Never worked	19.8	15.7	17.8	13.3	15.0
Worked continuously	14.6	13.0	11.4	11.9	9.0
Worked before marriage, left LF after marriage	4.7	7.8	14.9	23.5	26.9
Worked before marriage, left LF after marriage, re-entered after birth of last child	9.4	14.3	14.2	17.8	19.9
Worked before marriage, left LF between birth of first and last child, then re-entered LF	1.0	0.0	2.5	1.7	1.7
Worked only after birth of last child	21.4	22.6	22.8	14.4	13.6
Other patterns (including not working before marriage but working at some point after marriage)	29.1	26.6	16.4	17.4	13.9
Total	100.0	100.0	100.0	100.0	100.0

Notes

Percentages are based on the number of women in each cohort; total sample size is 1,065.

LF: Labor Force.

extremely unusual for older women (only 5 percent demonstrated this pattern) but has become the modal one for young women. Of course, it is possible that these young women will re-enter the labor force once they finish childbearing, which would move them out of the modal category and into the second most popular pattern, non-labor force activity for a period after marriage and childrearing and re-entry to the labor force after one's last child is born. This would mean that the pattern of temporary "retirement" from the labor force during the heavy childrearing years would become even more common, continuing the trend seen across cohorts in Table 12.2. Even so, the "modern" Western pattern of continuous labor force participation remains less common among younger than among older women, and is much less common than any of the other major patterns: never working, working only before marriage, working before marriage and again after the birth of the last child, working up until the birth of the first child and again after the birth of the last child, or working only after the last child is born.

These results do not support the modernization perspective's prediction of the increasing commonality of women's continuous labor force participation across the life cycle. Instead, they accord with marginalization theorists' expectation that discontinuous life-cycle patterns of work will dominate women's lives.

Movement between the formal and informal sectors

We use event-history methods to analyze the factors that affect women's movement into and out of the labor force at different points in their life cycle as well as their shifts between the formal and informal sectors. The dependent variable is the instantaneous rate of transition between states, which may be regarded as a function of duration in the state and of population heterogeneity.[12] The models for women's work before as well as after marriage examine women's entry into the labor force and into the formal sector upon completion of schooling as a function of duration in states and a number of other explanatory variables.[13]

Compared with conventional cross-sectional analyses, event-history methods allow us to capture the dynamics of a process occurring over time (Blossfeld *et al.* 1989). In our analyses, we also use cohort variables to indicate historical change. Cohort is a major concept in the analysis of social change (Elder 1974; Glen 1977; Ryder 1965), since "cohorts are most sharply differentiated in the course of rapid change, and represent a vehicle of social change to the extent that successive cohorts differ in life patterns" (Elder 1974: 169). But cohort is often confounded with other factors such as life-cycle stage or age. By applying event-history methods, we can control for factors confounded with cohort. For example, in the analyses of women's work before marriage, cohort is likely to be confounded with the length of the interval women are exposed to the "risk" of entry into the economy.[14] We control for such confusion by specifying the rate of movement as a function of the duration in states as well as other explanatory variables. Similarly, in the analyses of married women's entry into work, our analyses control for confounded age and cohort effects.

The informal sector includes "all those work situations characterized by the absence of clear separation between capital and labor, a contractual relationship between both, and a labor force that is paid wages and whose conditions of work and pay are legally regulated" (Portes and Sassen-Koob 1987: 31). Although this definition is conceptually clear, empirical analyses are usually confronted with limited information to measure sector at the detailed level. Variables often used to measure sector include detailed employment status and the size of enterprise (ILO 1972; Portes and Sassen-Koob 1987). Employment status is the most convenient and commonly used way of measuring informal sector participation, and we adopt this approach in examining women's work before marriage. We categorize paid employees into the formal sector, while others (employers, self-employed, and family-enterprise workers) are classified into the informal sector.[15]

Defining sector based only on employment status poses more serious limitations in examining women's work after marriage. In South Korea, some married women employees who engaged in production work during industrialization carried out these activities in their own homes, reporting regularly to an employer.[16] Although these home-based production workers received remuneration from their employers, the mode of their employment resembles that of informal sector labor: unprotected and unregulated. Therefore, in examining women's work after marriage, we included these home-based workers in the informal sector.[17]

We use four types of explanatory variables in the analysis of women's work before and after marriage. First, cohort measures the extent of historical change in women's participation. Second, women's resources are measured by educational attainment level and, in the analyses for post-marital work, women's work experiences before marriage. Both education and prior labor force experience are strong predictors of women's labor force participation in industrialized countries (Goldin 1990). The relationship between education and married women's labor force participation has been shown to be more complex during the process of industrialization (Goldin 1995; Ram 1980; Standing 1976, 1978) and our results below support those from other studies on South Korea that demonstrate this (Brinton *et al.* 1995; Kim 1990). We measured work experience in two ways: whether women worked in the formal sector, informal sector, or did not work at all; and the occupations in which women worked (versus not working). We ran separate models to include these two ways of measuring work experience, because employment status (formal or informal sector employment) and occupation are highly correlated with each other. We included age at marriage as a control variable, because it has been found in other studies to have a significant effect upon the pattern of women's employment after marriage.[18] This effect is often interpreted to stem from differences in the amount of women's resources (such as education) that are related to marriage age.[19]

The third group of variables measures the socioeconomic status of a woman's family. This includes the educational attainment of a woman's father and mother (in the analyses for women's work before marriage) and husband's education (in the analyses of women's work after marriage). From the integration or modernization perspective, parents' education should have a positive effect on women's entry into both the labor force and the formal sector before marriage. This occurs not only through its effect upon women's educational attainment level but also through its effect upon women's age at marriage,[20] which is related to a longer interval prior to marriage, when women are most available to engage in economic activities. By contrast, marginalization theory would predict that single women with less well-educated parents enter the labor force at a faster rate than those who can afford to stay out. However, parents' education is likely to have a positive effect on a single woman's entry into the formal sector given that she has entered the labor force at all. As for the socioeconomic resources of married women, husbands' income has been found generally to have a negative effect on wives' economic participation, and this effect is often particularly strong during the process of economic development (Goldin 1995). The marginalization thesis would be consistent with this finding, since it predicts that women with the least rather than the most resources are in the labor force and also that they would be relegated to the informal sector. The modernization perspective does not clearly predict what effect husbands' income may have on women's entry into work following marriage.[21]

In addition to all of these variables that measure a woman's characteristics and circumstances, we also include variables that measure the characteristics of her residential location: the size of the labor force (population aged fourteen and over) and the percentage of the labor force in manufacturing within the city. By accounting for differences in the local labor market, these variables are used to control for differences in the amount of labor demand, especially in manufacturing (Finegan 1975; Waite 1980).[22]

Results

Tables 12.3 and 12.4 show the results of our analyses on Korean women's entry into the economy before and after marriage. Holding constant across cohorts the characteristics such as education, women in successively younger cohorts are more likely to work prior to marriage and to be in the formal sector (Table 12.3).

These cohort effects are statistically significant for the youngest cohorts. In addition, the processes of single women's entry into the labor force and

Table 12.3 Estimates of models for South Korean urban women's work prior to marriage

	Entry into labor force		*Entry into formal sector*	
Age cohort				
30–34	0.91**	(0.19)[a]	0.81**	(0.27)
35–39	0.74**	(0.19)	0.48	(0.28)
40–44	0.33	(0.20)	0.59*	(0.29)
45–49	−0.09	(0.22)	0.19	(0.34)
50–54	–		–	
Education				
Less than middle school	–		–	
Middle school	0.03	(0.12)	0.76*	(0.16)
Vocational high school	0.71**	(0.18)	1.43**	(0.22)
Academic high school	0.65**	(0.15)	1.18**	(0.18)
Some college or more	1.05**	(0.21)	1.78**	(0.23)
Father's education				
Less than primary school	–		–	
Primary school	0.12	(0.12)	0.02	(0.15)
Middle school	0.25	(0.17)	−0.05	(0.19)
High school	−0.01	(0.19)	0.15	(0.21)
Some college or more	0.24	(0.24)	0.06	(0.25)
Mother's education				
Less than primary school	–		–	
Primary school	−0.07	(0.13)	0.02	(0.15)
Middle school	−0.30	(0.23)	−0.14	(0.25)
High school or more	0.07	(0.23)	0.06	(0.24)
City size	0.02	(0.06)	0.02	(0.08)
Manufacturing as percent of city labor force	1.78**	(0.65)	0.43	(0.83)
Chi-square	159.960		146.791	
d.f.	17		7	
N	956		493	

Notes

a Numbers in parentheses are standard errors.

* $p<0.05$; ** $p<0.01$.

into the formal sector are similar. Women with more education show a faster rate of both types of move. The major difference is that city industrial structure has a strong effect upon women's entry into the labor force, while it has no significant effect upon their conditional entry into the formal sector. Controlling for women's education, the educational attainment level of women's parents has no significant effect in either model.

For married women as well, once a number of variables are controlled, the youngest cohorts are more likely to work after marriage than are the older cohorts (Table 12.4).

Table 12.4 Estimates of models for South Korean urban women's work after marriage

	Entry into labor force		*Entry into formal sector*	
	Model 1	*Model 2*	*Model 1*	*Model 2*
Age cohort				
30–34	1.13** (0.17)[a]	1.13** (0.17)	2.94** (0.35)	2.97** (0.35)
35–39	0.81** (0.17)	0.78** (0.17)	2.19** (0.33)	2.20** (0.33)
40–44	0.32 (0.17)	0.31 (0.17)	1.41** (0.32)	1.42** (0.32)
45–49	0.26 (0.16)	0.25 (0.16)	0.33 (0.31)	0.34 (0.31)
50–54	–	–	–	–
Education				
Less than middle school	–	–	–	–
Middle school	−0.20 (0.11)	−0.20 (0.12)	−0.12 (0.19)	−0.12 (0.19)
Vocational high school	−0.49* (0.23)	−0.34 (0.24)	−0.68 (0.42)	−0.73 (0.46)
Academic high school	−0.50** (0.17)	−0.44* (0.18)	0.22 (0.25)	0.21 (0.27)
Some college or more	0.03 (0.27)	0.09 (0.29)	0.71 (0.38)	0.74 (0.41)
Employment status prior to marriage				
No work	–	–	–	–
Worked in formal sector	0.11 (0.11)	–	0.48* (0.16)	–
Worked in informal sector	0.06 (0.12)	–	0.12 (0.20)	–
Occupation prior to marriage				
No work	–	–	–	–
Agriculture	–	0.08 (0.13)	–	0.15 (0.21)
Production	–	0.15 (0.12)	–	0.48* (0.18)
Sales or service	–	0.24 (0.20)	–	0.25 (0.33)
Clerical	–	−0.25 (0.19)	–	0.52 (0.32)
Professional	–	0.35 (0.26)	–	0.32 (0.38)

Husbands' education								
Less than middle school	–		–		–		–	
Middle school	−0.09	(0.12)	−0.09	(0.12)	−0.37	(0.20)	−0.38	(0.20)
High school	−0.26*	(0.12)	−0.27*	(0.12)	−0.23	(0.20)	−0.22	(0.20)
Some college or more	−0.87**	(0.22)	−0.84**	(0.22)	−0.79*	(0.35)	−0.79*	(0.36)
Age at marriage	0.06**	(0.02)	0.06**	(0.02)	0.10**	(0.03)	0.10**	(0.03)
City size	−0.02	(0.05)	−0.02	(0.05)	0.22*	(0.09)	0.23*	(0.09)
Manufacturing as percent of city labor force	0.30	(0.56)	0.27	(0.56)	0.25	(0.99)	0.25	(1.00)
Chi-square	130.606		136.734		173.563		172.957	
d.f.	16		19		16		19	
N	945		945		580		580	

Notes

a Numbers in parentheses are standard errors.

* $p<0.05$; ** $p<0.01$.

This may seem contradictory to the finding in Table 12.2 that a greater percentage of younger than older women left the labor force after marriage and have not returned. The apparent contradiction may be explained in the following way: As Table 12.4 shows, women with more education, at least up to the level of academic high school, are less likely than others to be employed after marriage. Educational levels of Korean women have risen extremely rapidly across the period we are considering (Brinton and Lee 2001; Ministry of Education, Korea 1995), so the youngest cohorts are much better educated than the older ones. Given the negative association between high school education and labor force participation for married women shown in Table 12.4, when the educational composition of different cohorts is held constant, younger cohorts show a higher propensity for post-marital labor force participation. We note that it is striking that high school education has this negative relationship with participation in the labor market for married women and also that women's work experience prior to marriage has no predictive effect on whether they will work following marriage; in short, it is not the case that married women with the most human capital and with work experience prior to marriage are the ones most likely to work following marriage, as modernization theory would have had us believe. In addition, the dampening effect of husbands' income on married women's work is strong, showing that women married to high-earning husbands are the least likely to be employed.

Given that a married woman is in the labor force, education does not have a clear predictive effect on whether she will be in the formal versus the informal sector. Women's prior work experience does have an effect: women who worked in the formal sector prior to marriage and specifically in production (manufacturing) jobs are more likely than other women to be in the formal sector if they are working at all following marriage. As with entry into the labor force, the more highly educated a woman's husband, the less likely she is to be employed in the formal sector. In addition, city size shows a significant positive effect on married women's conditional entry into the formal sector.

In sum, there are some major differences in the factors that affect single and married women's entry into the economy. Most importantly, while single women with higher education enter the labor force and the formal sector at a faster rate than less well-educated women, this is not the case for married women. In addition, while the socioeconomic status of a woman's family has no significant effect on single women's moves, once we control for women's own education, it has a significant negative effect on married women's entry into both the labor force and the formal sector. The effects of resources (women's own, and those of their husbands) therefore differ markedly for single and married women.

Overall, these results show mixed support for each theoretical framework. Modernization theory is supported by the analyses of single women's entry into the economy: younger cohorts of women as well as women with more education enter the labor force and the formal sector faster than others. However, results for married women's entry are much less consistent with modernization theory. Once we control for the different characteristics of cohorts, younger married women do move into the labor force and into the formal sector faster than older cohorts, as modernization theory would predict. However, contrary to the modernization perspective, a married woman's education, at least up to academic high school, has a negative rather than a positive effect upon her rate of movement into the labor force and has no significant effect upon her entry into the formal sector. The observed life-cycle variation and the effect of women's and husbands' education on married women's movement into the economy generally follow the marginalization argument, as less well-educated women with less well-educated husbands are the most likely to be in the labor force.

However, our results show one important contradiction to marginalization theory. This concerns the assumption that formal sector workers are a select group out of all women in the labor force. Our analyses show that married women workers in the formal sector are more or less representative of working women as a whole, with the proviso that women who have prior work experience in manufacturing and who reside in a larger city are more likely than others to be in the formal sector.

The similarities and differences between married women in the formal and informal sectors are further elucidated in Table 12.5, which shows the characteristics of currently working women in our sample. The human

Table 12.5 General characteristics of urban married women workers by sector

	Formal sector	*Informal sector*
Education		
Primary school	54.0%	48.0%
Middle school	24.6%	28.3%
Vocational high school	4.1%	7.5%
Academic high school	8.8%	11.4%
Some college	1.5%	0.5%
Junior college	2.3%	0.7%
University or more	4.7%	3.2%
Labor force experience (in months)	105.9	118.7
Job tenure (in months)	40.7	61.7
Age (in years)	39.5	38.9
Weekly work hours	58.4	60.2
Child under 6	21.7%	37.4%
Number of women	341	562

Note
Values other than percentages are means.

capital (education and labor force experience) of women in the two sectors is surprisingly similar. The educational distribution for formal sector workers is more polarized, with higher proportions of formal sector workers having either minimal or high educational attainment and higher proportions of informal sector workers having high school education. Workers' mean years of schooling are about the same in the two sectors (7.7 for those in the formal sector and 7.9 for those in the informal sector). Unlike in the United States where the self-employed tend to be older and to work more hours than wage workers, workers in the two sectors in urban South Korea are similar in age, and the difference in their weekly work hours is not notable. Informal sector workers have spent a longer time in their current job than have formal sector workers. More informal than formal sector workers have young children. Overall, we cannot conclude that married female informal sector workers are significantly less advantaged than formal sector workers in terms of human capital.

The absence of strong distinctions in the characteristics of married women who work in the two sectors leads us to question an assumption implicitly held by both theories: that the formal sector is "better" than the informal sector. Is this so in the context of South Korea?

The "good" formal sector and "bad" informal sector?

To measure whether women working in the formal sector are better-off than those in the informal sector, we look at earnings in the two sectors. Ideally one would also like to have respondents' own self-evaluation of the job as well as information on job stability, safety, and benefits. We recognize that earnings by themselves are not sufficient to evaluate the "goodness" of one's employment. But they nevertheless provide a measure of the overall standing of one's occupation in the economy and a measure of the economic resources women gain from working. Moreover, our data provide an unusual opportunity to compare women's earnings in formal and informal sector employment, as most surveys do not ask about informal sector earnings.

Table 12.6 compares the monthly earnings of married women currently working in each sector, with the informal sector including employers and self-employed, family enterprise workers, and home-based employees. Surprisingly, informal sector workers have significantly *higher* average monthly earnings than do workers in the formal sector ($t=3.28$, $df=882$). Earnings of workers in the informal sector also show a much larger variance than do earnings of formal sector workers. Calculating the 75th, 50th, and 25th percentiles for each sector, it is clear that the women in the top quartile of the earnings distribution in the informal sector dominate in producing the relatively higher mean for workers' monthly earnings in that sector. This may be seen also by the fact that if we take the natural log of

Table 12.6 Monthly earnings of urban married women workers by sector

	Formal sector	*Informal sector*
Mean	163,905	195,427
Standard deviation	110,642	174,680
75th percentile	200,000	250,000
50th percentile	140,000	150,000
25th percentile	100,000	80,000
Distribution		
Less than 100,000	31.9%	36.1%
110,000–200,000	48.4%	33.2%
210,000–300,000	13.4%	16.4%
310,000–500,000	4.5%	10.2%
510,000–800,000	1.5%	2.9%
More than 810,000	0.3%	1.3%
Mean of logged earnings	11.81	11.76
Standard deviation of logged earnings	0.69	1.03
Number of women	335	549

Note
Unit is Korean wŏn (in 1985).

earnings (thereby bringing in the "tails" of the earnings distribution), mean earnings are statistically indistinguishable between formal and informal sector workers (t = 0.78, df = 882).

Of course, the earnings of workers in the two sectors are not directly comparable to each other in a strict sense, because the earnings of non-wage workers include non-labor returns (returns to capital) as well as labor returns. Our data include a question on the amount of capital used to start the business in the case of employers and the self-employed. In the extreme case where women reported no capital (N = 31), their monthly earnings (211,282 won) were still significantly higher than the mean for women working in the formal sector (163,905 won). This provides some assurance that our results regarding the relative economic standing of formal and informal sector workers are valid.

In sum, our findings generally contradict the argument made by both modernization and marginalization theory that the informal sector consists of workers with the lowest socioeconomic status, waiting to enter the formal sector. Married urban female South Korean workers of various socioeconomic statuses are located in the informal sector; they cannot be considered more "marginal" than married women who work in formal sector jobs. They are more likely to be high school graduates, to have somewhat longer labor force experience, and to have worked in their jobs for longer periods than women in formal sector jobs. Further, their monthly earnings are not lower on average than those of formal sector workers. In fact, married women in the top quartile of the informal sector earnings distribution earn considerably more than comparable formal sector workers.

Does formal sector employment appear similarly unprofitable or, to put it more positively, does informal sector employment appear similarly lucrative, for single Korean women as for married women? Additional descriptive analyses shed light on what formal and informal sector employment means for single vs. married women. Since earnings data are not available for jobs held in previous life-cycle stages by the women in our sample, we approximated earnings based upon occupational information from previous life-cycle stages. We did this by combining information from the 1985 Occupational Wage Survey and our data.[23] Using the approximated occupational wage rate, the mean monthly earnings of women who worked in the formal sector before marriage were 206,342 wŏn, while the earnings of women who worked in the informal sector before marriage was 193,328 won. Not only are the mean monthly earnings of women who worked in the formal sector prior to marriage higher than those of women who worked in the informal sector, they are higher than those of married women in either sector. Furthermore, the greater earnings for single women in the formal sector contrast with our finding of greater earnings for married women in the informal sector. This does not mean that the earnings potential in the informal sector is good in absolute terms for married women; rather, it indicates that married women working in the formal sector have very low earnings. It is not an exaggeration to say that in the mid-1980s following two decades of high economic growth, the formal sector was "better" in earnings terms than the informal sector for single but not for married women. Married women could achieve the same earnings on average in the informal as in the formal sector, and some married women could achieve significantly more than they could in the formal sector.

Table 12.7 sheds further light on the differences in work experiences of single and married women in the formal sector. The top half of the table shows the occupational distribution of women who worked in the formal sector prior to marriage, by birth cohort. The bottom half of the table shows the occupational distribution for married women in the formal sector, also by birth cohort. While almost half of all women who worked in the formal sector prior to marriage were either in professional or clerical occupations, this goes down to just 8 percent for women working in the formal sector following marriage.[24] Instead, many more women work in sales or service occupations following marriage. (We did not include the administrative/managerial category due to the simple – and, we feel, highly significant – fact that no women reported having worked in these occupations either prior to or following marriage).

We note that the "marriage bar" in white-collar occupations in South Korea was extremely strong during the 1970s and 1980s. A survey of 150

Table 12.7 Distribution of occupations among urban women working in the formal sector prior to and after marriage (%)

(a) Occupational distribution of women working prior to marriage

		Birth cohort				
		1931–1935	*1936–1940*	*1941–1945*	*1946–1950*	*1951–1955*
		Age in 1985				
		50–54	*45–49*	*40–44*	*35–39*	*30–34*
Occupation						
Professional	11.5	37.5	9.1	10.2	13.5	8.8
Clerical	32.4	18.8	13.6	32.2	27.1	39.2
Sales or services	10.4	6.3	13.6	3.4	13.5	11.1
Agriculture	0.3	6.3	–	–	–	–
Production	45.3	31.3	63.6	54.2	45.8	40.9
Total	100.0	100.0	100.0	100.0	100.0	100.0

(b) Occupational distribution of women working after marriage

		Birth cohort				
		1931–1935	*1936–1940*	*1941–1945*	*1946–1950*	*1951–1955*
		Age in 1985				
		50–54	*45–49*	*40–44*	*35–39*	*30–34*
Occupation						
Professional	3.9	–	6.2	3.8	5.2	3.1
Clerical	2.6	4.8	–	1.9	1.7	4.6
Sales or services	40.2	38.1	56.2	37.7	46.6	29.2
Agriculture	8.7	14.3	3.1	11.3	8.6	7.7
Production	44.5	42.9	34.4	45.3	37.9	55.4
Total	100.0	100.0	100.0	100.0	100.0	100.0

public offices and large companies in Seoul in the early 1980s showed that 73 percent of personnel officers required women to be single if they were hired into clerical work, and 51 percent had this requirement for professional occupations as well. (Obviously this restriction on marital status did not apply to male workers: just 2 percent of clerical positions and 3 percent of professional positions had a marital status requirement for men; see KWDI 1983). Discrimination against women in white-collar occupations has occurred not only in hiring but throughout the life cycle, as few female workers in white-collar occupations have received equivalent on-the-job training and promotional opportunities to males (KWDI 1983). Therefore, even if women do find employment in white-collar occupations, the probability of building a career is low unless they are in one of a select number of professional occupations such as education, pharmacology, or nursing.[25]

Given this context, it makes sense that working in one's own business or in a family business has been a strategic choice for many married women, especially in the years covered by our micro-level data. Jobs in the manufacturing sector not only have low earnings for women but also carry low social status, whereas self-employment may permit more autonomy and flexibility. Moreover, although the financial risks may be high, our results demonstrate that some types of self-employment bring women higher earnings than they would achieve in the formal sector. Even among home-based employees, many women may prefer to continue their work rather than find employment in the formal sector. Earnings for this group are lower than in the formal sector, but working in one's own home is especially convenient for married women with young children, particularly given long commuting times in a city such as Seoul. In a survey of home-based married female workers in Seoul, 77 percent said they took their job because it allowed them to easily combine earnings activities with housework. About 70 percent of women had no intention of changing jobs, and about half of these women cited the advantage of coordinating earnings activities and housework as the major reason (KWDI, 1989).

Discussion

We have shown that urban women's life-cycle patterns of labor force participation changed surprisingly little across the first twenty-five years of rapid economic growth in South Korea. Very few women worked continuously throughout marriage and childrearing; the majority left the labor force around the time of marriage, and many re-entered at some later point in their lives. South Korea has continued to share this "M-shaped" life-cycle pattern of female labor force participation into the twenty-first century with only one other country in East Asia: Japan (Brinton 2001; Brinton *et al.* 1995). This pattern is more in accord with the marginalization perspective on women's work than with modernization theory, particularly given the nature of the work married women engage in if they do return to the labor force.

Our study shows that women's access to formal sector employment did increase for younger cohorts of women during South Korea's rapid industrialization, and that this happened for both single and married women. This supports the tenets of modernization theory. The more education a woman has, the more likely she is to be in the labor force prior to marriage and to be in the formal sector. The expanded formal sector opportunities for single women have been generated mainly in white-collar occupations, especially clerical work. These results are consistent with both of the theoretical perspectives we have discussed in this chapter.

However, we have found important differences between the characteristics of single and married employed women in the Korean formal sector that are not predicted by either modernization or marginalization theory. Married women with at least a high school education have been less likely to participate in the labor force than those with less education, and through 1985 those with a college education were no more likely to work than elementary school graduates. This is consistent with the marginalization perspective. However, contrary to both the modernization and marginalization frameworks, given that married women do work, it has not been the more educated women who have greatest access to the formal sector, nor has it been the case that the formal sector is "better" in terms of income generation. Our empirical results show that whether married women work in the formal or informal sector cannot be predicted from their educational level. The increased employment of married women in the formal sector over time has come mainly from the expansion of jobs in sales, services, and manufacturing, all of which provide lower earnings than white-collar work. As a result, the average earnings of married women working in the formal sector are lower than those working in the informal sector. The reverse is true for single women, whose increased participation in formal sector work has allowed them to generate higher earnings on average than they could in the informal sector.

These results show that women's absorption into the South Korean urban economy has been complicated, especially given the continued size of the informal economy, the diversity of types of work within it, and the barriers to married women's participation in white-collar work in the formal economy except for a few professions. As we mentioned in teasing out predictions from modernization and marginalization theories, careful examination of how historical cohort, women's own education and work experience, and life-cycle stage interact has not been developed in most studies on women and development, although some studies have nevertheless hinted at these complexities.[26] Using data on several cohorts of South Korean women and looking at their work experience across the stages of being single and married, we have demonstrated how critical it is for studies on women and economic development to make specific predictions about how the expansion of the economy and the particular development of the formal and informal sectors may affect women differentially at different life-cycle stages and with different amounts of human capital.

Both the modernization and marginalization perspectives also assume that women's informal sector labor is marginal and that formal sector employment is "better." Our results suggest that for South Korean married women, wage employment as a whole has not necessarily been better than other forms of employment, at least in terms of earnings. There exists a great deal of heterogeneity in the informal sector, which we alluded to by pointing out the wide variance in married women's earnings there.[27] An earlier study of married women's "informal earning activities" in Seoul found that lower-class women in this sector tend to be engaged in daily labor, while women in the middle class usually generate earnings in sales (mostly in self-employment), and women in the upper class often engage in "invisible jobs" such as money lending, real estate speculation, commodity speculation, and other opportunistic economic activities (Moon 1982).[28] This has been reported in other studies as well (Kim 1992). Managing tutorial or educational services is yet another way for highly educated Korean women to earn money in the informal sector, given the extreme educational competition in Korea and the large market for tutoring and exam-preparation services.

The invisibility of some income-generating activities of upper-class or upper-middle-class women means that some opportunities are not likely to be captured in our data, or in fact in any other dataset that collects earnings information based upon employment per se. Therefore, we can speculate that the mean earnings for our sample of informal sector married women might well increase if we could include all the "invisible jobs" carried out by relatively high-status married women.[29] This would widen even more the difference between married women's mean earnings in the informal and formal sectors.

In closing, we see strong indications in the Korean experience of the "status frustration" effect mentioned in some studies of the association between married women's education and labor force participation in industrializing societies (Goldin 1995; Standing 1976). Middle-class married women with higher education may experience considerable frustration and discouragement if their opportunities for wage employment in the white-collar sector are not commensurate with their educational qualifications. If employment discrimination means that the possibility of continuous employment in the formal sector is highest in low-wage, low-status jobs, many women may prefer to exit the labor force or to participate in informal sector activities that allow them to reap higher earnings. Our findings from survey data through the mid-1980s together with the current trends which we outlined at the beginning of this chapter suggest that the implications of these patterns for women's well-being and for the health of the economy remain important questions for South Korea in the early twenty-first century.

Notes

1 Among all OECD countries only Japan shows a comparable rate, at 34 percent.

2 We use the terms "modernization theory" and "integration theory" interchangeably in this chapter.

3 By setting out these two perspectives we do not mean to ignore the literature on changes in the level of female labor force participation itself during the process of economic development. Female labor force participation typically declines in the early stages of development with the shift in the locus of pro-

duction from the household to manufacturing establishments, and only later does it rise as women's educational attainment increases and the service sector expands (Durand 1975; Goldin 1995). Our focus is on how women are incorporated into the urban economy, and particularly into the formal sector, with economic development. We also note that in this chapter we do not distinguish the marginalization thesis from the exploitation perspective, which is slightly different and focuses more on the nexus between the patriarchal nuclear family and the labor demands of capitalism.

4 Comparable figures for other industrial economies range from 2.2 percent for the United Kingdom, 2.3 percent for the U.S., 3.3 percent for Germany, and 3.9 percent for France (ILO 1984).

5 For example, the contribution of exports to Korea's GNP increased from 18 percent in 1961 to 65 percent in 1983 (Mitchell 1988).

6 What has made this more prominent is the low degree of labor absorption by the leading industries, especially since the mid-1970s. During the early stage of industrialization, the fastest growing industries were labor-intensive, such as the electronics and garment industries, but since 1973, the focus of industrial development has been on capital-intensive heavy industries, which tend to have a relatively low degree of labor absorption.

7 Greece, Poland, Portugal, and Turkey also have relatively sizable proportions of the labor force engaged as family enterprise workers or as self-employed workers.

8 The life-cycle effect is also reflected in the aggregate statistics on Third World women's age-specific labor force participation rates. In most nations, the rates are the highest among women aged fifteen to twenty-four years, drop among women in the twenty-five- to thirty-four-year age group, and remain stable among older age groups (Tiano 1984, 1987). Since most informal activities are excluded in these data, the observed age-specific participation rates reflect the degree of formal sector involvement for different age groups of women. However, with such cross-sectional data, it is difficult to interpret how much of the observed age pattern stems solely from the life-cycle effect. We need longitudinal data on several different cohorts of women in order to disentangle life cycle and age effects.

9 For example, women in several Central/South American countries make up between 46 to 70 percent of the informal sector, while their representation in the formal sector is only around 20 percent (ICRW 1980b).

10 See the interesting discussion by Lu (2001) about wives of small business owners in Taiwan.

11 Given that women were asked about work in four life-cycle stages, altogether there are sixteen possible life-cycle patterns of work. We include in the table the six most common patterns, and group others into an "other" category.

12 Since our interest is in estimating the effect of explanatory variables on these rates rather than in modeling the form of duration dependence, we choose a non-parametric specification of duration dependence, the so-called Cox proportional hazards model (1972). The model specifies the rate as $r(t) = h(t)\exp(b_1X_1 + S + b_kX_k)$ where the X's are exogenous variables of interest, the b's are coefficients estimating the effects of these variables, and h(t) is an unknown nuisance function affecting every sample member in the same way.

13 Excluded in these analyses are those who completed schooling after marriage ($N = 17$) and those who started working before completion of schooling ($N = 56$). The sample for the analyses of work entry after marriage includes women who were not working at the time of marriage. This is 983 women, or 94 percent of our sample. Although 55 percent of women in the sample worked before marriage, the majority of them left the job before or at

marriage. Of the 574 women who worked before marriage, only seven were engaged in the same job at the time of the survey; 174 women left their job before marriage, 335 left with marriage, and fifty-eight left after marriage.

14 This is due to the fact that there is a linear relationship between cohort and age at marriage, and the latter determines the length of the interval. Mean age at marriage for Korean women increased from 21.6 in 1960 to 25.5 in 1990 (National Statistical Office, Population and Housing Census 1990).

15 In our data, 3.5 percent of women who were in the labor force at the time of the survey (twenty-six out of 748) classified themselves as employers. Thirteen of them had one employee, eight had two employees, four had three employees, and two had four employees. Only one of twenty-six employers had more than five employees.

16 In our data, 26 percent of the women who were working as employees at the time of the survey worked in their own homes.

17 The variable specifying place of work is available only for the current job. We impute place of employment for each job in women's work history by making a judgment based on occupation, using the information on women's work at the time of the survey. For each three-digit occupational category we looked at the distribution of employees who work in their own home. If this is more than 50 percent, we classify women in that occupation as being in the informal sector.

18 We measure age at marriage as a continuous variable in the analysis of women's work prior to marriage. In the analysis of women's work following marriage, however, age at marriage is the beginning time when women enter the risk set for the specific event. Therefore, we measure it with three categories instead of as a continuous variable, in order to avoid the problem of collinearity.

19 Early marriers are characterized by their own lower educational attainment as well as that of their husbands. The relatively low level of early marriers' resources pushes them to enter the labor force following marriage. Accordingly, they not only have a higher overall probability of entering the labor force following marriage but they enter the labor force at a faster rate than others (Elder and Rockwell 1976; Sorensen 1983).

20 Parents' education generally has a positive relationship to women's age at marriage (Elder and Rockwell 1974; Michael and Tuma 1985).

21 Of course, labor economists have established the negative effect that husbands' income generally has on married women's labor supply (Bowen and Finegan 1969; Mincer 1962; Smith 1980). If the husband's education is highly correlated with income, it will also have a negative effect. However, it is not clear to us what prediction modernization theory would make about these relationships. We note that the information in our data on husbands' earnings is for the time of the survey rather than at the time of marriage. Men's education and earnings are highly correlated in Korea, so we use husband's education as a proxy for earnings.

22 The data for these variables come from the 1980 Population and Housing Census. We need to make two assumptions in order to use these locational variables. The city where respondents lived at the time of the survey is assumed to be where they have lived continuously, at least since the completion of their schooling. We checked the feasibility of this assumption by computing the proportion of a woman's age (in years) that she has lived in her current city of residence. The proportion is 92 percent. This high proportion comes from the fact that our sample includes only women who have lived in urban areas since they were fourteen years old. We also assume that the 1980 city-level characteristics have been constant over time. While this is obviously a strong assumption, our main interest is in the relative ordering of cities in terms of these values rather than the exact numbers. Using the 1970 Census, we computed the

correlation coefficients for these city-level variables between 1970 and 1980. The coefficient is 0.99 for labor force size and 0.89 for the percent of the labor force in manufacturing. Therefore, it is reasonable to assume that the variation among cities has been constant over time. We wished to include a variable on the percentage of females in the labor force. However, the correlation coefficient for this variable between 1970 and 1980 was only 0.14, making it difficult for us to assume that the variation among cities has been constant over time. Therefore, we do not include this variable in our analyses.

23 The annual Occupational Wage Survey in Korea reports the monthly earnings and yearly bonus for each three-digit occupational category. However, this survey is based only on employees who are in workplaces of ten or more employees. Therefore, we used our data to calculate the earnings for each employment status within occupational categories.

24 We note the unusually high percentage of older women (50 to 54) who report having been in professional occupations prior to marriage. This most likely appears high because it is relative to clerical work and to production; both of these latter sectors expanded in subsequent decades. Professional occupations for both the early and later cohorts shown in Table 12.7 are predominantly in teaching.

25 In an effort to promote the employment of married women with higher education, the government encouraged several large companies to hire married women into white-collar occupations in 1981. The three largest companies in Korea hired sixty married women, limiting the qualifications to those who worked in professional occupations prior to marriage. In a survey of the women who were hired, about half expected to experience a promotion, but only 13 percent answered that they expected to be promoted to a managerial position (Kwon 1986).

26 Tiano, for example, notes: "Employment may be more liberating for young, relatively well educated women than for their older, unskilled counterparts. Such factors as these may underlie the divergent predictions of the exploitation and integration theses about women in the new international division of labor" (1987: 41).

27 We did not have sufficient space to pursue this issue further here, but in other work we disentangle this heterogeneity through comparing the earnings of South Korean women who run their own businesses vs. those who work in family enterprises or as home-based employees (Choi *et al.* 1993).

28 Class in this study was defined by women's own education, husband's education and earnings, and household income.

29 Moreover, married women's education and earnings may both contribute to their class identity and that of their households even if women are not incorporated into the formal sector in the way that the two theoretical traditions we have considered here would consider necessary (Abelmann 1997; Kim 1992).

References

Abelmann, Nancy. 1997. "Women's Class Mobility and Identities in South Korea: A Gendered, Transnational, Narrative Approach." *The Journal of Asian Studies* 56 (2): 398–420.

Amsden, Alice. 1989. *Asia's Next Giant: South Korea and Late Industrialization.* New York: Oxford University Press.

Anker, R. and C. Hein. 1985. "Why Third World Urban Employers Usually Prefer Men." *International Labor Review* 124: 73–90.

Arizpe, Lourdes. 1977. "Women in the Informal Labor Sector: The Case of Mexico City," in The Wellesley Editorial Committee (ed.). *Women and National Development: The Complexities of Change.* Chicago, IL: The University of Chicago Press, pp. 25–37.

Aronson, Robert L. 1991. *Self-employment: A Labor Market Perspective.* Ithaca, NY: ILR Press.

Bai, Moo Ki and Woo Hyun Cho. 1995. *Women's Wages and Employment in Korea.* Seoul: Seoul National University Press.

——. 1996. "Women's Employment Structure and Male–Female Wage Differentials in Korea," in Susan Horton (ed.). *Women and Industrialization in Asia.* London: Routledge, pp. 165–206.

Blau, David M. 1985. "Self-employment and Self-selection in Developing Country Labor Markets." *Southern Economic Journal* 52: 351–363.

Blossfeld, Hans-Peter, Alfred Hamerle, and Karl Ulrich Mayer. 1989. *Event History Analysis.* Hillsdale, NJ: Lawrence Erlbaum Associates.

Boserup, Ester. 1970. *Women's Role in Economic Development.* New York: St. Martin's Press.

Bowen, W.G. and T.A. Finegan. 1969. *The Economics of Labor Force Participation.* Princeton, NJ: Princeton University Press.

Brinton, Mary C. 1993. *Women and the Economic Miracle: Gender and Work in Postwar Japan.* Berkeley: University of California Press.

——. 2001. "Married Women's Labor in East Asian Economies," in Mary C. Brinton (ed.). *Women's Working Lives in East Asia.* Stanford, CA: Stanford University Press, pp. 1–37.

Brinton, Mary C. and Sunhwa Lee. 2001. "Women's Education and the Labor Market in Japan and South Korea," in Mary C. Brinton (ed.). *Women's Working Lives in East Asia.* Stanford, CA: Stanford University Press, pp. 125–150.

Brinton, Mary C., Yean-Ju Lee, and William Parish. 1995. "Married Women's Work in Rapidly Industrializing Countries: Examples from East Asia." *American Journal of Sociology* 93 (1): 1099–1130.

Castells, Manuel and Alejandro Portes. 1989. "World Underneath: The Origin, Dynamics, and Effects of the Informal Economy," in Alejandro Portes, Manuel Castells, and Laureen A. Benton (eds). *The Informal Economy: Studies in Advanced and Less Developed Countries.* Baltimore, MD: The Johns Hopkins University Press, pp. 11–37.

Cheng, Lu-Lin and Gary Gereffi. 1994. "The Informal Economy in East Asian Development." *International Journal of Urban and Regional Research* 18 (2): 194–219.

Choi, Moonkyung, Mihye Roh, and Mary C. Brinton. 1993. "Earnings Attainment of Married Women Workers in Korea." Paper presented at the American Sociological Association Annual Meetings, Miami, August.

Cox, D.R. 1972. "Regression Models and Life Tables." *Journal of the Royal Statistical Society* B34: 187–220.

Cumings, Bruce. 1984. "The Origins of Development of the Northeastern Asian Political Economy: Industrial Sectors, Product Cycles, and Political Consequences." *International Organization* 38: 1–40.

Davis, Kingsley. 1984. "Wives and Work: The Sex Role Revolution and Its Consequences." *Population and Development Review* 10: 397–417.

Deyo, F.C. 1989. *Beneath the Miracle: Labor Subordination in the New Asian Industrialization.* Berkeley: University of California Press.

Durand, J. 1975. *The Labor Force in Economic Development: A Comparison of International Census Data, 1946–66.* Princeton, NJ: Princeton University Press.

Elder, Glen H. Jr. 1974. "Age Differentiation and the Life Course." *Annual Review of Sociology* 1: 165–190.

Elder, Glen H. Jr. and Richard C. Rockwell. 1976. "Marital Timing in Women's Life Patterns." *Journal of Family History* 1: 34–54.

Elliott, Carolyn M. 1977. "Theories of Development: An Assessment," in Wellesley Editorial Committee (ed.). *Women and National Development: The Complexities of Change.* Chicago, IL: The University of Chicago Press, pp. 1–8.

Finegan, Aldrich. 1975. "Participation of Women in the Labor Force," in Cynthia B. Lloyd (ed.). *Sex, Discrimination and the Division of Labor.* New York: Columbia University Press, pp. 27–60.

Genda, Yuji and Seung-Yeol Yee. 1998. "Korea: Wage Determination and Labor Turnover," in Toshiaki Tachibanaki (ed.). *Wage Differentials: An International Comparison.* New York: St. Martin's Press, pp. 72–107.

Glen, Norval D. 1977. *Cohort Analysis.* Beverly Hills, CA: Sage.

Goldin, Claudia. 1990. *Understanding the Gender Gap.* New York: Oxford University Press.

——. 1995. "The U-shaped Female Labor Force Function in Economic Development and Economic History," in T. Paul Schultz (ed.). *Investment in Women's Human Capital.* Chicago, IL: University of Chicago Press, pp. 61–90.

Goode, W. 1970. "Industrialization and Family Change," in B. Hoselitz and W. Moore (eds). *Industrialization and Society.* The Hague: Mouton, pp. 237–259.

Hamilton, Gary G. and Nicole Woolsey Biggart. 1988. "Market, Culture, and Authority: A Comparative Analysis of Management and Organization in the Far East." *American Journal of Sociology* 94: S52–S94.

Hamilton, Gary G, William Zeile, and Wan-Jin Kim. 1990. "The Network Structures of East Asian Economies," in S.R. Clegg and S.G. Redding (eds). *Capitalism in Contrasting Cultures.* Berlin: Walter de Gruyter, pp. 105–130.

House, William J. 1984. "Nairobi's Informal Sector: Dynamic Entrepreneurs or Surplus Labor?" *Economic Development and Cultural Change* 32: 277–302.

Inkeles, Alex and David Smith. 1974. *Becoming Modern.* Cambridge, MA: Harvard University Press.

International Center for Research on Women (ICRW). 1980a. *Keeping Women Out: A Structural Analysis of Women's Employment in Developing Countries.* Washington, DC: Agency for International Development.

——. 1980b. *The Productivity of Women in Developing Countries: Measurement Issues and Recommendations.* Washington, DC: Agency for International Development.

International Labor Office (ILO). 1972. *Employment, Incomes and Equality: A Strategy for Increasing Productive Employment in Kenya.* Geneva: ILO.

——. 1984. *World Labor Report.* Geneva: ILO.

Ito, Takatoshi and Kyoungsik Kang. 1989. "Bonuses, Overtime, and Employment: Korea vs. Japan." *Journal of the Japanese and International Economies* 3: 424–450.

Jackson, Robert Max. 1998. *Destined for Equality: The Inevitable Rise of Women's Status.* Cambridge, MA: Harvard University Press.

Jacobs, Norman. 1985. *The Korean Road to Modernization and Development.* Urbana: University of Illinois Press.

Jacquette, Jane S. 1982. "Women and Modernization Theory." *World Politics* 34: 267–284.

Kim, Dae-Il and Robert H. Topel. 1995. "Labor Markets and Economic Growth: Lessons from Korea's Industrialization, 1970–1990," in Richard B. Freeman and Lawrence F. Katz (eds). *Differences and Changes in Wage Structures*. Chicago, IL: The University of Chicago Press, pp. 227–264.

Kim, Kyung-Keun. 1990. "Schooling and Married Women's Work in a Developing Country: The Case of the Republic of Korea." Ph.D. dissertation, The University of Chicago.

Kim, Myung-hye. 1992. "Gender, Class, and Family in Late-industrializing South Korea." *Asian Journal of Women's Studies* 1: 58–86.

Koo, Hagen. 1985. "Transformation of the Korean Class Structure: The Impact of Dependent Development." *Research in Social Stratification and Mobility* 4: 129- 148.

Korean Economic Planning Board (KEPB). 1970, 1980, 1985. *Population and Housing Census*. Seoul: KEPB.

——. 1984. *Report on the First Employment Structure Survey*. Seoul: KEPB.

——. 1987. *Report on the Second Employment Structure Survey*. Seoul: KEPB.

Korean Ministry of Labor. 1985. *Report on the Occupational Wage Survey*. Seoul: Ministry of Labor.

Korean Women's Development Institute (KWDI). 1983. *A Study of Social-Institutional Factors Inhibiting Women's Development*. Seoul: KWDI (in Korean).

——. 1985. *Survey on Women's Labor Force Participation: Focus on Married Women*. Seoul: KWDI (in Korean).

——. 1989. *Studies of Home-based Production*. Seoul: KWDI (in Korean).

Kwon, Young-Ja. 1986. "Study on Returning Married Female Workers." *Women's Studies* 4: 5–31. Seoul: KWD (in Korean).

Lee, Sunhwa. 1997. "Elite Education for Career or Marriage: The Case of Female University Graduates in South Korea." Ph.D. dissertation, Department of Sociology, University of Chicago.

——. 2001. "Women's Education, Work, and Marriage in South Korea," in Mary C. Brinton (ed). *Women's Working Lives in East Asia*. Stanford, CA: Stanford University Press, pp. 204–232.

Lee, Sunhwa, and Mary C. Brinton. 1996. "Elite Education and Social Capital: The Case of South Korea." *Sociology of Education* 69: 177–192.

Lim, Lin Lean. 1993. "The Feminization of Labor in the Asia-Pacific Rim Countries: From Contributing to Economic Dynamism to Bearing the Brunt of Structural Adjustments," in Naohiro Ogawa, Gavin W. Jones, and Jeffrey G. Williamson (eds). *Human Resources in Development Along the Asia-Pacific Rim*. Singapore: Oxford University Press, pp. 175–209.

Lu, Yu-Hsia. 2001. " 'The Boss's Wife' and Taiwanese Small Family Businesses," in Mary C. Brinton (ed.). *Women's Working Lives in East Asia*. Stanford, CA: Stanford University Press, pp. 263–297.

Marcouiller, Douglas, Veronica Ruiz de Castilla, and Christopher Woodruff. 1997. "Formal Measures of the Informal-Sector Wage Gap in Mexico, El Salvador, and Peru." *Economic Development and Cultural Change* 45: 367–392.

Michael, Robert T. and Nancy Brandon Tuma. 1985. "Entry into Marriage and Parenthood by Young Men and Women: The Influence of Family Background." *Demography* 22: 515–544.

Mincer, Jacob. 1962. "Labor Force Participation of Married Women," in H. Gregg Lewis (ed.). *Aspects of Labor Economics*. Princeton, NJ: Princeton University Press.

——. 1974. *Schooling, Experience, and Earnings*. New York: Columbia University.

Ministry of Education, Korea. 1995. *Statistical Yearbook of Education.* Seoul: Ministry of Education.

Mitchell, T. 1988. *From a Developing to a Newly Industrialized Country: The Republic of Korea, 1961–82.* Geneva: ILO.

Moon, Uhn Cho. 1982. "Married Women and Urban Employment in Korea: Class Differences in Income-Opportunities." Ph.D. dissertation, University of Hawaii.

Moore, Wilbert. 1970. "Industrialization and Social Change," in Bert Hoselitz and Wilbert W. Moore (eds). *Industrialization and Society.* The Hague: Mouton, pp. 299–370.

National Statistical Office. Various years. *Survey of Economically Active Population.* Seoul: KEPB.

——. Various years. *Korea Statistical Yearbook.* Seoul: KEPB.

——. 1985, 1995. *Social Indicators in Korea.* Seoul: KEPB.

——. 1992. "Social Statistics Survey." Seoul: KEPB.

OECD. 2000. *Pushing Ahead with Reform in Korea: Labor Market and Social Safety-Net Policies.* Paris: OECD.

——. 2002. *OECD Employment Outlook.* Paris: OECD.

Papanek, G. 1988. "The New Asian Capitalism: An Economic Portrait," in P.L. Berger and H.H. Hsiao (eds). *In Search of an East Asian Development Model.* New Brunswick: Transaction, pp. 27–80.

Papanek, Hanna. 1976. "Women in Cities: Problems and Perspectives," in I. Tinker and M Bramsen (eds). *Women and World Development.* Washington, DC: Overseas Development Council, pp. 54–69.

Portes, Alejandro. 1985. "The Informal Sector and the World-Economy: Notes on the Structure of Subsidized Labor," in Michael Timberlake (ed.). *Urbanization in the World Economy.* New York: Academic Press, pp. 53–62.

Portes, Alejandro and Lauren Benton. 1984. "Industrial Development and Labor Absorption: A Reinterpretation." *Population and Development Review* 10: 589–612.

Portes, Alejandro and Saskia Sassen-Koob. 1987. "Making it Underground." *American Journal of Sociology* 93: 30–61.

Portes, Alejandro and John Walton. 1981. *Labor, Class, and the International System.* New York: Academic Press.

Pyle, Jean Larson. 1990. *The State and Women in the Economy.* Albany: State University of New York Press.

Ram, Rati. 1980. "Sex Differences in the Labor Market Outcomes of Education." *Comparative Education Review* 24: S53–77.

Ryder, Norman B. 1965. "The Cohort as a Concept in the Study of Social Change." *American Sociological Review* 30: 843–861.

Schmink, Marianne. 1986. "Women and Industrial Development in Brazil," in June Nash and Helen I. Safa (eds). *Women and Change in Latin America.* South Hadley, MA: Bergin and Garvey, pp. 136–164.

Smart, Josephine. 1990. "Self-Employment vs. Wage Employment in Hong Kong: A Reconsideration of the Urban Informal Economy," in M. Estelle Smith (ed.). *Perspectives on the Informal Economy.* New York: University Press of America, Inc., pp. 251–280.

Smith, James P. (ed.). 1980. *Female Labor Supply: Theory and Estimation.* Princeton, NJ: Princeton University Press.

Sorensen, Annemette. 1983. "Women's Employment Patterns after Marriage." *Journal of Marriage and the Family* 45: 311–321.

Standing, Guy. 1976. "Education and Female Participation in the Labor Force." *International Labor Review* 114: 281–297.

——. 1978. *Labor Force Participation and Development.* Geneva: ILO.

Tiano, Susan. 1984. "The Public–Private Dichotomy: Theoretical Perspectives on 'Women and Development'." *Social Science Journal* 21: 11–28.

——. 1987. "Gender, Work, and World Capitalism," in Beth Hess and Myra Marx Ferree (eds). *Analyzing Gender.* Beverly Hills: Sage, pp. 216–243.

——. 1994. *Patriarchy on the Line: Labor, Gender, and Ideology in the Mexican Maquila Industry*. Philadelphia, PA: Temple University Press.

Teilhet-Waldorf, Earl and William H. Waldorf. 1983. "Earnings of Self-Employed in an Informal Sector: A Case Study of Bangkok." *Economic Development and Cultural Change* 31: 587–607.

Truelove, Cynthia. 1987. "The Informal Sector Revisited: The Case of the Colombian Mini-Maquilas," in Richard Tardanico (ed.). *Crises in the Caribbean Basin: Past and Present.* Beverly Hills, CA: Sage, pp. 95–100.

Waite, Linda. 1980. "Working Wives and the Family Life Cycle." *American Journal of Sociology* 86: 272–294.

Ward, Kathryn B. 1984. *Women in the World System.* New York: Blackwell.

——. 1988. "Women in the Global Economy," in Barbara Gutek, Ann Stromberg, and Laurie Larwood (eds). *Women and Work,* Vol. 3. Beverly Hills, CA: Sage, pp. 17–48.

——. 1990. "Introduction and Overview," in Kathryn Ward (ed.). *Women Workers and Global Restructuring.* New York: ILR Press, pp. 1–22.

Wood, Adrian. 1991. "North–South Trade and Female Labor in Manufacturing: An Asymmetry." *The Journal of Development Studies* 27: 168–189.

Yamada, Gustavo. 1996. "Urban Informal Employment and Self-Employment in Developing Countries: Theory and Evidence." *Economic Development and Cultural Change* 44: 289–314.

Yoon, Jin-Ho. 1987. "Social Characteristics of Urban Small Business," in Hyun-Chae Park (ed.). *Studies on the Korean Economy.* Seoul: Kkachi (in Korean), pp. 341–376.

Conclusion

South Korea: in pursuit of modernity

Chang Yun-Shik

The Industrial Revolution that first occurred in England (1750–1850) implied such a drastic break with the past that historian David Landes was led to say that it "has been like in effect to Eve's tasting of the fruit of the tree of knowledge: the world has never been the same" (1969: 12). In the latter part of the twentieth century, another industrial revolution took place in South Korea. It has been hailed as a "miracle on the Han River," and serves as a model to be emulated by those underdeveloped countries aspiring to modernize their economies. What impact has it had on Korean society? How far has an industrialized Korea moved away from its Confucian past? How similar is industrialized South Korea to the West? What discontinuities and continuities are there between traditional and modern Korea?

In 1945, Allied forces liberated Korea from thirty-five years of Japanese rule. Following the Soviet and American occupations and the creation of the Republic of Korea and the Democratic People's Republic of Korea in 1948, the two Koreas went through a modernization process which involved the adoption of mutually antagonistic socio-economic and political systems. Two very different countries emerged as each Korea took on some of the characteristics of the country it was trying to emulate. While the chapters in this volume that examine Chosŏn and colonial Korea deepen our understanding of North Korea, our focus has for the most part been on the origins and evolution of pre-1945 Korean and post-1945 South Korean modernity. The discussion that follows here largely adopts that framework of analysis.

Together with the task of nation-building, economic recovery and development became urgent tasks for the South Korean government. Toward the end of the 1950s, with the help of US advisers, the Korean government came up with its first comprehensive five-year economic development plan. The short-lived second republic (1960–1961) revised and expanded this plan but was unable to launch it due to the military coup led by Major General Park Chung Hee. Park's military government (1961–1979) focused on economic development and carried out three consecutive five-year economic development plans. Support for this economic growth project was overwhelming, and hence the government had little difficulty in legitimizing its development programs. Acute awareness of South Korea's economic backwardness was directly equated with a strong desire to catch up with industrially advanced nations. Despite mounting criticism against the military regime for its autocratic rule, there was a broad consensus backing *choguk kŭndaehwa,* or the modernization of the fatherland.

As a latecomer, South Korea quickly modernized its economy by mobilizing whatever resources – capital, technologies, manpower (capitalists, professional managers, skilled workers, and industrial laborers) – remained in the southern half of the peninsula after the Japanese returned to their homeland. The country also made use of what the industrially advanced countries – mainly the US and Japan – could offer to facilitate the development process (i.e., capital, technology, management skills, a development model, economic advisers and markets). It should also be noted that industrialization proceeded simultaneously with other modernization projects: educational expansion, democratization, and reproductive and family revolution.

Modernity, the end-product of this process, entails the selective Westernization of Korea. The British sociologist Anthony Giddens defines modernity as "modes of social life or organizations which emerged in Europe from about the seventeenth century onwards and which subsequently became more or less worldwide in their influence" (1990: 1). However, one should not simply assume that the new Western way of life has spread to the rest of the world in a uniform manner. Westernization is a selective process. Late-developers adopt only some, not all, modes of social life or organizations of the industrialized West. Some aspects of the indigenous cultures may not survive the Westernization process, while others may adapt with varying degrees of difficulty. What emerges from this process is a hybrid of Eastern and Western influences.

So vast and rapid was the growth and change brought about by these interrelated modernization processes that an attempt to assess their consequences is a challenge to social scientists. A comprehensive attempt to grasp the meaning of this historical event has yet to begin.[1] My aim here is not to enumerate the changes that occurred during Korea's industrialization but rather to explore the transformations South Korea has undergone by comparing South Korea's contemporary urban industrial state with the Chosŏn Dynasty's Confucian and agrarian society. I focus on four areas of social transformation that constitute major dimensions of Korean modernity – the rise of a capitalist market economy, democratization, globalization, and the legacies of Korean Confucianism.

The rise of the capitalist market economy

According to Paul Kuznets, "consistent, reliable economic data, available only since 1953, show slow GDP growth after the Korean War until the mid-1960s, then much more rapid growth afterward" (Chapter 3). This growth increased real per capita GDP fivefold after 1970, and tenfold since 1953 (Chapter 3). Output growth, combined with declining rates of population growth, raised incomes so that the average annual income reached US$10,000 in 1995. The percentage of the labor force engaged in agriculture decreased from 63 percent of the total employed in 1953 to 11.6 percent in 2000. This much-simplified numerical summary of South Korea's industrial growth speaks volumes about the impact of industrialization.

Toward an affluent society: work and wealth

For the first time in history, the average Korean today no longer feels poor. "Poverty estimates, where poverty is defined in absolute terms to include any income below that corresponding to the minimum necessary food consumption level," Kuznets writes, "show that in 1965, 41 percent of all Koreans were living in poverty. The estimate for 1982 was less than 8 [percent]" (Chapter 3).

During the Chosŏn Dynasty and for most of the twentieth century, poverty was a perennial feature of Korea's agrarian economy. Most peasant families had to go through what was known as the "barley hill" (*bori kogae*) or "spring poverty" (*ch'un'gung*), the period from when the rice they produced the previous year ran out and the time when the spring harvest of barley was ready. When they had a poor harvest, which was not infrequent, and usually due to flood or drought, a famine followed, with grass roots and tree bark as the only sources of food. Traditional folk wisdom is reflected in the adage "Even the government cannot save the poor" (*kanan kujenŭn nara do mothanda*).

Even *yangban* elites were not entirely free from poverty. Unlike in feudal society, where the aristocracy was a status system of inheritance, in Chosŏn Dynasty Korea the *yangban* status was, in theory, earned either through passing the Civil Service examination and thereby becoming a government official, or by being born into a family that had produced a government official within the past three generations (father, grandfather, and great-grandfather). In order to establish themselves as a status group with a collective cultural identity, they adopted the old Chou Dynasty idea of *sŏnbi* (literati) as the image to emulate; thus they became responsible for supplying candidates for government posts (Yi 1989).

The *sŏnbi* indulged himself in reading Confucian classics with the aim of grasping the deep meaning of what the ancient sages said about human virtues and ideal governance, thereby cultivating his mind and becoming an exemplary member of his community.[2] Learning was considered a lifelong process, in which the *sŏnbi* internalized the Confucian moral principles and cultivated his mind in order to become a man of virtue. According to these principles, virtuous is he who has acquired the sense of propriety, righteousness, honor and shame, and acts accordingly without ever compromising the principle. "The *sŏnbi* would rather die than accommodate the changing political situation (*siguk*)," says noted Confucian scholar Yi Chang-hi (1989: 35). The *sŏnbi*, therefore, cannot afford to be lax with learning. Even if he becomes poor, he should not stop reading books. To seek material gain is to lose his moral posture. The ultimate goal of the *sŏnbi* is to become a government official, and to serve the King by fully utilizing what he has learned to promote the welfare of all his subjects. In practical terms, the *sŏnbi* needed a certain amount of land and slaves to enable him to devote his time to reading books. The number of government positions available to aspirants, however, was limited, and many *yangban* elites never managed to become bureaucrats (in some cases even after they passed the Civil Service examination), remaining merely literati or "book-reading men" (*toksŏin*). If a man was not born into a rich landowning family, he was bound to face the problem of not being able to support his family adequately. In principle there was no rule against a *sŏnbi* engaging in farming when not in government service, but doing so would demote him to the rank of peasant commoner, risking the possibility of alienating him from other fellow *yangban* and preventing him from finding a spouse of equal status for his sons or daughters.

If a poor *yangban* refused to engage in farming, becoming involved in wealth accumulation activities through trade was unthinkable. This does not mean that *yangban* were not interested in money-making. In fact, many land-rich *yangban* elites were engaged in usury, but they rarely conducted such affairs directly, preferring to delegate the work to servants in the house. Others who were not as resourceful suffered poverty but could claim that they had not compromised themselves in order to maintain the *yangban* status. "Being poor but living a clean life" (*chŏngbin*) approximated to the ideal of the average literati. The Korean linguist Yi Hi-sung (1970: 37) describes the characteristics of the typical literati at the end of the nineteenth century as follows:

> Such a *sennim* (unsuccessful literati) does not go out very often. Whether he has his own outer room (*sarangbang*) or not, his daily work is to sit in a room alone, dressed properly even in a worn dress and broken hat, and read Confucian classics including the Four Books and Five Scriptures (*Sasŏ Ogyŏng*) continuously a hundred or thousand times. House-keeping couldn't be his concern. It is up to his wife to make smoke come out of the chimney, who either procures money through pawning or borrowing. This is how he survives.

Korea's industrial development after 1945 gradually brought about an open labor market with multiple occupational choices, free of the constraints previously imposed upon the employment options of the traditional elite. A broadening job market enabled individuals to earn a living, to become wealthy and to choose a career. Today, the traditional fatalistic attitude toward life has disappeared. Poverty is treated as something that can be overcome by individuals, not to be blamed on the system. Poverty has come to symbolize the ineptness and laziness of the one who suffers from it. As for those people who cannot help but remain poor, the government is capable and willing to take care of them.

One of the most important criteria for evaluating one's social status these days is an individual's income or wealth, whether inherited or acquired. Entrepreneurs and traders – those who are in the business of making money – have moved to the top of the occupational scale. These new categories of jobs and professions are often ranked above traditionally esteemed job categories such as bureaucrats and teachers, and are becoming more popular among those entering the workforce. The Mencian distinction between mental and menial work has not disappeared completely, but the wage-earning manual work of the corporate world has established itself as a job category that many of the less educated and fortunate are ready to choose. In contrast to the old adage quoted above, the title of the autobiography by a former economic planning board minister reads, "Poverty Relief is the Responsibility of the Government" (Kang 1992).

Work is now directly associated with the generation of income, and the pursuit of material gain has become a legitimate work motive. The launching of the economic development plan is all about making the nation and its individual citizens wealthy, at least ideally. One New Village Movement (*Saemaŭl*) song says, "It is about time we live well" (*chal sara bose*). To make a lot of money, to engage in unlimited acquisition, has come to be regarded as a patriotic action. The number-one exporter becomes a national hero, decorated with medals by the government. The government encourages people to become entrepreneurs and, since Park Chung Hee became leader, exporters. Contemporary Koreans are embracing the possibility of becoming opulent if they try (*hamyŏn toenda*). From *chaebŏl* chairmen down to factory workers, everybody works very hard to make money.

The first-generation entrepreneurs faced cut-throat competition in the domestic as well as the world market. With help and encouragement from the government, big corporate owners (who grew to be *chaebŏl*) and managers built up capital assets, imported technologies, provided training to workers, and took substantial risks by expanding production and capacity for export in pursuit of profits (Westphal 1978: 374). They were determined to accumulate wealth, prepared to establish a corporate empire, willing to participate in the national project-economic development plan, and ready to break into the world market largely dominated and carefully guarded by the advanced industrial countries. Government support and protection are partly responsible for the success of the big entrepreneurs, but they had to prove themselves worthy of the privileges accorded by the government (Jones and SaKong 1980: 276–277; see also Lie (Chapter 5, this volume) for a counter-argument).

In the 1980s, when the income of the government and semi-government officials was frozen, many elite bureaucrats and bankers went to big corporations for better salaries. As competition for well-paying jobs grows with the increasing number of university graduates, it has become a common phenomenon for university students to prepare for *chuijik* (employment) examinations in the occupations of diplomat and journalist, as law college students have been doing for *kodungoshi* (the higher Civil Service examination). Social prestige is still an important consideration in occupational or professional choice but it alone is not sufficient. In the old days, when law college students prepared for *kodungoshi*, they aimed to become judges or prosecutors for the power and prestige that those jobs accorded. Income that came with the job was of secondary concern, but the quest for a high salary is now an added feature in job-seeking efforts. The educated class displays very little of the old, altruistic *sŏnbi* spirit.

Factory workers, both men and women, work equally hard. In the 1970s, they worked more than ten hours a day under poor conditions with low wages. They tried to increase their income by working longer hours, sometimes without holidays and taking on double shifts. Mostly recruited from rural areas, factory workers regard their job in the city as a way out of farming and rural life, and are determined to stay on the job. More importantly, they have made efforts to improve their standing in terms of pay and working conditions by forming unions. The constitution and labor law guarantee their rights to demand pay increases and to negotiate collectively with the management, and to take collective action if and when negotiation fails. In 2003, some automobile factory workers earned higher wages than those accorded to university professors (*Weekly Chosun.com* 2003).

Even peasants have become farmer entrepreneurs. Profit-seeking is now a key tenet of a farming household. Farms are no longer self-sufficient operations, but rather enterprises focused on selling to the urban market at a profit. They are concerned with growing more profitable cash crops and increasing land productivity by a variety of means. Their expectations have risen, and they think it is possible to make big money in the urban agricultural market, or hope to sell their farmland some day to an industrialist for a large sum of money. Like urban workers, farmers also claim government income protection against natural disasters and the uncertain markets for agrarian products resulting from globalization. As Burmeister points out, those agricultural cooperatives that used to operate as a government control mechanism are now in the hands of farmers, protecting and promoting their interests (Chapter 2, this volume). People now have confidence to reach out for what they previously thought was out of their reach.

Mobile society

The capitalist market economy creates an open society where one can move up the ladder of success through one's own efforts, and reshuffling the social hierarchy is an ongoing process.

In the early Chosŏn Dynasty Korea, there were officially only two status groups: *yangin*, men of good status or free men, and *nobi*, low-born men, slaves or unfree men. There were four major occupational categories: scholar-official, peasant, artisan, and merchant, in order of hierarchical standing.

These four occupational categories were filled by commoner men; women, with few exceptions, were expected to take care of domestic affairs. *Nobi* were regarded as chattel property of the person or public office that owned them, and as "objects subject to purchase and sale" (Palais 1996: 212). Chosŏn Dynasty Korea was founded on agricultural fundamentalism: "if agriculture flourishes, the country will prosper; if agriculture declines then the country is on the road to ruin" (Dore 1960: 71). The country adopted a policy of restricting commerce and industry, preventing their expansion beyond what was thought necessary. Although *yangin* artisans were free and independent, most were employed by the agencies of central government, or by provincial governments or the district magistrate. They worked for a period of time for those agencies to fulfill their labor service obligation to make necessities or tribute products for the King and Court, and for the rest of the year operated as independent artisans producing artifacts for market.

As for commerce, there were two types of merchants or traders: (1) a small number of merchants (*sijŏn sangin*) who were licensed to run shops established by the central or local government, securing and providing necessities for the *yangban* and administrative office in the capital as well as for the local government (established at a later date); and (2) itinerant merchants and peddlers who serviced periodic markets nationwide. Although industry and commerce offered occupational roles for commoners, other than those merchants and artisans listed in the government register, they were not free to engage in industrial or commercial activities. Both registered artisans and merchants were conferred the right to prevent other commoners from becoming artisans and merchants.

From very early on, those families whose ancestors in the previous dynasty had served as government officials or subsequently produced government officials organized themselves into a group and claimed an elite status (i.e., above that of a commoner). Accordingly, the word *yangban*, which originally meant "two files of officials" (civil and military) in the royal Court, became a de facto status category with status privileges recognized by the government, but it was never an officially recognized status group. Government clerks and technical staff also established themselves in another status category, *chungin* (middle stratum), which gradually evolved into a hereditary status group. There thus evolved four status groups: *yangban, chungin, yangin,* and *nobi.*

During the 500 years of the Chosŏn Dynasty, the structure of the social status system went through significant changes, but it is rather difficult to generalize in terms of overall trends, since inter-status mobility took various forms. *Yangban* could lose their status and become slaves by committing serious crimes. The wives and children of *yangban* criminals could be made post-station slaves. Offspring of *yangban* men and commoner (or slave) concubines could not inherit elite status. However, illegitimate sons of *yangban* could purchase permission to take the civil service examinations. *Chungin* could achieve *yangban* status for themselves through arresting clerks who fled their posts, or secure it for their descendants through heroic military deeds or scholarly accomplishments. *Yangin* purchased official titles by contributing grain or money to the government. On the other hand, impoverished commoners commended themselves to powerful *yangban* as slaves in order to avoid heavy government duties.

As for *nobi,* there were a number of avenues through which they could overcome their base status: reporting runaway slaves, contributing grain to the government, purchasing commoner titles, supplying their owners with substitute slaves, or running away. Shortly after the Japanese invasion (1592–1598), the government granted some 60,000 slaves commoner status. The loss of slaves through these routes was compensated for by supply from other sources. We have already mentioned how both *yangban* elites and commoners could fall to the status of *nobi,* but the most important source was intermarriage and sexual relations between *yangban* men and slave women. In spite of the fact that the law at the beginning of the Chosŏn Dynasty prohibited intermarriage between slaves and commoners, it became so common that a law was instituted stipulating that "the children of slave mothers were claimed by the mother's owner whether the father was a commoner or a slave, while the offspring of slave fathers and commoner mothers went to the father's owner" (Shin 1974: 14). This law was later changed (in 1662) so that the offspring of commoner mothers and low-born fathers followed the mother's status. Under changing laws, "the slave owners arranged marriage between their slaves, or married them to commoners in order to retain their control over the children" (Shin 1974: 14). The complexity governing the status system does not allow for easy generalizations about the mobility patterns and trends that emerged during the Chosŏn Dynasty period. Dismissing the existing summary views, Edward Wagner (1974: 38) cautiously offers the following proposition:

> the Yi dynasty's first century was characterized by an important degree of fluidity and openness in its social class structure. Many forces were at work, however, that led the society toward the hardening of class lines for which Yi Korea justly has been known. The process toward

> rigid stratification went forward through the sixteenth century and throughout the seventeenth century as well.... Sometime after 1700 certain new patterns began to emerge that may have had a softening effect on what had come to be [a] tightly controlled, largely stagnant social class system. Fundamental change, however, was slow in coming and in the most meaningful areas had to await the closing years of the dynasty or even beyond.

The occupational structure also underwent changes, but its scope was not as pronounced as the shifts experienced in the status system. As mentioned above, any commoner who was qualified (i.e., educated in Confucian classics) was allowed to sit for Civil Service examinations and become *yangban*, but in reality it was practically impossible for peasant commoners or their sons, who were mostly tenants, to become bureaucrats, since it required a lengthy period of preparation, and time away from farming. Consequently the *yangban* class[3] came to dominate government posts. Within this limitation, the size of the *yangban* class expanded and the number of those who passed government examinations increased, but the number of government posts remained more or less unchanged until 1894, when administrative reform was introduced.

In the late nineteenth century commerce experienced some significant structural changes and growth, and lured away many landless commoners and slaves from farming. "Private merchants," writes Palais, "had begun to break free from restrictions, engage in both wholesale and retail trade ... and private artisans began to abscond from their state employers to produce goods for the market on their own" (1996: 16). Many peasant commoners became artisans to avoid starvation as poor tenants, but it is almost impossible to estimate the changing size of the artisan and merchant population. Important though this expansion and its changes in the structure of the industry and commerce were, the overall structure of the Chosŏn Dynasty economy was not significantly altered. At the end of the dynasty, Choson Korea still remained predominantly agricultural. The earliest statistical information available on the occupation structure of colonized Korea indicates that, in 1915, the agricultural population accounted for 83.1 percent of the entire population (Takahashi 1935: 162).

Industrial growth during the colonial period created the beginnings of an urban job market. According to the 1940 census (Chōsen sōtokufu 1944), 30.9 percent of the gainfully occupied population, which included Koreans and Japanese residents, engaged in non-agricultural work, but Koreans alone accounted for 28.5 percent of those workers in non-agricultural pursuits. Within the non-agricultural occupational domains, Koreans experienced very little upward mobility. The upper rungs of the occupational ladder were largely dominated by Japanese residents, while educated Koreans became low-ranking civil servants, lawyers, medical doctors, and secondary school teachers. Less well-educated Koreans were small-scale urban merchants, wage earners, and holders of unskilled jobs (Chang 1971).

When various forms of markets opened up in the wake of the industrial progress following liberation, there were very few structural constraints preventing any segment of the population from participating. South Korea entered the development era in the late 1960s as a relatively fluid, if not chaotic, society. Japanese colonialism had undermined the established *yangban* elites and some of the Chosŏn Dynasty's rigid social hierarchies. Liberation removed the top layers of the colonial establishment and discredited a small contingent of Korean collaborating elites. As Shin points out (Chapter 1, this volume), land reform and the Korean War virtually eliminated landlords by equalizing assets and breaking up the old pattern of social relations in rural areas. The war also destroyed the assets of the urban elites and of the small middle class, while monetary inflation during and after the Korean War further significantly reduced the value of financial assets that had survived the colonial period (Chang 1991: 113).

Within four decades following liberation, South Korea had transformed itself from a predominantly agrarian to a predominantly industrial society. The decline of the agricultural workforce from 68.5 percent of the total force in 1960 to 11.6 percent in 2000 may be taken as a rough measure of the scale of reallocation of work and the extent of social mobility that occurred in South Korea in less than a generation. Initially, farmers and their children, especially daughters, left their villages to find non-farming jobs in the cities. With the spread of school education, farm youths, like their city counterparts, went to school before entering the job market to look for non-farming jobs.

The achieving society: merit and patronage

In the Chosŏn Dynasty, education had been, at least partly, a means of testing qualifications for recruitment into the government bureaucracy; most other occupations such as farming, crafting, and trading did not recruit educated manpower.

During the colonial period, secondary and tertiary school education served similar purposes. The government looked for recruits mainly among graduates of high schools and colleges, institutions which were established largely for the purpose of training civil servants. Vocational high schools and professional schools at colleges produced the skilled manpower that the small modern sector of the economy required. New legal and medical institutions were imported from the West, together with professional schools that trained lawyers and doctors.

After liberation, public education became geared to the general population. Primary schooling was made compulsory at the inception of the republic in 1948, and by the late 1960s education at this level had become universal. Today, only a tiny minority of children fail to complete six years of education. Secondary education expanded to accommodate the growing number of children who graduated from primary school and aspired to move on to secondary school. By 1970 the majority of school-age youths received secondary education, and a considerable proportion (40 percent) of those who finished high school went on to college or university (Chang 1990).

This rapid educational expansion took place before society felt the impact of the industrial revolution during the 1960s and 1970s. Thus, when the urban industrial labor market was growing in the 1970s and 1980s, an educated workforce was abundantly available for it.

By the time corporate employers began to recruit workers in the 1970s, "entrance examinations granting access to higher education," as observed by Dore, became ever more severely competitive, suggesting that "entrance into the credential-requiring corporate sector is overwhelmingly the dominant ambition of the socially mobile, rather than aspiration to make their own way in the self-employed, small scale sector" (Dore 1976: 297). The school system came to represent more or less the institutionalization of qualification requirements into government and industrial corporations. The higher the level of one's educational attainment, the more likely one is to land a better-paying job. The intelligence that one is born with and the school education built on to it have become another form of asset, termed human capital.

Schooling that screens candidates for jobs is, however, only an eliminating process. The traditional ascriptive principles of patronage still operate to modify or amplify the workings of merit criteria in the allocation of jobs and promotion. Traditional personal connections, based on kinship and local community ties, and contemporary connections formed within the school or university, are very important; there is no sign that the use of personal connections is declining. Personal connections are sedulously cultivated, and the average urban Korean is a member of multiple networks of relatives, friends, and close acquaintances. If university education (especially at a prestigious university) is a guarantee of academic ability and occupational aptitude, personal networks serve as a guarantee of the continuing goodwill of the string-puller and of the inductee's good behavior. Sociologists only recently recognized such social connections as a form of capital (Bourdieu 1986; Coleman 1988; Lin 2001). In South Korea, social capital is as valued as human capital and the latter is not likely to replace the former, as appears to have happened in Japan.

Consumer society

"As the income level goes up," wrote Veblen (1952 [1899]: 72), "consumption becomes a larger element in the standard of living in the city than in the country." The self-sufficiency that characterized the traditional peasant economy is quickly replaced by the urban market economy that emphasizes consumption. Over the past several decades South Korea has rapidly developed into a consumer society.

During the Chosŏn Dynasty period most peasants were largely self-sufficient, living at subsistence level. Their basic needs were barely procured, and their consumption of goods produced outside of their communities was minimal. They sold only a minor portion of the grain and home (winter) products they produced (e.g., bags and straw shoes at the weekly periodic market, the main form of market that existed) in order to purchase what was necessary for farming (e.g., farm equipment) and daily living (e.g., combs) from other peasants or itinerant peddlers who serviced periodic markets nationwide. The latter also came to farming villages. Local landowning *yangban* elites with surplus could afford to purchase beyond the basic necessities, but what the local market offered was limited and they themselves did not go to the market. Instead, they let their slaves do the necessary shopping. The list of goods commonly found at local markets into the late nineteenth century included woven materials and their ingredients, fruit, ironware, ceramics, livestock, stationery, and products made of wood, bamboo, stone and brass, as well as herbal medicines and marine products (Mun 1941).

In the cities, licensed (and later unlicensed) shops called *sichon* serviced the government offices, the imperial house and *yangban* residents. Each *sichon* had the monopoly right to sell only one kind of product; products from the *sichon* may have been of better quality but they were also limited in kind and in number. Beyond the necessities for living, only a small number of luxury goods had a limited circulation. The Chosŏn Dynasty government, as mentioned above, adopted early the policy of suppressing commerce and handicraft industries, as they were considered base and commercial activities in pursuit of profit, and especially because they were considered to undermine agriculture by luring peasants away from farming and by corrupting their minds. Frugality, not consumption, was considered a virtue.

The traditional market system went through a drastic transformation during the colonial period. With the Korean economy linked to and eventually integrated with the Japanese capitalist economy, markets became more open, formalized, functionally diverse, and comprehensive. Both city residents and rural peasants became closely involved in market transactions, but in the countryside, peasant market participation was more forced than voluntary. After colonization, as Mun Chong-chang pointed out (1941: 118), the traditional periodic market became a place where urban factory owners collected manufactured industrial ingredients and peasants purchased goods manufactured by urban factories. Under Japanese authorities, agricultural productivity increased about sevenfold, but Korean peasants, the majority of whom became landless, remained impoverished. In other words, as the farm sector became closely linked with the emerging manufacturing industry as a supplier of ingredients, and as the market became a venue for the flow of factory-manufactured goods, peasants were forced to sell what they produced in order to buy the factory products. Given what purchasing power most peasants had, their needs were sufficiently met in the periodic market. In the cities, new markets developed to service those Japanese residents and a small number of rich Koreans and their children who purchased from a wide range of manufactured goods and services. Still, the majority of citizens were able only to afford to buy goods from the market for their basic daily needs. The new market became the source of information for what constituted the modern, Western lifestyle, and helped those who had the necessary resources to adopt a new Western lifestyle.

The consumer market grew rapidly in post-liberation South Korea, with economic growth based on the expansion of the manufacturing industry, the increase of the non-farm population, and rising income levels. With mass production, goods and services often exceeded demand.

In the initial stage of developmental growth in the 1960s, the government plced more emphasis on the production of manufactured goods for export than for domestic use, and hence urged people to be frugal and focus on saving. However, in the 1980s, the continuing growth of productivity made it necessary to increase domestic demand. The consumption of domestically produced goods became a more important ingredient for sustained development than adhering to a thrifty lifestyle focused on saving.

Numerous goods and services were sold in stores and shops of varying types, ranging from street vendors, corner grocery stores, convenience stores and supermarkets, to department stores and shopping malls, and most recently the electronic market. There were also movie theaters, amusement parks, exhibition halls, opera houses, and music-halls offering entertainment. Information on consumer goods has been aggressively distributed through advertising and media. Those who advertised also created constantly changing fashions for consumers, arousing curiosity and creating motives to purchase new products. Credit cards were introduced in the 1960s, enabling Korean consumers to purchase what they wanted to buy on credit at any time they desired. Also accessible – though limited to the upper income group – were the overseas markets. As more Koreans traveled overseas, they gained access to foreign markets for shopping.

Unlike other forms of market (marriage, education, labor, and political), the consumer market is open to everybody, directly or indirectly, and is becoming rapidly incorporated into the world market. Unfortunately, the consumption side of the South Korean economy has not been as closely explored as the production side. The study of consumer behavior is of recent origin in South Korea. It is not possible at this point to present a clear picture of the emerging South Korean consumer culture; however, two distinct features may be identified.

As many Western consumer behavior researchers have predicted (see Slater 1997), consumers in Korea are becoming more individualized. Koreans have increasingly more discretionary income to spend on themselves and have the freedom to buy whatever they want, without being forced to choose among certain goods and services sold by the government or others. Entering the market, consumers have to know what they want in order to choose from a wide range of goods and services. Consumption in the market therefore helps consumers become more aware of their own tastes, preferences, talents, and aptitudes. The consumer markets help people discover themselves and act according to their own will and need.

While Korean consumers spend their money as they choose, this does not preclude them from committing a large portion of it to others. There is an undying commitment on the part of parents to provide what is best for their children, especially the best education, formal as well as informal. Since schooling has become nearly universal to the level of high school, parents try to give their children the best education through private tutoring or cram schools, spending anywhere from one-third to one half of the household income on extra-curricular tutoring. Efforts are also made by Korean consumers to maintain and expand their interpersonal networks involving other relatives, friends, and acquaintances through gift giving, cash donations, social drinks, and so on. Social bonds and ties have traditionally been valued, and in the market society, a significant amount of people's wealth and time is expended on maintaining these and creating new ones. Social networking could be an end in itself, for simple reasons of pleasure; however, in a capitalist market society, social networks can play a significant utilitarian function. One can easily rely on one's social network to promote one's private interests by mobilizing resources in the form of information and the practical help embedded in it. Expenditure on the maintenance and creation of a social network is therefore considered a form of investment.

Democratization

If South Korea became an industrial society, it is also becoming, albeit slowly, a more democratic nation. Although democracy as a form of polity for Korea was adopted at the time South Korea became a republic in 1948, democratization was delayed by the authoritarian government that made itself the chief architect of economic modernization. The military was determined to stay in power through whatever means it could until the goal of economic development was achieved. Democratization happened only after a high level of industrial production had been achieved, and some of those politicians who served in the authoritarian government claim that industrialization cleared the path to democratization. Relationships between industrialization and democratization are rather complex, as de Schweinitz (1964) demonstrated, and given the fact that the way in which democratization occurs varies from country to country, the relationship between industrialization and democratization cannot be readily generalized. In the Korean context, we can retrospectively think of a number of preconditions for democratization that were established in the process of industrial growth. As mentioned above, popular support for the economic modernization project, designed to overcome chronic poverty, was overwhelming when it was first launched, and the authoritarian government that deprived ordinary citizens of their civic rights was tolerated in the hope of achieving this goal. But when poverty was no longer the major concern, people found the government too oppressive in managing the nation, including the economy, and found the democratic alternative that they once had more desirable.

Until recently, for a variety of reasons, rural voters tended to vote for ruling party candidates, presidential or national assembly, while urban voters tended to choose opposition party candidates. Thus the urbanization that accompanied industrial development posed a threat to the ruling party and the authoritarian government. The densely populated city with the rapid flow of news and information helped make it easier for criticism and discontent against the authoritarian government to consolidate into public opinion and create public space for collective action. Farmers scattered in small villages – the basic residential units – could not be readily mobilized for such mass rallies and demonstrations witnessed during the authoritarian period in big cities. Industrial organizations also served as a place for forming groups to protest against authoritarian owners and foremen. In the 1970s, young female factory workers organized themselves into informal protest groups and used the workplace as an arena for struggle to claim the three constitutional labor rights. The corporate business power that grew with the help of the state formed a large civic group that, in turn, competed against the former in controlling the economy and influencing the people. Their need to adjust to each other served as a mechanism for curbing the increase of power on each side.

But these contributions of industrialization to democracy were made in the form of necessary conditions, not of causes. Industrialization must have facilitated democratization but did not cause it.

The government played a decisive role in economic development through initiating, planning, and implementing it, and earned the name of developmental state. The developmental state was an authoritarian government – anti-democratic and developmentalist. The president first brought the other two branches of the government, the legislative and the judiciary, under his control, dismantling the local government, depriving the citizens of their constitutional rights, and silencing all the pressure groups that tried to restrict the arbitrary power of the government that came to be symbolized by the president and his administration. This authoritarian government sought legitimacy in economic growth, not in democracy.

Thus a dialectic process began. Authoritarian regime-building eliminated the majority of citizens from the political process, and blocked all avenues through which public opinion and demand could be channeled. With the loss of their constitutional rights, citizens' discontent increased gradually, and political dissension and opposition against the government eventually became widespread and consolidated into a growing anti-government or pro-democracy force. Anti-government groups first sprang up separately in reaction to the oppressive government, then united their forces into a people's democracy movement strong enough to bring down the government. This happened in 1960 (the April 19th Student Revolution), 1979 (the Pu-Ma Struggle that led to the assassination of Park Chung Hee by Kim Jae-kyu), and 1987 (the June Resistance, eventually resulting in the fall of the Chun Doo Hwan regime).

Democracy was revived as a result of citizens' struggle to save it from extinction. The struggle to regain their lost constitutional rights also helped people to appreciate and defend the virtues of constitutional democracy of which they had little understanding when it was first bestowed upon them, and to internalize democratic norms and values. As they fought for democracy, they also came to realize the weaknesses of the traditional person-oriented norm which had provided a moral basis for the authoritarian regime. As democracy as a political ideology began to assume a new moral authority among the anti-government forces, tension between the two forces increased, threatening the legitimacy of the authoritarian system.

Koreans have regained various constitutional rights conferred by the first constitution adopted by the Constituent Assembly in 1948, which transformed them into independent citizens from "loyal" subjects to the alien emperor. Koreans are endowed with three sets of rights which T.H. Marshall (1950) has identified as political, civil, and social. The civil category comprises "the rights necessary for individual freedom": the freedom of individual corporeal liberty, the freedom to change residence, the right to privacy, the right to worship as one chooses, freedom of speech, freedom of assembly, and the freedom of knowledge and art. The social category concerns "the whole range from the right to a modicum of economic welfare and security to the right to share to the full in the social heritage and to live the life of a civilized being according the standards prevailing in the society" (Marshall 1950: 12): the right to education, to the equality of men and women, and to basic labour rights, namely the right of the employee not to be unfairly discriminated against by the employer and to equality before the law. The political category refers to the right of the citizen to form a government that, in turn, guarantees these rights.

As full-fledged citizens, both Korean men and women are actively participating in politics. Citizens' participation in the political process has gone through a number of stages. It began by electing the president and lawmakers, but, as discussed above, the elected president turned into an authoritarian ruler whose administration governed the nation with little input from its citizens. Authoritarian regimes were not only unreceptive to policy demands and criticism from citizens, but were also unwilling to allow the existence of autonomous collective forces. Two such forces, labor unions and students, were quickly brought under government control after South Korea became a republic. Under Rhee the national labor organization, the Korean Federation of Trade Unions, became closely linked with the government. As a strong organized collective supporter of Rhee, readily lent its support for government policies. During the post-Rhee period, union activities were strictly suppressed by the government by way of facilitating frictionless capitalist development.

Students were organized nationwide into the Student Patriotic Association, an organization designed by the government to promote "patriotic spirits." At the level of high school and above they received military training as part of the school (high school and above) curriculum and were expected to devote their energies to defending the country. Students were the first group to become a force of civic disobedience. As is well known, in 1960 they led the struggle for democracy that eventually brought down the Rhee regime, and they continued to play the key role in subsequent democracy movements.

In the early 1970s, factory workers began a campaign to regain their constitutional labor rights and to establish an autonomous labor union. Dissident church leaders also actively participated in both democracy and labor movements, which led to the downfall of the authoritarian government.

Increasingly these days, citizens organize themselves to promote the public interest. There are some 2,000 civic groups expressing their concerns about various social issues, nuclear power, the environment, women's equal rights, clean elections, and so on, which are emerging as influential pressure groups. More fundamentally, democratic constitutionalism demands that Koreans challenge traditional personalist ethics by upholding new political ideals such as human rights, the rule of law, social justice, and equality – those public goods that go beyond one's own interests or those of friends and acquaintances.

Globalization and new nationalism

Chosŏn Dynasty Korea remained isolated from the world, having little interaction with foreign countries other than China and Japan. Today, however, South Korea is fully integrated with the world capitalist system. Until quite recently political economists argued that this process of joining – often by force – the world capitalist system would have the effect of subjecting less developed economies to exploitation by the more advanced economies, keeping the former underdeveloped and dependent upon the latter. South Korea, however, has become a successful late-developer. Daniel Chirot points out that "if it [South Korea] had sealed itself off from the global market and not become so dependent on exporting to the rest of the world, it would have been in as ruinous a condition as North Korea's economy" (Chapter 10, this volume).

In the 1960s, South Korea adopted an outward-looking development strategy. Export of manufactured products was regarded as the key to development. South Korea now trades with more than 100 foreign countries. Corporate firms are manufacturing products not primarily for the domestic market but for the world market, but as wage levels go up and trade unions become stronger, companies are increasingly moving their manufacturing operations out of the country in search of cheaper labor elsewhere. In 1998, 435 Korean corporate groups had 3,637 branch offices in seventy-six countries. Medium-sized companies are mostly focusing their overseas business ventures on Southeast Asia and China to take advantage of inexpensive labor there, while big businesses tend to focus on the US and Europe for the purpose of penetrating those markets. Corporate economic expansion has been paralleled by government efforts to extend the country's diplomatic and international networks, even to those countries known to be friendlier with the north than with the south. As of 1998, the Republic of Korea had diplomatic relations with 183 countries, fifty-two memberships in intergovernmental organizations, and 1,250 memberships in international intergovernmental organizations (Kim 2000: 265).

At the same time, Korea opened up its domestic market in response to external pressures, especially from the US and Japan. South Korea now imports more than it exports. Direct investment of foreign capital, which the government long resisted, is now allowed, and foreign capitalists are buying up a significant proportion of Korean stocks listed in the domestic and international stock-market. Multinational corporations are opening up branch offices in South Korea. The McDonald's fast food chain, Starbucks coffee shops, Kentucky Fried Chicken and others are expanding throughout the country, doing booming business. There is internal structural pressure to open up the labor market to foreign workers and to open up consumer markets to cheaper foreign products. In February 2003, there were 67,158 foreign workers in South Korea (Seol and Han 2004: 45). A bill was recently passed by the National Assembly, giving foreign workers some limited constitutional labor rights. The ban on importing foreign liquor and Japanese movies, among other things, was recently lifted. Farmers continuously have rallies protesting against opening up the domestic market to foreign agricultural products.

Koreans are also traveling to foreign countries in increasing numbers, as representatives for international events, visitors, or tourists. Government officials and civilians are redefining Korea's role and responsibilities in the world commensurate with its relative standing in the global hierarchy. The ROK Army has been deployed overseas during the Vietnam and Gulf Wars, and has participated in peace-keeping operations in Somalia, West Sahara, Angola, India, and Pakistan. South Korea hosted the 1986 Asian Olympics, the World Olympics in 1988, and the World Cup (with Japan) in 2002. South Korea is now an aid-giving country. Also worth mentioning are the large number of Koreans who have settled in other countries. Overseas Koreans are estimated to number 5.4 million: two million in China; 1.5 million in Japan; 1.3 million in the US; 400,000 in the former Soviet republics; and the remainder in 140 countries all over the world (Yu 2003).

South Korea has shed its one-time moniker of "hermit kingdom," and has increasingly become an open society with growing connections to other nations. South Korea's linkages with the world community have grown so extensive that "local happenings are shaped by events occurring many miles away and vice-versa" (Giddens 1990: 64). South Korea's incorporation into the world community has subjected it to the international standards, rules and regulations, norms and ethics, which do not always conform to the local equivalents.

It has been a century since Korea broke its exclusive ties with China and started to join the wider world. The globalization process has extensively transformed Korea from a relatively undifferentiated agrarian society into a highly differentiated industrial society. As many scholars believe (Kim 2000: 4), this may have effected the effacing of national boundaries, identities, stability, and solidarity. A related idea considers the Korean as an individual becoming more a global citizen rather than remaining a "Korean" with little concern for what happens outside the country. Contrary to such expectations, the globalization process, instead of eroding national frontiers and diluting national sentiments, has helped strengthen them.

According to popular beliefs, ones which in recent years have been promoted in the media and in purportedly academic works on Korean "history," Koreans are the descendants of a single "race" originating from Tangun, who founded an ancient Korean Kingdom more than 5,000 years ago. "Korea" is portrayed as a monolithic political entity from the time the three kingdoms were unified under Silla in the seventh century until the country was divided in 1945. The country's territorial boundaries have remained largely unchanged, it is argued, and thus Koreans have a clear collective identity and speak the same language with little variation in dialect. Such arguments have been reinforced by assertions that Koreans' ethnic identity has been well-preserved because they rarely had occasion to marry other ethnic groups.

The slow course of globalization that began after Korea was forced by invading Western and Japanese forces to open its doors to the world beyond China has been, in a sense, a process of bolstering the strength of the nation, reinforcing national sentiments, and building a new identity. The process began with a breakaway from Korea's Confucian past. In the early twentieth century, many nationalist elites became very critical of the country's Confucian heritage and attributed the fall of the Chosŏn Dynasty and Korea's "backwardness" to it. Both the Chosŏn government and civic leaders saw Western-style education as a way of enlightening people and strengthening the nation. Some historians rewrote the history of Korea not as a small middle kingdom but as an independent country with its own founding fathers and unique culture, highlighting those historical events which produced military heroes who saved the country from foreign invasions, and cultural achievements which were distinctly of Korean character – such as the invention of *han'gŭl* (the Korean alphabet), movable type, and the rainfall gauge. Self-trained linguists devoted themselves to promoting the use of *han'gŭl* in place of Chinese characters by standardizing spelling and establishing its grammatical basis with the help of those Christian missionaries trained in Western linguistics. A group of reform-minded intellectuals published a newspaper called *The Independent* (*tongnip sinmun*). The ultimate goal of these nationalist intellectuals was to foster the "spirit of independence" and to create a "national consciousness" or identity. After Korea became a colony of Japan, the colonial authorities made deliberate efforts to Japanize Koreans by rewriting the history of Korea. They did this by emphasizing Korea's old ties with Japan as a colony in ancient times, making Japanese the official language and by forcing Koreans to adopt Japanese-style names, to learn Japanese history, to attend Shinto shrines, to observe Shinto rituals at home, to serve the Japanese army, and to recite the "oath of the imperial subject." Surrendering their national sovereignty and facing the threat of extinction of their cultural identity, Korean elites carried on their struggles within Korea and overseas until liberation in 1945.

The two Koreas that emerged after 1948 continued nationalist campaigns, but in different directions. For the South Korean authoritarian regime, economic development was more than a program to lift people out of poverty. It was a way for the military leadership of the country to establish legitimacy for the government they created through their military coup. "Legitimacy," says Jung-en Woo,

> is a matter of creating and reinforcing politically expedient myths. For economic growth to substitute for legitimacy, it has to be transformed into a symbol that appeals to some collective primordial sentiment – such as, for instance, nationalism. That symbol in Korea was a number: a talisman double digit GDP growth figure that was the Korean score in the race to catch up with Japan and also to surpass the DPRK economic performance.
>
> (Woo 1991: 98)

At the personal level, South Koreans remain strong nationalists. There is an awareness of distinction between "us," Koreans, and others. Reischauer (1977: 401–421) and Dore (1979–80: 604–606) wrote about the Japanese sense of separateness, the absence of a certain fellow-feeling with other ethnic groups or nations. One can speak of Koreans in similar vein. South Korea as a state may have become a member of the United Nations and the global community but this global membership has yet to make South Koreans feel and act as members of the larger community. Mindful of this fact, a noted political scientist-statesman, Lee Hong-ku, asked: "How many foreign residents does Seoul have among its population of 10 million? Or how would most of your neighbors react if a foreigner moved into your neighborhood? Finally, how would you answer if someone asked you why Seoul does not have a Chinatown?" (1994: 86). The responses to these questions, Lee implied, would make us feel ill-at-ease: Koreans might not feel comfortable with a foreign neighbor or might be relatively unconcerned about events occuring outside the country, such as the sufferings of others in civil conflicts in, say, Bosnia or Rwanda. When two Korean youths volunteered in 2001 to go to Iraq to be part of a human shield against the US army that was about to invade the country, the gesture evoked little public sympathy. Additionally, the Korean abroad is often expected not to act as an individual but as a Korean sharing national responsibility for the nation's good name. It will take time before Koreans can become full members of a global community.

Confucian modernity?

In the above sections, I have attempted to assess the extent to which Korea has moved away from its Confucian past over the course of its modernization process. Since Korean leaders took over the modernization project from the Japanese authorities following liberation, it has taken about a generation for the economy to develop and to mature.

If the modernization of Korea was largely a process of Westernization, it was at the same time a process of de-Confucianization. The effort to purge Confucianism from Korean society was deliberate on the part of the Korean political and cultural elites, since Confucianism was widely thought to be the cause of Korea's "backwardness" and an impediment to development. After a long period of contented isolation, the country had to grapple with this legacy when it was forced to open up to the industrial West and to Japan. Except for the initial resistance by those orthodox Confucianists who were eager to defend and protect the "Confucian way," the de-Confucianization process has been relatively painless.

Korea's modernization has been extensive and thorough. In the 1970s, however, a nationalistic and nativistic reaction occurred. In 1973, the Park government established the "filial piety prize" as a way to promote the tradition of filial piety. Shortly before his death in 1979, Park emphasized in a speech the importance of moral education and urged that it be based on "traditional spiritual culture." Ironically, he recognized humanism as the core of the Korean traditional spiritual culture, and went on to assert that the concept of filial piety should form the foundation of Korean humanism. Briefly in the early 1980s, filial piety became a favorite subject among those moralists who were concerned with the wane of traditional Confucian ethics in the wake of rapid industrialization and urbanization (Chang 1996; Chi 1997; Chon 1994: 30–34; Han 1990; Kim 1999; Son 1997; Song 1995). Some corporate organizations even tried to inculcate the spirit of loyalty into their employees by invoking the virtues of filial piety.

Indeed, the government has for some time been making efforts to preserve and revive traditional cultural heritage. Most notably, together with academic institutions, it launched a long-term plan of translating historical records, documents, and archives originally written in Chinese characters into *han'gŭl*, to make them more accessible to those who have no command of classical Chinese – that is, the majority of contemporary Koreans. There is also growing interest in noted Confucian philosophers such as Yi Toegye, Yi Yulgok, and Chong Ta-san. The government has erected statues of many famous Chosŏn Dynasty Confucian philosophers and politicians, together with other historical heroic figures. Their descendants and scholars are organizing study groups to render modern interpretations of their work. Some Confucian relics are now designated as National Treasures by the government.

Impressed by these efforts to preserve the Confucian heritage as part of the Korean tradition, Harvard Confucian philosopher Tu Weiming has remarked on the revival of Confucianism: "Whether or not competition with Japan is an important motivating force in Korea's search for her own roots, the Koreans' concerted effort to engage themselves in reanimating the old (Confucian past) as a way of defining their own cultural identity anew is noteworthy" (Tu 1991: 759). He went on to predict that "the Korean Confucian revival may well become the model for similar efforts in the rest of East Asia" (Tu 1991: 767). Here Professor Tu is clearly overstating the case for the Confucian revival in South Korea. What he regards as a Confucian revival is only a part of the nationwide effort to rediscover and appreciate Korean tradition, broadly defined as a counter-movement to sweeping Westernization, and to redefine the Korean past or identity in terms of things Korean rather than by means of re-establishing the Confucian identity. This is more nationalistic in character than Confucian. The government project of building statues of historical figures is not confined to Confucian scholars, but rather includes noted military generals, artists, poets, and others. The idea of National Treasures is conceived as a way of preserving the traditional culture: history, arts, music, dance, ceramics, and cooking. While the writings of Confucian scholars are being translated, numerous books on Korean history, especially on ancient times, and books on culture, are also being published. Some of them are becoming bestsellers. Men's traditional Korean dress in modernized form is making a comeback. Various traditional Korean liquors, cold drinks, food dishes, and teas are being "rediscovered" and are catching consumers' attention. As Tu himself is aware, there are still many Koreans who are critical of the Confucian past.

More importantly, references to Confucianism as the moral foundation of post-liberation Korea are nowhere to be found in the constitution, the National Charter of Education, government offices, or school classrooms (Koh 1996: 195). Nor are Confucian ethics formally taught, and knowledge of the Confucian classics has long ceased to be a requirement for sitting the Civil Service examinations. The majority of contemporary Koreans cannot read the classical Chinese in which most of the books by Chosŏn Dynasty scholars were written; hence the knowledge of the Confucian past is at most selective and limited. A small number of Korean scholars study Chosŏn Dynasty Confucianism, but they do not claim to be Confucian thinkers. "In short," says Koh Byoung-ik, a noted Korean historian, "Confucianism today (in Korea) is hardly visible on the surface and rarely manifests itself in any organization or institution. It survives only at the most basic level of the popular consciousness and in the routines of daily life" (1996: 194).

How far have Koreans moved on from their Confucian past? Has Confucian thinking completely disappeared from everyday life? This question does not have a simple answer. Very few Koreans identify themselves as Confucianist when they are asked about their religious affiliation. According to the *Manual of Korean Religion* published in the 1980s, the self-claimed "Confucianists" accounted for about 2 percent of the entire population. In 1995, it was less than 0.4 percent (1995 Population Census). But, as Koh Byong-ik points out, regardless of their professed religious affiliation – be it Shamanism, Buddhism, Confucianism, Protestantism, or Catholicism – the majority of Koreans are still Confucians in their "conviction" (1996). He cites as evidence the results of a survey that asked 2,000 respondents about their religious affiliations and value orientations.[4] Although only 2 percent said they were Confucianists, to the question on value orientation, all the respondents answered that they were "Confucians." Evidence is limited, but Koh concludes that "Confucianism is declining with respect to the number of those who identify themselves as followers, but it is surviving as the basis of the beliefs and practices of the majority of the Korean population, in spite of the fact that they often turn to other religions for salvation" (1996: 200). This survey result, in a way, confirms a major assumption that underlies the whole discourse on Asian values and their role in Asian development: that post-Confucian Asia remains Confucian. This should not, however, be interpreted to mean that Confucian values and norms still remain intact.[5] It only means that while the Confucian way of life and social organizations have more or less disappeared, and while some Confucian norms, particularly those governing filial piety and chastity, are no longer as widely practiced and enforced as they were during the Chosŏn Dynasty period (Chang 1989), Koreans still remain largely Confucian in their "habits of mind." Put another way, the Confucian value system that Koreans adopted during the Chosŏn Dynasty period may have become weaker in influence, but it has not been replaced by another value system.

If Koreans have embraced modern forms of government and socio-economic organization without adopting Western values, and have retained aspects of Confucian culture, how did Confucian values accommodate themselves to this structural transformation?

As for the Industrial Revolution, there is a growing debate among scholars as to what role, if any, "post-Confucian" ethics played in the process. It is true that, as Weber pointed out, Confucian ethics failed to give "birth to economic and technical revolution from within itself" (Giddens 1976: 4). But once industrial development came to be regarded as the only way of catching up with the advanced industrial West and Japan, and was accepted as a national goal by the government and the majority of the populace, Confucian values proved to be much more accommodating than other religious values. Perhaps the most important fact is that Korean elites were able to abandon certain Confucian values that were seen as inimical to economic development such as a low regard for commercial and craft activities, and for material wealth. Various scholars have identified "post-Confucian" values that are believed to have played roles in the formation of a work ethic, mobilization of physical and human capital, industrial management, the creation of the "developmental state" bureaucracy, commercial transaction, and innovative technology.[6]

Given the fact that a second wave of industrialization occurred in Northeast Asia, a region predominantly under Confucian influence, it is tempting to say that post-Confucian characteristics played a key role, but as several authors in this volume have pointed out, when we look at each country separately, the evidence for that assumption is not definitive. On the other hand, Confucian "habits of mind" have been more susceptible to Westernization. Post-Confucian South Korea has achieved remarkable economic success and has established a brand of Asian-style capitalism. Perhaps we can agree with the conclusion reached by Kim Uchang that Korean Confucian culture contained an important element of collectivism that provided a moral climate in which capitalism could grow, and that this could possibly "be modulated into the ideal of equality, an important component of the democratic ideal as conceived in the West" (Chapter 8, this volume).

Democracy, on the other hand, did not have an easy time establishing roots in Confucian Korea. As shown above, politicians once elected into government office were reluctant to leave after their term of tenure, as the constitution stipulated. On numerous occasions, they amended the constitution to stay in power. After three decades of struggle, led by students and dissident church leaders, South Korea returned to democratic rule. Confucian values, in the form of what I called the personalist ethic, proved initially to be rather incompatible with those democratic values embodied in the constitution, but the same ethic served later as a means to solidify the anti-authoritarian democratic forces. South Korean democracy is now being consolidated, and here again, Koreans, with their Confucian ways, are accommodating themselves to democratic institutions, thereby producing a "Korean" form of democracy (Chan 2003). We witness numerous Confucian values absorbed into the system: the personalized style of party politics, widespread personal networks within the power structure, voting behavior guided more by personality factors of candidates than by their political orientation or policy stance. Particularism continues to prevail in democratic politics, and there is increasing tension within the democratic system between particularistic and universalistic value orientations. Internalization of the latter is necessary for Korean democracy to fully establish human rights, social justice, equality, the rule of law, or moral autonomy as virtues. These represent the value orientations that are considered to be Western, to which Koreans are not quite accustomed. This is not simply a Korean problem but one that other "Confucian" nations – Japan, Taiwan, Hong Kong, and Singapore – have to tackle. This is a challenge imposed by the Asian modernization process.

Faced with this challenge, some scholars in the field of Confucian studies claim to have found in classical Confucian writings some evidence of values akin to various concepts associated with Western democracy, implying that Confucian values are not necessarily incompatible with democratic values and that they could be reinstated to provide a hospitable climate to the democratic system when it is imported (Bell 2000; Chan 2003; de Bary 1983, 1998; de Bary and Tu 1998; Metzger 1991). There may be no exact equivalent for John Locke's theory, but values similar to aspects of Western conceptions of human rights may be found in Asian cultural traditions. "The notion of *ren* in Confucianism, for example," Daniel A. Bell writes, "expresses the value of impartial concern to relieve human suffering" (2000: 50). Other scholars go even further, arguing for a creative adaptation. Efforts to adapt Confucian values to democratic polity should be accompanied by an attempt to overcome the shortcomings of the individualistic Western democracy: family breakdown, atomization, alienation, and depersonalization. Uchang Kim is one scholar who advocates an Asian form of democracy that emphasizes the group-oriented Confucian concept of the individual rather than the Western individualistic concept of the individual. Tu Wei-Ming is more ambitious, in that his list of Asian or Confucian values to be accommodated to a new democratic political system is longer: humanity, sympathy, reciprocity, civility, responsibility, public-spiritedness, and communality

(Bell and Hahm 2003). Given the anti-Confucian sentiment among cultural elites in post-Confucian industrial Korea, will Korea undertake another Confucian revival project?

Acknowledgment

I am indebted to Steven Lee for his thoughtful comments and editorial assistance.

Notes

1 The project "Studies in the Modernization of the Republic of Korea," undertaken by the Korean Development Institute, is perhaps the most systematic attempt so far to explain the meaning of the economic development project. But this study was conducted largely from an economics perspective, paying little attention to the cultural and social sides of the transformation.

2 This characterization of *sŏnbi* is based on Chŏng (2002, 2003), Kum (2000), and Yi (1989).

3 Sons of those government officials who usurped government treasure, sons and grandsons of those women who remarried or were known for their moral impropriety, and sons of concubines were all prohibited from sitting the government examinations.

4 The survey included twelve items on value orientations, including filial piety and loyalty; three cardinal virtues and five ethics; benevolence, righteousness, courtesy, and wisdom; self-cultivation and family ordering; veneration of the ancient sages and wise men; and inviolability of tradition (Koh 1996: 197).

5 It requires a major study to assess differences between the pre-modern and post-modern Confucian values held by Koreans.

6 The list is very long and includes ideas relating to self-confidence, social cohesion, subordination of the individual education for action, bureaucratic tradition, and moralizing certitudes (MacFarquhar 1980). Others have included different emphases on these values (Berger 1988: 7–8; Dore 1996; Jones and SaKong 1980; Tu 1996: 40–41).

References

Bell, Daniel A. 2000. *East Meets West: Human Rights and Democracy in East Asia.* Princeton, NJ: Princeton University Press.

Bell, Daniel A. and Hahm Chai-bong (eds). 2003. *Confucianism for the Modern World.* Cambridge: Cambridge University Press.

Berger, Peter L. 1988. "An East Asian Development Model," in Peter L. Berger and Hsin-huang Michael Hsiao (eds). *In Search of an East Asian Model.* New Brunswick: Transaction Books, pp. 3–11.

Bourdieu, Pierre. 1986. "The Forms of Capital," in John G. Richardson (ed.). *Handbook of Theory and Research for the Sociology of Education.* New York: Greenwood Press, pp. 241–258.

Chan, Joseph. 2003. "Giving Priority to the Worst Off: A Confucian Perspective on Social Welfare," in Daniel A. Bell and Hahm Chai-bong (eds). *Confucianism for the Modern World.* Cambridge: Cambridge University Press, pp. 236–253.

Chang, Ki-kun. 1996. *Todŏk, yulli, hyodo ŭi wŏlli wa silchŏn* (The Theory and Practice of Morals, Ethics and Filial Piety). Seoul: Churyu Ilnyomsa.

Chang, Yun-Shik. 1971. "Colonization as Planned Change: The Korean Case." *Modern Asian Studies* 5: 163–186.

——. 1980. "The Growth of Education: Causes and Consequences," in Chang Yun-Shik (ed.). *Korea: A Decade of Development.* Seoul: Seoul National University Press, pp. 79–107.

——. 1989. "From Filial Piety to the Love of Children," in the Korean Christian Academy (ed.). *The Third World Community in Post-Industrial Society I: Changing Families in the World Perspective.* Seoul: Wooseok Publishing, pp. 77–94.

——. 1990."Education, Equality and Society: A Comparision of North and South Korea." *California Sociologist* 13: 87–121.

——. 1991. "The Personalist Ethic and the Market in Korea." *Comparative Studies in Society and History* 33: 106–129.

Chi, Kyo-hon. 1997. *Han'guk ŭi hyo sasang* (The Principle of Filial Piety in Korea). Seoul: Minsokwon.

Chon, Byong-che. 1994. "Hyŏndae kajogŭn wiki'inga (Is the Modern Family in Crisis?)," in *Wigi e sŏn kajok* (The Family in Crisis). Seoul: Tasan Chulpansa, pp. 11–44.

Chŏng, Kwang-ho. 2003. *Sŏnbi: Sosin kwa ch'ŏsin ŭi salm* (Literati: Their Belief and Way of Life). Seoul: Nulwa.

Chŏng, Ok-cha. 2002. *Uri Sŏnbi* (Our Literati). Seoul: Hyŏnamsa.

Chōsen sōtokufu. 1944. *Shōwa 15 nen kokusai chosa kekka yoyaku* (A Summary of the Results of the 1940 National Census). Seoul: Chōsen sōtokufu.

Coleman, James S. 1988. "Social Capital in the Creation of Human Capital." *American Journal of Sociology* 94: S95–S121.

de Bary, Wm. T. 1983. *The Liberal Tradition in China.* Hongkong: The Chinese University, and New York: Columbia University.

——. 1998. *Asian Values and Human Rights.* Cambridge, MA: Harvard University Press.

de Bary, Wm. T. and Tu Wei-Ming (eds). 1998. *Confucianism and Human Rights.* New York: Columbia University Press.

de Schweinitz Jr, Karl. 1964. *Industrialization and Democracy: Economic Necessities and Political Possibilities.* New York: The Free Press of Glencoe.

Dore, Ronald P. 1960. "Agricultural Improvement in Japan: 1810–1900." *Economic Development and Cultural Change* 9, Part II: 69–91.

——. 1976. *The Diploma Disease.* Berkeley: University of California Press.

——. 1979–1980. "The Internationalization of Japan." *Pacific Affairs* 52 (1): 595–611.

——. 1996. "Confucianism, Economic Growth and Social Development," in Josef Kreiner (ed.). *The Impact of Traditional Thought on Present Day Japan.* Monographien 11, Phillip-Franz-von-Siebold-Stiftung, Deutschen Institut for Japan Studies, pp. 17–30.

Giddens, Anthony. 1976. "Introduction" to Max Weber, *The Protestant Ethic and the Spirit of Capitalism,* trans. Talcott Parsons. London: George Allen & Unwin.

——. 1990. *The Consequences of Modernity.* Stanford, CA: Stanford University Press.

——. 1991. "Introduction," in Max Weber. 1976 (1904–1905, 1930). *The Protestant Ethic and the Spirit of Capitalism,* trans. Talcott Parsons. London: George Allen & Unwin, pp. 1–12.

Han, Taewon. 1990. *Han'guk ŭi hyo wa hyohaeng* (Filial Piety and Its Practices in Korea). Seoul: Namdo.

Jones, Leroy P. and Il SaKong. 1980. *Government, Business and Entrepreneurship in Economic Development: The Korean Case.* Cambridge, MA: Council on East Asian Studies, Harvard University.

Kang, Kyŏng-sik. 1992. *Kanan kujenŭn naraka handa* (Poverty Relief is the Responsibility of the Government). Seoul: Sarm kwa Kkum.

Kim Chong-kŭn. 1999. *Saram taun saram'i toenŭn il* (The Way for a Human Being to Become Truly Human). Seoul: Yurim munhwasa.

Kim, Samuel S. 2000. *Korea's Globalization.* Cambridge: Cambridge University Press.

Koh, Byong-ik. 1996."Confucianism in Contemporary Korea," in Tu Wei-Ming (ed.). *Confucian Traditions in East Asian Modernity.* Cambridge, MA: Harvard University Press, pp. 191–203.

Kum, Chang-tae. 2000. *Han'guk ŭi sŏnbi wa sŏnbi chŏngsin* (Korean Literati and Literati Spirits). Seoul: Seoul Daehakkyo Chulpanbu.

Landes, David S. 1969. *The Unbound Prometheus.* Cambridge: Cambridge University Press.

Lee Hong-koo. 1994. "Attitudinal Reform Toward Globalization." *Korean Focus* 2 (2): 85–98.

Lin, Nan. 2001. *Social Capital: A Theory of Social Structure and Action.* Cambridge: Cambridge University Press.

MacFarquhar, Roderick. 1980. "The Post-Confucian Challenge." *The Economist,* February: 67–72.

Marshall, T.H. 1950. *Citizenship and Social Class.* Cambridge: Cambridge University Press.

Metzger, Thomas A. 1991. "Confucian Thought and the Modern Chinese Quest for Moral Autonomy," in Silke Krieger and Rolf Trauzettel (eds). *Confucianism and the Modernization of China.* Mainz: Van Hase and Koehler Verlag, pp. 266–306.

Mun, Chong-chang. 1941. *Chōsen no sijō* (The Market in Korea). Tokyo: Nihon Hyoronsha.

Palais, James B. 1996. *Confucian Statecraft and Korean Institutions: Yu Hyong Won and the Late Chosŏn Dynasty.* Seattle: University of Washington Press.

——. 2002. "Confucianism and Economic Development in South Korea," in Benjamin A. Elman, John Duncan, and Herman Ooms (eds). *Rethinking Confucianism.* Los Angeles, CA: Asia Institute, UCLA, pp. 490–517.

Reischauer, Edwin. 1977. *The Japanese.* Cambridge, MA: Harvard University Press.

Seol, Dong-Hoon. 1974. "Past and Present of Foreign Workers in Korea 1987–2000." *Asian Solidarity Quarterly* 2 (6): 6–31.

Seol, Dong-Hoon and Geon-Soo Han. 2004. "Foreign Migrant Workers and Social Discrimination in Korea." *Harvard Asia Quarterly* 3 (1): 45–50.

Shin, Susan. 1974. "The Social Structure of Kumhwa County in the Late Seventeenth Century." *Occasional Papers on Korea,* No. 1: 9–35.

Slater, Don. 1997. *Consumer Culture and Modernity.* Cambridge: Polity Press.

Son, In-su. 1997. *Han'guk ŭi hyodo munwha* (The Filial Piety Culture of the Korean). Seoul: Munumsa.

Song, Kyu-taek. 1995. *Saesidae ŭi hyo* (Filial Piety in the New Era). Seoul: Yonse Daehakkyo Chulpanbu.

Takahashi, Kamekichi. 1935. *Kendai Chōsen kezairon* (A Study of Modern Korean Economy). Tokyo: Chikura shobo.

Tu Wei-Ming. 1991. "The Search for Roots in Industrial Asia: The Case of the Confucian Revival," in Martin E. Marty and R. Scott Appleby (eds). *Fundamentalisms Observed.* Chicago: University of Chicago Press, pp. 740–781.

——. 1996. "The Confucian Discussion in the East Asian Development Model," in Josef Kreiner (ed.). *The Impact of Traditional Thought and Present-Day Japan.* Monographien 11, Philip-Frana-von-Siebold-Stiftung Deutsche Institute for Japan Studies, pp. 31–48.

Veblen, Thorstein. 1952. *The Theory of the Leisure Class.* New York: Mentor Books (first published 1899).

Wagner, Edward. 1974. "Social Stratification in the Seventeenth-Century Korea: Some Observations from a 1663 Seoul Census Register." *Occasional Papers on Korea,* No. 1: 36–54.

Weber, Max. 1958. *From Max Weber: Essays in Sociology,* translated, edited and with an Introduction by H.H. Gerth and C. Wright Mills. New York: Oxford University Press.

Weekly Choson.com. 2003.

Westphal, Larry E. 1978. "The Republic of Korea's Experience with Export-Led Industrial Development." *World Development* 6: 347–382.

Woo, Jung-En. 1991. *Race to the Swift.* New York: Columbia University Press.

Yi, Chang-hi. 1989. *Chosŏn sidae ŭi sŏnbi yŏn'gu* (A Study on the Literati in Chosŏn Dynasty Korea). Seoul: Pagyŏngsa.

Yi, Hi-sung. 1970. "Ttalkkak bari," in his *Pongŏri naegkasum* (The Frozen Heart of the Deaf). Seoul: Ilchokak, pp. 35–39 (originally published 1956).

Yu, Eui-Young. 2003. "Hanin kyohoe wa iminsahoe 1965 nyŏn ihulul chungsimŭro" (The Korean Church and the History of Immigration: With a Focus on Post-1965). Unpublished manuscript.

Index

For Product Safety Concerns and Information please contact our EU
representative GPSR@taylorandfrancis.com
Taylor & Francis Verlag GmbH, Kaufingerstraße 24, 80331 München, Germany

www.ingramcontent.com/pod-product-compliance
Lightning Source LLC
LaVergne TN
LVHW011108300926
849160LV00008B/307
* 9 7 8 0 4 1 5 5 4 6 9 5 9 *